Financial Accounting and Reporting

Also by Robin John Limmack

Joint adaptor (with John Boyle) of British edition of Weston and Brigham's *Managerial Finance*

FINANCIAL ACCOUNTING AND REPORTING

An Introduction

Robin John Limmack

MACMILLAN

© Robin John Limmack 1985

All rights reserved. No reproduction, copy or transmission of this publication may be made without written permission.

No paragraph of this publication may be reproduced, copied or transmitted save with written permission or in accordance with the provisions of the Copyright Act 1956 (as amended).

Any person who does any unauthorised act in relation to this publication may be liable to criminal prosecution and civil claims for damages.

First published 1985

Published by
Higher and Further Education Division
MACMILLAN PUBLISHERS LTD
Houndmills, Basingstoke, Hampshire RG21 2XS
and London
Companies and representatives
throughout the world

Printed in Hong Kong

British Library Cataloguing in Publication Data
Limmack, Robin John
Financial accounting and reporting.
1. Accounting
I. Title
657′.48   HF5635
ISBN 0–333–34639–4
ISBN 0–333–34640–8 Pbk

Contents

Preface ix

1 INTRODUCTION: THE SCOPE AND HISTORICAL BACKGROUND OF ACCOUNTANCY **1**
   1.1 Introduction 1
   1.2 Sub-groupings within accountancy 2
   1.3 Development of financial accounting and financial reporting 6
   1.4 Summary 11
       Questions 12

2 USERS AND OBJECTIVES OF FINANCIAL INFORMATION **13**
   2.1 Introduction 13
   2.2 Users of financial accounting information 13
   2.3 Objectives of financial reporting 20
   2.4 Desirable characteristics of financial reporting 23
   2.5 Summary 23
       Questions 24

3 ACCOUNTING PRINCIPLES AND PRACTICE **26**
   3.1 Introduction 26
   3.2 Approaches to accounting theory construction 27
   3.3 Accounting income and economic income 30
   3.4 Historic cost accounting 32
   3.5 Summary 37
       Questions 38

4 FINANCIAL STATEMENTS AND INCOME MEASUREMENT **40**
   4.1 Introduction 40
   4.2 The Balance Sheet and income measurement 41
   4.3 The Income Statement and income measurement 49
   4.4 Summary 56
       Questions 58
       Problems 59

5 THE ACCOUNTING RECORDING PROCESS (I) — 62
- 5.1 Introduction — 62
- 5.2 Double-entry book-keeping — 62
- 5.3 Flow of information — 74
- 5.4 Summary — 75
  - *Appendix* Comprehensive illustration to Trial Balance stage — 76
  - *Questions* — 80
  - *Problems* — 87

6 THE ACCOUNTING RECORDING PROCESS (II) — 91
- 6.1 Introduction — 91
- 6.2 Control accounts — 91
- 6.3 Adjusting entries — 100
- 6.4 Work sheet — 108
- 6.5 Accounting for non-trading organisations — 112
- 6.6 *Summary* — 116
  - *Questions* — 116
  - *Problems* — 118

7 FIXED ASSET MEASUREMENT (I) — 122
- 7.1 Introduction — 122
- 7.2 Asset valuation and accounting income — 122
- 7.3 Fixed assets and depreciation — 125
- 7.4 Summary — 136
  - *Questions* — 136
  - *Problems* — 138
  - *Appendix* Asset valuation and economic income — 139
  - *Appendix Questions* — 146

8 FIXED ASSET MEASUREMENT (II) — 147
- 8.1 Introduction — 147
- 8.2 Tangible fixed assets — 147
- 8.3 Intangible assets — 154
- 8.4 Investments — 157
- 8.5 Capital allowances and investment grants — 159
- 8.6 Summary — 162
  - *Questions* — 163
  - *Problems* — 164

9 CURRENT ASSETS (I) — 167
- 9.1 Introduction — 167
- 9.2 Stocks and work-in-progress — 167
- 9.3 Flow of costs — 182
- 9.4 Manufacturing accounts — 184
- 9.5 Departmental accounts — 186
- 9.6 Summary — 189
  - *Questions* — 190
  - *Problems* — 191

10	**CURRENT ASSETS (II)**		**194**
	10.1	Introduction	194
	10.2	Inventory cost recognition	194
	10.3	Long-term contracts and work-in-progress	197
	10.4	Cash and other liquid assets	201
	10.5	Summary	209
		Questions	210
		Problems	212
11	**FORMS OF BUSINESS ORGANISATION (I): SOLE TRADERS AND PARTNERSHIPS**		**215**
	11.1	Introduction	215
	11.2	Sole traders	215
	11.3	Value added tax	227
	11.4	Partnerships	231
	11.5	Summary	237
		Questions	237
		Problems	238
12	**FORMS OF BUSINESS ORGANISATION (II): INCORPORATED BUSINESSES**		**241**
	12.1	Introduction	241
	12.2	Features of incorporated businesses	241
	12.3	Forms of share capital	245
	12.4	Debenture capital	247
	12.5	Security issues	249
	12.6	Accounting for security issues	253
	12.7	Summary	257
		Questions	258
		Problems	258
13	**CORPORATE FINANCIAL REPORTING REQUIREMENTS**		**260**
	13.1	Introduction	260
	13.2	Financial disclosure requirements	261
	13.3	Distributable profits	273
	13.4	Company taxation	274
	13.5	Summary	276
		Appendix A Format of financial statements	276
		Appendix B Octagon plc: notes to the accounts	287
		Questions	294
		Problems	294
14	**ANALYSIS OF ACCOUNTING STATEMENTS**		**299**
	14.1	Introduction	299
	14.2	Ratio analysis	301
	14.3	Funds flow analysis	313
	14.4	Preparation of a statement of sources and applications of funds (as per SSAP 10)	315
	14.5	Cash flow statements	323

	14.6	Summary	326
		Questions	326
		Problems	328
15	**ACCOUNTING FOR INFLATION**		**333**
	15.1	Introduction	333
	15.2	The history of inflation accounting	333
	15.3	Inflation and historic cost accounting	335
	15.4	Current purchasing power accounting	338
	15.5	The Sandilands Committee	339
	15.6	SSAP 16: Current cost accounting	342
	15.7	Summary	351
	Appendix	Preparation of Current Purchasing Power (CPP) Statements	352
		Questions	359
		Problems	360
16	**GROUP ACCOUNTS**		366
	16.1	Introduction	366
	16.2	Historical developments	366
	16.3	Balance Sheet consolidation	371
	16.4	Profit and Loss Account	376
	16.5	Associated companies	385
	16.6	Merger accounting	386
	16.7	Summary	390
		Questions	391
		Problems	393

Notes and References   396

Glossary of Terms   406

Index   409

Preface

This textbook is intended to provide an introduction to the theory and practice of financial accounting and external reporting. Intended readership includes accountancy students in the first year of undergraduate degree and HND programmes together with those students preparing for the foundation examinations of professional accountancy bodies.

The book commences by distinguishing financial accounting from the broader discipline of accountancy. The principal factors leading to the development of current financial accounting practice are then identified.

Chapter 2 introduces the role of financial reporting to the users of financial accounting information, with particular reference to external user groups. The role of external financial reporting is shown to have expanded from the early, narrow, stewardship view of reporting to owners into the much wider role currently claimed for financial reporting as 'the provision of information for users in order to assist them in making economic decisions'.

Thus at the outset accountancy is identified as a 'service' discipline, providing information for users, with the external user group being one such group who are provided with part of their information requirements through the medium of financial accounting statements.

Chapter 3 briefly examines alternative approaches to the development of a theory of accounting, before identifying those concepts and principles which are fundamental to historic cost accounting. Much of the remainder of the text is then concerned with the application of historic cost accounting concepts to the process of asset valuation and income measurement. Wherever relevant, attention is also drawn to the limitations of historic cost accounting. Additionally, Chapter 15 examines alternatives to historic cost accounting within the context of accounting for the effects of inflation.

Throughout the text, emphasis is given not only to the principles of historic cost accounting but also to the application of these principles. The dual aspect of accounting transactions is first introduced in Chapter 4 and then extended into the procedural aspects of a system of double-entry book-keeping in Chapters 5 and 6. Subsequent chapters give emphasis not only to the measurement aspects of accounting but also to the recording aspects.

Chapters 11 to 13 identify the recording and reporting requirements of different forms of business enterprise. Although not an accounting problem of unincorporated businesses alone, Chapter 11 also examines the features of accounting for VAT. Chapter 13 considers, in particular, the reporting requirements placed on companies by the Companies Acts 1948 to 1981.

All chapters include discussion questions on the text and many chapters also include multiple choice questions as well as comprehensive review problems. A glossary of terms used in the early chapters of the text is included at the end of the book for use by students.

As the final stage of study of the text students are recommended to re-read the first three chapters in order to reconsider the ideas expressed in the light of the subsequent chapters.

A number of colleagues have commented on the book, suggesting amendments and alterations. In particular, Dr Alan Goodacre made detailed comments and suggestions, many of which were incorporated into the text. Thanks are also due to A. C. Storrar and D. P. Stopforth for helpful advice given in various sections and to Elissa, Elenor and Elspeth for secretarial help.

Helpful comments were also received from a number of external reviewers of preliminary and later drafts of the textbook. As with all texts, the author must accept final responsibility for errors whether of commission or omission.

Thanks are due also to John Winckler, the original sponsoring editor, and to Steven Kennedy, Anthea Brodrick, Keith Povey and Keith Eady, who completed this task.

The extract from the 1981 Companies Act included in Appendix A to Chapter 13 is reproduced with the permission of the Controller of Her Majesty's Stationery Office.

Finally, I wish to thank my wife for her patient support and encouragement especially during the typing and editing of the manuscript.

University of Stirling   R. J. LIMMACK

NOTE: A booklet of suggested solutions to many of the end of chapter questions and problems is available to lecturers in accountancy on payment of a small fee. Requests should be addressed to the author at The Department of Accountancy and Business Law, University of Stirling, Stirling, FK9 4LA, Scotland.

1 Introduction: The Scope and Historical Background of Accountancy

1.1 Introduction

The use of accountancy and accounting information permeates all aspects of modern society. We could not live in the type of world we know today without accountancy. Decisions made on the basis of accounting information affect the lives of countless millions in one way or another, whether at the individual level in the pricing of particular commodities or in wage negotiation, or at the macro level involving the economic strategies of governments. The rules governing accountancy are considered sufficiently important as to warrant government intervention from time to time, whether in the form of legislation or in the appointment of committees to consider special issues.[1]

In common with many other disciplines,[2] the nature of the definition of accountancy arouses disagreement among practitioners and academics alike. Simple attempts to define accountancy may make reference to the functions of accountants, e.g., 'accountancy is what accountants do'.[3] Apart from being tautological, such definitions are so vague as to be devoid of meaning. Accountants are found in a wide variety of occupations undertaking work of a very different nature from what the majority of individuals would regard as the province of accountancy. Even within the so-called accountancy profession, there are accountants who occupy roles as management consultants, financial and investment advisers, training officers, systems analysts, as well as those occupying the more traditional roles of auditors, tax specialists, financial controllers, transaction recorders and information communicators. At the other end of the spectrum of definitions, accountants are described more succinctly as 'professional keepers or inspectors of records'.[4] Hence, accountancy might be seen in its narrowest form as the art of keeping or inspecting records.

Which, if either, of these extremes is correct? The answer, not surprisingly, is neither. Accountancy is neither so wide as to encompass all that accountants might possibly do nor is it yet such a narrow discipline to include only the recording and verifying of records.

1

A more useful definition than the above is that given by E. Kohler in his *Dictionary for Accountants*. Kohler uses the term accountancy to include 'the entire body of knowledge associated with the discipline' namely: 'the theory and practice of accounting; its responsibilities; standards, conventions and activities generally'.[5]

Within the broad discipline of accountancy there are a number of sub-groupings of which financial accounting, the subject matter of this text, is but one. Each sub-grouping is described briefly in the next section.

1.2 Sub-groupings within accountancy

Financial accounting

Financial accounting is concerned with the recording, classifying, summarising and reporting of those transactions undertaken by an organisation, which are of a financial nature. It is also concerned with the construction of a theory of accounting, with identification of rules of measurement, and with regulation of the content of financial reports.

Elements of financial accounting include:

(a) the recognition and recording of financial transactions;
(b) the design of information systems and the processing of accounting information;
(c) the introduction of internal controls and safeguards, both over the accuracy of the recording process and over the security of the resources owned;
(d) summarising information and preparation of financial reports for use by internal and external users.

There are two major financial accounting statements prepared at periodic intervals; the Balance Sheet which identifies the resources owned by a business and the claims on those resources; and the Income Statement which identifies the profit or loss earned over an accounting period. Other financial accounting statements are also prepared, either to meet specific requirements of internal users or to meet the more general requirements of external users.

Auditing

Although this area might perhaps be included within the boundaries of financial accounting, falling as it does under the headings of 'professional examination of financial statements' (external auditing), and 'continuous critical testing of transactions' (internal auditing) as identified by Kohler,[6] the duties of an auditor are sufficiently distinct from other aspects of financial accounting to warrant separate examination at a level beyond the scope of this text.

Externally appointed auditors are involved in an examination of the underlying books, vouchers and other accounting records of a business in order to ascertain:

(i) whether the Balance Sheet provides a true and fair representation of the state of affairs of the business on the Balance Sheet date; and

Introduction: the scope and historical background of accountancy

(ii) whether the Income Statement provides a true and fair view of the profit or loss for the financial period.

Whenever a company publishes financial statements, it must also publish the external auditor's report with those statements. The auditor's report should state 'whether in the opinion of the auditors, the financial statements comply with the Companies Acts 1948–81 and give a true and fair view of the state of the company's affairs at the balance sheet date and of its profit or loss for the year ended on that date'.[7] Amongst other requirements, the auditor must also state in the report if proper accounting records have not been kept or if the financial statements presented are not in agreement with the underlying accounting records. Hence the auditor must have expert knowledge of the principles and practices of financial accounting and financial reporting. The 1948 Companies Act gave belated recognition to this need by requiring auditors to be members of one of the bodies of accountants recognised for this task by the Department of Trade and Industry, namely;

The Institute of Chartered Accountants in England and Wales.
The Institute of Chartered Accountants of Scotland.
The Institute of Chartered Accountants in Ireland.
The Association of Certified Accountants.

Other individuals in special circumstances, have been approved as recognised auditors by the Department of Trade and Industry, including those with similar qualifications gained outside the United Kingdom.

When considering his task, the externally appointed auditor examines the internally created systems of checks and safeguards on the financial accounting procedures of an organisation. Such checks and safeguards are built into accounting systems in an attempt to ensure the accuracy of the information output and to prevent irregularities or fraudulent manipulation of the system. There have been many examples of accounting systems being set up in an inadequate form which later proved to be capable of manipulation, one notable example being the case of Equity Funding Corporation of America. This Corporation, a modestly sized financial services company, grew rapidly by fraudulent means over a period of ten years into a major insurance group. The fraud involved the inclusion of non-existent business in financial statements and subsequent reinsurance with other companies by the addition of false data to computer files. The fraud only came to light when a dismissed employee informed on the company to State insurance officials.[8] The case is an illustration of how auditors, unfamiliar with computerised systems, can easily be fooled.

Internal auditors are employees of a business appointed to provide a continuous system of review of the operations and accounting records of the business. Unlike the externally appointed auditors who are answerable to shareholders or other owners, the internal auditors report to the management.

Most businesses operate a system of internal control over the resources owned and the accounting recording process. Checks will normally be included in the system of internal control whereby the work of one employee is proved independently of, or complementary to, the work of another. The duties of the internal auditor will include, amongst others, a review of the systems of accounting and internal control operated by the business.

Cost and managerial accounting

Cost and managerial accounting is concerned primarily with the organisation and collection of financial data for the internal management of an organisation to aid in the areas of decision making for which they are responsible. Although there are instances of industrial book-keeping records being kept in the United Kingdom in the centuries before the Industrial Revolution, it is generally accepted that cost accounting came into existence after 1800.[9]

Initially, industrial records were concerned more with providing controls over the physical usage of materials and labour, including wastage, rather than with the identification of unit product cost. Only when competition between producers became more fierce did the identification of production cost become more important as an aid to both product pricing and cost control. For a time the problem of the allocation of factory overheads[10] to product cost was largely ignored and attention was focused on prime cost, consisting of direct material and labour costs. By the turn of the nineteenth century, however, the importance of the issue of overhead allocation had been recognised and this period witnessed the beginnings of the debate on allocation procedures which continues to this day. The Institute of Cost and Management Accountants (formerly the Institute of Cost and Works Accountants) was itself incorporated in 1919 and granted a Royal Charter in 1975. This developed as a separate body to promote the needs and interests of cost and management accountants.

Since the commencement of the twentieth century, the role of cost and managerial accounting has expanded considerably. There is virtually no area within the attention of business management that does not require the use of accounting data, whether it be planning, marketing, personnel or financial management. Areas of involvement include cost control, pricing, performance measurement, budgetary planning, and long and short-term decision making. In an introductory text on financial accounting there is obviously limited space to devote to such a wide ranging topic although later chapters on depreciation and inventory valuation will include some aspects of this area of accountancy. Indeed, complete separation of financial and managerial accounting is impossible as the same primary data is used in both accounting systems. Additionally, while the final product may be aimed at different parties, namely external and internal users, the implications of decisions made on the basis of internal reports will ultimately be reflected in the financial accounts.

Taxation

The major portion of government revenue in the United Kingdom is raised through taxation, whether directly as a tax on the income of organisations or indirectly by the addition of a tax charge to the cost of a transaction.

For the employees of an organisation, direct taxation is borne through the

'Pay As You Earn' system (PAYE) with income tax being deducted where relevant, by the employer from the wages of the employees. The employer must then account to the government for the income tax so deducted. In the case of owners' of both incorporated and unincorporated businesses, tax liability is computed by reference to the 'taxable profits' of the business. Companies may pay Corporation Tax on taxable profits; as far as unincorporated businesses are concerned, each owner's share of taxable profits is subject to income tax and assessed by reference to the various Income and Corporation Taxes Acts. The determination of taxable profits of business organisations is closely related to the determination of accounting profits but with certain adjustments which are briefly explained in Chapters 8 and 13. To that extent, therefore, taxation might be viewed as a branch of financial accounting. Additionally, a large proportion of the indirect taxation gathered by government is also determined by reference to the financial records of organisations, e.g., value added tax and excise duties are indirect taxes, the liability for which is determined by reference to the receipts and expenditures of a business.

The field of taxation is now so complex, with changes taking place at such a rapid pace as a result both of government legislation and subsequent case law, that a special 'breed' of taxation expert has emerged. Often these experts are members of recognised accountancy bodies, or at the very least will have gained some experience in financial accounting. Since 1930 there has also been a separate Institute of Taxation which has its own specialised examination syllabus.

It is impossible to write a text on financial accounting or indeed to teach an introductory course on financial reporting without including some analysis or discussion of taxation. Hence, various chapters will include reference to the taxation aspects of the subject under discussion, but at a level which is introductory rather than exhaustive.

Financial management

The decision to place financial management at the end of this introductory section was not taken because of any low degree of importance attached to this area, but rather it reflects the relative youth of this area of accountancy. Indeed many people, accountants and non-accountants alike, view the subject area as one distinct from accountancy as such. This view may stem partly from the use of analytical tools, such as mathematical and economic modelling, by financial managers.

In the United Kingdom, financial management or finance is a much less well developed subject discipline than it is in the United States. Initially the function of financial management was seen as one of aiding in the provision of funds for industrial organisations and, as part of the function of the management accountant, the control of funds within the organisation. Gradually the role of financial management has widened until it encompasses not only the raising of funds, including the identification of the optimal capital structure for an organisation, but also the disposal of those funds, including the capital investment decision-making process. Indeed studies undertaken in finance theory are now finding their way into financial accounting with implications for financial policy making, e.g., as an aid in the choice amongst competing accounting treatments. Nowadays all the major accountancy bodies devote at least one examination paper to financial management.

1.3 Development of financial accounting and financial reporting

Early developments

It is unreasonable and also perhaps dangerous, to claim too great an antiquity for the foundations of modern accountancy; otherwise accountancy might be thought to be a static subject, unfitting and unresponsive to the needs of modern society. Nevertheless, it is a discipline possessing fairly ancient antecedents. As students and researchers of accountancy history have demonstrated, traces can be observed in the records of the earliest known civilisations, Sumerian, Egyptian, Greek and Roman included. Furthermore, some of the earliest known writers on accountancy have been recognised as being amongst the most intellectually gifted of their generation.[11]

In practice, however, early record-keeping often involved merely preparing a list of goods owned, without any concern for any of the modern concepts of 'value' or 'income measurement'. These records were often required of stewards as evidence of their good faith in the handling of goods owned by their masters. An impetus to the development of accountancy came in the Middle Ages with the needs of the merchant traders who required more sophisticated systems of record-keeping which would be based on monetary values. Records were maintained, however, essentially by and for the owners of business enterprises, and normally without any requirement for either external reporting or for measurement of profit (or loss). These records merely detailed information which was of use to the merchant or tradesman in pursuit of his own business affairs.

Although the exact origin is unknown, it appears that at some time around the turn of the thirteenth century, the recording process which came to be known as double-entry book-keeping made its appearance. The earliest known surviving study on the subject was written in 1494 by Luca Pacioli, an eminent Franciscan monk and scholar. This study describes a system which had been in operation for the previous two hundred years in Venice and presumably in other Italian merchant states.[12]

The development of the system of double-entry book-keeping provided a number of advantages over earlier methods of record keeping as follows:

(i) the records were kept in a more orderly and comprehensive form;
(ii) the duality of transactions upon which the system was based provided a convenient (although not comprehensive) check on the accuracy and completeness of the records;
(iii) the records made available by such a system contained the materials for later development of statements of financial position and statements of profit.[13]

However, for some centuries thereafter, such accounting practices as existed were designed to meet the needs of merchants and others actively connected with the management of their own businesses. No standardised conventions existed to govern either the valuation of assets or the calculation of profits, if indeed either task was required at all. Instead, the governing philosophy in the recording of financial transactions was simply to record information in whatever manner was most useful to the owners of the business. Balance Sheets were prepared at irregular intervals, if at all, and usually only for the purpose of checking the accuracy of the recording process. Profit and Loss Accounts were also closed at irregular intervals according to the whim of the individual owner and appear often 'to have been the rag-bag into which unwanted account balances were thrown',[14] rather than providing a thorough attempt at determination of periodic income.

Following on from the introduction of double-entry book-keeping, the next important stage in the development of accountancy came around the time of the Industrial Revolution. At this time two new categories of incorporated bodies emerged; firstly, registered companies and secondly, those registered companies which possessed limited liability.

Nineteenth-century developments

The Industrial Revolution in Britain brought about a change in the size of productive units as well as in the method of production. Many traditionally smaller, cottage-type industries were replaced by larger factories requiring substantial levels of capital investment. In some instances it was possible to provide the financial resources needed to finance the new industrial organisations out of a single pocket, but in many cases the combined investment of a large number of previously unrelated individuals was necessary. The process by which these individuals might combine and achieve corporate status was cumbersome until the passing of the 1844 Joint Stock Companies Act, which removed the need to pass specific Acts of Parliament or to obtain a Royal Charter. Instead it allowed incorporation of businesses by the relatively simple process of registration.

The passing of the 1844 Act also imposed specific accounting requirements on the directors of newly registered companies with the aim of providing information for the 'protection' of creditors and shareholders (i.e., owners):

(i) books of account were to be kept;
(ii) a 'full and fair' Balance Sheet was to be presented at each ordinary meeting of shareholders;
(iii) auditors were to be appointed from amongst the members to report on the Balance Sheet and were to be given access to the books of account and the opportunity to question officers of the company;
(iv) a copy of the Balance Sheet was to be filed with the Registrar of Companies.

Although retained profit figures were available from an examination of the Balance Sheet, there was no requirement laid down by the Act to produce a Profit Statement of any kind, nor was there any specification of the information to be included in the Balance Sheet.

The attractiveness of investing in the new registered companies was increased after the passing of the 1855 Joint Stock Companies Act. This Act limited shareholders' liability for debts of the company to the amount unpaid, if any, on the shares held by them. The passing of this Act had the effect, however, not only of increasing the risks to creditors of such companies, but also of removing the limited accounting requirements of the 1844 Act when both Acts were subsequently consolidated in the 1856 Joint Stock Companies Act.

The general philosophy of parliamentary legislators at the time appears to have been one of adopting a policy of placing minimum restrictions on business enterprises and to leave the responsibility for obtaining information on business matters with the shareholders and creditors who were deemed to have freely entered into transactions with limited liability companies. Not until the beginning of the twentieth century would accounting disclosure requirements be reintroduced for all classes of limited liability companies.

Although the above seems to indicate an almost cavalier attitude by parliament to the needs of shareholders and creditors, three further factors must also be considered in order to obtain a balanced view of the state of nineteenth century corporate reporting:

(i) The importance of limited liability companies to the economy was not significant until the later decades of the century, except in specific industries, such as banking, to which specific accounting disclosure requirements did indeed apply.

(ii) Accounting conventions were developed by the emerging accountancy profession along what was considered to be conservative lines, with general acceptance of asset measurement based on historic, i.e., acquisition, cost. These accounting conventions will be considered further in Chapter 3.

(iii) A distinction emerged, both through commercial practice and case law, between what is known as capital and revenue items,
   (a) for the purposes of identifying profits available for dividend distribution and hence for creditors' protection;
   (b) to produce some indication for absentee shareholders of the profitability and 'soundness' of their investments.

Hence, some of the protection lost to creditors (and shareholders) through the withdrawal of disclosure requirements was reintroduced through case law.

With the granting of limited liability status to companies, shareholders had received a significant safeguard against the possibility that they would be called upon to meet unlimited claims for debts incurred by companies of which they were members. In granting this benefit to shareholders, some recognition was given, although not enacted, of the need to offer safeguards to creditors of such companies, e.g., funds available to meet the repayment of debts were not to be utilised in the repayment of shareholders funds through dividend distributions.

It became the accepted practice of the courts and of the majority of businesses after 1844 to allow payment of dividends only out of profits 'earned'; a distinction was drawn between capital introduced by the owners, and revenue or profits generated by the business enterprise. However, no ready definition emerged as to the nature and measurement of 'profits', although some guidelines were evolving.

As dividends were payable out of liquid resources, there was a tendency to link profits with the increase in net current assets.

'Changes in either direction in the current value of fixed assets not realised by actual sales were not included in the profit calculation.'[15] When accountants eventually began to recognise the fall in fixed assets values by setting aside depreciation provisions, these provisions were initially made to provide funds for the replacement of assets and not to charge the loss in value against profits earned. It was not until much later that the practice was adopted of making a regular and systematic allocation against profits of part of the acquisition cost of fixed assets. Accounting profits available for distribution to shareholders became identified as any excess remaining after maintenance of total net assets, i.e., owners' initial investment.[16]

The view that a dividend payment could not be made if it led to a reduction in net asset values was overturned by a legal decision in 1889. In the case of *Lee* v. *Neuchatel Asphalte Company* it was first argued that, in declaring a dividend, the company could not ignore the decline in the value of its principal asset, a quarry concession expiring in 1907, although the articles of association apparently permitted this. In the Court of Appeal, however, it was ruled by Lindley LJ that there was nothing in the then existing companies legislation to define either how profits were to be reckoned or how dividends were to be paid: 'the Companies Acts do not require the capital to be made up if lost'.[17] The inference from the above judgement was that the courts did not wish to impose rules on the business world which they were less able to make than the business world itself. Additionally, the then existing practice of allowing dividends to be paid only after maintaining the monetary value of shareholders capital was overturned.

In a later ruling Lindley confirmed this new legal doctrine whilst distinguishing between fixed capital which may be 'sunk and lost' and 'circulating capital' which must be made good (maintained) before a dividend could be declared.[18] This distinction required, for example, a charge for the replacement of goods sold before the calculation of profit, but not for the replacement of expired usefulness of fixed assets.

The effect of the above two decisions was to erode the already fragile protection offered to creditors of limited liability companies. Further legal decisions were made allowing for the payment of dividends out of profits of one accounting period without requiring losses from previous periods to be made good.[19] The balance created by earlier legal decisions between the interests of the shareholders and those of the creditors had been tipped against the interests of creditors.

The issue of distributable profits will be taken up again in Chapter 13 when the effects of recent corporate disclosure requirements will also be considered.

1900–1967

The last two decades of the nineteenth century saw the emergence of a much more important investment community which now existed on a wider scale and with greater strength. Pressure was exerted by the investing community, amongst others, to reintroduce the accounting disclosure requirements of the 1844 Companies Act. This pressure paid off when in 1900, a new Act was passed reintroducing the requirement for an annual audit for registered companies. A later Act, passed in 1907, reintroduced the requirement for public companies to file their audited Balance Sheet with the Registrar of Companies. A similar requirement was eventually made for private companies in the 1948 Companies Act, but even then certain companies were exempted.

Presentation of an annual Profit and Loss Account to shareholders of public companies at the annual general meeting became a requirement after the 1928 Companies Act. However, it was not until after the 1948 Act was passed that the Profit and Loss Account was required to be filed with the Registrar of Companies. There had been a lot of pressure against the publication of Profit and Loss Accounts, stemming from a widely held view that such publication would be against the interests of shareholders in providing information to competitors which could damage the company concerned. Consequently even by 1948 the amount of information disclosed in both Balance Sheet and Profit Statements was minimal.

One significant aspect of the 1948 Act, however, was the introduction of a requirement that the annual audit was to be performed by professionally qualified persons rather than by persons appointed from amongst the shareholders of the company concerned as had happened previously.

1967 to the present

Since 1967, there has perhaps been a greater number of forces for change in financial accounting and financial reporting than in all the previous periods combined. A redirection of the emphasis of financial reporting has also taken place sufficient to cause more than one writer to describe this period as a 'revolution in financial accounting'.[20]

(a) *Company legislation*
The first impetus for change has come from the traditional area of company legislation in the form of the 1967 and subsequent Acts, particularly the 1981 Companies Act, which not only increased the disclosure requirements of registered companies but have laid down requirements about the form in which information is to be provided. Companies are now obliged to provide not only detailed information on how profits have been calculated, including the accounting policies adopted, but also information on asset valuation and profitability based on valuation methods additional to historic cost. Some degree of international harmonisation of disclosure requirements is also taking place across member states of the European Economic Community (EEC) which the United Kingdom joined in 1973.

(b) *Statements of Standard Accounting Practice*
Secondly, the accounting profession has itself entered the area of financial regulation by introducing Statements of Standard Accounting Practice

(SSAPs) which businesses are normally expected to follow, or else face various penalties including qualification of the audit report. These statements lay down not only requirements as to the information which should be disclosed but also the way in which the information is to be aggregated and presented.

(c) *Inflation accounting*

Thirdly, the impact of inflation on business profitability has given rise to demands for a different approach to income determination other than one based on historic cost. It is perhaps inevitable that these demands have not yet been resolved in a manner satisfactory to all parties concerned, given the varied needs of different users of accounting information. For the last few years companies have been required to prepare additional financial statements based on a 'current cost' method of accounting, in an attempt to incorporate and reflect the effects of inflation on business results.

(d) *Accounting policy determination*

The fourth force for change involves a difference in emphasis in the way in which the choice amongst competing accounting practices is resolved, i.e., the manner by which accounting policy is determined. Until recently, accounting policy determination has been motivated by the choice amongst competing accounting treatments on the basis of reporting, in the most accurate manner possible, the 'underlying reality'. Latterly, however, a shift in emphasis has taken place towards an 'information perspective in which selection from amongst accounting alternatives is made on the basis of social choice involving trade-offs'.[21] The description of the process as one of social choice recognises that different users of accounting information have different information needs and that there may be little or no consensus of agreement amongst users on the best accounting method. Much more weight has been given to the needs of users of accounting information than in the past, with the body of potential users being widely defined to include all these groups in whose interests 'the activities of an organisation impinge or may impinge'.[22]

(e) *Computerisation*

Finally, the growth of new technologies has revolutionised much of the day-to-day work involved in the collection and organisation of financial data. It has introduced new possibilities for solving perennial accounting problems and for a greater integration of external financial reporting and internal managerial information systems. The introduction of new technology has not been without its problems for accountancy particularly in the area of computerised fraud. Hence, the modern accountant must be equipped with a much greater variety of skills than his predecessors of even ten years ago.

1.4 Summary

In this first chapter, the nature of accountancy itself has been introduced. A distinction has been drawn between the broad discipline of accountancy and the sub-groupings within the discipline, of which financial accounting is but one. Although the remainder of this text will focus attention on the financial accounting role within the firm and reporting to external users, a brief description of the other sub-groupings within accountancy, namely auditing, management accounting, taxation, and financial management, has demonstrated that the lines of demarcation between the different groupings are not always capable of precise definition.

The influences on accounting have been briefly outlined and will be considered further in later chapters.

Questions

1. Identify for each of the following, three uses of accounting information:

    (a) a shop-keeper,
    (b) a self-employed plumber,
    (c) a manufacturer,
    (d) central government.

2. What are the advantages/disadvantages of limited liability status to the following groups?

    (a) Shareholders.
    (b) Creditors.
    (c) The public at large.

3. What are the functions of an external auditor?
4. To what extent has the voluntary disclosure of accounting information been insufficient to satisfy the needs of external users?
5. For what reasons would the internal management of a business wish to place restrictions on the amount of financial disclosure to external groups?

2 Users and Objectives of Financial Information

2.1 Introduction

Financial accounting information is produced by many different types of organisation to meet a multitude of different needs throughout the world. Both communist and non-communist societies require and make use of information prepared from financial accounting records.[1] Within a mixed economy which includes both public and privately owned enterprises (such as in the UK), some organisations will function on a profit oriented basis whilst others, including such diverse entities as schools, hospitals and religious bodies, will have different orientations.

Even within the profit-oriented sector of the UK economy there are many different forms and sizes of organisations, ranging for example from small owner-run organisations, such as the traditional corner shop, to giant international companies such as ICI, IBM and Unilever. Each organisation will have its own internal requirements for financial accounting information; the way in which each presents information to various user groups outside the organisation will also differ.

In summary therefore, there is no unique set of financial accounting information that will satisfy the needs of every organisation. In order to bring any examination of financial accounting and financial reporting to manageable proportions, a general framework must be identified which is applicable to most situations but which is capable of modification to meet the needs of particular groups. The content of this chapter is therefore organised as follows:

(i) to identify the users of financial accounting information and their general information requirements;
(ii) to define the objectives of financial reporting;
(iii) to describe the desired characteristics of financial statements.

2.2 Users of financial accounting information

It is possible to identify two broad groups of users of financial accounting information produced by business organisations:

(i) those users, internal to an organisation itself, who require financial information in order to help make their contribution to the achievement of the overall aims and objectives of that organisation;

(ii) those users, external to the organisation, who require information either in order to follow their own personal goals or else the goals of other organisations which they represent or serve.

The accounting system implemented by an organisation must be capable of meeting the information needs of both groups of users. Specific reports may be needed by internal users whilst more general reports are normally prepared for external users. The dual role of the accounting system is represented in Figure 2.1 which shows that although the same primary data flows into the organisation, it will be used for different purposes by each user group and to produce different reports. Some feedback of reporting results will also take place between the internal and external user groups, with particular information relevant to the internal users also incorporated into external systems, e.g., in measurement of the values of resources owned. Additionally, the results identified in reports to external users will have implications for internal decision making and may be expected to influence the decisions made.

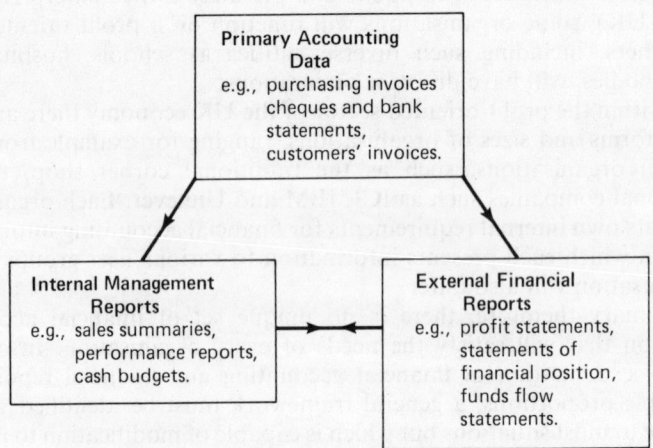

FIGURE 2.1 *The dual role of accounting reporting systems*

Internal users

In any organisation the degree of complexity of the financial accounting system will depend to a great extent on the degree of complexity of the organisation itself, both in terms of the internal structure of the organisation and also the variety of transactions undertaken.

Businesses are formed and run for a variety of different reasons, not all of which are explicitly 'profit-motivated'. Some businesses are founded by individuals or groups who have a desire for pre-eminence in their chosen field, e.g., a desire to be known as the manufacturer of top quality furniture; others may be formed to satisfy a desire for independence from interference from more senior management or owners.[2] Whatever the explicit reasons few organisations, if any, will be able to achieve these other objectives without paying a minimum degree of attention to financial criteria.

Therefore, although the overriding objective may not be profit-maximisation there will normally be some implicit goal of at least 'profit-satisficing', i.e., the achievement of a sufficient level of profits to allow other objectives (if any) to be pursued. The goal of profit achievement, at whatever level, will not be concerned exclusively or even necessarily with the short-term but with the long-term future; there are many opportunities to improve short-term profits at the expense of long-term profitability, e.g., by continually postponing necessary maintenance work, which reduces charges against current profits but which may mean that the earnings power of an organisation is permanently damaged. Management information requirements will therefore include details, not only of day to day operations but also of the long-term implications of current decisions.

A simplified structure of a business organisation is presented in Figure 2.2. Examples of accounting information requirements are then considered in turn for each section of the business illustrated.

(a) *The purchasing section* is concerned to ensure that the necessary amounts of raw materials and other factors of production are bought (or hired) at the required times; that the correct quality of goods are acquired on the best terms possible, including not only cost but also the required dates of payment. Budgeted amounts available to be spent will also be required to be specified and should be compared with amounts actually spent and amounts committed for future expenditure, both for planning and control purposes.

The financial accounting information system must also identify amounts of raw materials currently in stock, the times at which reordering should take place and the amounts which should be reordered. Additional information must be available concerning the terms of trade of different suppliers and the amounts owed to existing suppliers of materials and other services.

(b) *Manufacturing section.* Managers responsible for the manufacturing

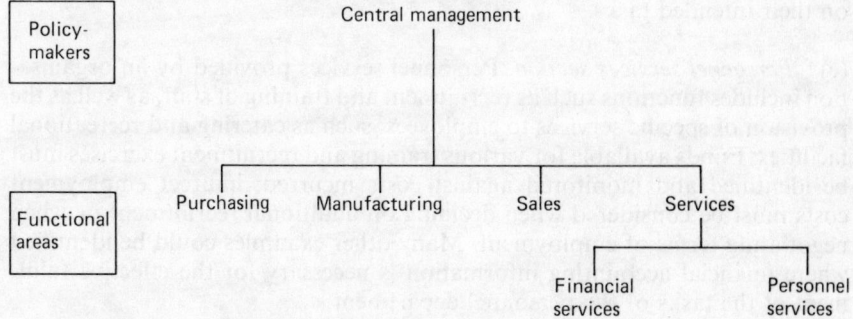

FIGURE 2.2 *Simplified business structure*

function in an organisation have to identify requirements for raw materials, labour and other factors of production including plant and machinery. Regular reports are also required to enable production management to identify whether they are operating within the guidelines set for both the volume and costs of production. Records must be kept of the amount and value of materials used and of goods in production or fully completed. Periodic reports are therefore useful both in planning, control of costs, and in measurement of performance.

(c) *Sales section.* Within this section are those responsible for:

(i) marketing the goods and services of a firm, including advertising;
(ii) actual sales contact with customers;
(iii) recording and monitoring transactions.

Markets available for the products and services of an organisation must be identified together with likely sales potential both in volume and in money terms; sales targets must be identified for individual sales representatives and their performance monitored and periodically reported to them. Control must be exercised over customers' accounts, particularly those with overdue accounts or those whose credit limits have been exceeded, in order to identify potential or actual bad debts.

(d) *Financial service section.* Financial services includes the raising of funds required by an organisation at the times required and on the best possible terms. Additionally, the operation and control of the financial accounting (and management accounting) systems of the organisation will come within the responsibility of this section. The financial accounting system must be constructed to meet the individual needs of the other sections within the organisation and also to co-ordinate the various activities both in the planning stage and also in the production of periodic financial reports for external users. It is also the responsibility of financial services to ensure that the only information presented to specific management will be that which is relevant to their particular needs. The temptation often exists to provide so much information (particularly since the computerisation of accounting systems) that managers are often given more information than they can cope with and are unable either to make rational decisions or spend sufficient time on their intended tasks.

(e) *Personnel services section.* Personnel services provided by an organisation includes functions such as recruitment and training of staff, as well as the provision of specific services to employees, such as catering and recreational facilities. Funds available for various training and recruitment exercises must be identified and monitored against costs incurred; indirect employment costs must be considered when deciding on additional recruitment or when negotiating terms of employment. Many other examples could be identified where financial accounting information is necessary for the effective fulfilment of the tasks of the personnel department.

(f) *Central management.* Central management is responsible for planning future activities in order to aid in the achievement of organisational goals, as well as monitoring on-going activities. It needs to ensure that the different functional areas are working together to achieve overall organisational objectives rather than merely pursuing their own individual objectives, e.g., the production of large quantities of unwanted goods in excess of sales requirements. Financial services will provide valuable help to central management by the production of individual reports relating to specific areas and also of integrated reports relating to all activities.

External users

The traditional view of the role of financial reporting is that of stewardship; directors and/or managers reporting to the owners of a business on their use of resources entrusted to their care. Reporting for stewardship involves two aspects:

(i) it involves satisfying the owners that there has been no misappropriation of resources;
(ii) it involves reporting on the efficiency of the utilisation of resources entrusted to the care of the stewards.

The first aspect of stewardship has long been recognised by legislation as a requirement of financial reporting, but not the second. Early acceptance of this second role is nevertheless evidenced elsewhere; for example, in the parable of the unfaithful steward recorded in the Gospel of Luke, where the owner required an account, from the steward, not only of the resources (talents) initially entrusted to the steward, but also of the gains from using these resources.[3]

As mentioned in Chapter 1, the legal requirements for corporate financial disclosure identified minimum levels of disclosure, but placed more emphasis on the publication of reports showing that funds entrusted to directors by owners/shareholders had not been misappropriated (or used for activities outside of the defined functions of the company). Little or no emphasis was placed on reporting on the efficiency of utilisation of resources,[4] so much so that the general requirement to publish a Profit and Loss Account was not introduced until 1948. The United Kingdom continues to lag behind other countries, particularly the United States, in the quality and amount of information which companies are required to publish to help others in the determination of the efficiency of their operations. Nevertheless there is now an increasing awareness of the need to provide a greater amount of information and to a wider section of the community.

A number of studies, including *The Corporate Report*,[5] have emphasised the duty of business organisations and others to report on their actions to the public at large, as well as to those to whom a legal obligation is identifiable. *The Corporate Report*, a discussion paper published in 1975 by the Accounting Standards Steering Committee, examined the wider role required of published financial reports. This report considered that the responsibility to report is wider than that recognised by legal requirements,[6] and that 'a reasonable right to information exists where the activities of an organisation impinge or may impinge on the interests of a user group'.[7]

Seven different groups were identified in *The Corporate Report* as having a reasonable right to information which ought to be recognised by general purpose corporate reports, including not only the basic financial statements but also all the other forms of information which 'most completely describes an organisation's economic activity'.[8] The seven groups are as follows.

(i) *The equity investor group* This group includes not only existing but also potential ordinary shareholders and holders of other securities. Information is required by this group to help make decisions involving investment or disinvestment in the reporting company and in making comparisons with investments in other companies. Hence, information ought to be provided in a form which is comparable with other business organisations. In particular shareholders will require information on future earnings power and dividend paying potential; to the extent that this may be reflected by past earnings, the presentation of historic data is useful. Additionally, a greater detail of information is called for in order to assist in the assessment of the performance of both the current management team and the company as a whole.

(ii) *The loan creditor group* This group includes both those who have made long-term loans to an organisation and those short-term creditors to whom the organisation owes money in the course of business, e.g., for supplies bought on credit terms.

Long-term loan creditors have much of the same information requirements as the equity investor group. They will be concerned in particular with the long-term viability of the organisation as well as current liquidity; profitability as such may only be of secondary importance. Specific interest will focus on an assessment of the likelihood of corporate default as well as the possible consequences that this might have for the lender's security. Additionally, the lender will be concerned to ensure that the borrower has complied with any restrictions laid down in any loan agreement between them.

Short-term creditors are concerned not only with the security of their loans but also with the likelihood of future business with the borrowing organisation.

(iii) *The employee group* This group is interested in obtaining information concerning the prospects for continuing employment and information for the purposes of collective bargaining. *The Corporate Report* recognised that information currently provided in an aggregated form may not be as useful to the employee group as disaggregated information which would report on sub-groupings within a business organisation, e.g., on a factory basis rather than a company-wide basis.

(iv) *The analyst–adviser group* This group includes not only financial analysts and investment analysts but also journalists, statisticians and others who provide information for other groups of users, including those already mentioned. The needs of this group are similar to the needs of the groups which they serve but their capacity to absorb more complex and sophisticated information should be greater. Indeed, it has even been argued that the current trend towards simplifying accounting reports to the level of the naive investor is unnecessary given the existence of sophisticated investment analysts.[9]

(v) *The business contact group* This group includes a number of different parties who may be affected in some way by the activities of the reporting entity. For example, suppliers may wish to know the likelihood of continued, or indeed of increased, trade with the organisation; customers dependent on the finished product wish to be assured of continued supplies and the likelihood that any expansionary plans of their own may be hindered by a lack of supplies. The continued prosperity and even the survival of many otherwise separately controlled businesses are often interrelated. For example, when the De Lorean Motor Assembly Plant went into liquidation in 1982, a number of other businesses either supplying components to De Lorean or selling their cars, also went into liquidation.[10]

One often expressed fear, and supposed deterrent to disclosure of financial and other information, is the possibility that competitors will benefit in some way from the release of otherwise confidential information. This fear appears to be more prevalent in the UK than in the United States where greater disclosure of information takes place (particularly if the information is expected to improve share price ratings). However, it is acknowledged that there will be occasions when demands for additional information have to be weighed against likely harm done to the reporting entity *vis-à-vis* its competitors.

(vi) *Government* Both at local and at central government level certain information is required from business organisations concerning not only specific governmental needs (e.g., tax paying potential) but also in order to ensure that organisations meet the more general needs of acting in the public interest. Various government bodies monitor business organisations to ensure that they comply with statutory regulations, involving not only taxation and other levies, but also payment of minimum levels of wages to employees, youth training programmes and anti-pollution activities. Statistical and other information is required by other government bodies to enable planning and forecasting functions to be undertaken, as well as providing information to help monitor the effectiveness of government policies.

(vii) *The general public* The final group identified in *The Corporate Report* as having a right to information do so for reasons arising from the status of business organisations within the community, i.e., 'they are afforded special legal and operational privileges, they compete for resources of manpower, materials and energy and they make use of community owned assets such as roads and harbours'.[11]

One further group with an interest in financial accounting information, but not identified as a separate group in *The Corporate Report*, is the financial accounting community itself. This group has special status as the preparers of financial reports and has a vested interest both in the continued output of such reports and in the maintenance of public confidence in the content of financial statements. Additionally there is an increased awareness by the accountancy profession of the possibility of being involved in expensive court cases for negligent advice on auditing/reporting activities. A cynic might see some conflict of interest between the desire of the accountancy profession to improve standards and the fear that increased complexity and scope of reporting exposes the accountant to a greater risk of loss through court actions.

As a postscript to this section on the users of financial accounting reports, it is worth mentioning that *The Corporate Report* recommends among other things, the development of a system of current value accounting (of which more will be said in Chapter 15) and that six additional statements be provided. These additional recommended statements are listed below in Table 2.1 but as yet only the last has been accepted as a reporting requirement by company legislation, while the first has also been recommended by the ASC. A number of the larger UK companies also produce the additional reports on a voluntary basis, particularly the value added and employment reports.

TABLE 2.1 *Additional statements recommended by* The Corporate Report

1. A statement of value added.
2. An employment report.
3. A statement of money exchange with government.
4. A statement of transactions in foreign currency.
5. A statement of future prospects.
6. A statement of corporate objectives.

2.3 Objectives of financial reporting

There is potentially an almost unlimited number of ways in which financial transactions may be recorded and aggregated to produce financial reports. Without any rules or guidelines as to how these reports should be prepared, accountants would be faced with an impossible task in preparation, and users would have little confidence in their content. Unlike physics which possesses a determinable set of natural laws which are discoverable, e.g., Newton's law of gravity, accountancy is not a pure science.[12] Rather, the guidelines which should govern accountancy and more specifically financial reporting, must be those which help in the achievement of overall objectives. Hence, overall objectives first need to be identified before the rules and guidelines can be formulated. However, as the objectives of financial reporting may change over time, it is possible that the guidelines which helped the achievement of objectives in one time period will no longer be relevant in later time periods. In this sense accountancy is a continually evolving discipline and not a stagnant dogma.

Various attempts have been made over the last few years to formulate the objectives of financial reporting. Early statements and views on objectives emphasised the stewardship role of financial reporting by managers to owners (and also creditors). Later studies tended to place greater emphasis on the responsibility of the representatives of business organisations to report to other user groups also. Attempts have also been made to deal with the problems raised by potential conflicts of interest between the information needs of different user groups, although no satisfactory resolution to this problem is as yet in sight.

The Corporate Report mentioned earlier, described the fundamental objective of reporting (including financial reporting) as 'to communicate economic measurements of and information about the resources and performance of the reporting entity useful to those having a reasonable right to such information'.[13] The role of financial information is wider than that of stewardship reporting according to this view; users are to be provided with information that will help them judge the efficiency of the utilisation of resources and likely future utilisation, as well as other factors of both a quantitative and a qualitative nature.

There is a greater volume of written evidence available in the United States on the deliberations of the accountancy profession concerning the objectives of financial reporting. One major pronouncement, APB Statement No. 4,[14] which considered the basic concepts and principles underlying the preparation of financial statements, also included a section on objectives. Three levels of objectives were identified:

(i) the basic objective underlying all others, namely 'to provide financial information about individual business enterprises that is useful ... in making economic decisions'.[15]
(ii) general objectives which determine the appropriate content of financial accounting information, including:
   (a) reliable financial information about the economic resources and obligations of a business enterprise and about changes in these resources and obligations;
   (b) financial information which may assist in the estimation of the earnings potential of the enterprise;
   (c) other information relating to the nature of the information provided, including the accounting policies adopted by the enterprise.
(iii) qualitative objectives, defining the desirable characteristics of the financial information to be provided, and which serve to make that information useful (see Section 2.4).

A later study group, the Trueblood Committee, formed by the American Institute of Certified Public Accountants, was given the goal of making the objectives of financial reporting more explicit.[16] This Committee reaffirmed in its report that the fundamental function of financial reporting was 'to provide information useful for making economic decisions'.[17] Subordinate objectives were also identified as means of achieving the overall objective, including the satisfaction of information needs of various user groups, the type of financial statement to be provided, and the information to be provided in these statements.

In APB 4 and the report of the Trueblood Committee, recognition was given both to the possible conflicts of interest between the information needs of the various user groups and also to the requirement that financial reporting should also serve the public interest.

A number of writers have suggested that the fundamental objective should be expanded to recognise the broader implications of financial reporting by the addition of the rider '[with] an objective of maximisation of social welfare'.[18] This addition was suggested because it was recognised that conflicts would arise from time to time between the needs of different user groups. Unless one group was to be recognised as having an overriding claim on the reporting function, e.g., the existing shareholders, some means of weighting the various competing claims needed to be identified. Hence there has emerged a view that the choice amongst competing accounting alternatives is one of 'social choice' and not merely a question of deciding upon the most theoretically 'correct' accounting model. Needless to say, this view has not received universal acceptance.[19]

Although not everyone would agree with the conclusions of the Trueblood Committee the report produced the foundation for later discussion and subsequent proposals of the Financial Accounting Standards Board (FASB).[20]

In the United Kingdom a recent development has been the commissioning and subsequent publication of a report into 'the possibilities of developing an agreed conceptual framework for setting accounting standards and the nature of such a framework'.[21] This objective was refined by the author of the report, Professor Macve, to consider a framework for financial accounting and reporting in general, rather than one for accounting standards. The identification of a 'conceptual framework' is intended to provide the structure for considering what the objectives of financial reporting are and 'how alternative accounting practices are likely to help achieve these objectives'.[22]

Macve suggests in his report that there is little agreement on specific objectives of financial reporting or of the means to achieve objectives. Three major reasons are given for this lack of agreement:

(i) uncertainty about what information is actually useful and how it is useful;
(ii) variety of needs (as already explained different users have different information needs);
(iii) conflicts of interest, making the establishment of objectives and a conceptual framework a political or social issue as well as a technical matter.

In summary, Macve suggests 'that it is unlikely that an agreed "conceptual framework" can be found that will give explicit guidance on what is appropriate in preparing financial statements'.[23] However, he does suggest that in any consideration of a particular accounting problem the effect of possible solutions on different user groups should be considered and that the areas where the exercise of professional judgement is needed should be more clearly identified.

2.4 Desirable characteristics of financial reporting

A number of studies, including those mentioned in Section 2.3, have considered those characteristics which would be deemed to be most desirable in financial reports. These studies have tended to identify similar characteristics and help provide broad guidelines for the nature of financial information and financial reports. The following seven desirable characteristics have been identified:

(i) *Objectivitity (or neutrality)*. This implies that the measures used in financial reporting should not be biased towards the needs of particular users but should be directed towards the common needs of all user groups (if at all possible).
(ii) *Relevance*. The information included should be that which is likely to be of use to users in their decision making function. Only information which is of material importance should be included.
(iii) *Understandability*. The manner in which information is presented must be capable of being understood by the users. Not only must the information be comprehensible but it must also be sufficiently detailed to satisfy the needs of different users.
(iv) *Reliability*. Reports may not be capable of 100 per cent accuracy or complete objectivity but users must be able to determine how much confidence to place in a particular report. In this respect the verification of reports by independent accountants, i.e., auditors, should increase confidence in reports.
(v) *Timeliness*. In order to be of maximum usefulness, the date of publication of financial reports should be as soon as possible after the period or event to which they relate. Information which arrives too late to have any effect on decisions made will have no value to the users. This attribute of timeliness may, in fact, be considered to be another aspect of the attribute of relevance.
(vi) *Comparability (or consistency)*. The same accounting treatment should be adopted for the same event or transaction wherever possible. This applies not only within reporting entities and from one period to another, but also across different reporting entities in so far as similar treatment does not produce misleading or illogical results.
(vii) *Completeness*. All the information which is necessary to meet user needs should be included in financial reports.

The last desirable characteristic listed above is another reminder of the dilemma facing any search for reporting objectives. Sufficient disclosure to meet the needs of one group of users may be considered excessive disclosure, and thereby harmful, by another group of users.

2.5 Summary

In order to begin to provide a framework for later examination of basic accounting rules and principles, this chapter has attempted to identify users and objectives of financial accounting information. Two broad groups were first identified, namely internal users and external users of accounting information. Using an illustration of a simple form of business organisation various internal uses of financial accounting information were identified. External users were classified into seven groups using the headings identified in *The Corporate Report*.

After a discussion of the information requirements of each external user group, an examination was made of various stated objectives of financial reporting. A primary objective was identified as 'the provision of information useful for making economic decisions', with the addition of a term to allow some method of choosing from amongst competing alternatives, namely 'with the objective of maximisation of social welfare'. Subordinate objectives, identifying how the primary objective might be achieved, were also considered.

Finally, desirable attributes of published financial reports were described.

Questions

1. Identify the types of accounting records and information that would assist each of the following groups of internal users in the performance of their task:

    (a) the stock controller;
    (b) production management;
    (c) the cashier's office;
    (d) the purchasing department;
    (e) the sales department;
    (f) personnel function;
    (g) central management

2. Explain what is meant by the expression 'reporting on the stewardship role'. What should this reporting function involve?
3. Describe the seven groups which the *Corporate Report* identifies as having a reasonable right to corporate information. Specify briefly the major accounting information requirements of each group.
4. To what extent do you agree with those who argue that business organisations have a duty to report on their actions to the public at large? What limitations, if any, should be placed on that duty?
5. For what purpose have various committees sought to identify the objectives of financial reporting? Describe the various categories of reporting objectives which have been identified.
6. To what extent may the information requirements of the following pairs of user groups conflict?

    (a) Existing and potential shareholders;
    (b) Shareholders and employees;
    (c) Shareholders and creditors;
    (e) Managers and shareholders.

    For what other groups of users might information requirements be in conflict?
7. Describe what is meant by the expression 'conceptual framework for accounting'. What are the functions of a conceptual framework?

8. Identify the desirable characteristics of financial statements and explain the significance of each.
9. To what extent does the introduction of a notion of social welfare into the objectives of financial reporting contradict the desirable attribute of objectivity or neutrality?

3 Accounting Principles and Practice

3.1 Introduction

In Chapter 2 both the objectives of financial reporting and the users of financial accounting information were introduced. A broad definition of the overall objective of financial reporting was identified as 'the provision of information to various user groups for the purposes of making economic decisions'. As there are a variety of external (and internal) user groups each with specific needs which sometimes overlap and sometimes conflict, an addition was made to the above objective in accordance with the suggestion of May and Sundem, i.e., 'with the objective of maximisation of social welfare'.[1]

Having arrived at this rather grand definition it might be asked whether this is actually the objective of financial reporting in practice or rather what academics believe it should be. There is sufficient evidence in the writings of accountancy bodies and academics, particularly in the United States, to confirm that this definition is what many of them believe that the objective should be, but that it is not the objective accepted for financial reporting by accounting practitioners. Indeed, one major problem with the definition is that there is no accepted theory of social preference which is capable of ranking user needs in terms of social desirability. It may well be that in many situations the achievement of the goal of the maximisation of social welfare may be accomplished by the pursuit and satisfaction of the goals of the investor group only, but this will not necessarily be the case in all circumstances; it may be socially more acceptable to pursue reporting policies which stabilise the reported profits of an organisation if by doing so this guarantees continued investment, even when such a reporting policy may cause loss to certain groups of investors.[2]

In fact, there is no universal acceptance of the above objective within the financial reporting community. Financial accounting and reporting has developed from a narrowly defined stewardship perspective and not from the wider 'information usefulness' perspective. In the United Kingdom, the basis on which accounting principles and reporting policies have largely developed is that of accounting for the performance of the managers of business enterprises, in part including measurement of business income, but in

Accounting principles and practice

particular, on their legal duties of acting in trust and with good faith. Indeed until recently, little attention was focused on reporting on the other major duty of stewards, i.e., that of dealing efficiently with the resources entrusted to them.

Early analyses of the nature of accounting and attempts to develop a unifying theory have largely taken what is known as the 'classical approach', which involves attempts to identify the measurement rules which give the 'correct' definition of accounting income (see below). Only recently have theoreticians and practitioners begun to recognise explicitly that the scope of financial reporting has widened beyond the requirement to satisfy stewardship obligations. Recognition is now being given to the need to consider the requirements of other groups of users in addition to investors, and also the economic consequences of adopting particular accounting policies. Such consideration of economic consequences implies that choice amongst alternative accounting methods should be based not merely on which accounting treatment is the most 'correct', but also on the effect which the adopted reporting procedure will have on allocation of resources within the economy (see Section 3.2(c) below). Although the scope of financial accounting and reporting has now widened, many of the fundamental accounting principles have their origin in the development of the stewardship role of financial reporting. Criticisms have been raised of the inapplicability of these principles to modern needs and also to the contradictory nature of some of them.

There have been a number of attempts over recent years to develop a unifying theory of accounting in an attempt to define the rules by which practice may be guided. As with the attempt to identify an overall objective for accounting, many of these theories do not accord with what accountants do in practice. The fault for this may lie with the theories themselves or it may lie with current accounting practice, or perhaps the fault, if any, is shared between the two. The following sections describe attempts made to define a unifying theory of accounting and the different approaches available to theory construction. The importance of income measurement is then considered together with a brief comparison of existing accounting practice, under what is described as the historic cost basis of accounting, with measures of business income derived from economic theory.

3.2 Approaches to accounting theory construction

One of the most widely quoted documents on accounting theory in recent years is the American Accounting Association publication, 'Statement of Accounting Theory and Theory Acceptance'.[3] As described in its preface, the document is not a statement *of* accounting theory but a statement *about* accounting theory and theory acceptance. The document records the deliberations of a committee which was formed with the brief of considering whether it was possible to identify a single universally accepted basic accounting theory, i.e., a conceptual framework for accounting. The committee concluded in its report that no such universally accepted theory was capable of identification. Instead, three different approaches to theory formulation were identified and an argument was put forward by the committee that these represented competing or distinct approaches to theory formulation. The three approaches identified are:

(a) The classical approach;
(b) The decision usefulness approach;
(c) The information economics approach.

(a) *The classical approach*

This approach is itself based on two different schools of thought, namely deductive theorists and inductive theorists,[4] each providing a theory of financial reporting for the assessment of the stewardship role. Deductive theorists argue for the primacy of a particular method of income measurement, one which would ideally meet the information needs of all users. Deductive theorists are for this reason often given the title of the 'ideal or true income' school. They use concepts derived from neo-classical economic theory and attempt to formulate theoretical income (and wealth) concepts which are also capable of practical adoption.

Inductive, or positive, theorists on the other hand, take as their starting point observations of existing accounting practice, and attempt to deduce broad accounting principles from these observations. Although this latter approach has been criticised as one supporting the maintenance of the status quo in accounting, it has been justified on the grounds that it helps in the identification of areas where changes are both needed and are also capable of being achieved.[5]

Both the deductive and the inductive forms of classical theory are consistent with what has been described as an 'accountability' approach to financial reporting which has as the central purpose of accounting reporting 'the measurement of the economic performance of the accountor'.[6]

(b) *The decision usefulness approach*

The second approach to accounting theory construction differs from the classical approach in that the primary concern is with the usefulness of the information provided, rather than the relationship of the accounting income measure adopted to 'ideal income'. Again two broad schools of thought have emerged, those concerned chiefly with the construction of decision models and the identification of required information inputs to these models, and those concerned more with the decision makers themselves, i.e., the users of accounting information.

In the decision-model school, 'information relevant to a decision model or criterion is isolated and various accounting alternatives are compared to the data presumably necessary for implementing these decision models'.[7] Among the difficulties encountered in this approach is the problem of specifying the decision models used by the various user groups and identifying the information inputs required by each model. Additionally, different accounting methods may well be suitable for different models, although little evidence is available to support this view as to date the only user group effectively considered by this approach has been the investor group.

The alternative, decision-maker, approach involves an examination of the reaction of the decision makers themselves, either in the aggregate or individually, to alternative accounting data, in order to derive preferred reporting practices. At the aggregate level the approach has chiefly examined the effect of different accounting data on security prices. Research in this area has relied heavily on what is known as the Efficient Markets Hypothesis (EMH), a theory of capital market efficiency. According to the semi-strong form of the EMH, share prices fully reflect all publicly available information about the securities, including published accounting information;[8] security prices are said to react quickly and in an unbiased manner to any new information which is relevant to security prices. Hence, the information content of different sets of accounting data may be tested by reference to the security market reaction to that data, i.e., the share price movements. One limitation of this particular approach to accounting research is that analysis is restricted to current reporting methods only and appears unable to examine whether other methods, not currently under consideration or in use, would be superior.

At the individual level, the decision-maker approach has been described as behavioural accounting research, being concerned as it is with the reaction of individual users to various forms of accounting information. The objective of this approach appears to be the identification of general statements about human behaviour which would then be incorporated into the design of accounting reports useful to users generally.

(c) *The information economics approach*

The third approach to theory formulation differs from the other two in that accounting information is given a value in these earlier approaches only if it helped in any decision-making process, whereas in the latter approach, information is itself treated as 'an economic commodity, the acquisition of which constitutes a problem of economic choice'.[9] This approach is concerned with the costs and benefits of information itself; benefits may result from improved decision making but the attendant costs of providing the relevant accounting information, it is argued, must also be considered before accounting policy decisions are made. It is argued by proponents of this approach that financial accounting theory should make explicit recognition of the possible economic and social consequences of the various accounting methods advocated. Indeed, there is a considerable body of evidence to support the view that in the realm of accounting policy making at least (i.e., the choice amongst competing methods of reporting), the likely economic consequences of particular reporting methods have been major factors in determining whether a particular accounting treatment is adopted or not. In the United States, for example, the choice of which accounting method should be adopted for dealing with oil exploration costs has been determined largely by the likely effect on future levels of investment in the industry.[10]

Although the consideration of economic consequences is present (implicitly) in classical approaches to accounting theory in that decisions are presumably made on receipt of financial reports by owners which have economic effects – even a decision to do nothing will have an economic impact – the explicit recognition of economic consequences has been criticised as effectively 'politicising' accounting. A number of critics have argued that accounting theory should be concerned rather with the production of guidelines for the measurement of performance etc. which users may be able to apply as standards.[11]

One conclusion of the above committee was that the three approaches outlined above are in conflict with each other and consensus agreement on a unifying theory of financial accounting and financial reporting cannot be found. A contrary view held by K. V. Peasnell, Professor of Accountancy at the University of Lancaster, is that 'the three accounting theory approaches identified by the Committee represent the dominant interests of key researchers in the development of accounting thought' and that 'each time the objects of direct interest ... has [sic] shifted. First it was the accounting practices, then it moved to users' decision outcomes; and now to economy-wide costs and benefits. Put differently, the scope of accounting theory has steadily widened'.[12] The view expressed by Professor Peasnell has much to commend it and has implications for the continued role which accounting income theorists still have to play, either in the identification of information which users *should be* concerned with or with the identification of accounting treatments which *should be* adopted in particular circumstances, subject to the constraints imposed by the consideration of the economic consequences of their adoption. Fundamental concepts in economic income will therefore be considered briefly in the following section before going on to consider how accounting income and net asset values are measured in practice.

3.3 Accounting income and economic income

The classical approach to accounting theory formulation mentioned above attempts to define and measure the income of an enterprise by reference to economic theory. One of the major sources of inspiration has been the writings of J. R. Hicks. Hicks' definition of personal income has been widely adopted by income theorists; 'we ought to define a man's income as the maximum value which he can consume during a week, and still expect to be as well off at the end of the week as he was at the beginning'.[13] Although this definition was made for personal income it is generally accepted that it is applicable also to the measurement of enterprise income, i.e., in its most simple form:

$$I_t = W_t - W_{t-1} \tag{1}$$

where I_t = income for time $t-1$ to t, W_t = wealth time t, W_{t-1} = wealth time $t-1$.

Adjusting for any increase or decrease in investment by the owners of the enterprise over the time period studied, equation (1) becomes

$$I_t = W_t - W_{t-1} + C_t - A_t \tag{2}$$

where C_t = disinvestment (consumption) for period $t-1$ to t, A_t = additional investment for period $t-1$ to t.

Not all economists agree with the distinction made in equation (2) between consumption and income; a number of economists actually define income as the amount consumed during a period. Most economists and accounting theorists, however, do agree with the above distinction and the subsequent

Accounting principles and practice

definition of business income as the increase in wealth as identified in equation (2). Where no general agreement exists amongst theorists, however, is on the question of how wealth or 'well-offness' is to be defined and measured. A number of valuation bases have been proposed by different schools of thought, with three main valuation bases identified as follows.

Discounted present value basis

This valuation base owes its origins to the work of the economist Irving Fisher,[14] and others who have refined his ideas.[15] Wealth at any point in time is calculated under this approach by the summation of the discounted values of all net cash inflows which are expected to be earned by the existing assets of a business. 'Discounting' is the process by which cash flows of different time periods may be equated to a single sum of money which would have equal value if received immediately. The process recognises that £1 received in one year's time is less valuable than £1 received today, and that individuals or businesses would normally require some compensation, e.g., in the form of interest receipts, for delay in consumption.

Illustration 1

Mr A is given the opportunity of receiving £x today or £100 in one year's time. Assuming that he requires compensation in the form of interest at 10 per cent for any delay in consumption, then to be indifferent between receiving £x today and £100 in one year,

£x is equal to $\frac{£100}{(1+r)}$

where r = required interest rate of 10 per cent = 0.1.

i.e., £$x = \frac{£100}{(1+0.1)} = £100 \times 0.9091 = \underline{\underline{£90.91}}$

Hence, the present value of £100 received at the end of one year given a discount rate of 10 per cent will be £90.91. The present value of £100 received in one year will differ for different discount rates, i.e., for rates higher than 10 per cent, the present value will be less than £90.91 and for rates lower than 10 per cent, the present value will be higher than £90.91.

In order to calculate wealth using present values at least two factors must be specified:

(i) The expectations of future cash flows; and
(ii) The appropriate discount rate.

The present value approach has been criticised on a number of grounds including subjectivity (in choice of discount rate, etc.) and the uncertainty attached to the expected future cash flows. However, as will be explained later, subjectivity and uncertainty are present to a greater or lesser extent in all valuation bases.

Current market basis

Because of the practical difficulties attached to the present value approach, a number of accounting theorists have suggested wealth valuation based on market prices, e.g., current replacement cost,[16] or net realisable value.[17] Market prices are therefore used as approximations of discounted present values, with different schools of thought arguing as to which form of market price represents the closest approximation. The use of current market values as proxies for economic or present values in income determination is considered in more detail in the Appendix to Chapter 7.

Original or historic cost basis

Although not everyone would agree with the identification of original cost as a valuation base, it must be acknowledged that cost must have represented value, in the case of purchased assets at least, at one particular point in time, i.e., at the date of purchase. By this school of valuation, wealth increases or decreases are measured in relation to the monetary amount of ownership capital invested in the business at the beginning of a period of time.

Original, or historic cost, is the valuation base traditionally used by accountants in the determination of periodic business income and is introduced more fully in the next section.

3.4 Historic cost accounting

Introduction

The stewardship perspective of financial reporting identified earlier may at first sight be thought to be concerned with the reporting of past events as an end in itself. By contrast, the decision usefulness perspective appears to be concerned solely with future events. However, this arbitrary distinction is too simplistic as past events often have a significant influence on future events. Indeed, reporting on the stewardship function implies that decisions will be based on the information reported, e.g., to retain one's investment, to replace managers, to make a distribution of profits to the owners, etc.

Two major aspects of reporting on stewardship have been recognised, first, the provision of a measure of business and management performance, and secondly, a presentation of the financial condition of the reporting entity. The first aspect has been recognised as involving something more than merely recording cash flows, but rather involving primarily the measurement of business income. This aspect has traditionally been satisfied by the preparation of what is known as a Profit and Loss Account or Income Statement. The second aspect involves reporting on the economic resources owned or controlled by the reporting entity and also on the claims exercised on these resources by outside parties. Attempts to satisfy this second aspect involve the preparation of what is known as a Balance Sheet or Statement of Financial Position.

Two criteria in particular appear to have dominated the selection of data to be included in the above two financial statements. First, the recipients of the statements (the users) had to be able to express confidence in the reliability of the information included, and secondly, any doubt over choice from amongst equally acceptable alternative accounting methods was to be resolved by reference to the alternative which produced the most conservative results, i.e., that which minimised the reported income and ownership interest.

Why should these two criteria have played so important a role in the development of financial accountancy? The answer to this question may be found partly by reference to the business environment in the second half of the nineteenth century. Limited liability status was a relatively new phenomenon and one which was not without its opponents; experience of recent business scandals had made investors wary of possible fraudulent reporting activities. Additionally, as explained earlier, reporting of financial performance was considered to be less important than reporting on financial stability. During this same period, the newly emerging accounting bodies were also seeking to establish themselves in the eyes of the general public as a profession with all the attendant standards of behaviour and performance. It was (and is) essential that users could place confidence in the figures provided in financial statements. Adoption of a system of financial reporting based on original or historic cost appeared to satisfy these two basic requirements of objectivity and conservatism. Transactions undertaken and resources acquired were recorded at the cost to the enterprise, with increases in value not normally recognised in the accounting statements until these were realised, e.g., through the disposal of the resources. As will be seen in later chapters, adoption of this historic cost valuation base has often resulted in *ad hoc* and haphazard solutions to accounting problems, some of which are neither objective nor conservative in nature. Indeed original cost itself is not always a well-defined concept, especially when goods are acquired as a result of part-exchange. Additionally, allocations of cost to more than one accounting period often give rise to a considerable element of subjectivity. However, the historic cost system of accounting is now firmly entrenched in the activities of accountants. The fundamental principles on which this system is based will now be examined.

Basic accounting principles

Until relatively recently, formal specification of what constitutes the basic postulates or principles for historic cost accounting are remarkable mainly for their absence. Company legislation has identified a general obligation to prepare financial statements in order to portray 'a true and fair view' of the enterprise being reported upon.[18] This has often been interpreted as meaning the preparation of accounts in accordance with 'generally accepted accounting practices' but with no formal statement of what these practices consist of. From time to time a sufficiently large crisis emerged in the operations of a specific company or group of companies to produce a reaction in the form of government inquiry, followed often by subsequent fresh legislation. Accounting reporting practices have therefore developed partly in response to the needs of the time and also partly in response to the latest scandal.[19] In an attempt to take the initiative in establishing guidelines for financial accounting and financial reporting, the Accounting Standards Committee (ASC) was formed in 1969 by the Consultative Committee of Accounting

Bodies.[20] One of the first statements issued by the ASC dealt with four concepts which were identified as underlying the production of periodic financial statements.[21] Recently, the 1981 Companies Act has reinforced the importance of these concepts, requiring company accounts to be prepared in accordance with these fundamental concepts.[22] The four concepts identified as fundamental are:

(a) Going-concern.
(b) Prudence.
(c) Accruals.
(d) Consistency.

The ASC recognised that the above concepts did not represent 'an exhaustive theoretical approach'[23] to financial accounting, which would have included many more propositions than the four referred to. Although not everyone would agree with their choice of the above as 'the four fundamental concepts of accounting', each will be examined in turn before identifying other concepts which might also lay claim to the title of fundamental concept.

(a) *Going-concern*

Under this concept business entities are considered to operate for the foreseeable future in the absence of any evidence to the contrary. Without making such an assumption the valuation of resources would presumably have to be made on a net realisable value basis. Various commentators have questioned both the likelihood of indefinite business life and also of the need to assume continuity at all.[24] However, it is unquestionable that the 'going-concern' rule is an implicit assumption in the minds of those who prepare financial statements. It is also one of the main arguments used in support of the historic cost accounting system, although one authority on accounting theory has pointed out that 'the mere fact that we assume that a firm will not be forced into liquidation does not justify valuations based on historic cost; other valuations may be more relevant'.[25]

(b) *Prudence, or conservatism, concept*

This concept requires that revenues and profits are not anticipated but are recognised only when realised in cash form or where their ultimate realisation in cash form can be assessed with a reasonable degree of certainty. Provision must, however, be made for all known liabilities, i.e., expenses and losses, whether the amounts involved are known for certain or are based on the best estimate of ultimate liability in the light of the available information.

Application of the prudence concept actually allows wide scope for the exercise of subjective judgement, both with regard to the identification of the time at which revenues may be deemed to be reasonably certain of realisation and also with regard to the likelihood, and ultimate amount, of potential or contingent liabilities. Support is also given to the historic cost accounting system by the application of this concept, as no unrealised gains in resources would normally be recorded until realised and resources are thereby recorded at original cost even when their current values have risen substantially. (In practice revaluations of fixed assets do take place, even within an historic cost system.) Unrealised losses on the other hand, are anticipated and charged against revenues at the earliest opportunity in accordance with a 'lower of cost or market value' rule, i.e., assets are recorded at acquisition cost or current market value, whichever is lower.

Recognition of the prudence concept is given by acceptance of the general principle of choosing that accounting method which maximises expenses and liabilities or minimises revenues and resources when faced with *equally acceptable* alternative accounting treatments.

The prudence concept has received more criticism than most other aspects of accounting, with critics arguing that deliberate understatement of profits and undervaluation of resources is equivalent to misrepresentation and can be as harmful to owners and others as deliberate overstatement. Adoption of this concept is arguably a poor reaction to uncertainty about the future; its application has been criticised as producing inconsistent results which hinder interpretation of financial statements and which can lead to less than full disclosure of relevant information to users.[26]

In defence of the concept, it has been argued that its presence is necessary to offset the undue optimism often expressed by managers and owners, and that understatement is preferable to overstatement as the latter is believed to be potentially more dangerous, especially to ill-informed users of accounting information.

In summary, there are several arguments to suggest that the adoption of the prudence concept has provided one of the major cornerstones for the development of an historic cost acounting system. On the other hand, the concept may have its roots more firmly fixed on pragmatic, rather than on theoretical, foundations and may have led to inconsistencies in accounting treatments which have often been resolved by appeal to 'professional' i.e., subjective, judgement. One influential accounting academic, Professor R. R. Sterling has described conservatism as 'the fundamental principle of valuation in the Accounting Tradition' and 'the premise, often tacit, from which other rules of valuation are derived'.[27] Indeed, SSAP 2 states that 'where the accruals concept is inconsistent with the prudence concept, the latter prevails'.[28]

(c) *Accruals concept*

By this concept, revenues and expenses are matched with one another in so far as this is justified. They are included in the Profit and Loss Account of the period to which they relate, whether or not this is the period in which costs are incurred or receipts collected.

To understand this concept a number of the basic terms used in accounting must first be defined and distinguished.

An *asset* is an economic resource owned by an enterprise which gives rise to a claim to potential future benefits or services, e.g., the ownership of a motor vehicle gives rise to potential benefits either in the use of the vehicle or the disposal of it.

A *liability*, in contrast to an asset, is a measure of future reduction in economic benefits of an enterprise 'arising from present obligations of a particular entity to transfer assets or provide services to other entities in the future as a result of past transactions or events'.[29] In other words, a liability represents a drain on the resources of an enterprise or a debt owed to parties other than the owners of an enterprise. A bank overdraft is a liability, as is money owed to suppliers for goods received, or money owed to the Gas Board on an unpaid bill.

An *expense* is the reduction in value of assets, or increase in liabilities, of an enterprise in the process of earning *revenues*, which are by contrast, increases in the economic resources of an enterprise i.e., reduction in liabilities or increases in assets. The accruals concept distinguishes expenses and revenues, which involve changes in the amount of resources owned by an enterprise, from *costs* and *receipts* which do not; the latter merely involve, in accounting terminology at least, the exchange of one type of resource for another.

Illustration 2
The purchase of a ticket on a train involves a cost, i.e., the price paid in exchange of one asset, cash, for another, namely, the right to travel on a specified journey. No expense is incurred until the journey is actually undertaken. Similarly, the receipt of cash by the railway authorities is not strictly revenue until the journey has been made (and the ticket handed in); until that time arises the holder of the ticket still has the opportunity to reverse the previous exchange transaction and resell the ticket.

Despite the emphasis on the primacy of the prudence concept over the accruals concept, the allocation of expenses and matching with revenues earned implicitly involves postponement of the recognition of losses. Certain expenditures are not charged against profits immediately they have been incurred but instead are treated as assets, even if only for a short period of time. Revenues may similarly be recognised even before cash is received, although this would not be the case if the prudence concept was strictly applied. Instead, where there is a reasonable degree of certainty that cash or its equivalent will eventually be received, revenues earned may be recognised by inclusion in the Income Statement. The accruals concept may be thought of as a modifying influence on the prudence concept. However, without the emphasis placed on the latter the inclusion of gains on revaluation of assets before their disposal, as part of revenues, might be more acceptable to the accounting profession than is currently the case.

(d) *Consistency concept*
This concept requires that similar items and transactions should be treated in a consistent manner within any one accounting period and from one period to the next. Similarly, consistency of treatment should be adopted whenever possible for the same transaction across different firms.

The choice of consistency as a fundamental accounting principle appears rather peculiar. It is one of the desirable characteristics of accounting information defined in Chapter 2 but has no particular claim for pre-eminence amongst these desirable characteristics. Its justification appears to be that consistency of treatment allows for greater comparability of data and hence makes accounting information more amenable to interpretation. Also consistency of treatment increases the acceptability of accounting reports by the general public. At most, consistency should be seen as a constraint on the selection from amongst equally valid alternative treatments.

Accounting principles and practice 37

(e) *Further concepts*

The above list of so-called fundamental accounting concepts differs in a number of respects from what many accountants would identify as fundamental. In particular assumptions regarding the nature of the environment in which the firm operates, the environmental postulates described by Moonitz,[30] are absent. Two such environmental postulates, or conventions, are: (i) the entity convention; and (ii) the money measurement convention.

With regard to the nature of the entity itself there must be clear specification of which transactions and events are to be recorded and reported on, and which are to be ignored. The *entity convention* allows each accounting entity to be treated as a distinct or closed system for accounting purposes, with separation of the transaction relating to each entity from those relating to the owners or to other business entities. The entity concept may be applied either to the whole of a business organisation or indeed to sub-sets within the organisation, e.g., subsidiaries of an investing company. Financial transactions undertaken by the entity are 'accounted for' in relation to their impact on the entity itself.

The *money measurement convention* identifies which events or transactions are to be accounted for and reported on. Only those transactions which are measurable in money terms may be recorded in the accounting system. Hence, existing accounting practice does not normally allow for the recording of the acquisition of human skills when new employees are recruited.[31]

One final principle promulgated for inclusion as a fundamental accounting concept, but one which like consistency appears to be a desirable attribute of information is *materiality*. Recognition of the degree of subjectivity in identification of revenues and expenses, and of the potential for information overload, allows items which are not considered to be material in size and in importance to be dealt with by accounting treatments which may not be in line with the four fundamental accounting concepts. For example, the purchase of pencils by a major company should in theory be treated as the acquisition of an asset and expensed only when used. Such treatment however, is unnecessarily complicated and expensive when compared to the additional benefit to the user of the accounting statements that such treatment may provide.

3.5 Summary

Financial accounting and reporting has developed in the United Kingdom from a stewardship perspective and not from an 'information usefulness' perspective. Attempts to fit current accounting practice into a theoretical framework without recognition of this fact are fraught with dangers. On the other hand, adoption of a wider perspective for financial reporting than that advocated in the stewardship approach may mean that many of the existing accounting practices are no longer relevant.

Three approaches to the determination of an all-embracing theory of accounting were identified:

(a) the classical approach;
(b) the decision usefulness approach; and
(c) the information economics approach.

Each approach may be further subdivided according to the method of reasoning adopted by their advocates, i.e., deductive versus inductive reasoning. According to some observers the approaches represent mutually inconsistent views while according to others they represent a broadening of the scope of accounting theory.

The classical approach to accounting theory formulation has been, until very recently, the most widely embraced approach. It rests heavily on economic theory in its deductive aspect at least, attempting to define enterprise income by reference to measurement of changes in enterprise wealth. Unfortunately the approach is hampered by lack of unanimity over the basis to be adopted for the valuation of wealth. Alternative bases include present values, market values, and historic cost, with the latter being the alternative currently adopted by accounting practitioners.

SSAP 2 identified the four fundamental postulates of historic cost accounting as going concern, prudence, accruals, and consistency. To these may be added the so-called environmental postulates of separate entity and money measurement.

Finally six of the basic concepts or terms used in accounting were introduced and distinguished, namely,

(a) *assets*, economic resources giving rise to potential future benefits or services,
(b) *liabilities*, claims on the resources of an entity,
(c) *expenses*, a reduction in the net asset value,
(d) *revenue*, an increase in the net asset value of an entity,
(e) *cost*, amount expended in exchanging one asset or liability for another,
(f) *receipt*, amount received in exchange of one asset or liability for another.

Questions

1. Identify the major limitations of the definition given for the overall objective of financial reporting at the end of Chapter 2.
2. Distinguish between the three major approaches to the determination of a unifying theory of accounting. Identify also the major characteristics and merits of each approach.
3. Explain what is generally meant by the expression 'the economic consequences of financial reporting'. To what extent may consideration of these economic consequences conflict with the achievement of a 'true and fair view' in financial reporting?
4. Compare the relative merits of historic cost and other potential valuation bases, for the provision of financial accounting information to the following user groups: (a) investors, (b) creditors, (c) competitors.
5. Summarise the reasons for the adoption of an historic cost basis of valuation in financial reporting. To what extent do these reasons still remain valid?
6. Describe the four fundamental accounting principles identified in SSAP 2. Explain whether you agree with the inclusion of consistency as a fundamental principle rather than merely a desirable attribute.
7. How compatible is the prudence concept with the desirable attribute of neutrality in financial reporting?

Accounting principles and practice 39

8. Distinguish inductive from deductive approaches to theory formulation.
9. Categorise each of the following according to their effect on assets, liabilities, revenues and expenses:
   (a) purchase of flour by a bakery;
   (b) payment of employees' wages;
   (c) opening a bank loan account;
   (d) payment of motor car insurance;
   (e) sale of goods by a trader;
   (f) amount owed to supplier for goods received.
10. Which of the following involves an expense?
    (a) the cost of building new office premises;
    (b) the rent paid on shop premises;
    (c) the purchase of goods for resale;
    (d) the payment to a supplier for goods received.

4 Financial Statements and Income Measurement

4.1 Introduction

As demonstrated in the previous chapter, business income may be measured by calculating the difference between ownership interest in the business at the beginning and end of a period of time after adjusting for any changes in the level of investment by the owners. When business income is measured over the life of an entity, the above method of income determination provides a relatively unambiguous measure. Unfortunately, the various groups of users of accounting information, including the owners, require information concerning the level of business or enterprise income at much more frequent intervals, i.e., annually or even semi-annually. As will be demonstrated throughout this textbook, many of the problem areas for accounting arise because of the need to measure income at periodic intervals rather than over the life of an enterprise.

Application of the historic cost basis of valuation requires ownership interest in a business to be measured by reference to the original cost of the assets and liabilities of the business, rather than by reference to current market values or any other valuation base. Increases in asset values are not normally recognised as income until the increases are realised by disposal of the assets, if indeed they are recognised even then. Any loss or reduction in asset value must, however, be recognised whenever it has been identified, although the accruals concept requires that, wherever possible, the loss or reduction in value of assets should be matched with any revenues which the use of these assets has generated. Accounting income is determined through a process of allocating gains or losses, i.e., revenues and expenses, to the time periods to which they relate. Problems arise when there is no unambiguous method of allocation available, and these problems are compounded by the existence of uncertainty regarding the future, e.g., when an asset is purchased to provide services for more than one future accounting period, but the exact service life of the asset is unknown. In such situations there are no exact rules which can be applied in historic cost income measurement, and the exercise of subjective judgement is often called upon. It is in the exercise of judgement that different bases of allocation may be used by different accountants in the same situation, occasionally giving rise to vastly different income figures, as for example in the identification of depreciation expense (see Chapter 7).

4.2 The Balance Sheet and income measurement

Introduction

One method by which ownership interest in a business enterprise, and hence business income, may be measured is by the production of periodic Balance Sheets or Statements of Financial Position. A Balance Sheet provides a summary of the assets owned by a business enterprise at one point in time and the claims on those assets. The Balance Sheet may be viewed as a photograph of the financial position of an organisation at that one particular point in time. It includes the resources owned by the organisation, although not necessarily all the resources controlled by the organisation, or indeed the values of the resources owned except as measured on a historic cost basis. Balance Sheets are statements showing the accumulated results of past financial transactions, hence their name, which denotes the summarised listing of balances on financial accounts. Each subsequent financial transaction undertaken by an organisation will cause an alteration in the Balance Sheet.

Adoption of the entity convention allows a model to be constructed which can demonstrate the relationship pictured in the Balance Sheet between the assets of an organisation and claims on those assets. The model is known as the Accounting Model of the Firm and in its simplest form is described by equation (1):

$$\text{Assets} = \text{Equities} \qquad (1)$$

Equities include all the claims on the assets whether these arise through ownership investment or through funds borrowed from other parties. Borrowed funds are known collectively as liabilities and include such diverse items as money owed to suppliers for goods provided, wages and other expenses not yet paid, bank loans and overdrafts and funds borrowed on a long-term basis. Hence,

$$\text{Assets} = \text{Owners' interest} + \text{Liabilities} \qquad (2)$$

One of the important effects of viewing an enterprise as a closed system is that any financial transaction undertaken by an organisation may be incorporated into the accounting model, and subsequently into the recording process, but in its *dual aspect*, i.e., there will be two aspects to every transaction which must be recorded to allow the model to balance or remain in equilibrium. Each transaction capable of being recorded must have this dual aspect, a giving as well as a receiving; each aspect being recorded to maintain the equilibrium of the model.

Illustration 1
Mr Jones decides to set himself up in business as the XYZ Trading Company, using £11 500 of his own money and £5500 of money borrowed by means of a bank loan. The following purchases are made for the new business: freehold property at a cost

of £10 000, motor vehicles at a cost of £4500 and a stock of goods for resale at a cost of £1850.

Using the accounting model described in equation (1) the above transactions are analysed as follows:

(i)	Increase in Assets: cash	+£11 500
	Increase in Owners' interest	+£11 500
	(Amount invested by Mr Jones in the business.)	
(ii)	Increase in Assets: cash	+£5500
	Increase in Liability: bank loan	+£5500
(iii)	Decrease in Assets: cash	−£16 350
	Increase in Assets: freehold property	+£10 000
	motor vehicles	+£4500
	stock of goods	+£1850

The effect of the above transactions on the accounting model will be as follows:

Assets		=	Owners' interest	+ Liabilities
Property	£10 000		Capital	+ Bank
Motor vehicles	4 500		introduced	loan
Stock	1 850			
Cash	650			
	£17 000	=	£11 500	+ £5500

Table 4.1 shows a simple Balance Sheet for the XYZ Trading Company summarising the information given in the above equation.

TABLE 4.1

XYZ Trading Company Balance Sheet

Assets	£
Freehold property	10 000
Motor vehicles	4 500
Stock of goods for resale	1 850
Cash in hand	650
	£17 000

Equities	
Owners' interest	11 500
Bank loan	5 500
	£17 000

Balance Sheet structure

There are a number of different forms in which a Balance Sheet may be presented. Within these different forms, varying levels of detail are also possible. Professor Yamey, in an historical analysis of nineteenth-century Balance Sheets, notes an example of a Balance Sheet which extended for 14 pages and had only one sub-heading. He contrasts this with Balance Sheets consisting of two headings only, 'To sundries' and 'By sundries'.[1] Clearly, if Balance Sheets are to be of use to their readers, the information presented must be intelligible and relevant to their needs but with the disclosure of significant amounts only. A recommendation on accounting principles, issued in 1968 by the Institute of Chartered Accountants in England and Wales (ICAEW) stated that 'the function of a Balance Sheet is to give a true and fair view of the state of affairs of the company as on a particular date' and that 'a true and fair view implies appropriate classification and grouping of the items'.[2] Although this recommendation has now been withdrawn, the principle of classification and grouping of information under relevant sub-headings still applies.

Assets are generally grouped in Balance Sheets under two main headings, namely current assets and fixed or long-lived assets.[3] *Current assets* are those which are either intended to be held for periods of less than one year or which are expected to be completely exhausted within one complete operating or trading cycle; *fixed assets* include all other assets.

The same type of asset may be considered to be a fixed asset in one organisation and a current asset in another organisation depending on the type of business conducted. For example, motor vehicles may be considered to be fixed assets when they form part of a delivery fleet for a bakery company but would be considered to be a current asset by a motor trader who buys and sells them in the ordinary course of business. Similarly, a building in the course of construction would be considered to be a current asset if owned by a building contractor other than for his own use, but a fixed asset if otherwise, or if owned by another type of organisation such as a manufacturing or trading firm.

Liabilities are also grouped under two headings depending on whether they are due for repayment within one year, i.e., *current liabilities*, or at some later date, i.e., *long-term liabilities*. It is not uncommon for an amount originally borrowed on a long-term basis to be reclassified as a current liability in the year in which it is due for repayment.

Incorporating the above sub-divisions of assets and liabilities, the accounting model becomes:

Fixed assets + Current assets
= Owners' interest + Long-term liabilities + Current liabilities

(3)

A distinction is often made in Balance Sheets between capital initially invested in a business and profits subsequently retained in the business by the owners. The distinction is perhaps an artificial one for an unincorporated business but presents a legal requirement for UK registered companies and will be considered more fully in Chapter 13.

One point worth noting about the ordering of the assets (and the equities) in the Balance Sheet of the XYZ Trading Company is that the accepted convention in the UK and many other countries, but not in the USA, is to list items in order of their degree of permanence to the business: hence, the freehold property, provided it is held for use and not resale, is anticipated to be owned by the business longer than the motor vehicles, which are in turn expected to be owned longer than the goods held for resale or even the cash in hand. One advantage of accepting this convention, or even its reverse, is that it is easier to determine the liquidity position of an organisation, i.e., the ability to meet ongoing financial obligations. Fixed assets are therefore shown in order of their decreasing life expectancy, within the business while current assets are similarly shown in order of the increasing speed at which they are likely to be converted into cash.

For example, in a manufacturing organisation raw materials remain in store until they are introduced into the manufacturing stage, when they are converted to a stock of work in progress; when the goods are completed they will lie in the warehouse until sold. When the completed goods are sold, a debt will normally be created with money owed to the business by the customer. Only when this debt is paid by the customer will cash be received which is then used to buy more raw materials. There is therefore a cycle of cash generation as follows:

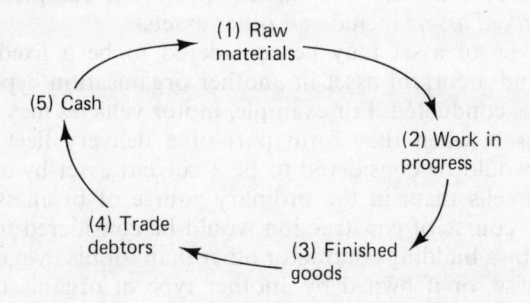

```
         (1) Raw
         materials
   ↗              ↘
(5) Cash          (2) Work in
                  progress
   ↖              ↙
   (4) Trade
   debtors    ← (3) Finished
                  goods
```

As goods are sold at point (4) but cash is not received until point (5) there will be a difference between the cash flow and the income flow of the business. There will also normally be a difference between the point at which raw materials were acquired and the point in time at which they are paid for.

There are two principal forms of Balance Sheet adopted in the UK, the vertical form and the horizontal form. Within these two forms there are a variety of different methods of presentation. Tables 4.2 and 4.3 show the same information for the ABC Company, a manufacturer of office furniture using first the vertical, then the horizontal form of presentation. Each presentation uses the following extension of the accounting model:

Fixed assets + Current assets
   = Capital introduced + Retained profits + Long-term liabilities
   + Current liabilities

(4)

Alternative methods of presentation would use some variation of equation (4), e.g.,

Fixed assets + (Current assets − Current liabilities)
   = Capital introduced + Retained profits + Long-term liabilities

(4a)

or

Table 4.2

The ABC Company
Balance Sheet (vertical form) at 31 December 1984

			£000
Fixed assets			
Freehold land and buildings			82
Plant and equipment			36
Motor vehicles			14
			132
Current assets			
Stocks:			
Raw materials	8		
Work-in-progress	11		
Finished goods	17	36	
Trade debtors		49	
Cash in hand and at bank		7	
			92
			£224
Owners' interest			
Capital introduced			100
Retained profits			57
			157
Long-term liability			
Mortgage on land and buildings			35
Current liabilities			
Trade creditors			32
			£224

Table 4.3

The ABC Company
Balance Sheet (horizontal form) at 31 December 1984

Owners' interest	£000	Fixed assets		£000
Capital introduced	100	Freehold land and buildings		82
Retained profits	57	Plant and equipment		36
	157	Motor vehicles		14
				132
Long-term liability		**Current assets**		
Mortgage on land and buildings	35	Stocks:		
		Raw materials	8	
		Work-in-progress	11	
Current liabilities		Finished goods	17	36
Trade creditors	32	Trade debtors		49
		Cash in hand and at bank		7
				92
	£224			£224

Fixed Assets + (Current assets − Current liabilities) − Long-term liabilities

= Capital introduced + Retained profits (4b)

Note that an increase in an asset does not of itself cause an increase in owners' interest, nor does an increase in owners' interest necessarily result in an increase in assets. Additional assets may be acquired by means of borrowed funds while additional investment by owners may result in repayment of outstanding liabilities. Similarly, one asset may be acquired or disposed of in exchange for another. In this latter case, only when the value of the asset acquired differs from the value of the asset disposed of, will there be any change in ownership interest, i.e., a profit or loss resulting from the transaction.

Illustration 2

The Balance Sheet illustrated in Table 4.1 showed goods held by XYZ Company for resale which originally cost £1850. Assume that the following transactions take place:

(i) the goods are sold subsequently for £3000
(ii) additional goods are purchased for resale at a cost of £2000.

The first of the above transactions involve a net increase in assets and owners interest as follows:

Stock of goods for resale	−£1850
Cash in hand	+ 3000
Net increase in assets and owners' interest	+ 1150

The second transaction, however, involves no net change in assets or owners' interest, but rather the exchange of one asset for another as follows:

Cash in hand	−£2000
Stock of goods for resale	+ 2000
Net increase in assets and owners' interest	Nil

After these two transactions are completed the Balance Sheet of the XYZ Company becomes

XYZ Trading Company
Balance Sheet

Fixed assets		£
Land		10 000
Motor vehicles		4 500
Current Assets		
Stock of goods for resale	2000	
Cash in hand	1650	
		3 650
		£18 150
Owners' interest		12 650
Bank loan		5 500
		£18 150

Financial statements and income measurement

If in transaction (ii) above, goods had been bought on credit terms and not immediately for cash, then there would still have been no change in ownership interest or in net assets, i.e.,

	£	
Stock of goods for resale (asset)	2000	increase
Money owed to supplier (liability)	2000	increase
Net increase (i.e., assets less liabilities)	Nil	

The ownership interest in a business is a function of the total assets minus total liabilities, not of total assets alone. Any change in ownership interest arises either through profits or losses on transactions undertaken or else through changes in the level of funds invested by the owners, i.e., additional investments or withdrawals. The change in ownership wealth during any time period, and hence business enterprise income, will be the sum of the profits and losses on individual transactions undertaken during that time period.

As unrealised gains and losses do not strictly arise as a result of completed transactions, they should be excluded from the determination of historic cost business income. Application of the prudence concept, however, requires all foreseeable losses to be provided for as soon as they are identified. Hence losses on revaluations, although unrealised, will be included as a charge on business income in the period in which they are identified. Gains on revaluations will not be included in business income until realised, if then, but will normally be recorded by means of a credit entry to a Capital Reserve.

Income determination

It is possible, although not normal, to measure business income[4] by comparison of opening and closing Balance Sheets after adjusting for withdrawals of funds or additional investment by the owners. For example, consider the Balance Sheets of the Thompson Trading Company illustrated in Table 4.4. At the beginning of the year, the owners' interest was equal to:

Total assets − Total liabilities = £30 000 − £5 000
   = £25 000

At the end of the year, the owners' interest was equal to:

Total assets − Total liabilities = £31 600 − £5 500
   = £26 100

The income of the business for the year can now be calculated as:

Owners' interest (31.12.XX) − Owners' interest (1.1.XX)
 = £26 100 − £25 000
£1100

The above calculation has assumed that there was no additional investment of funds by the owners during the year and that likewise, no withdrawal of funds took place. If however, additional funds of £500 had been invested by the owners, then the increase in owners' interest could not be attributed

Table 4.4

The Thompson Trading Company
Balance Sheet

	1 January 19XX £	31 December 19XX £
Fixed assets:		
Shop premises and fixtures	21 000	21 000
Current assets		
Stock of goods available for resale	6 200	9 100
Cash in hand and at bank	2 800	1 500
	£30 000	£31 600
Owners' interest	25 000	26 100
Current liabilities		
Bank loan	5 000	5 500
	£30 000	£31 600

solely to the business income earned over the year but must include the additional investment also. The calculation of business income would therefore need to be adjusted as follows:

Business Income = Owners' interest 31.12.XX −
(Owners' interest 1.1.XX + Additional investment)
= £26 100 − (£25 000 + £500)
= £600

Similarly, if during the year the owners had withdrawn funds or other assets from the business amounting to, say, £4000, then the ownership interest at 31 December 19XX would have been reduced by this amount. In the absence of any such withdrawal of assets, the owners' interest in the business at 31 December 19XX would have been £30 100, i.e., £(26 100 + 4000). Business income actually earned for the year may now be calculated as:

$$\begin{bmatrix} \text{Owners' interest 31.12.XX} \\ + \text{Withdrawals} \end{bmatrix} - \begin{bmatrix} \text{Owners' interest 1.1.XX} \\ + \text{Additional investment} \end{bmatrix}$$

= £[26 100 + 4000] − £[25 000 + 500]

= £30 100 − £25 500

= £4600

The above illustration demonstrates that business income can be measured for a particular time period by reference to change in owners' interest in that business, and without reference to the transactions giving rise to the change. This approach is feasible whether an historic cost basis of valuation is adopted or some other basis, for example, current market values.

The major drawback in the above approach to the measurement of business income is that it demonstrates how much has been earned but not how it has been earned. Insufficient information would be given to users of financial statements if managers of business merely reported income as change in owners' interest after adjusting for withdrawals of funds and additional investment. Users would also wish to receive information which would help them form an opinion as to whether the business appears to be run efficiently or not, and whether there is any room for improvement. In order to provide the additional information required, an Income Statement must be prepared.

4.3 The Income Statement and income measurement

Introduction

The Income Statement is given a number of different names including Earnings Statement or Profit and Loss Account. In essence though, these statements are produced with the objective of summarising those transactions which have given rise to profits or losses and hence to changes in owners' interest.

The profit or loss on an individual transaction is calculated by deducting the cost of resources disposed of, or otherwise exhausted, in the acquisition of revenues, from the value of the resources obtained in exchange, i.e.,

$$\text{Profit (Loss)} = \text{Revenue} - \text{Expense} \tag{5}$$

The income for a business enterprise over a specified time period may be calculated by aggregating all revenues earned and all expenses incurred during that time period and offsetting one against the other. Accountants normally measure enterprise income by reference to the transactions undertaken by a business during a particular time period and not directly by reference to changes in owners' interest over the time period. Although both methods will provide the same figure for enterprise income, the first method is able to provide information for inclusion in an Income Statement which will demonstrate *how* the income has been earned as well as *how much* has been earned.

Note that adoption of an historic cost basis of valuation means that neither of the above methods will be able to measure change in owners' wealth over a particular period of time as unrealised gains arising on revaluation of assets will not be included. Nor does the figure shown in a Balance Sheet as owners' interest necessarily reflect the amount realisable by owners if their investment in the business were to be withdrawn. The realisable amount depends partly on whether the business was to be disposed of as a going concern or on the basis of the disposal of individual assets, and also on the amounts obtainable on disposal, which would probably be very different from the Balance Sheet values based as they are on original or historic cost.

The complete form of the accounting model (as described in equation (6)) can be obtained as follows:

Owners' interest$_t$
$= [\text{Fixed assets} + \text{Current assets}]_t - [\text{Long-term liabilities}$
$+ \text{Current liabilities}]_t \tag{6}$

But,

Owners' interest$_t$
 = Owners' interest$_{t-1}$ + [Revenues − Expenses] + [Additional investment − Withdrawals]

Hence,

[Owners' interest$_{t-1}$ + (Revenues − Expenses) + (Additional investment − Withdrawals)]

= [(Fixed assets + Current assets) − (Long-term liabilities + Current liabilities)]

Transaction analysis

Using the accounting model as the basis for the analysis of transactions, the dual aspect of every accounting transaction can be further demonstrated.

Illustration 3
The sale of goods for cash involves the following transaction:

Increase in current assets	i.e. cash
Increase in revenues	i.e. cash sales

Sale on credit, or delayed payment terms, involves the following transaction:

Increase in current assets	i.e. trade debtors
Increase in revenues	i.e. credit sales

Illustration 4
The purchase of goods for resale would initially involve a cost as follows:

Increase in current assets	i.e. stocks
Increase in current liabilities	i.e. trade creditors

Payment to the supplier for the goods acquired involves the following transaction:

Decrease in current assets	i.e. cash
Decrease in current liabilities	i.e. trade creditors

Neither of the above two transactions involves the owners' interest and hence neither can be deemed to be an expense. An expense arises when the goods are sold to the customer:

Decrease in current assets	i.e. stock
Increase in expenses	i.e. 'cost of goods sold'

An accounting transaction involving the increase in the value of one asset must be accompanied by one of the following:

(i) decrease in the value of a second asset,
(ii) increase in a liability,
(iii) increase in the owners' interest

Illustration 5
Increase in the current asset, cash at bank, may be accompanied by one of the following

Financial statements and income measurement

a payment by a trade debtor, i.e. (i) above
borrowing from a finance company, i.e. (ii) above
additional investment in the business by the owners, i.e. (iii) above

The above categories of transactions involve a dual aspect. Certain complex transactions might appear to have more than two aspects. However, on careful examination, these transactions may be broken down into a number of simpler transactions, each of which has only two aspects.

Illustration 6
The purchase of a motor car on credit terms normally involves the payment of a cash deposit plus the acceptance of a liability to make further payments in the future. On inspection, this complex transaction is actually seen to be made up of two simple transactions as follows:

(i) the acquisition of the motor car and acceptance of liability for the total purchase consideration
   i.e. Increase in asset, motor vehicle.
   Increase in liability, amount owed to vendor.
(ii) the payment of the cash deposit in partial settlement of the liability
   i.e. Decrease in asset, cash.
   Decrease in liability, amount owed to vendor.

Revenues, expenses and income determination

Revenues are increases in the economic resources of an enterprise arising from sale of goods or provision of services. Adoption of the conservative, or prudence, concept allows revenues to be recognised only (i) when they have been earned; and (ii) when they are reasonably certain of realisation.

The actual time when revenues may be said to be earned is a moot point. For example, consider a company manufacturing and distributing goods: should revenues be recognised when the goods are manufactured or when the goods are sold? Strictly speaking, the revenues are earned by both activities but to recognise revenues before a sale takes place would conflict with the prudence concept, e.g., recognition of realisable values of stocks of finished goods available for sale would produce a Balance Sheet value higher than original or imputed cost, and record a gain which may never be realised if the goods remain unsold. Hence, the normal procedure under the historic cost accounting system is to recognise revenues only when a sale has been made, i.e., when the ownership of the goods passes to the purchaser. Exceptions do exist to this principle, for example, in the case of long-term construction contracts where revenues may be apportioned over the life of the contract, but on a very conservative basis. Similarly, on some contracts involving hire purchase or other financial agreements, revenues may be recognised before ownership of the goods finally changes hands.

There are also situations where the reverse may be necessary, i.e., where it may not be prudent to recognise the revenues until payment is actually received from the customer or client.

An expense involves the use or consumption of economic resources of an enterprise in the process of earning revenues. When an expense is incurred it will be manifested by a reduction in the net assets of an enterprise, i.e., either assets will fall, or liabilities rise, or both.

The choice of an historic cost valuation base means that many expenses must be computed by reference to their original acquisition cost, if any, or the value of goods given in exchange for services acquired. The actual timing of an expense may on some occasions coincide, at least approximately, with the date of original acquisition or payment, e.g., in the case of sales force salaries, but in many circumstances the expenses of a business may be reported in periods differing from that in which the original acquisition or expenditure took place. In these latter circumstances there is a need to allocate, or apportion, the original acquisition cost to the periods in which revenues have arisen as a result of these expenditures. In other words the process of expensing costs should be undertaken wherever possible on the basis of *matching* the expenses with the revenues which they can reasonably be said to have generated.

Sometimes it may be possible to allocate expenses directly against revenues, but on other occasions the allocation will have to be undertaken on an indirect basis. For example, sales commissions may be directly related to revenues earned but other sales expenses, including travel and motor expenses may not be capable of identification with specific revenues. Even the 'cost of goods sold expense' may not be capable of direct matching with revenues as the goods sold may have been acquired at various prices and may be of a homogeneous nature making specific identification impossible. In fact, the majority of expenses must be matched with revenues on an indirect basis, with time apportionment being a common basis used.

Illustration 7
McEwen Ltd have an accounting year ended 31 December but incur charges for property insurance payable annually in March for the following twelve months to 31 March. In March 1982, property insurance was paid for the year to 31 March 1983, amounting to £4400. This amount will be apportioned and expensed on a time basis as follows:

Accounting year ended 31 December 1982: $\frac{3}{4} \times £4400 = £3300$

Accounting year ended 31 December 1983: $\frac{1}{4} \times £4400 = £1100$

A similar apportionment will also take place in future years. For example, assuming that the property insurance paid in March 1983 amounted to £5200, then the amount will be apportioned and expensed as follows:

Accounting year ended 31 December 1983: $\frac{3}{4} \times £5200 = £3900$

Accounting year ended 31 December 1984: $\frac{1}{4} \times £5200 = £1300$

Hence the total property insurance expense for the accounting year ended 31 December 1983 will amount to £5000, i.e., £1100 + £3900. At 31 December 1982, the amount of property insurance paid in respect of the following year i.e., £1100, will be shown in the Balance Sheet as a current asset, namely a *prepaid expense*. Similarly, in the Balance Sheet at 31 December 1983, an amount of £1300 will be described as a prepaid expense and included in current assets.

Any expenses actually paid in the year *following* that to which they relate are

Financial statements and income measurement

included in the Balance Sheet of the year in which they were expensed under current liabilities and described as *accrued expenses*.

Illustration 8
If an electricity bill was due to be received by McEwen Ltd for the quarter ended 31 January 1983 and the bill was expected to be £1200, then an amount of

$$2/3 \times £1200 = £800$$

would be expensed in the 1982 Income Statement and subsequently included as an accrued expense under the heading of current liabilities in the Balance Sheet at 31 Deember 1982.

Illustration 9
Suppose that electricity bills paid during 1983 by McEwen Ltd totalled £5300 including the bill outstanding at the beginning of the year, and that a further bill was outstanding at the end of the year for the quarter ended 31 January 1984, and estimated at £1500. Again an apportionment would be made of the bill outstanding, probably on a time basis, unless actual electrical usage had been recorded. An amount of $\frac{2}{3} \times £1500 = £1000$ would then be expensed in the 1983 Income Statement and again this amount would be shown as an accrued expense in the Balance Sheet at 31 December 1983. The total electricity expense charged in the 1983 Income Statement would be:

Cash paid	£5300
Add accrued expense 31.12.83	1000
	6300
Less accrued expense 31.12.82	800
(relating to 1982 Income Statement)	
Total expense for 1983	£5500

Matching of expenses with revenues on a time basis, as in the above illustrations, is often justified either on the basis that it is a close approximation to what the allocation would be if a more exact and costly allocation was undertaken, or else because many of the costs occur on a recurring basis with the difference in cost from one year to the next not sufficiently large to distort income. While recognising the merits of these arguments, it should be remembered that allocation on a time basis, as with all other indirect allocation methods, is only an approximation of the matching process. Hence, the determination of income cannot be considered to be a precise process, but rather one involving 'best approximations' based on the subjective judgement of the accountant.

The accounting model of the firm and the dual aspect of accounting transactions: a comprehensive illustration

Arnold Hobbitt, who has recently been made redundant, decides to satisfy a lifetime ambition and set himself up in a retailing business, Hobbitt Enterprises, with the purpose of selling historical books. The following transactions all take place in June 1984.

1 June. Hobbitt opens a bank account in the name of the new business. He deposits in the account £20 000, the proceeds from the sale of his house plus his redundancy payments. Recording this transaction:
    Increase in current asset: cash at bank, £20 000
    Increase in owners' interest: capital introduced, £20 000

2 June. Hobbitt pays a cheque for £2400 relating to one year's rent on business premises:
    Increase in current asset: pre-paid rent, £2400
    Decrease in current asset: cash, £2400

2 June. Hobbitt receives a stock of books costing £6500 from his suppliers on credit terms:
    Increase in current asset: stock of books, £6500
    Increase in current liability: trade creditor, £6500

At the completion of the above transactions, the financial position of Hobbitt Enterprises, using the following simplified accounting model format, is:

	Current assets =	Capital introduced	+	Current liabilities
stock	£6 500			
prepaid rent	2 400			
cash	17 600			
	26 500 =	£20 000	+	£6500

During the remainder of the first month of business, the following (summarised) transactions take place:

(i) Books sold for cash, £4200:
    Increase in current asset, cash, £4200
    Increase in revenues, £4200

(ii) Books sold on credit terms, £450:
    Increase in current asset, trade debtors, £450
    Increase in revenues, £450

(iii) Estimated cost of books sold, £3255:
    Decrease in current asset, stock, £3255
    Increase in expenses, cost of goods sold, £3255

(iv) Payment made to book distributors, £4800:
    Decrease in current asset, cash, £4800
    Decrease in current liability, trade creditor, £4800

(v) Payment of wages to assistant, £220:
    Decrease in current asset, cash, £220
    Increase in expenses, wages, £220

In addition, the following transactions are recorded:

(vi) Expiry of one month's rent:
    Decrease in current asset, prepaid rent, £200
    Increase in expenses, rent, £200

(vii) Estimated bills for heat, light and telephone for the month (not yet received), £150:

Increase in current liability, expenses accrued, £150
Increase in expenses, heat, light and telephone, £150
(viii) Withdrawal by Hobbitt from the bank for his own personal use, £250:
Decrease in current asset, cash at bank, £250
Decrease in owner's interest, drawings, £250

The effect of the above transactions on the accounting model for Hobbitt Enterprises is as follows:

Current assets = Capital introduced + [Revenues[3] − Expenses[4] − Drawings] + Current liabilities[5]

[Stock[1] + Trade debtors + prepaid rent + cash[2]]

i.e. £[3245 + 450 + 2200 + 16 530] = £20 000 + £[4650 − 3825 − 250] + £1850

i.e., £22 425 = £22 425

Notes
1. Stock = £(6500 − 3255) = £3245
2. Cash = £(17 600 + 4200 − 4800 − 220 − 250) = £16 530
3. Revenues = £(4200 + 450) = £4650
4. Expenses = £(3255 + 220 + 200 + 150) = £3825
5. Current liabilities = £(6500 − 4800 + 150) = £1850

From equation (5):
Profits = Revenues − Expenses,
= £4650 − £3825
= £825

Income statement presentation

In addition to knowing how much profit has been achieved during the month of June, Hobbitt will also wish to know how this profit has been achieved. Other parties may also wish to receive a statement showing the revenues and expenses of the business in a more detailed form than that available using the accounting model. For example, if Hobbitt approaches his bank manager at some future date with an application for overdraft facilities, he will probably be required to produce statements of profit (or loss) for a number of past years together with an up-to-date Balance Sheet.

An Income Statement will provide Hobbitt with information showing, in a summarised form, revenues earned and expenses incurred in June 1984. Table 4.5 illustrates one method of presentation of an Income Statement in a vertical form, using the information from the previous illustration.

Additionally, a statement can be prepared showing the movements in retained income from 1 June to 30 June, as in Table 4.6.

An alternative presentation of the Income Statement in the so-called horizontal form is given in Table 4.7. This presentation also shows separately

TABLE 4.5

Hobbitt Enterprises
Income Statement for the month ended 30 June 1984

	£	£
Sales		4650
Deduct expenses:		
Cost of goods sold	3255	
Wages	220	
Rent	200	
Heat, light and telephone	150	
		3825
Net income for month		£825

TABLE 4.6

Hobbitt Enterprises
Statement of Retained Income at 30 June 1984

	£
Retained income, 1 June 1984	—
Add Net income for month	825
	825
Deduct Withdrawals by owner	250
Retained income, 30 June 1984	£575

the gross margin of the business in what is often described as the Trading Account. The separation of gross margin from net income is also possible using the vertical form. The Statement in Table 4.7 also includes a statement of retained income as an addition to the Income Statement, showing how much of the income earned has been reinvested in the business by Hobbitt.

Finally, the Balance Sheet for Hobbitt Enterprises at 30 June 1984 is presented in vertical form in Table 4.8.

4.4 Summary

The current chapter introduced the two major financial accounting statements, namely the Balance Sheet and the Income Statement. Two methods of calculating business income were proposed using each of these statements in turn. The first method, using the Balance Sheet, was rejected in favour of a more informative method which utilised the Income Statement in which total revenues earned and expenses incurred during an accounting period were offset one against the other.

The structure of the Balance Sheet was shown to be based on an equation known as the Accounting Model of the Firm, namely:

Fixed assets + Current assets

= Capital introduced + Retained profits + Long-term liabilities + Current liabilities

(4)

Financial statements and income measurement

TABLE 4.7 *Alternative presentation of Income Statement and Statement of Retained Income using the horizontal format*

Hobbitt Enterprises
Income Statement for the month ended 30 June 1984

	£		£
Opening Stock	—	Sales	4650
Purchases	6500		
	6500		
Less closing stock	3245		
Cost of goods sold	3255		
Gross margin c/d	1395		
	£4650		£4650
Wages expense	220	Gross margin b/d	1395
Rent expense	200		
Heat, light and telephone expense	150		
Net income c/d	825		
	£1395		£1395
Withdrawal by owner	250	Net income b/d	825
Transfer to retained income	575		
	£825		£825

TABLE 4.8

Hobbitt Enterprises
Balance Sheet at 30 June 1984

	£
Current assets	
Stock	3 245
Trade debtors	450
Prepaid rent	2 200
Cash	16 530
	£22 425
Owners' interest	
Capital introduced	20 000
Retained income	575
	20 575
Current liabilities	
Trade creditors	1700
Accrued expenses	150
	1 850
	£22 425

Transactions were analysed using various forms of the above model and the dual aspect of each accounting transaction was illustrated.

Problems of revenue recognition were introduced together with associated problems of matching expenses with revenues generated. Expenses outstanding, i.e., accruals and prepaid expenses, were described together with their effect on periodic income and their basis of inclusion in the Balance Sheet.

Questions

1. Explain the functions of the following financial statements: (a) an Income Statement; (b) a Balance Sheet.
2. To what extent is a Balance Sheet prepared on an historic cost basis, a residual statement summarising outstanding balances?
3. Distinguish between: (a) revenue and receipt; (b) cost and expense.
4. What effect do the following transactions have on owners' interest?

	Increase	Decrease	No effect
(a) Introduction of cash by owner:			
(b) Purchase of equipment on credit terms:			
(c) Purchase of goods for cash:			
(d) Payment of wages to employees:			
(e) Sale of goods which originally cost £3000 for £4500:			
(f) Payments made on behalf of owner:			

For each of the following questions, **circle** the *letter* of the *best choice* from amongst the possible solutions presented.

---

5. The effect of payment for goods received previously on credit terms is:
   (a) decrease in total assets and increase in liabilities;
   (b) increase in total assets and increase in liabilities;
   (c) decrease in total assets and total liabilities;
   (d increase in total assets and decrease in total liabilities.
6. The total assets of a business would be increased by:
   (a) purchase of equipment by means of a long-term loan;
   (b) cash received in satisfaction of customer's account;
   (c) sale of motor vehicle at its book value;
   (d) each of the above.
7. An end-of-period adjustment for prepaid expenses would:
   (a) increase assets and owners interest;
   (b) increase liabilities and decrease assets;
   (c) decrease assets and liabilities;
   (d) decrease assets and owners interest.
8. Owners' interest would be increased by:
   (a) sale of goods on credit terms;

(b) purchase of goods for cash;
(c) repayment of a bank loan;
(d) none of these.

9. Arcadian Enterprises operate an accounting year to 31 December annually. Annual property insurance is paid in advance on 30 April each year, with payments of £2100 made in 1983 and £2400 in 1984. Property insurance expense for 1984 is:

(a) £2100,
(b) £2200,
(c) £2300,
(d) £2400.

10. During their accounting year ended 30 June 1983, Lever Products made payments for heat and lighting totalling £4200, including a payment of £900 for the three months ended 31 July 1982.

During the accounting year ended 30 July 1984, heat and light payments totalled £5600, including a payment of £1050 for the three months to 31 July 1983. Lever Products heat and light expense for the year ended 30 June 1983 is:

(a) £5550,
(b) £5700,
(c) £4250,
(d) £4300.

Problems

1. Summarised Balance Sheets for Walsh Traders at the beginning and end of the 1983 accounting year are as follows:

Balance Sheet	Opening £	Closing £
Fixed assets	12 500	16 200
Current assets	11 300	14 350
	£23 800	£30 550
Owners' interest	16 500	21 960
Current liabilities	7 300	8 590
	£23 800	£30 550

During the year the owners withdrew for personal use, goods valued at £1700 and cash of £1100. Additional assets had been purchased by the owners on behalf of the business at a cost of £2500.

Calculate the business income earned by Walsh Traders during 1983.

2. The following information is available for the first year of operations of Rendel Traders:

Capital introduced by owner	£17 500
Assets owned at end of year	£26 400
Liabilities at end of year	£1 350
Amount withdrawn by owner during year	£960

(a) Calculate the business income for the first year of operations.
(b) Prepare a summarised Balance Sheet at the end of the first year of operations.

3. (a) Using the following form of the accounting model

   Assets = Owners' interest + Liabillities

   analyse the following transactions for Olympic Products undertaken during the first month of operations:

   (i) Cash introduced by owners, £5000.
   (ii) Purchased assets on credit terms, £4200.
   (iii) Sold assets, which originally cost £1100, for £1550 in cash.
   (iv) Used up assets during the course of business, £500.
   (v) Paid £4200 for assets received earlier on credit terms.
   (vi) Cash withdrawn by owner, £400.

   (b) Draw up a summarised Balance Sheet for Olympic Products at the end of the first month of trading.

4. The summarised Balance Sheet of the Minerva Trading Company at 31 January 1984 was:

		£
Fixed assets		17 400
Current assets:		
Stock	7 200	
Trade debtors	4 650	
Cash	2 820	14 670
Total assets		£32 070
Owners' interest		27 220
Current liabilities:		
Trade creditors		4 850
Total equities		£32 070

(a) Analyse the effect of the transactions listed below, which were undertaken during February 1984, on the opening Balance Sheet figures:

For example, transaction (i) involves
          decrease in cash   £1100
          decrease in current liability   £1100

   (i) Payment of £1100 to trade creditors.
   (ii) Purchase of goods for resale on credit terms, £3060.
   (iii) Sale of goods for £6200. These goods were originally acquired at a cost of £2750.
   (iv) Payment of wages for month, £375.
   (v) Payment of property insurance for the year commencing 1 February 1984, £480.
   (vi) Payment of motor expenses for February, £246.
   (vii) Purchase of additional fixed assets on credit terms, £2400.
   (viii) Withdrawal of cash by owner, £420.

(b) Prepare a summarised Income Statement for the Minerva Trading Company for the month of February 1984 and a Balance Sheet at 29 February 1984.

5. The assets and equities relating to the Apollo Company at 31 December 1983 are as follows:

	£
Trade creditors	12 420
Owners' interest	?
Buildings	17 500
Land	12 400
Prepaid expenses	3 910
Cash	3 200
Stock of goods	5 750
Trade debtors	4 650

From the above list prepare a Balance Sheet at 31 December 1983 using the style illustrated in Table 4.2.

6. Mr Brown is made redundant by his firm and given £1500 in compensation. He takes this money and decides to set himself up in business as a mobile grocer.

The following day he borrows £500 from his bank and carries out the following transactions:
(a) Purchase of a second hand van for £1000 in cash.
(b) Payment of one year's road tax and insurance on the van, £120 cash.
(c) Purchase of stock of groceries for the van, £800 cash.

At the end of the first month's trading, he takes stock of his situation and finds that he owns the following items:

Van, valued at month end, £960
Stock of goods for resale, at cost £250
Cash in hand, £1250

He is also owed £130 by customers who bought goods on credit. Mr Brown also owes trade suppliers £250 in respect of goods which he has bought on credit terms for resale in his business. The bank loan is still outstanding and interest on this loan for the month amounts to £9. In addition to the above, Brown has withdrawn £50 per week for four weeks for personal expenditure.

Prepare the following for Mr Brown:
(a) A statement of income for the first month of operations.
(b) A Balance Sheet at the end of the first month of operations.

7. The following additional information is available for the second month of trading for Mr Brown (Problem 6 above):
   (i) Cash purchases of goods amounted to £1300.
   (ii) Purchases of goods on credit amounted to £250. These goods had not been paid for at the end of the month.
   (iii) Cash sales amounted to £1140.
   (iv) Credit sales amounted to £1130. Of these sales, £1000 were paid for by customers before the end of the second month.
   (v) The cost of goods sold amounted to £1100.
   (vi) Motor expenses paid in cash amounted to £470.
   (vii) Payment of interest on bank loan for 2 months, £18.

(a) Analyse the above transactions using a suitable accounting equation format.
(b) Prepare, in good form, an Income Statement for the second month of operations, and a Balance Sheet at the end of the second month of operations.

5 The Accounting Recording Process (I)

5.1 Introduction

In the previous chapter financial transactions were analysed and recorded within the framework of an accounting equation, or model, of the firm. The accounting equation is a useful aid in demonstrating the dual aspect of accounting transactions but cannot be used as a sophisticated recording process. There are practical difficulties involved in any attempt to apply the equation to situations involving a large number of transactions, often including many different categories of assets, liabilities, revenues and expenses. Instead of the accounting model, another system of recording has developed which does, however, recognise the dual aspect of every accounting transaction. This system, which is widely adopted by accountants, is known as Double-Entry Book-keeping and is thought to have developed in Europe during the Middle Ages.

5.2 Double-entry book-keeping

Debits and credits

Double-entry book-keeping utilises two types of accounting entries, namely debits and credits. By convention, debits are entered on the left-hand side of accounts while credits are entered on the right-hand side. There is, though, no inherent value attached to the description of an entry as a credit as opposed to a debit entry (contrary to normal usage of the terms).

The traditional form of double-entry book-keeping uses what is known as 'T' accounts, so named after the original shape of the account (see Table 5.1). Although computerisation may have altered the shape of the account itself, the principle involved in its use still applies. Each account lists all relevant debit and credit entries on the appropriate side, and periodically, the totals of each side will be ascertained and the excess of one side over the other either transferred to another account or else transferred to the following accounting period (see later in the chapter).

The dual aspect of accounting transactions requires that for every debit

TABLE 5.1 *Illustration of a 'T' account*

Name of Account

Debit Entries	£ XXX	Credit Entries	£ YYY

entry in one account, there is an equal, but opposite, credit entry in some other account (or accounts) and vice versa. As with the accounting model used earlier, recording of the dual aspect ensures that the total of all debit entries equals the total of all credit entries and that the total of debit balances on accounts at any point in time will equal the total of credit balances.

The basis on which debit and credit entries are made can be demonstrated by adjusting the accounting model of the firm shown below in the form described in equation (1):

Fixed assets + Current assets = Capital introduced + Retained profits + (Revenues − Expenses) − Distributions to owners + Current liabilities + Long-term liabilities

(1)

and rearranging it as follows:

Fixed assets + Current assets + Expenses + Distributions = Capital introduced + Retained profits + Revenues + Current liabilities + Long-term liabilities

A debit entry is the recording of that aspect of an accounting transaction which increases one of the constituents of the left-hand side of the above equation. A credit entry is the recording of that aspect of an accounting transaction which increases one of the constituents of the right-hand side of the above equation. Reductions to each constituent will be recorded by means of an entry corresponding to the opposite of that described above. Table 5.2 explains the effect of a debit and credit entry on the above accounting categories.

TABLE 5.2 *Effect of debit and credit entries on accounting categories*

	Debit entry	Credit entry
Assets	increase	decrease
Expense	increase	decrease
Owner's interest	decrease	increase
Revenues	decrease	increase
Liabilities	decrease	increase

Illustration 1
Consider the following simple accounting transactions.

(a) Michael Jones opens a bank account for his new business, Jones Industries, and deposits £50 000.
(b) Freehold premises are bought for £37 000 in cash.
(c) £12 000 is borrowed from a well-wisher, J. Fold.

The above three transactions are recorded in T accounts as illustrated in Table 5.3.

TABLE 5.3

Jones Industries

M. Jones
Owner's Interest a/c

	(a) Cash £50 000

Cash at bank a/c

	£		£
(a) M. Jones	50 000	(b) Premises	37 000
(c) Loan	12 000		

Freehold Premises a/c

	£
(b) Cash	37 000

J. Fold
Loan a/c

		£
	(c) Cash	12 000

Journal Entries

One way of illustrating accounting transactions and the accounts in which the entries are to be recorded is by means of what are known as Journal entries. The Journal was originally a book of account in which the relevant debit and credit aspects of all accounting entries were recorded before they were transferred or 'posted' to the relevant 'T' accounts. A commentary is normally added to the journal entry to explain to later readers of the record what has actually taken place.

A typical page in a Journal would include the following headings:

Journal Page

Date	Description	Account Number	Debit £	Credit £

The accounting recording process (I)

Illustration 2

Mary Stuart forms a new business, Tartan Endeavours. On day 1 she deposits £13 000 in a bank account opened in the name of the business and buys business premises for £20 000 with an initial payment of £2000 leaving £18 000 payable in six months time. Journal entries to record the above transactions are shown in Table 5.4.

TABLE 5.4

Tartan Endeavours
Journal Entries

Date	Description	Account number	Debit £	Credit £
Day 1 (a)	Cash at bank Owner's interest Capital introduced by M. Stuart	1 2	13 000	13 000
(b)	Business premises Cash at bank Deposit paid on business premises	3 1	2 000	2 000
(c)	Business premises Creditor Amount owed for business premises, payable in six months	3 4	18 000	18 000

The Journal entries provide an exact image of the way in which the transactions would be recorded in the 'T' accounts. Table 5.5 shows the T accounts relevant to the above transactions.

Transactions (b) and (c) were identified separately in Table 5.4 to illustrate the dual aspect of each accounting transaction but in fact they may have been represented by means of a more complex Journal entry, i.e.,

		£	£
Debit	Business premises	20 000	
Credit	Cash		2 000
	Creditor for premises		18 000

Payment of deposit on business premises and balance due to be paid in six months

The use of complex Journal entries often serves to present an overall picture of the event being recorded and also shortens the recording process. They should only be used, however, in respect of related transactions and where the user is certain of the correct presentation of the transactions. In all other cases simple Journal entries should be used.

Books of prime entry

Apart from the Journal itself there are a number of other accounting records

TABLE 5.5

Tartan Endeavours: T-accounts

M. Stuart
Owner's interest a/c

			£
		(a) Cash	13 000

Cash at bank a/c

	£		£
(a) M. Stuart	13 000	(b) Premises	2 000

Business premises a/c

	£
(b) Cash	2 000
(c) Creditor	18 000

Creditor for premises a/c

		£
	(c) Business premises	18 000

where transactions may be recorded initially before being posted to the relevant 'T' accounts. These preliminary records, or 'books of prime entry' include the Sales and Purchases Journals, or Day Books, Sales Returns and Purchase Returns Journals, as well as Cash Receipts and Cash Payments Journals. The primary purpose of these record books is to summarise similar accounting transactions and to transfer only periodic totals to the relevant 'T' accounts. Without the use of such records the recording of every individual sale transaction in the sales account, for example, would soon result in overburdened accounting records. Although the advent of both mechanised and computerised accounting records has taken much of the tedium out of the recording process and altered the form of the Day Book, present systems still retain the same features as are illustrated below.

Illustration 3
The following sales were made by Turpin Fabrics on credit terms:

Day 1:	to A. Stack	£7500
	to B. Cross	£3180
	to C. Breeze	£ 946
	to D. Lite	£1123

Each of the above transactions were recorded by means of a debit entry in the relevant customer's account. The credit entry was not, however, immediately recorded but rather the sale was entered in the Sales Journal as shown in Table 5.6.

The accounting recording process (I)

TABLE 5.6

Turpin Fabrics
Sales Journal

Date	Account	Account number	Amount
Day 1	A. Stack	S1	7 500
	B. Cross	C1	3 180
	C. Breeze	B1	946
	D. Lite	L1	1 123
			£12 749

At regular intervals, the amount column in the Journal will be totalled and this total transferred to the credit of the sales account, thus completing the double entry.

A Purchase Journal may also be utilised in a similar form with the possible addition of extra columns to enable the type of purchase to be analysed. Expenses incurred may also be included in the Purchase Journal although in the case of irregular expenses the amounts are normally posted to the relevant 'T' account immediately without waiting for the periodic totalling of the expense column.[1]

Illustration 4
The following transactions were undertaken by Turpin Fabrics on Day 2 and recorded in the Purchase Journal:

Purchased goods for resale from G. Day	£762
Incurred electricity expense	£110
Purchased packaging materials	£ 84
Purchased goods for resale from R. Mee	£458
Paid wages	£560
Purchased goods for resale from J. Tar	£923
Purchased packaging materials	£126

Table 5.7 shows a typical Purchase Journal used to record the above transactions. Various forms of the Purchase Journal exist and the number of columns used for analysis may be altered to suit the needs of the business concerned. In particular, a column may be added to show the number of the invoice to which the transaction related.

Posting of the transactions recorded initially in the Purchase Journal in Table 5.7 will be as follows:

(a) As with the Sales Journal, only the entry relating to the supplier of goods will be made initially,
  e.g., Credit the account of G. Day £762
(b) At the end of the relevant period, columns will be totalled and the amount of £2143 will be debited to a Goods Purchased Account (G1).
(c) A similar treatment will be utilised for the transactions relating to the purchase of packaging materials with the accounts of suppliers (P2) being credited with £84 and £126 respectively and an amount of £210 debited to

TABLE 5.7
Turpin Fabrics
Purchase Journal

Date	Particulars	Account Number	Total	Goods Purchased	Packaging	Expenses	Account Number
			£	£	£	£	£
Day 2	Purchases: G. Day	D 1	762	762			
	Electricity	E 1	110			110	E 2
	Packaging materials	P 2	84		84		
	Purchases: R. Mee	M 1	458	458			
	Wages	W 1	560			560	W 2
	Purchases: J. Tar	T 1	923	923			
	Packaging materials	P 2	126		126		
			£ 3023	2143	210	670	
				G 1	P 1		

Packaging Materials Expense Account (P1). If the materials had been purchased for cash the credit entries would have been made to the Cash Account and not to the Suppliers Accounts.

(d) Accounts for electricity and wages payable, E1 and W1, would have immediately been credited with amounts of £110 and £560 respectively. Corresponding debit entries would also have gone to the Electricity Expenses and Wages Expense Accounts, E2 and W2.

On a practical note, the total column is a useful device to cross-check the accuracy of other additions. It is also good practice not to write the account number into the relevant column in the Journal until after the posting has been made. Any posting omissions should then be capable of immediate identification.

Where businesses are continually purchasing and selling similar types of goods it is not uncommon to find a steady volume of goods being returned either from customers or to suppliers. If the volume is considered significant, separate Sales Returns and Purchase Returns Journals may be kept. Relevant entries from these Journals would be:

Debit Sales Returns (or Sales Account)
Credit Customer's Account
with the sales value of any goods returned by customers;

Debit Suppliers Account
Credit Purchase Returns (or Purchase Account)
with the cost of any goods returned to suppliers.

Cash book

If a business generates a large volume of cash transactions, separate Cash Receipts and Cash Payments Journals may also be maintained. These Journals may be maintained separately or more commonly be combined to

The accounting recording process (I)

form one Cash Book. The Cash Book will replace the Cash Account. The following illustration incorporates both Journals into one Cash Book and also assumes for the moment no distinction between Cash and Bank Accounts.

Illustration 5
Kyla Company undertakes the following cash transactions on the same day:

(i) Pays J. Owens for goods received, £947
(ii) Makes cash sales of £1650
(iii) Pays electricity bill, £218
(iv) Receives cash from customer, M. Bell, £1300
(v) Pays wages, £484
(vi) Pays H. Richmond for goods received, £950
(vii) Receives cash from customer, G. Burns, £580
(viii) Receives cash from customer, A. Souter, £760

At the start of the day the balance of cash on hand amounted to £1245. The above transactions are entered into the Cash Book as shown in Table 5.8.

As the Cash Book represents the Cash Account, the recording of each transaction therein involves one aspect of the transaction. The complementary aspect is completed by recording the corresponding debit or credit in the relevant T account. For example,

Receipt from cash sales involves:

Debit Cash Account	£1650	
Credit Sales Account		£1650
Payment of electricity bill involves:		
Debit Electricity Payable Account	£218	
Credit Cash Account		£218
Receipt from credit customer, M. Bell involves:		
Debit Cash Account	£1300	
Credit Customer's Account, M. Bell		£1300

The closing balance of cash in hand at the end of day 1 is identified by totalling all debits and all credits separately and deducting one from the other. In this case there is a greater amount on the debits side than on the credits, i.e., an excess of cash receipts over cash payments, producing a balance of cash on hand amounting to £2936 at the end of day 1 which will be carried down to day 2. The way in which this balance is carried down is in fact to credit the old period, i.e. day 1, with £2936 and to debit the new period, day 2, with £2936. The correctness of this entry can be verified by observing that the cash in hand represents an asset to the business as indicated by a debit balance on the account, in accordance with the convention explained earlier. If there had been an excess of cash payments over cash receipts (including the opening balance), this would have resulted in a cash overdrawn position, i.e., money owed, hence a liability which would have been represented by a credit balance at the commencement of day 2.

The balancing of asset and liability accounts involves the relevant debit or credit balance being carried down from one period to the next. Balancing, or closing, of revenue and expense accounts on the other hand, requires that the net amount standing to the credit or debit of the relevant account be

TABLE 5.8 Kyla Company Cash Book

Date	Description	Account Number	Trade Debtors	Others	Total	Date	Description	Account Number	Trade Creditors	Others	Total
			£	£	£				£	£	£
1	Opening balance			1245	1245	1	J. Owens	O1	947		947
,,	Cash sales	S1		1650	1650	,,	Electricity	E1		218	218
,,	M. Bell	B1	1300		1300	,,	Wages	W1		484	484
,,	G. Burns	B2	580		580	,,	H. Richmond	R1	950		950
,,	A. Souter	S2	760		760	,,	Balance c/d	c/d			2936
			£2640	£1650	£5535				£1897	£702	£5535
2	Balance	b/d			2936						

transferred to a Profit and Loss Account summarising all the revenues and expenses.

Illustration 6
Assume the total on Sales Revenue Account stood at £41 950 at the end of a particular accounting period. As this balance would be shown as a credit in the Sales Account the relevant closing entry would involve:

Debit Sales Revenue Account	£41 950
Credit Profit and Loss Account	£41 950

Similarly, if the balance on the Wages Expense Account stood at £3750, this Account would be closed by the following entry:

Debit Profit and Loss Account	£3750
Credit Wages Expense Account	£3750
Being the transfer of expense for the period ended ...	

Ledger accounts

In most of the above illustrations individual accounts were assigned a number as well as being named. Many businesses will also assign a number, or folio, to the relevant accounts of suppliers and customers. In fact, different types of accounts may often be kept in different books, or ledgers, both for ease of access and also for control purposes.

For example, accounts which are personal to the owners of a business or those of a confidential nature, may be kept in what is known as the Personal Ledger with access limited to the owners or their nominees. Accounts relating to assets, liabilities, revenues and expenses are normally kept in what is known as the Nominal or Impersonal Ledger. Other ledgers will be maintained by the business as size and circumstances dictate. For example, many businesses maintain one or more Sales Ledgers and Purchases Ledgers (or Creditors Ledgers) in which the individual accounts of customers and suppliers are maintained. One of the main reasons for the separation of accounting records in this way is not in fact for the sake of convenience but rather in the interests of control; the separation of the recording of cash movements, for example, from the recording of the purchases or sales to which they relate in order to minimise error and fraud. With the use of computerised accounting records a simple form of control is to maintain each Ledger, Daybook and Cash Book on separate files with access to each file restricted to different operators.

Trial balance and recording errors

Correct recording of the dual aspect of every accounting transaction will automatically ensure that the relationship described in the accounting model will always hold, i.e.,

Total of debit balances = Total of credit balances

Unfortunately human error often creeps into the recording process causing errors which may even maintain the balance while making incorrect recordings. Errors may be of two forms, i.e., errors of practice and errors of principle. The first form of error involves a different amount being recorded as debit entry to that recorded as credit entry or one entry being omitted completely, while the second form of error involves entries in the wrong accounts.

(a) *Errors of practice*

To help identify the first form of error, errors of practice, it is often useful to prepare a Trial Balance before undertaking the preparation of the final accounting statements. The Trial Balance involves a summary listing of all the credit and debit balances of a business at one point in time. If the total of debit balances equals the total of credit balances then there are either no errors of practice, or else there are compensating errors, i.e., there may be an accumulation of incorrect entries which by coincidence balance one another out. A typical Trial Balance is shown in Table 5.9 in which the total of the debit balances exceed the total of credit balances by £54.

The fact that the difference is £54 gives a clue to the possible error which may have occurred. Where the digits in a number are transposed in error the difference between the correct and the incorrect number will give rise to a balance whose digits will add to 9 or multiples of 9. For example, if £471 is debited to one account but £417 incorrectly credited, then an excess of

TABLE 5.9 *Illustration of Trial Balance (with error)*

Account Name	Debit balances	Credit balances
	£	£
Freehold premises	32 000	
Motor vehicles	7 400	
Owner's interest		38 400
Bank loan		15 000
Stock of goods for resale	11 240	
Cash at bank	3 587	
Prepaid expenses	111	
Debtors' accounts:		
J. Jones	27	
M. Smith	145	
A. Donald	79	
Creditors' accounts:		
H. Watt		226
M. Philipps		417
R. Brown		84
Accrued expenses		408
	54 589	54 535
Error		54
	£54 589	£54 589

£(471 − 417) = £54 will result for the total of debit balances. The sum of the digits of this excess balance, 5 + 4 = 9. Hence the existence of the error of £54 gives prima facie, but not conclusive, evidence of an error of this sort. To confirm or otherwise the existence of such an error requires all recorded transactions to be checked to ensure that the transposition error has not taken place, and all balances transferred to the Trial Balance similarly checked.

An alternative form of error could be the complete omission of a credit entry of £54. This error would be much more simple to track down requiring only that the postings of transactions in the amount of £54 be confirmed.

One other possible cause of the unbalanced Trial Balance may be the recording of an entry as a debit when it should have been recorded as a credit or even the inclusion of an account on the Trial Balance itself on the wrong side. Again with a difference of £54 this would require an error of exactly half that amount, i.e., £27 to explain it. Thus re-examination of accounting entries should be carried out to identify whether any transactions amounting to £27 have been incorrectly recorded by means of two debit entries, rather than one debit and one credit entry. Similarly, any closing debit balances amounting to £27 should be checked carefully to ensure that they are not in fact credit balances. One common source of error on customer or suppliers accounts is to misread the balance especially when the balance itself is unusual, i.e., a debit balance for a supplier or a credit balance for a customer. Such unusual balances are not unknown and occur when returns are credited to customers or by suppliers after the goods have been paid for.

(b) *Errors of principle*

Errors of principle occur when transactions are recorded in the wrong account. They will not normally be observable by an imbalance in a Trial Balance. An example of a simple form of error of principle involves debiting the account of J. Smith for goods sold to him when in actual fact the goods had been sold to J. Johnson. Errors of this kind are often not found until an irate customer complains about incorrect statements or when a customer ignores the incorrect amount and pays only the correct balance, leaving abnormal or irregular balances remaining until the error is spotted. This simple type of error has now largely been eradicated through the use of mechanised and computerised accounting systems which automatically enter the transaction in the 'book' of prime entry and at the same time post the entry to the relevant accounts. Unfortunately, as recipients of the occasionally incorrect bank statements will find, even the most sophisticated accounting system is still subject to human error.

More serious forms of errors of principle involve the treatment of what is known as a revenue item as a capital item and vice versa. This type of 'error' results mainly from the allocation problem which was discussed in the previous chapter and which will be further considered in later chapters. It arises either when expenditures incurred and costs arising in the course of generating current revenues are incorrectly capitalised, i.e., treated as assets of one form or another, rather than being treated as revenue items, i.e., expensed immediately, or else when capital items are incorrectly expensed. This form of error of principle may therefore be considered to arise in the main as a result of the imprecise nature of historic cost accounting allied to errors of judgement by the accountant.

5.3 Flow of information

Introduction

Accounting systems may be adapted to meet the individual information needs of all types of business. Typically, though, five stages will be involved in the flow of information as follows:

   (i) Initiating a transaction;
  (ii) Receipt of transaction data;
 (iii) Entering transaction into books of prime entry;
 (iv) Posting transaction to ledger accounts;
  (v) Reporting summarised transactions to users.

Stage (i) may involve, for example, receipt of an order from a customer, or a request from the factory to purchase more materials. At this stage no transaction will be recorded but information must be transmitted to initiate further action, e.g., delivery of goods to customers, or transmission of order to supplier.

Stage (ii) occurs when data is supplied concerning actions initiated in stage (i), e.g., sending out invoices and subsequently statements of account to customers; receipt of delivery notes and/or invoices from suppliers; payments made to suppliers and others; cash received from customers and others. As soon as the transaction data has been received, stage (iii) will be initiated with the transaction recorded in the books of prime entry.

Stage (iv) will involve periodic postings from books of prime entry to relevant ledger accounts. In the case of relatively small businesses, stage (iv) may be undertaken immediately on receipt of transaction data without recourse to books of prime entry other than the cash book.

Finally, stage (v) will involve summarising the transaction data in whatever form is required by the ultimate recipients, whether these are internal or external users.

Flow of sales information

The flow of information relating to sales made by a trading organisation is illustrated in Figure 5.1.

Stage 1 involves the receipt of an order from a customer. This may be received via one of the traders sales representatives or it may be received directly from the customer. An order form is then completed and transferred to the warehouse. From there the goods will be shipped to the customer (stage 2) and a delivery note signed by the customer will then be transferred to the sales ledger clerk who will record the sale, i.e.

   debit   customer a/c
   credit   sales revenue a/c
     with the selling price of the goods.

The accounting recording process (I)

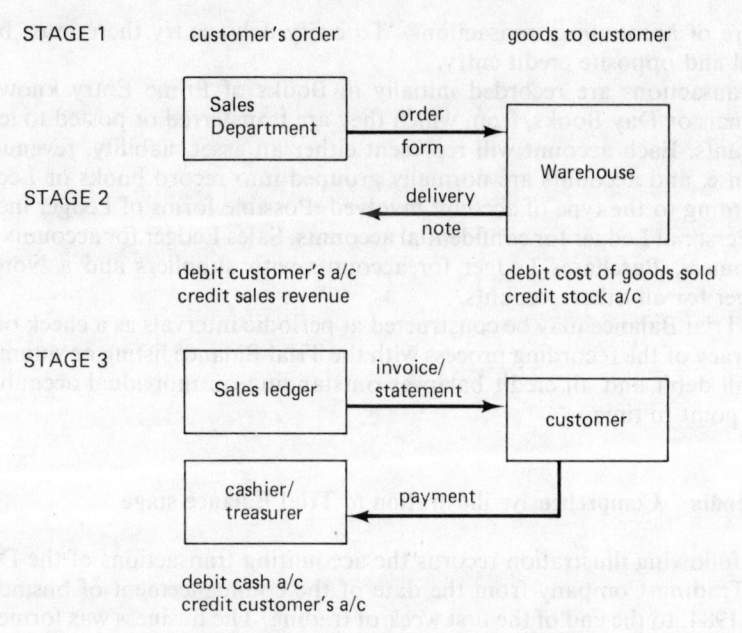

```
STAGE 1    customer's order              goods to customer

           ┌─────────────┐    order      ┌─────────────┐
           │    Sales    │    form       │             │
           │  Department │──────────────▶│             │
           │             │               │  Warehouse  │
STAGE 2    └─────────────┘    delivery   │             │
                              note       │             │
                          ◀──────────────│             │
                                         └─────────────┘
           debit customer's a/c          debit cost of goods sold
           credit sales revenue          credit stock a/c

STAGE 3    ┌─────────────┐   invoice/
           │    Sales    │   statement
           │    ledger   │──────────────▶┌─────────────┐
           └─────────────┘               │             │
                                         │  customer   │
           ┌─────────────┐    payment    │             │
           │   cashier/  │◀──────────────│             │
           │  treasurer  │               └─────────────┘
           └─────────────┘

           debit cash a/c
           credit customer's a/c
```

FIGURE 5.1 *Flow of information: sales*

Sales invoices will then be transmitted to customers.

The clerk in charge of stock records will also record the outflow of goods by the following entry,

    debit   cost of goods sold
    credit   stock a/c
       with the cost price of the goods sold.

Eventually a statement of account will be sent to the customer showing a summary of all transactions with the trader since the date of the previous statement. Statements are normally sent out on a monthly basis and often on the same day each month. The statement will also indicate terms and method of payment, including any discount available and the date by which payment must be completed. Finally, in Stage 4 the customer will pay the balance due on the account in accordance with the terms indicated on the statement and the final accounting entry will be recorded as,

    debit   cash a/c
    credit   customer a/c
       with the payment received.

5.4 Summary

Double-entry book-keeping is a recording system which builds on the dual nature of accounting transactions. 'To every debit entry there must be an equal and opposite credit entry.'

Transactions are recorded initially in Books of Prime Entry known as Journals or Day Books, from which they are transferred or posted to ledger accounts. Each account will represent either an asset, liability, revenue, or expense, and accounts are normally grouped into record books or Ledgers according to the type of account involved. Possible forms of Ledger include the Personal Ledger for confidential accounts, Sales Ledger for accounts with customers, Purchases Ledger for accounts with suppliers and a Nominal Ledger for all other accounts.

A Trial Balance may be constructed at periodic intervals as a check on the accuracy of the recording process with the Trial Balance listing or summarising all debit and all credit balances outstanding on individual accounts at that point in time.

Appendix Comprehensive illustration to Trial Balance stage

The following illustration records the accounting transactions of the Dunedin Trading Company from the date of the commencement of business, 1 July 1984, to the end of the first week of trading. The business was formed by Graham Hunter as a retail shoe shop. Hunter has kept a complete set of accounting records from day 1, including Journal, Day Books, Columnar Cash Books and Personal and Nominal Ledgers. As goods are sold on cash and credit terms to selected customers, a Sales Journal, or Day Book, and a Sales Ledger are also kept, together with a Purchase Journal, or Day Book, and Purchases Ledger.

The Purchase Journal and Purchase Returns Journal are shown in Tables A5.1 and A5.2. Only two analysis columns have been used in the Purchase

TABLE A5.1
Dunedin Trading Company
Purchase Journal

Date	Particulars	Account Number	Total	Goods Purchased	Expenses	Account Number
			£	£	£	
July 1	Rent	NL/5	400		400	NL/9
,, 1	Goods: D. Levy	PL/L1	4850	4850		
,, 2	Goods: G. Sepe	PL/S1	1760	1760		
,, 2	Telephone	NL/6	80		80	NL/10
,, 2	Stationery	NL/7	236		236	NL/11
,, 3	Goods: D. Straw	PL/S2	2490	2490		
,, 5	Wages	NL/8	160		160	NL/12
,, 5	Goods: L. Tron	PL/T1	1570	1570		
			£11546	£10670	£876	

NL/3

TABLE A5.2

Purchases Returns Journal

Date	Particulars	Account number	Amount
July 2	D. Levy – faulty goods	PL/L1	£184
July 5	D. Straw – incorrect goods	PL/S2	210
July 5	D. Levy – faulty goods	PL/L1	62
			£456
			NL/3

Journal as most expenses are of an irregular variety and do not warrant particular attention. The list of account numbers to the left of the total column indicate the account which will be credited with the amount owed by the Dunedin Trading Company. Account numbers on the right-hand side of the journal page and to the bottom of the 'goods purchased' column indicate expense or asset accounts which will be debited.

Postings will be undertaken in the reverse manner for the items listed in the Purchase Returns Journal. Thus the account of D. Straw will be debited with goods returned to him, with a subsequent credit being made in the Purchases Account.

Sales Journal and Sales Returns Journal are shown in Tables A5.3 and A5.4. Here the list of account numbers to the left of the amount column indicate debtors accounts which will be debited with the amount owed to the Dunedin Trading Company. The corresponding credit entry is obtained by transferring the total of the column to the credit of the sales account in the Nominal Ledger, i.e., NL4.

Similarly postings from the Sales Returns Journal are undertaken in the

TABLE A5.3

Dunedin Trading Company
Sales Journal

Date	Account	Number	Amount
			£
July 1	A. Been	SL/B1	180
July 1	B. Nash	SL/N1	75
July 2	L. Bryant	SL/B2	63
July 3	R. Mosbie	SL/M1	111
July 4	A. Been	SL/B1	47
July 4	B. Nash	SL/N1	94
July 5	L. Bryant	SL/B2	196
July 5	A. Been	SL/B1	125
			£891
			NL/4

TABLE A5.4

Dunedin Trading Company
Sales Returns Journal

Date	Account	Number	Amount
July 5	A. Been	SL/B1	£95
			NL/4

reverse manner to that effected from the Sales Journal itself, i.e., the account of A. Been will be credited with £95, the selling price of goods returned to the company, while the sales account will be debited with a corresponding amount.

The business's Cash Book is illustrated in Table A5.5. As the Cash Book itself represents the Cash Account, all transactions recorded within it will represent one aspect of the transaction leaving only the complementary aspect to be recorded. Hence, all items recorded on the debit side of the Cash Book must be accompanied by a corresponding credit in the account referred to in the folio column. Similarly items recorded on the credit side of the Cash Book must be accompanied by a corresponding debit in the relevant account. Exceptions are made for one debit item in the Cash Book and two credit items which are not posted to other accounts immediately but are cross-referenced to the first page in the Journal from which postings to the relevant accounts are made. These exceptions are included separately in the Journal (see Table A5.6) as they are sufficiently important to warrant this special attention. A number of accountants would post all transactions through the Journal, in effect performing four entries for every transaction, but this practice is unnecessary if clear cross-references to postings are provided in the relevant Day Books.

The accounts to which transactions have been posted are also shown. Tables A5.7 and A5.8 (p. 82) illustrate the Private Ledger and Nominal Ledger Accounts while Tables A5.9 and A5.10 (pp. 84–5) illustrate the Purchase Ledger and Sales Ledger Accounts.

Two groups of accounts are apparent in the Nominal Ledger; the first relating to the liability which has arisen, e.g., wages payable, and to the eventual satisfaction of the liability, i.e., by payment of cash. The second group indicates the expense itself which will ultimately be transferred to the Profit and Loss Account at the end of the accounting period to which it relates. The separation of liability and expense accounts is not undertaken in all book-keeping systems but is recommended as a means of simplifying many of the problems which will arise later in more complex recording situations.

It would not normally be necessary to balance accounts at weekly intervals but the balances have been 'drawn', or calculated, in the illustration in order to construct an interim trial balance which is shown in Table A5.11 (p. 86).

The Trial Balance itself does not form any part of the double entry recording process but merely summarises the balances outstanding on all accounts. Note that although the account of D. Levy is in the Purchases

TABLE A5.5 *Dunedin Trading Company: Cash Book*

Date	Description	Folio	Amount	Date	Description	Folio	Amount
			£				£
July 1	Capital introduced	Jn/1	50 000	July 1	Freehold premises	Jn/1	24 000
,, 1	Cash sales	NL/4	324	,, 2	Furniture and fittings	Jn/1	6 000
,, 2	Cash sales	NL/4	286	,, 3	Stationery	NL/7	236
,, 3	Cash sales	NL/4	292	,, 3	Rent	NL/5	400
,, 3	B. Nash	SL/N1	75	,, 5	D. Levy	PL/L1	4 666
,, 4	Cash sales	NL/4	310	,, 5	G. Sepe	PL/S1	840
,, 5	A. Been	SL/B1	85	,, 5	Wages	NL/8	160
,, 5	Cash sales	NL/4	408	,, 5	Balance	c/d	15 478
			£51 780				£51 780
,, 6	Balance	b/d	15 478				

TABLE A5.6
Dunedin Trading Company: Journal

Date	Description	Account Number	Debit £	Credit £
July 1	Cash	CB/1	50 000	
	Owner's interest	P/1		50 000
	Being capital introduced by owner			
,, 1	Freehold premises	NL/1	24 000	
	Furniture and fittings	NL/2	6 000	
	Cash	CB/1		30 000
	Being purchase of shop and fittings			

TABLE A5.7
Dunedin Trading Company
Private Ledger

Pl. Owner's interest a/c

Date		Folio	Amount £
July 1	Capital introduced	Jn/1	50 000

Ledger and would normally be expected to show a credit balance, if any, at this particular point in time it shows a debit balance because of the goods returned to D. Levy after the payment for goods received. As proof of the apparent accuracy of the posting of the transactions the total of debit and credit balances in the Trial Balance are equal, at £57 266. As mentioned earlier in the chapter, however, it is possible for the Trial Balance to 'balance' and yet have either compensatory errors or errors of principle.

Questions

1. If the totals of debit and credit balances shown on a trial balance are equal does this prove the accuracy of the recording process?
2. Describe the purpose of:
   (a) Ledger accounts;
   (b) Books of prime entry.
3. It has been argued that the primary advantage of double-entry book-keeping is the creation of 'order from chaos'. To what extent do you agree with this statement?
4. Outline each stage in the flow of accounting information for a wholesaling organisation, relating to the purchase of goods from a manufacturer.
5. Does the recording of a credit entry generally indicate a favourable event and a debit entry an unfavourable one?

The accounting recording process (I)

6. Indicate whether each of the following is true or false:

   (a) an increase in an asset account is recorded by a credit entry;
   (b) a decrease in a liability account is recorded by a credit entry;
   (c) an increase in an expense account is recorded by a debit entry;
   (d) a decrease in a revenue account is recorded by a debit entry.

7. Give examples of transactions which achieve each of the following:

   (a) an increase in assets and owners' interest;
   (b) a decrease in liabilities and assets;
   (c) an increase in expenses and a decrease in assets;
   (d) an increase in assets and liabilities;
   (e) an increase in one asset and a decrease in another.

In each of the following questions **circle** the *letter* alongside the *best choice* from amongst the possible solutions presented.

8. When goods are purchased on credit terms, the appropriate entry is:

   (a) none;
   (b) debit expense account, credit cash;
   (c) debit stock account, credit cash;
   (d) debit stock account, credit trade creditors.

9. ABC Company sold goods which had originally cost £400. The selling price was £1000, of which £400 was collected immediately, and £600 remained outstanding at the Balance Sheet date. The effect of the transaction on the Balance Sheet would be:

   (a) no change in the total amount of assets and equities;
   (b) an increase in total assets and total equities;
   (c) a decrease in total assets and total equities;
   (d) a decrease in total assets and increase in total equities.

10. XYZ Company always pays its £24 000 annual rent in advance by equal quarterly instalments on 31 December, 31 March, 30 June and 30 September. The company's financial year end is 31 August. The Balance Sheet of XYZ at 31 August will show:

    (a) Accrued rent   £4000;
    (b) Accrued rent   £2000;
    (c) Prepaid rent   £4000;
    (d) Prepaid rent   £2000.

11. A payment of £150 to a supplier has been incorrectly posted to an expense account. To correct this error the required entry is:

    (a) Debit expense account, credit suppliers account with £150;
    (b) Credit expense account, debit suppliers account with £150;
    (c) Debit expense account, credit suppliers account with £300;
    (d) Credit expense account, debit suppliers account with £300.

12. The closing stock of LMN Traders was £10 000 higher at the end of the year than at the commencement. Sales for the year were £250 000 and purchases were £140 000. As a result:

    (a) Cost of goods available for sale was £130 000;
    (b) Cost of goods sold was £150 000;
    (c) Gross profit was £130 000;
    (d) Gross profit was £120 000.   *[Questions cont. on p. 86.]*

TABLE A5.8
Dunedin Trading Company
Nominal Ledger

NL/1 Freehold Premises a/c

Date	Description	Folio	Amount £
July 1	Cash	Jn/1	24 000

NL/2 Furniture and Fittings a/c

Date	Description	Folio	Amount £
July 1	Cash	Jn/1	6 000

NL/3 Purchases a/c

Date	Description	Folio	Amount £	Date	Description	Folio	Amount £
July 5	Purchase Journal	PJ/1	10 670	July 5	Returns Journal	PR/1	456
				" 5	Balance	C/d	10 214
			£10 670				£10 670
July 5	Balance	b/d	10 214				

NL/4 Sales a/c

Date	Description	Folio	Amount £	Date	Description	Folio	Amount £
July 5	Returns Journal	SR/1	95	July 1	Cash sales	CB/1	324
" 5	Balance	c/d	2 416	" 2	"	CB/1	286
				" 3	"	CB/1	292
				" 4	"	CB/1	310
				" 5	Sales Journal	SJ/1	891
			£2 511				£2 511
				" 6	Balance	b/d	2 416

NL/5 Rent Payable a/c

Date	Description	Folio	Amount £	Date	Description	Folio	Amount £
July 3	Cash	CB/1	400	July 1	Purchase Journal	PJ/1	400

NL/6 Telephone a/c

Date	Description	Folio	Amount £	Date	Description	Folio	Amount £
				July 2	Purchase Journal	PJ/1	80

NL/7 Stationery Payable a/c

Date	Description	Folio	Amount £	Date	Description	Folio	Amount £
July 2	Cash	CB/1	236	July 2	Purchase Journal	PJ/1	236

NL/8 Wages Payable a/c

Date	Description	Folio	Amount £	Date	Description	Folio	Amount £
July 5	Cash	CB/1	160	July 5	Purchase Journal	PJ/1	160

NL/9 Rent Expense a/c

Date	Description	Folio	Amount £	Date	Description	Folio	Amount £
July 1	Purchase Journal	PJ/1	400				

NL/10 Telephone Expense a/c

Date	Description	Folio	Amount £	Date	Description	Folio	Amount £
July 2	Purchase Journal	PJ/1	80				

NL/11 Stationery Expense a/c

Date	Description	Folio	Amount £	Date	Description	Folio	Amount £
July 2	Purchase Journal	PJ/1	236				

NL/12 Wages Expense a/c

Date	Description	Folio	Amount £	Date	Description	Folio	Amount £
July 5	Purchase Journal	PJ/1	160				

TABLE A5.9 Dunedin Trading Company Purchase Ledger

PL/L1 D. Levy a/c

Date	Description	Folio	Amount £	Date	Description	Folio	Amount £
July 2	Returns Journal	PR/1	184	July 1	Purchase Journal	PJ/1	4 850
" 3	Cash	CB/1	4 666				
			£4 850				£4 850
July 5	Returns Journal	PR/1	62				

PL/S1 G. Sepe a/c

Date	Description	Folio	Amount £	Date	Description	Folio	Amount £
July 5	Cash	CB/1	840	July 2	Purchase Journal	PJ/1	1 760
" 5	Balance	c/d	920				
			£1 760				£1 760
				July 6	Balance	b/d	920

PL/S2 D. Straw a/c

Date	Description	Folio	Amount £	Date	Description	Folio	Amount £
July 5	Returns Journal	PR/1	210	July 3	Purchase Journal	PJ/1	2 490
" 5	Balance	c/d	2 280				
			£2 490				£2 490
				July 6	Balance	b/d	2 280

PL/T1 L. Tron a/c

Date	Description	Folio	Amount £	Date	Description	Folio	Amount £
				July 5	Purchase Journal	PJ/1	1 570

TABLE A5.10 Dunedin Trading Company Sales Ledger

SL/B1 A. Been a/c

Date	Description	Folio	Amount £	Date	Description	Folio	Amount £
July 1	Sales Journal	SJ/1	180	July 5	Returns Journal	SR/1	95
,, 4	,, ,,	SJ/1	47	,, 5	Cash	CB/1	85
,, 5	,, ,,	SJ/1	125	,, 5	Balance	c/d	172
			£352				£352
July 6	Balance	b/d	172				

SL/B2 L. Bryant a/c

Date	Description	Folio	Amount £
July 2	Sales Journal	SJ/1	63
,, 5	,, ,,	SJ/1	196
			£259

SL/M1 R. Mosbie a/c

Date	Description	Folio	Amount £
July 3	Sales Journal	SJ/1	111

SL/N1 B. Nash a/c

Date	Description	Folio	Amount £	Date	Description	Folio	Amount £
July 1	Sales Journal	SJ/1	75	July 3	Cash	CB/1	75
July 4	,, ,,	SJ/1	94				

TABLE A5.11

Dunedin Trading Company
Trial Balance at 5 July 1984

Account	Folio	Amount £	Amount £
Owner's interest	PL/1		50 000
Freehold premises	NL/1	24 000	
Furniture and fittings	NL/2	6 000	
Purchases	NL/3	10 214	
Sales	NL/4		2 416
Telephone payable	NL/6		80
Rent expense	NL/9	400	
Telephone expense	NL/10	80	
Stationery expense	NL/11	236	
Wages expense	NL/12	160	
D. Levy	PL/L1	62	
G. Sepe	PL/S1		920
D. Straw	PL/S2		2 280
L. Tron	PL/T1		1 570
A. Been	Sl/B1	172	
L. Bryant	SL/B2	259	
R. Mosbie	SL/M1	111	
B. Nash	SL/N1	94	
Cash in hand	CB/1	15 478	
		£57 266	£57 266

Questions *cont.*

13. Star Traders price their goods on the basis of 'cost plus 25 per cent'. The gross profit is therefore:

    (a) 25 per cent;
    (b) 20 per cent;
    (c) $33\frac{1}{3}$ per cent;
    (d) none of these.

14. A cash payment from a credit customer was incorrectly posted to sales revenue account. To correct this error the required entry is:

    (a) Debit cash, credit sales revenue;
    (b) Credit cash, debit sales revenue;
    (c) Credit trade debtors, debit sales revenue;
    (d) Debit trade debtors, credit sales revenue.

15. A payment of £400 was posted to the wrong side of the cash account. The trial balance will be overstated by

    (a) £200 in the total of debit balances;
    (b) £200 in the total of credit balances;
    (c) £800 in the total of credit balances;
    (d) £800 in the total of debit balances.

The accounting recording process (I)

Problems

1. (a) Record the following transactions in journal entry form:
    for Paragon Products for July 1984:
    (i) Payment of £3600 in respect of three months rent;
    (ii) Purchase of office equipment for £6000, cash;
    (iii) Receipt of £1150 from credit customers in respect of accounts outstanding;
    (iv) Purchase of goods for resale, £5300, on credit terms;
    (v) Payment of employees salaries for month, £646;
    (vi) Motor expenses incurred, but not yet paid, £325;
    (vii) Sale of goods on cash terms, £4960;
    (viii) Sale of goods on credit terms, £7150;
    (ix) Cost of goods sold, £6418;
    (x) Depreciation on motor vehicles, £1120.

    (b) Prepare an Income Statement for July 1984 based on the information provided in (a).

2. The following trial balance was extracted from the records of Kite Company at the year end.

Kite Company
Trial Balance as at 31 December 1983

	£	£
Cash	200	
Stock of goods for resale	12 600	
Prepaid insurance	300	
Shop equipment	11 800	
Accumulated depreciation on equipment		3 400
Trade creditors		4 100
Owners' capital		19 500
: withdrawals during the year	4 400	
Sales		65 200
Purchases	40 200	
Sales returns	100	
Salaries	15 700	
Rent expenses	5 500	
Advertising expense	1 250	
Telephone expense	150	
	£92 200	£92 200

The following additional information is also relevant:

(a) Ending stock, £11 700;
(b) Expired insurance for the year, £180;
(c) Estimated depreciation on shop equipment for the year, £1200;
(d) Accrued salaries at 31 December 1983, £250.

You are required to prepare in good order:

(a) An Earnings Statement (Profit and Loss Account) for the year; and
(b) The Balance Sheet at 31 December 1983.

3. James James has a plumber's business which he wishes to sell. A prospective buyer has asked him for up to date accounts and James asks you, as his accountant, to prepare a Profit and Loss Account for the year ended 30 September 1983 and a Balance Sheet at that date.

His Balance Sheet at 30 September 1982 was as follows:

	£	£		£	£
Owners' interest		6 200	Fixed assets		
			Fixtures and fittings		1 800
			Motor vehicles		2 200
Loan		2 000			4 000
Current liabilities			Current assets		
Trade creditors	3400		Stock of materials	3900	
Accrued rent	400		Debtors	2700	
		3 800	Prepaid expenses:		
			Insurance		
			(1.10.82 to		
			31.12.82)	200	
			Rates		
			(1.10.82 to		
			31.3.83)	300	
					500
			Cash		900
					8 000
		£12 000			£12 000

In the course of checking his books and papers, etc., you extract the following information for the year ended 30 September 1983:

1. Cash receipts for year

	£
Cash sales	5 200
Cash received from credit customers	23 500

2. Cash payments made during year

To suppliers for materials purchased on credit	8 700
Wages	7 500
Motor vehicle expenses	2 800
Rent	1 600
Postage, stationery and advertising	600
Secretary's salary	1 400
Telephone	300
Electricity	200
Miscellaneous expenses	520
Repairs	400
Interest on loan	200
Bank charges	100
Insurance (for year ended 31.12. 83)	600
Rates (for period 1.4.83 to 31.3.84)	600
Van (bought 1.10.82)	1 000

3. Credit sales for year — 24 800
4. Materials received on credit from suppliers — 9 000
5. Invoices for period ending 30.9.83 but unpaid at that date:

Rent	400
Telephone	100

6. Depreciation for year
   Motor vehicles – 25% of book value
   Fixtures and fittings – 10% of book value

7. Mr James's drawings for year totalled   2 000
8. Stock of materials on hand at 30.9.83   3 300

Required
Prepare a Profit and Loss Account for year ended 30 September 1983 and a Balance Sheet at that date.

4. The following information was extracted from the accounting records of Brin Traders for 1984:

	March £	April £	May £
Sales to customers	20 000	25 000	30 000
Purchases	15 000	22 000	19 000
Operating expenses	3 000	3 500	5 000

Closing stocks of unsold goods at the end of each month were:

	£
February 29	9 000
March 31	11 000
April 30	14 000
May 31	12 000

(a) Prepare summarised monthly Income Statements for March, April and May 1984 from the above information.

(b) It was later discovered that the following errors had occurred in the above stock figures:

  (i) March 31 closing stock should have been £12 500
  (ii) April 30 closing stock should have been £13 500

What effect have the *errors* had on reported monthly income figures?

5. Trial balances for Rocky Products at the beginning and end of the 1983 accounting year are as follows:

	January 1 £000	December 31 £000
Land	120	120
Buildings (net)	60	58
Equipment (net)	45	48
Stock of goods	71	76
Trade debtors	40	45
Prepaid expenses	11	10
Cash	10	20
	357	377
Capital introduced	140	140
Retained earnings	54	66
Long-term loan	60	75
Trade creditors	82	79
Interest payable	2	3
Accrued expenses	19	14
	357	377

An analysis of the cash account for 1983 revealed the following:

Receipts:	£000
For cash sales	45
Collections from trade debtors	286
Increase in long-term loan	15
	346

Payments:	
To trade creditors	186
For operating expenses	109
Interest on loan	17
Purchase of equipment	24
	336

(a) Reconstruct the relevant ledger accounts for Rocky Products for 1983.
(b) Prepare an Income Statement for Rocky Products for the year ended 31 December 1983, and a classified Balance Sheet at that date.

6 The Accounting Recording Process (II)

6.1 Introduction

Preparation of final accounting statements from an interim trial balance should be a relatively straightforward matter provided that no errors have crept into the recording process. The current chapter identifies techniques available to minimise and correct various errors of practice that may have arisen and also explains the adjusting entries required to convert an interim trial balance into a statement from which the Balance Sheet and Income Statement may be prepared.

There are many organisations operating in the United Kingdom which are classified as non-trading organisations. Preparation of an Income Statement and Balance Sheet in the form described to date is often an inappropriate way of communicating information to interested parties. Forms of financial statements which may be more appropriate to the needs of these non-trading organisations are described in the final section of this chapter.

6.2 Control accounts

Introduction

The potential for errors in the recording of financial transactions is magnified within the accounting departments of large firms, which deal on a regular basis with many thousands of accounts for customers and suppliers. One way in which potential errors may be minimised or at least localised is by the use of Control Accounts for sections of the accounting records. The use of control accounts is fairly common for sales and purchase ledgers, and indeed individual business circumstances may warrant more than one control account for each, with the ledgers being subdivided, perhaps on an alphabetic basis.

Within a control account will be debited and credited the total of all transactions debited and credited individually to the ledger accounts to which the control accounts relate. If individual postings have been made correctly the total balance shown on the control account should equal the sum of the balances on the individual accounts. If there is a discrepancy between the two, then the search for posting errors may be confined to the individual accounts covered by the control account.

The use of control accounts serves at least two functions:

(i) they act as a safeguard on the accuracy of postings made to the individual accounts and help identify areas in which errors have been made, or in which fraud has occurred;
(ii) the control account balance may be substituted for the individual account balances when the trial balance is drawn up.

Control accounts may be included within the double-entry book-keeping system in which case they normally relegate the individual accounts to memoranda, or else the control accounts may themselves be used as memorandum accounts outside of the double-entry system.

Whether the decision is taken to include the control accounts within the double-entry system or exclude them, the same postings will be made. The following illustration considers the use of a control account as a memorandum account for the sales ledger of the Dunedin Trading Company, illustrated in the Appendix at the end of Chapter 5.

Illustration 1

The Dunedin Trading Company (Chapter 5) operated a sales journal and sales ledger. In order to introduce a sales ledger control account the following additional postings would need to be made:

(i) Debit the Sales Ledger Control Account with the periodic total of sales recorded in the Sales journal;
(ii) Credit the control account with the periodic total of returns recorded in the sales returns journal;
(iii) Credit the control account with the periodic amount of cash received from debtors. (In the case of the cash book of the Dunedin Trading Company this has required the inclusion of an additional column for identifying total cash receipts from trade debtors.)

The net result of the above transactions is as follows:

Sales Ledger Control Account

Date	Folio	£	Date	Folio	£
July 5 Sales Journal	SJ1	891	July 5 Sales Returns	SR1	95
			July 5 Cash	CB1	160
			July 5 Balance	c/d	636
		£891			£891
July 5 Balance	b/d	636			

The balance shown on the control account at 5 July may be compared with the sum of the balances on the individual accounts as follows:

SL	B1	A. Been	£172
"	B2	L. Bryant	259
"	M1	R. Mosbie	111
"	N1	B. Nash	94
			£636

The accounting recording process (II)

Agreement between the totals helps to confirm the accuracy of the recording process.

Discounts received and allowed

As money tied up in debtors' balances is an unproductive asset many businesses follow the practice of allowing cash discounts to customers who settle their accounts promptly. In order to maintain the accuracy of the accounting records discounts received from suppliers and allowed to customers must also be recorded.

In order to record discounts the following steps should be taken:

(i) Two additional columns should be included in the cash book, one on the debit side for discounts allowed to customers, the other on the credit side for discounts received from suppliers.
(ii) The periodic total of discounts received should be transferred to the credit of a Discounts Received Account. The complementary aspect of this transaction will be completed by posting the individual discounts received to the debit of the relevant suppliers account in the purchase ledger.
(iii) The periodic total of discounts allowed should be transferred to the debit side of a Discounts Allowed Account. The complementary aspect of this transaction will be completed by posting the individual discounts allowed to the credit of the relevant customers' account in the sales ledger.
(iv) The total of discounts received should be posted to the debit of the purchase ledger control account.
(v) The total of discounts allowed should be posted to the credit of the sales ledger control account.

Illustration 2
Helen Matthews operates a builders' merchants business, H. Matthews Merchandising Company, buying goods from manufacturers on terms which allow her to deduct a 2 per cent discount if payment of account is made within the approved period. The record of transactions undertaken with one of her suppliers, G. O. Gail, for the month of May 1984 is as follows:

May	1	Opening balance	£1100
	3	Cash paid to clear balance	1078
	7	Goods purchased	1400
	15	Goods purchased	850
	20	Cash paid	1372
	20	Discount received	28

The account with G. O. Gail for the month of May, 1984 is shown in Table 6.1.

Illustration 3
Customers of Matthews Merchandising (above) also receive a cash discount, of 1 per cent, for payment of accounts within ten days of receipt of goods. The record of transactions undertaken with one customer, Oban Builders, who always claim the discount, is given below for the month of May 1984.

			£
May	1	Opening balance	650
May	7	Goods sold	1250
May	10	Cash received	1881
May	16	Goods sold	800

May 23   Goods sold   640
May 25   Cash received   792

The account with Oban Builders, recording the above transactions is shown in Table 6.2. An extract from the cash book of H. Matthews Merchandising Company incorporating the transactions identified in illustrations 2 and 3, is given in Table 6.3.

Once the discounts have been incorporated into the recording process the next problem to address is how to deal with the balances on the discount received and discounts allowed accounts. A number of different treatments are possible of which the following are the major forms:

(i) To offset the balance shown on one account against the balance shown on the other account and to carry forward any resulting balance to later accounting periods; this treatment has little to commend it as the problem is merely transferred to later periods in the belief that the excess of one form of discount over the other is a random event, which will eventually even itself out.

(ii) To deduct discounts received from the cost of purchases and discounts allowed from sales revenue in order to show net cost and net revenues; this treatment has its opponents who point out the resulting distortion of trading margins and confusion of financial charges with trading expenses.

TABLE 6.1   *H. Matthews Merchandising Company: extract from Purchase Ledger*

G. O. Gail a/c

1984		£	1984		£
May 3	Cash	1078	May 1	Balance b/d	1100
3	Discount received	22			
		£1100			£1100
May 20	Cash	1372	May 7	Purchases	1400
20	Discount received	28			
31	Balance c/d	850	15	Purchases	850
		£2250			£2250
			June 1	Balance b/d	850

TABLE 6.2   *H. Matthews Merchandising Company: extract from Sales Ledger*

Oban Builders a/c

1984		£	1984		£
May 1	Balance b/d	650	May 10	Cash	1881
7	Sales	1250	10	Discount allowed	19
		£1900			£1900
May 16	Sales	800	May 25	Cash	792
			25	Discount allowed	8
23	Sales	640	31	Balance c/d	640
		£1440			£1440
June 1	Balance b/d	640			

TABLE 6.3 H. Matthews Merchandising Company: extract from Cash Book

1984		Discount Allowed	£	1984		Discount Received	£
May 10	Oban builders	19	1881	May 3	G. O. Gail	22	1078
„ 25	Oban builders	8	792	„ 20		28	1372
					Balance c/d		223
		£27	£2673			£50	£2673

Debit:
Discounts
Allowed a/c
Credit:
Sales
Ledger
Control a/c

Credit:
Discounts
Received a/c
Debit:
Purchase
Ledger
Control a/c

(iii) To show discounts allowed and discounts received either separately, or as a net figure, in the profit and loss account, identifying discounts as a financing charge (or revenue) separate from trading and operating activities; this last treatment appears to be the one most commonly adopted, especially by businesses operating in industries where the giving and/or receiving of discounts is a regular occurrence.

One final problem has at times been raised over outstanding balances on accounts on which it is likely that discounts will be received or allowed. Again accountants differ on the treatment of future discounts; some make what is known as a provision for discounts to be allowed or received while others make no adjustment at all. One argument in favour of providing for discounts on outstanding balances is that the balances would otherwise overstate the respective assets and liabilities of the business. Arguments against, include the concept of prudence in not anticipating the revenues from discounts until received, together with the requirement of consistency of treatment of similar items of discounts received and allowed. Overall it appears that both treatments are possible, particularly as the amounts involved will not normally be of sufficiently significant size as to cause distortions in the financial statements. One way of minimising distortions is to require consistency in application of whatever treatment has been adopted from one accounting period to the next.

As a final point on the discussion of discounts, it should be emphasised that the above discussion is concerned with cash discounts only and not *trade discounts*, which are reductions in the price of goods allowed to members of certain trades or vocations. The receipt of a trade discount, or granting of one, will result in the purchase cost, or sales revenue, being recorded at a price which is *net* of the trade discount but *gross* of any cash discount which may subsequently occur.

Bad and doubtful debts

Most, if not all, businesses will from time to time suffer from customers who appear to be either unwilling or else unable to pay their debts. The numbers involved will vary from industry to industry and will depend on the prevailing economic climate. Apart from legal remedies which may be available to achieve collection of money owed, the accountant may also consider whether any adjustment is necessary in the accounting records and to the amount shown as trade debtors in the balance sheet. An additional consideration will be the experience of many that balances outstanding on customers accounts for extended periods often have a tendency of being overlooked when the annual financial statements are prepared and hence create balancing problems.

When the balance on a debtors' account is considered to be uncollectable, possibly because the customer has been declared bankrupt or moved to an unknown address, the normal procedure adopted is to 'write-off' the uncollectable balance, i.e., to transfer the balance on the debtors account to a Bad Debts Expense Account:

Debit   Bad debts expense a/c
Credit   Debtors' account

As an additional move the debtors account may itself be physically transferred from the sales ledger and stored separately, often after the errant customer's name has been added to a 'black-list' of persons to avoid extending further credit to.

Illustration 4
Included in the total of £14 860 trade debtors of the Monograph Company at the end of their 1984 accounting year, was an amount of £1240 owed by a customer who had subsequently been declared bankrupt. As it appears unlikely that the customer will repay any of the debt owed, the accountant of the Monograph Company has decided to write off the debtor's balance as a bad debt expense.

The relevant journal entry is:

		£	£
Debit	Bad debts expense	1240	
Credit	Trade debtors' a/c		1240
Being specific debtors' balance written off as uncollectable			

The effect of the above journal entry will be to reduce profits for the year (or increase losses) by £1240 and also to reduce trade debtors by the same amount to £13 620.

Where some doubt remains as to whether the balance on an account is likely to prove uncollectable or not, the normal procedure is to make no entry in the relevant customer's account (apart from perhaps a note relating to future credit limits), but rather to open two new accounts as follows:

Debit   Doubtful debts expense account
Credit   Provision for doubtful debts a/c

The accounting recording process (II)

with the estimated amount of the likely uncollectable debt. Alternatively, the debit entry may have been made in the bad debts expense account.

The doubtful debts expense will be debited in the profit and loss account along with any amounts standing to the debit of the bad debts expense account. The balance on the provision for doubtful debts will be used as a deduction from the total of trade debtors in order to include in the Balance Sheet only the estimated recoverable amount from trade debtors.

Should any debtor for which specific provision has been made subsequently be confirmed as bad, then the appropriate entry is:

Debit   Provision for doubtful debts a/c
Credit   Debtors' account

With the amount involved.

Illustration 5

Cartwright Traders produce accounts annually to 31 July. At the end of the accounting year ended 31 July 1983 trade debtors outstanding amounted to £17 847.

Included in the above debtors' figure were three balances on accounts which were unlikely to be received, the amounts involved being £140, £186, and £152 respectively. Accordingly, the accountant made a specific provision for doubtful debts of £478 by the following entry:

		£	£
Debit	Doubtful debts expense a/c	478	
Credit	Provision for doubtful debts a/c		478
Being specific provision on doubtful debts at 31 July 1983			

The amount shown in the Balance Sheet as a current asset under trade debtors was:

	£	£
Trade debtors	17 847	
Less provision for doubtful debts	478	
		17 369

During the accounting year to 31 July 1984 one of the above doubtful debt accounts amounting to £152 subsequently proved to be bad. A second account for £140 was paid by the debtor. The third balance, originally amounting to £186, remained outstanding at 31 July 1984 apart from a small payment of £24 received during the year; the remaining balance was still considered to be doubtful.

Total amount of trade debtors at 31 July 1984 amounted to £21 467 including any balances remaining on the above three accounts. An additional debtors' balance of £324 was also considered to be doubtful at that date.

Accounting entries in respect of the above at 31 July 1984 are as follows:

			£	£
(i)	Debit	Provision for doubtful debts a/c	152	
	Credit	Trade debtors a/c		152
	Being bad debt previously considered doubtful			

(ii) Debit   Provision for doubtful debts a/c   164
    Credit Doubtful debts expense a/c   164
    Provision no longer required for doubtful debts
    (£140 + £24)

(iii) Debit   Doubtful debts expense a/c   324
    Credit Provision for doubtful debts a/c   324
    Additional provision for doubtful debt at 31 July
    1984

The effect of the above transactions on the relevant accounts is:

Provision for doubtful debts a/c

1984		£	1983		£
31 July	Debtors a/c	152	1 Aug.	Balance b/d	478
31 July	Doubtful debt expense	164	1984 31 July	Doubtful debt expense	324
	Balance c/d	486			
		£802			£802
			1984 1 Aug.	Balance b/d	486

Doubtful debts expense a/c

1984		£	1984		£
31 July	Provision	324	31 July	Provision	164
			31 July	Profit and Loss Account	160
		£324			£324

The amount shown in the Balance Sheet as a current asset under trade debtors at 31 July 1984 is:

	£	£
Trade debtors	21 467	
Less provision for doubtful debts	486	
		20 981

The provision represents a specific amount set aside on two debtors' balances of £162 from the previous year (£186 − £24) and £324 from the current year.

Many managers find a specific identification of doubtful debts difficult, if not impossible, but prefer instead to make what are described as *general provisions*. Some managers even make general provisions in addition to specific provisions.

For example, if it is estimated that, on average, 1 per cent of all debtors' balances of a business will subsequently prove to be bad, then at the end of each accounting period the provision for doubtful debts should be adjusted to 1 per cent of the amount of trade debtors outstanding at that time. First, though, any debtors' accounts which have been identified as bad during the accounting period just ended should be dealt with as follows:

The accounting recording process (II)

Debit   Provision for doubtful debts a/c
Credit Debtors' account

Secondly, the doubtful debts provision should be adjusted to the required level by means of the following entry in those cases where the provision needs to be increased:

Debit   Doubtful debts expense a/c
Credit Provision for doubtful debts a/c

In those cases where the provision needs to be reduced then the reverse of the above entry will be necessary.

Finally, there are occasional pleasant surprises when debtors' balances previously written off as bad are subsequently paid. The appropriate entry in these circumstances is:

Debit   Trade Debtors' account
Credit Bad debts expense a/c

with the amount identified as recoverable, and

Debit   Cash a/c
Credit Trade debtors' account

with the amount actually recovered.

Illustration 6
Brindlewood Chemicals suffer from a relatively high proportion of uncollectable accounts. As not all are easily identifiable, the accountant makes both specific and general provisions for doubtful debts on 31 December at the end of each accounting year.

At 31 December 1982, trade debtors amounted to £14 783

At 31 December 1983, trade debtors amounted to £16 206

Included in the total at the end of 1983 were two accounts which have been identified as uncollectable. One of the accounts amounting to £483 had been the subject of a specific provision in 1982, the other balance of £196 was identified only in 1983. Both of these account balances are now to be written off as bad debts.

A specific provision is also to be made against a debtor's balance outstanding at 31 December 1983 and amounting to £427. A general provision is maintained at 1 per cent on the total of all balances not specifically provided for.

Finally, a cheque for £214 was received in 1983 from an old customer whose account balance had been written off as a bad debt two years previously. The amount received had been posted to a suspense account,[1] in anticipation of an end-of-year adjustment.

Journal entries relating to the above transactions for 1983 are recorded in Table 6.4.

The accounts in which the entries shown in Table 6.4 were recorded are also shown in Table 6.5, with a debtors' control account included, rather than individual debtors' accounts.

The balance on the provision for doubtful debts account at 31 December 1983 represents a specific provision on the debt of £427 and a general provision of 1 per cent of all other debtors balances, i.e. $1\% \times £(15\,527 - 427) = £151$. The amount of

TABLE 6.4 *Brindlewood Chemicals: Journal*

Date		Debit £	Credit £
1983 Dec. 31	Bad debts expense a/c Trade debtors a/c Uncollectable account balance written off as bad debt	196	196
„ 31	Provision for doubtful debts a/c Trade debtors Uncollectable balance written off; specific provision made previously.	483	483
„ 31	Doubtful debts expense a/c Provision for doubtful debts a/c Specific provision made for debt of £427, general provision on remaining balance, £151, less amount previously provided, £143	435	435
„ 31	Suspense a/c Trade debtors' a/c Transfer of amount recovered from account, previously identified as uncollectable	214	214
„ 31	Trade debtors' a/c Bad debts expense Adjustment for over-provision of expense, in previous years	214	214

the provision will reduce the total of trade debtors to be shown in the Balance Sheet at 31 December 1983 as follows:

Trade debtors	£15 527
less provision for doubtful debts	578
Net estimate of collectable balances	£14 949

Because of the recovery of the debt previously thought bad, there is a credit balance on the bad debts expense account. As the amount is not significant it may be deducted from the doubtful debts expense to produce a net expense of £417 in the Income Statement.

6.3 Adjusting entries

Before transferring the figures shown in an interim trial balance to the final accounting statements it is normally necessary to undertake what are known

TABLE 6.5 *Extracts from Ledger Accounts of Brindlewood Chemicals*

Bad debts expense a/c

1983		£	1983		£
Dec. 31	Trade debtors	196	Dec. 31	Trade debtors	214
„ 31	Profit and Loss Account	18			
		£214			£214

Provision for doubtful debts a/c

1983		£	1983			£
Dec. 31	Trade debtors	483	Jan. 1	Gen. Prov. b/d		143
			Jan. 1	Spec. Prov. b/d		483
„ 31	Balance c/d	578	Dec. 31	Doubtful debts		435
		£1061				£1061
			1984			
			Jan. 1	Gen. Prov. b/d		151
			Jan. 1	Spec. Prov. b/d		427

Doubtful debts expense a/c

1983		£	1983		£
Dec. 31	Provision	435	Dec. 31	Profit and Loss account	435
		£435			£435

Trade debtors control a/c

1983		£	1983		£
Dec. 31	Balance b/d	16 206	Dec. 31	Bad debts expense	196
„ 31	Bad debt expense	214	„ 31	Provision for doubtful debts	483
			„ 31	Suspense a/c	214
			„ 31	Balance c/d	15 527
		£16 420			£16 420

1984		
Jan. 1	Balance b/d	15 527

as adjusting entries. These entries fall under two main categories; first, the adjustment of cash related transactions to an accruals basis, and second, the allocation of previously incurred asset costs to relevant time periods.

Accruals and prepayments

The nature of accrued and prepaid expenses has already been described in Chapter 4. Accrued expenses are expenses relating to the current accounting period which are still unpaid at the balance sheet date; conversely, prepaid expenses are expenses paid in advance of the accounting year to which they relate. The accounting treatment of accruals and prepayments may be rendered more easy if it is remembered that an expense account should be represented by a debit balance: an adjustment to the current year's expense to take account of an amount accrued but not yet paid will involve a debit entry, while an adjustment to take account of an amount paid in the current period but relating to some future period will involve a credit entry.

(a) *Accruals*

Where a business operates an accounting system with accounts to record separately an expense and a liability outstanding the relevant entries are as follows:

Current year:
Debit   Expense a/c
Credit Expense payable a/c

with the amount of the accrued expense.

Following year:

When the expense is actually paid, the above entry is reversed, i.e.

Credit Expense a/c
Debit   Expense payable a/c

Illustration 7
(i) Hunter Enterprises began business on 1 January 1982. For the first year of operations rent on premises amounted to £4800, payable quarterly in arrears on 8 April, 8 July, 8 October, and 8 January.

The first three rental payments were all passed through the purchase journal, and the cash payment subsequently recorded by means of the appropriate entries, i.e.

debit	Rent expense a/c	£1200	
credit	Rent payable a/c		£1200

followed by:

debit	Rent payable a/c	£1200	
credit	Cash account a/c		£1200

Finally, an adjusting entry was necessary for the accrued rent expense not yet included in the purchase journal, i.e.

debit	Rent expense a/c	£1200	
credit	Rent payable a/c		£1200

Note. The above adjusting entry may have been replaced by a similar entry made through the purchases journal.

(ii) During the second year of operations the rent was increased to £6000 per annum, payable on the same dates.

Payment made on 8 January 1983 was recorded by:

debit	Rent payable a/c	£1200	
credit	Cash a/c		£1200

The accounting recording process (II)

The rent expense for 1983 was duly recorded through the purchase journal by means of the appropriate entry, i.e. three entries, each of

    debit   Rent expense a/c   £1500
    credit   Rent payable a/c   £1500

Rental payments were also recorded, i.e. three entries each of

    debit   Rent payable a/c   £1500
    credit   Cash a/c   £1500

Finally, an adjusting entry was necessary for the accrued rent expense, not yet included in the purchase journal i.e.

    debit   Rent expense a/c   £1500
    credit   Rent payable a/c   £1500

Rent expense and rent payable accounts for 1982 and 1983 are illustrated in Table 6.6.

Not all accounting systems operate separate accounts to record the expense and any amounts payable in respect of the expense, nor do they necessarily record expenses in the purchase journal. If such a system had not been adopted by Hunter Enterprises an alternative accounting treatment (in summary) for 1982 and 1983 would have been:

For 1982
(i)   debit   Rent a/c   £3600
      credit   Cash a/c   £3600
      Rental payments made in 1982

(ii)   debit   Rent a/c 1982   £1200
      credit   Rent a/c1983   £1200
      Payment outstanding at 31 December 1982

iii)   debit   Profit and Loss a/c   £4800
      credit   Rent a/c   £4800
      Rent expense for year ended 31 December 1982

For 1983
(i)   debit   Rent a/c   £5700
      credit   Cash a/c   £5700
      Rental payments made in 1982

(ii)   debit   Rent a/c 1983   £1500
      credit   Rent a/c 1984   £1500
      Payment outstanding at 31 December 1983

(iii) debit   Profit and Loss a/c   £6000
      credit   Rent a/c   £6000
      Rent expense for year ended 31 December 1983

TABLE 6.6

Hunter Enterprises
Rent expense a/c

1982		£	1982		£
Mar. 31	Rent payable	1200	Dec. 31	Profit and	
June 30	,,	1200		Loss a/c	4800
Sep. 30	,,	1200			
Dec. 31	,,	1200			
		£4800			£4800
1983			1983		
Mar. 31	,,	1500	Dec. 31	Profit and	
June 30	,,	1500		Loss a/c	6000
Sep. 30	,,	1500			
Dec. 31	,,	1500			
		£6000			£6000

Rent payable a/c

1982		£	1982		£
Apr. 8	Cash	1200	Mar. 31	Rent expense	1200
July 8	,,	1200	June 30	,,	1200
Oct. 8	,,	1200	Sep. 30	,,	1200
Dec. 31	Balance c/d	1200	Dec. 31	,,	1200
		£4800			£4800
1983			1983		
Jan. 8	Cash	1200	Jan. 1	Balance b/d	1200
Apr. 8	,,	1500	Mar. 31	Rent expense	1500
July 8	,,	1500	June 30	,,	1500
Oct. 8	,,	1500	Sep. 30	,,	1500
Dec. 31	Balance c/d	1500	Dec. 31	,,	1500
		£7200			£7200
			1984		
			Jan. 1	Balance b/d	1500

The relevant accounts using the above system of recording are shown in summary in Table 6.7.

(b) *Prepayments*

Adjusting entries for prepaid expenses may be made in one of two ways as follows:

(i) By opening a prepaid account and transferring the prepayment to this account from the relevant expense account:

    i.e. debit   Prepaid expense a/c
        credit Expense a/c

(ii) Alternatively, the adjusting entry may take the following form:

    credit Expense a/c current year
    debit   Expense a/c following year

The accounting recording process (II)

TABLE 6.7

Hunter Enterprises
Rent expense a/c

1982		£	1982		£
	Cash	3600		Profit and	
	Rent a/c 1983	1200		Loss a/c	4800
		£4800			£4800
1983			1983		
	Cash	5700		Rent a/c 1982	1200
	Rent a/c 1984	1500		Profit and	
				Loss a/c	6000
		£7200			£7200
			1984		
				Rent a/c 1983	£1500

Illustration 8

Stewart Traders operate a business with an accounting year ended 30 June. Property insurance is paid annually on 1 February for the year commencing on that date. Insurance for 1982/83 amounting to £1800 was paid on the due date. At 30 June 1982 the adjusting entry for the prepayment may be recorded by one of the following entries:

either

debit	Prepaid insurance a/c	£1050	
credit	Insurance expense a/c		£1050
7 months insurance paid in advance of the accounting year ended 30 June 1983			

or

debit	Insurance expense a/c 1983	£1050	
credit	Insurance expense a/c 1982		£1050

If the first of the two adjusting entries was made, then a reversing entry would be required on 1 July 1982

i.e.

debit	Insurance expense a/c	£1050	
credit	Prepaid insurance a/c		£1050

The principle involved whichever form of adjusting entry is used is to ensure that the Profit and Loss account for one year is not charged with an expense relating to the following year.

Allocation of asset cost

(a) Depreciating assets

The second category of adjusting entry differs from the first in degree rather than kind. Both categories, at their heart, involve the adjustment of cash related transactions to an accruals basis; the second category merely involves allocations of expenditures, which may have been incurred in previous periods, over more than one accounting period.

The concept of depreciation will be considered in more detail in the following two chapters. It is sufficient to recognise for present purposes that the accruals concept requires that the loss in value of an asset incurred in producing revenues or providing services should be matched with the revenues generated or services provided. Hence, if expenditure incurred on acquisition of long-lived assets may be considered to be a pool of prepaid expenses, adjusting entries are required to allocate a portion of these prepaid expenses to the accounting periods in which they generate revenues or provide services. The allocation of prepaid expenses involving tangible fixed assets is normally described as *depreciation*, while allocation of intangible assets is described as *amortisation*. For present purposes both will be described as *depreciation*.

In order to enact the adjusting entries required to depreciate assets two accounts must first be opened for the asset, or category of assets:

(i) Depreciation expense account to which the expense charged for the year in question will be allocated;
(ii) Accumulated depreciation account in which the sum of all depreciation charges will be credited over the life of the asset.

The second account is created, rather than merely reducing the balance shown on the asset account by crediting the depreciation expense directly; the balance standing on the accumulated depreciation account at any point in time will be deducted from the asset cost to ascertain the net book value of the asset, i.e. the unallocated balance of asset cost. The net book value of the asset must then be shown in each Balance Sheet, usually by means of disclosing

Asset cost	XXX
less accumulated depreciation	XXX
net book value	XXX

Illustration 9
Batty Products occupy premises acquired on 1 January, 1983 on a twenty-year lease at a cost of £100 000. Annual depreciation expense is calculated as (£100 000 ÷ 20) = £5000, with the expenses for the year ended 31 Deember 1983 recorded as follows:

debit	Depreciation expense a/c	£5000	
credit	Accumulated depreciation a/c		£5000
Being depreciation expense on lease for 1983			

The relevant accounts for Batty Products are illustrated below:

Leasehold Premises a/c
£
1983   Cash   100 000

The accounting recording process (II)

                Depreciation Expense a/c (Leasehold Premises)
1983   £
Dec. 31   Accum.
              depn   5000

                Accumulated Depreciation a/c (Leasehold Premises)
                                   1983   £
                                   Dec. 31   Depn.
                                                  exp.   5000

Included under fixed assets in the Balance Sheet at 31 December 1983 will be the following information relating to the leasehold premises:

	£
Leasehold premises, at cost	100 000
less accumulated depreciation	5 000
net book value	95 000

(b) *Other assets*

In addition to the adjusting entries required for depreciating assets, there are other assets acquired by a business during one accounting period the stock of which may not be completely exhausted by the end of that period.

One major example of this is the stock of goods purchased either for resale, or for conversion into other products. Many businesses operate what is known as a perpetual stock recording, or inventory, system in which the cost of goods sold or consumed is continually being expensed through the accounting system. A number of businesses, particularly smaller ones, operate an inventory system which records the cost of any goods sold or consumed at the end of the accounting period, i.e. periodically, by means of adjusting entries. In the case of goods which have been resold during the year the relevant adjusting entry in the periodic inventory system is:

    debit   Cost of goods sold
    credit   Stock a/c

with the cost of goods sold or consumed.

Any balance remaining on the stock account will represent the stock of goods unsold at the end of the accounting year and will be disclosed as a current asset in the Balance Sheet. Both perpetual and periodic inventory systems are considered further in Chapter 10.

Other assets for which similar adjusting entries may be required to identify stock on hand at the end of an accounting period include stationery, cleaning materials, and even spare parts for equipment. For each the relevant adjusting entry will be similar to that described above.

Illustration 10
Letford Motors buy their stationery in bulk. During their first year of operations

stationery costing £1400 was bought. Stock on hand at the end of the accounting year amounted to £250.

The entry to record the original purchase of stationery would have been:

debit	Stationery supplies a/c	£1400	
credit	Cash a/c		£1400
	Being stock of stationery acquired		

The relevant adjusting entry at the end of the year is

debit	Stationery expense a/c	£1150	
credit	Stationery supplies a/c		£1150
	Being stationery used during the year		

Rather than opening a separate stationery expense account, especially if no other entries were to be recorded in this account, it would be possible to debit the expense directly to the Profit and Loss Account, i.e.

debit	Profit and Loss a/c	£1150	
credit	Stationery supplies a/c		£1150

6.4 Work sheet

Many accountants prefer to make adjusting entries, and corrections to earlier recording errors, on what is known as a work sheet before recording the entries in the books of account. The work sheet forms no part of the double-entry accounting system but is prepared to help ensure the accuracy and completeness of the information to be included in the final accounting statements. It is not a foolproof check but merely part of the total system of control and check over the recording process.

Work sheets may be adopted to suit the size and complexity of any accounting system but all take the general form illustrated in Table 6.8. The account balances from the interim trial balance are listed first followed by one (or more) pairs of columns in which the adjusting entries will be recorded.

One variety of work sheet also includes a pair of columns into which all prepayments and accruals are separated, but this refinement is not absolutely necessary. Then follows two columns into which the adjusted trial balance is extended, thus checking that the dual aspect of all adjusting entries has been recorded. Finally, two pairs of columns are included for the Income Statement and Balance Sheet, the first pair into which expense and revenue balances are extended, the second into which asset and equity balances are extended. Any profit or loss calculated in the Income Statement should also be included in the Balance Sheet columns, either as a credit, if a profit, or as a debit, if a loss.

When the accountant is assured of the accuracy and completeness of the adjustments made in the work sheet and the figures included in the final accounts, then the relevant adjustments should be repeated, but this time in the underlying books of account themselves.

Illustration 11

Burton Traders Ltd prepare accounts annually to 30 June. An interim trial balance is first prepared and necessary adjusting entries are then made on a work sheet as shown in Table 6.8.

Adjusting entries, in journalised form, for the year ended 30 June 1984 are as follows:

(i)	debit	Heat and light expense a/c	NL/ 7	£140	
	credit	Electricity payable a/c	NL/14		£140
		Estimated electricity expense outstanding at 30 June 1984			

(ii)	debit	Prepaid rent a/c	NL/15	£600	
	credit	Rent expense a/c	NL/ 6		£600
		Six months rent payable in advance			

(iii)	debit	Bad debt expense a/c	NL/ 8	£249	
	credit	Trade debtor's a/c	SL		£249
		Uncollectable account written off			

(iv)	debit	Doubtful debts expense a/c	NL/19	£147	
	credit	Provision for doubtful debts a/c	NL/17		£147
		Increase in provision for doubtful debts to 0.8 per cent of outstanding debtors' balances			

(v)	debit	Depreciation expense a/c	NL/16	£800	
	credit	Accumulated depreciation motor vehicle a/c	NL/2		£800
		Depreciation on motor vehicles allocated for current year			

(vi)	debit	Cost of goods sold expense a/c	NL/12	£41 536	
	credit	Purchases inventory a/c	NL/3		£41 536
		Transfer of original cost of goods sold during the year			

(vii)	debit	Supplies expense a/c	NL/13	£793	
	credit	Supplies inventory a/c	NL/ 5		£793
		Transfer of supplies used during the year			

(viii)	debit	Wages expense a/c	NL/10	£189	
	credit	Motor expense a/c	NL/11		£189
		Transfer of payment originally debited to the wrong account			

After completing the work sheet and recording the adjusting entries in the books of account, the only task remaining to the accountant before prepar-

TABLE 6.8 Illustration of Work Sheet for the accounting year ended 30 June 1984

Burton Traders Ltd

Account	A/c No.	Initial Trial Balance		Adjusting Entries		Final Trial Balance		Income Statement		Balance Sheet	
		Debit £	Credit £	Debit £	Credit £	Debit £	Credit £	Debit £	Credit £	Debit £	Credit £
Owners' interest	PL/1		17 450				17 450				17 450
Motor vehicles	NL/1	6 400				6 400				6 400	
Accumulated depn – motor vehicles	NL/2		1 600		800		2 400				2 400
Cash at bank	CB/12	20 829				20 829				20 829	
Trade debtors control	SL	7 349			249	7 100				7 100	
Provision for doubtful debts	NL/17		421		147		568				568
Trade creditors control	PL		6 124				6 124				6 124

		Dr	Cr	Dr	Cr	Dr	Cr	Dr	Cr
Purchases inventory	NL/3	45 830						4 294	
Sales revenue	NL/4		89 507				89 507		
Supplies inventory	NL/5	924						131	
Rent expense	NL/6	1 800			1 200				
Heat and light expense	NL/7	5 367				5 507			
Bad debts expense	NL/8			140	249				
Doubtful debts expense	NL/9			147		147			
Wages expense	NL/10	21 923			189	22 112			
Motor expenses	NL/11	4 680				4 491			
Cost of goods sold expense	NL/12			41 536		41 536			
Supplies expense	NL/13			793		793			
Electricity payable	NL/14				140				600
Prepaid rent	NL/15			600				600	
Depreciation expense	NL/16			800		800			
Profit for year	PL/2					12 672			12 672
		115 102	115 102	44 454	44 454	116 189	116 189	39 354	39 354
							89 507	89 507	

111

ing the annual financial statements, is to transfer the balances on the various revenue and expense accounts to the Profit and Loss Account and from there either to retained earnings or owners' interest account. This procedure described as 'closing the accounts' is demonstrated for Burton Traders Ltd by the following summary journal entries:

			£	£
debit	Sales revenue a/c	NL/4	89 507	
credit	Profit and Loss a/c	PL/2		89 507

Being revenue earned for the year ended 30 June 1984

			£	£
debit	Profit and Loss a/c	PL/ 2	76 835	
credit	Rent expense a/c	NL/ 6		1 200
	Heat and light expense a/c	NL/ 7		5 507
	Bad debts expense a/c	NL/ 8		249
	Doubtful debts expense a/c	NL/ 9		147
	Wages expense a/c	NL/10		22 112
	Motor expenses a/c	NL/11		4 491
	Cost of goods sold expense a/c	NL/12		41 536
	Supplies expense a/c	NL/13		793
	Depreciation expense a/c	NL/16		800

Being expenses incurred for the year ended 30 June 1984

			£	£
debit	Profit and Loss account	PL/2	12 672	
credit	Owners' interest a/c	PL/2		12 672

Being transfer of profit for the year ended 30 June 1984

6.5 Accounting for non-trading organisations

Introduction

There are many thousands of organisations operating in the United Kingdom who do not trade as businesses and who do not operate with a basic objective that is profit orientated. Nevertheless many of these organisations receive and expend financial resources and are required to account for these, for example:

Charities, of which there are well over 100 000 registered in England and Wales alone, are required by the Charities Act 1960 to keep proper records of account and prepare periodic income statements;
Clubs are normally required by their constitution to prepare annual accounts for the benefit of their members;
Under Section 10 of the Trade Union and Labour Relations Act, 1974, unions are also required to keep proper accounting records and to submit an annual return including a Statement of Revenues and Expenses and Balance Sheet.

The accounting recording process (II)

Many of the above-named organisations will not, however, have the resources or the necessity to maintain fully integrated book-keeping systems. In fact, many of these organisations will probably maintain records on a single-entry cash basis and convert these, if desired, on to an accruals basis at the end of the year.

Receipts and Payments Account

The simplest and most convenient form of accounting statement which a non-trading organisation may choose to prepare is known as a Receipts and Payments Account. This account provides a summary of the Cash Book, with receipts entered on the left-hand side of the account and payments entered on the right-hand side. The account is opened by debiting in turn the amount of cash on hand and cash at bank held at the commencement of the year. The final entry in the account will include a credit entry for any closing balances of cash in hand or at bank (unless the amounts are overdrawn, in which case the closing balance will be recorded as a debit entry).

If a summary of cash movements is all the accounting information that the organisation wishes, or is required, to provide then a Receipts and Payments Account will be perfectly adequate. Table 6.9 illustrates a typical Receipts and Payments Account prepared by the gala committee of Fairport town.

Income and Expenditure Account

For many non-trading organisations a Receipts and Payments Account will not be sufficient. Even for the organisation whose accounts are illustrated in Table 6.9 the amount of information disclosed may be insufficient. The accounts give no indication of any assets owned by the gala committee nor, indeed, any liabilities outstanding at the end of the year. For many organisations it may prove necessary to prepare financial statements that are adjusted to an accruals basis and which include a periodic Balance Sheet, or Statement of Financial Position.

A number of organisations may choose to report on what may be

TABLE 6.9

Fairport Gala Committee
Receipts and Payments Account for the year ended 31 August 1985

1 Sept. 1984	£		£
Balances b/f			
Cash in hand	15	Hire of hall	120
Cash at bank	206	Stationery and postage	197
Donations	150	Printing of programmes	54
Entry fees for competitions	275	Advertising costs	216
Entrance monies	421	Prizes	582
Sale of programmes	69	Balances c/f 31 Aug. 1985	
Sponsorship	100	Cash in hand	17
		Cash at bank	50
	£1236		£1236

described as a 'modified accruals basis', i.e. converting outputs on to an accruals basis but retaining all or some of the inputs on a cash basis.

For example, a golf club may wish to include as income for a period amounts receivable in respect of ticket sales for the annual dinner dance whether paid for or not, but may wish to include in subscription income only amounts actually received.

Different organisations will adopt different practices regarding the treatment of inflows depending on the degree of certainty with which the eventual receipt is viewed. Assuming that the organisation wishes to include all inputs and outputs on to an accruals basis then it will be necessary to prepare an Income and Expenditure Account. The Receipts and Payments Account may be used as the starting point with adjustments being made to convert cash receipts and payments to the amounts receivable or payable for the period.

Opening and closing balances of cash will be excluded from the Income and Expenditure Account but depreciation to be charged on any fixed assets held should be included.

Records should be kept of assets and liabilities owned by the non-trading organisation at the end of each accounting period. From these records annual Balance Sheets will be prepared with any accumulated surplus of income over expenditures transferred, not to owners' accounts, but to an Accumulated Fund. The Accumulated Fund represents the book value of the net resources available to the members of the organisation (or to the charity) in order to help pursue the objectives of that organisation.

Illustration 12

Assume that the following additional information is available in respect of the Fairport Gala Committee mentioned earlier:

(i) Stocks of stationery held were:

at 1 September 1984   £46
at 31 August 1985   £85

(ii) Amounts outstanding at 1 September 1984 in respect of advertising costs were £84 while the corresponding amount outstanding at 31 August 1985 was £42.

(iii) Sponsorship monies of £150 in respect of the year ended 31 August 1985 was received in September 1985.

(iv) Office equipment owned by the Gala Committee was valued at £400 on 1 September 1984. An estimate of £100 was made in respect of the depreciation for this equipment in the year to 31 August 1985.

From the above information and that provided in Table 6.9 an Income and Expenditure Account may be prepared for the year ended 31 August 1985. All amounts shown on the debit side of the Receipts and Payments Account, other than cash balances, will be transferred to the credit side of the Income and Expenditure after adjusting for item (iii) above.

All amounts shown on the credit side of the Receipts and Payments Account, other than closing cash balances, will be transferred to the debit of the Income and Expenditure Account after adjusting for items (i), (ii) and (iv) above. Table 6.10 illustrates the Income and Expenditure Account for the year ended 31 August 1985.

The balance on the Accumulated Fund at the beginning of the current year may

Table 6.10

Fairport Gala Committee
Income and Expenditure Account for the year 31 August 1985

	£		£
Hire of hall	120	Donations	150
Stationery and postage	158	Competition fees	275
Programme printing	54	Entrance money	421
Advertising	174	Programme sales	69
Prizes	582	Sponsorship	250
Depreciation of equipment	100	Excess of expenditure over income for the year transferred to Accumulated Fund	23
	£1188		£1188

be calculated by identifying the book value of assets less liabilities held at 1 September 1984, i.e.

	£
Cash in hand	15
Cash in bank	206
Office equipment	400
Stationery stock	46
	667
Less: Advertising costs outstanding	84
	583

The Balance Sheet at 31 August 1985, including the balance on Accumulated Fund is shown in Table 6.11.

Table 6.11

Fairport Gala Committee
Balance Sheet at 31 August 1985

	£	£
Fixed assets		
Office Equipment	400	
Less amount written off	100	300
Current assets		
Cash in hand	17	
Cash at bank	50	
Sponsorship debtor	150	
Stationery stock	85	
	302	
Less current liabilities	42	260
		560
Accumulated Fund:		
Balance at 1 September 1984		583
Deficit for the current year		(23)
Balance at 31 August 1985		560

6.6 Summary

Control accounts are often used within an accounting function, either as part of the double-entry system in place of individual accounts, or for use in memorandum form. Their purpose is to maintain an independent check on the completeness of the recording of transactions relating to sections of the accounting system. By means of control accounts, errors in practice may be localised to one section of the accounting system.

Modifications to the basic recording process introduced earlier in Chapter 5 may involve the inclusion of additional columns in the cash book to record discounts allowed to customers and discounts received from suppliers.

Before preparing final accounting statements it is normally necessary to make adjusting entries either to convert cash expenses to an accruals basis or to allocate asset cost to relevant accounting periods. Additional entries required may include adjustments for bad debts expense and doubtful debts provision, transfer of cost of goods sold, and the expensing of other inventories. One aid often used by accountants, before finalising financial statements is the *work sheet*, used as a summary memorandum of all outstanding balances, adjusting and correcting entries, and of closing entries plus final accounts.

A Receipts and Payments Account summarises all cash inflows and outflows of an organisation. This statement may be an appropriate means of communicating financial information concerning simple forms of non-trading organisations. Where an accruals basis of accounting is considered to be more appropriate, then the non-trading organisation may prepare an Income and Expenditure Account and Balance Sheet.

Questions

1. Prepare a diagram illustrating the flow of accounting information for a trading organisation from the point of recognition of a credit sale to the payment of the account by the debtor.
   Include in your diagram a debtor's control account, but as a memorandum account only.
2. Explain whether you agree with the distinction adopted in the current chapter between the recording of cash discounts and trade discounts.
3. Summarise the major arguments for and against the recognition of an annual provision for discounts allowable on outstanding trade debtors.
4. The inclusion of prepaid expenses as current assets appears to be an exception to the conservatism or prudence concept. What other examples of such exceptions can you identify? To what extent is the overriding nature of the prudence concept, as identified in SSAP 2, contradicted by the above exceptions?

For each of the following questions **circle** the *letter* alongside the *best choice* from amongst the possible solutions presented.

5. Sales returns amounting to £156 were posted in error to the wrong side of the sales ledger control account. The required adjustment to the control account to correct the error is:

(a) debit £156;
(b) credit £312;
(c) debit £312;
(d) credit £156.

6. A payment of £720 to a supplier has been incorrectly posted to the sales ledger control account. The effect of this error is:

   (a) to overstate debtors' balances by £720 and understate creditors' balances by the same amount;
   (b) to understate both debtors' and creditors' balances by £720;
   (c) to overstate both debtors' and creditors' balances by £720;
   (d) to understate debtors' balances by £720 and overstate creditors' balances by the same amount.

7. A customer whose account was written off as a bad debt has recently paid a cheque for £400 in settlement of the account. A suitable journal entry to record the payment is:

   (a) debit cash, credit bad debts provision;
   (b) debit cash, credit sales revenue;
   (c) debit cash, credit trade debtors control account;
   (d) debit cash, credit bad debts expense.

8. Trade debtors of Oxford Products at 31 December 1983 amounted to £15 600. A debtors' balance of £300 is to be written off as a bad debt, while the provision for doubtful debts which currently stands at £145 is to be maintained at 1 per cent of outstanding debtors. The total charge in the Income Statement for 1983 for bad and doubtful debts is:

   (a) £289;
   (b) £300;
   (c) £308;
   (d) £311.

9. Fixit Garages stock a supply of spare parts for which accounting records are maintained on a periodic inventory valuation basis. Stock levels at the beginning and end of the recent financial year were £7250 and £8190 respectively. Spare parts purchased during the year amounted to £16 750. The spare parts expense to be charged in the annual Income Statement is:

   (a) £17 690;
   (b) £16 750;
   (c) £15 810;
   (d) none of these.

10. A debit balance on a suppliers' account has been wrongly included in the closing list of debtors' balances. The effect of this error is:

    (a) an overstatement of the list of debtors in relation to the correct amount shown on the debtors' control account;
    (b) an understatement of the list of creditors in relation to the correct amount shown in the creditors' control account;
    (c) both (a) and (b) above;
    (d) none of the above.

11. Closing stock of unsold goods was estimated at £5600 for ABC Traders at the end of their 1983 accounting year. Assuming that the actual level was £5150, the effect of the error is to:

(a) overstate profits for both 1983 and 1984 by £450;
(b) overstate the profit for 1983 by £450 and understate the profit for 1984 by £450;
(c) understate the profit for 1983 by £450 and overstate the profit for 1984 by £450;
(d) understate profits for both 1983 and 1984 by £450.

12. The accounting records of Ramage Products for the year ended 31 December 1983 revealed the following:

	1.1.83	31.12.83
Trade creditors	£ 7 450	£8 360
Stock of goods	£11 380	£9 260

Payment made to suppliers during the year were £32 470. Cost of goods sold for the year was:

(a) £35 500;
(b) £34 590;
(c) £33 380;
(d) £31 260.

Problems

1. The following transactions of the Wade Company for June 1984 relate to goods acquired on credit terms:

			£
June	1	Purchases from D. Owen	1750
	3	Purchases from S. Smith	875
	8	Returns to D. Owen	90
	13	Purchases from D. Owen	830
	17	Purchases from R. Nelson	842
	24	Returns to S. Smith	35
	26	Purchases from R. Nelson	1240
	28	Payment to D. Owen	1620
	28	Discount received from D. Owen	40

Record the above transactions in the relevant books of prime entry and prepare journal entries to record the postings to the appropriate ledger accounts, including a memorandum purchase ledger control account.

2. Further transactions for the Wade Company for July 1984, relating to goods acquired on credit terms were:

			£
July	3	Purchases from S. Smith	460
	7	Payment to S. Smith	825
	7	Discount received from S. Smith	15
	11	Purchases from D. Owen	936
	18	Returns to S. Smith	20
	21	Payment to R. Nelson	2070
	26	Purchases from S. Smith	538
	28	Returns to R. Nelson	35

(a) Record the above transactions in the books of prime entry prepared for Problem 1.

(b) Prepare journal entries to record the postings at the end of July to the appropriate ledger accounts.
(c) Post the journal entries for June (Problem 1) and July to the ledger accounts, including the purchase ledger control account.
(d) Reconcile the balance at the end of July in the purchase ledger control account with the sum of the individual balances on trade creditors' accounts.
(e) Explain how the balance on the account of R. Nelson should be described in a Balance Sheet prepared for the end of July.

3. The following list of balances was extracted from the records of the Terra Nova Company for the year ended 30 June 1984:

	£
Land and buildings, at cost	40 000
Plant and machinery, at cost	30 000
Accumulated depreciation, plant and machinery	5 000
Sales for the year	261 500
Sales returns	700
Stock of goods for resale 1.7.83	40 000
Purchases	129 100
Purchase returns	3 300
Wages expense	38 500
Insurance expense	6 000
General expenses	28 500
Trade debtors	45 000
Balance at bank	7 000
Owners' capital introduced	40 000
Retained profits 1.7.83	25 200
Trade creditors	29 800

Further examination of the records revealed that adjusting entries were required for the following items:

(i) Stock of goods for resale 30.6.84 £36 750;
(ii) Wages due but not yet paid £1 560;
(iii) Included in the insurance payments made during the year was an amount of £1800 relating to insurance on property for the twelve months ended 31 March 1985.
(iv) Depreciation of £2500 is to be charged on plant and machinery.
(v) A payment to a supplier, amounting to £1230 was wrongly included in general expenses.
(vi) A debtors account for £700 has been identified as a bad debt and is to be written off in the current year. In addition a provision for doubtful debts is to be opened amounting to 1 per cent of all debtors' balances at the end of the year.

Required

(a) Prepare a work sheet in a form similar to that illustrated in Table 6.8 and enter the account balances in the initial trial balance columns.
(b) Prepare journal entries to record the adjusting entries and enter the amounts in the work sheet.
(c) Complete the work sheet and prepare a Trading and Profit and Loss Account for the year ended 30 June 1984 and a Balance Sheet at that date.

4. G. Allan commenced business on 1 January 1982. At the end of the first year of operations trade debtors amounted to £17 420, including an account for £350 which was considered to be a bad debt. In addition, a general provision for doubtful debts of £420 was considered necessary.

At the end of the second year of business trade debtors amounted to £19 635, including two accounts totalling £560 which were considered to be doubtful. The doubtful debts provision is to be adjusted to make specific provision for the doubtful debts identified and to reduce the general provision to £250.

Required

(a) Prepare journal entries to record the adjustments, required by G. Allan in respect of bad and doubtful debts for 1982 and 1983.
(b) Show the bad debts expense and provision for doubtful debts accounts for the two years.
(c) Identify the amount to be shown for trade debtors in the Balance Sheets prepared at the end of 1982 and 1983.
(d) Should G. Allan be faulted for allowing doubtful debts to arise?

5. The Balance Sheet of Tinsley Traders at 31 July 1983 was as follows:

Fixed assets:	£	£
Land and buildings		63 000
Plant and equipment	24 000	
Less accumulated depreciation	6 000	
		18 000
		81 000
Current assets:		
Stock	5800	
Trade debtors	7240	
Prepaid rates	1500	
Cash at bank	1130	
		15 670
		£96 670
Owners' interest:		
Capital introduced		40 000
Retained profits		20 660
		60 660
Long-term loan (10%)		24 000
Current liabilities:		
Trade creditors	11 450	
Interest payable	200	
Accrued heat and light	360	
		12 010
		£96 670

During the year ended 31 July 1984 the following transactions were recorded:

(i) Purchase of goods for resale £263 500;
(ii) Payments made to suppliers £257 480;

(iii) Cash received from customers £471 900;
(iv) Payment of operating expenses £164 360;
(v) Purchase of additional equipment for £22 000 on 1 March, 1984 with payment to be made by an immediate deposit of £4000 followed by twelve equal monthly instalments beginning on 1 April, 1984;
(vi) Payment of quarterly interest payments on the long-term loan, of £600 on 30 September, 31 December, 31 March and 30 June;
(vii) Payments made out of the business bank account on behalf of the owner, of £17 430;

Inspection of the records at the end of the year revealed the following additional information:

(viii) Trade debtors at 31 July 1984 amounted to £9230.
(ix) Included in the operating expenses was an amount of £3600 relating to rates on the business premises for the year to 31 March 1985.
(x) An electricity bill for £840 was received in September 1984 relating to three month to 15 September 1984.
(xi) Depreciation of £7100 is to be charged on plant and equipment.
(xii) Closing stock of goods at 31 July 1984 amounted to £8200.

Required

(a) Record the above transactions and information in the relevant T accounts.
(b) Prepare a Trading and Profit and Loss Account for the year ended 31 July 1984 and a Balance Sheet on that date.

7 Fixed Asset Measurement (I)

7.1 Introduction

The measurement of asset values for accounting purposes is inseparable from the determination of business income. Business income has been described earlier as the increase in owner's wealth or owner's interest over a period of time. Owner's interest itself represents residual claims on the net assets of an organisation, i.e.

$$\text{Business income} = \text{Owner's interest}_{t2} - \text{Owner's interest}_{t1}$$

where

$$\text{Owner's Interest}_t = \text{Assets}_t - \text{Liabilities}_t$$

Hence the determination of periodic business income is based on the values assigned to the assets and liabilities of the business. The accounting determination of income is not, however, normally undertaken through a process of valuation but through the allocation of the revenues earned and expenses incurred to each accounting period. Asset values are only indirectly included in an historic cost system of accounting. For example, the change in value of goods sold during an accounting period is recognised by crediting the Profit and Loss Account with the revenues received on sale of goods and debiting with the cost of acquiring, or manufacturing, those goods. The valuation or measurement of other assets (and liabilities) remaining in the business at the end of an accounting period has not yet been considered explicitly. The accounting treatment of *fixed assets* held but not disposed of by the end of an accounting period is the subject matter of Chapters 7 and 8, while the treatment of *current assets* is the subject matter of Chapters 9 and 10.

7.2 Asset valuation and accounting income

Introduction

Traditional accounting treatment of asset valuation differs markedly from that resulting from the application of economic theory. Although assets were often recorded at market or other valuation prior to the mid-nineteenth century, for most of the last 80 to 100 years the accepted doctrine has been to record assets at original, i.e., historic, cost or lower. The practice of recording depreciation, although observable before 1900 was not itself accepted as sound accounting practice until after a number of judgements in legal cases in the early part of the twentieth century.[1]

Accounting rules have developed along lines which are loosely identifiable with the idea of measuring income after ensuring the maintenance of the owner's wealth. Wealth, or capital, maintenance was identified by reference to the monetary amount of capital invested by the owners, not the earnings capacity of the business. Similarly, assets were valued either by reference to the actual amount expended in their acquisition, or else the cost of goods given in exchange for them, or exhausted in their creation.

The reasons for the general acceptance of an historic cost basis of accounting have already been referred to in an earlier chapter. Two particular reasons are, however, worthy of re-examination, namely: (i) the desire for objectivity; and (ii) the overriding emphasis placed on conservatism.

Historic cost valuation satisfies the desire for objectivity in asset valuation, to the extent that the cost of acquisition is verifiable by reference to invoices, or other primary data sources. The element of objectivity is not normally present, however, in the case of those assets acquired in exchange for other assets, or those obtained through the exhaustion or conversion of existing assets, e.g., machinery produced by the firm for its own use. Additionally, whether an asset is acquired for cash or in any other way, the element of objectivity is no longer present when valuing assets in years subsequent to acquisition.

The doctrine of conservatism, similarly, *may* be satisfied by adherence to the historic cost valuation process, but it *need not be* in all circumstances. Non-recognition of higher replacement costs of assets may impair the future earnings capacity of a business and even the ability to repay debts incurred, and may eventually lead to business failure. Acceptance of a doctrine merely because it satisfies the requirements of objectivity and conservatism is insufficient; the doctrine must also satisfy the functions for which accounting statements are prepared. Recent discussion of the deficiencies of historic cost accounting in the business and academic world suggest that user needs may not be satisfied by continued adherence to the historic cost basis of asset measurement and income determination, particularly during periods of rapidly changing prices.

The allocation problem

The accountants' notion of an asset has been compared by A. L. Thomas to the economists' concept of an economic good, i.e., 'goods that can be bought and sold in a market – goods that command a price'.[2]

The classification of economic goods used by Thomas and adopted in the following section, identifies two forms of economic goods:

Monetary goods consisting either of cash or else legally enforceable claims to receive cash;
Non-monetary goods, including all others.

Non-monetary goods are further divisible into three classes, namely:

(i) *Unlimited life goods.* These are goods which have an unlimited service life and which are normally recorded in financial statements at original cost, e.g., freehold land.

(ii) *Single-period goods.* These goods are acquired, and disposed of, within the same accounting period. One example of a single-period good is office heat and light expenditure paid for, and relating to, a period between two Balance Sheet dates.

If single-period goods are disposed of in the acquisition of some other non-monetary goods, then their acquisition cost will be included in the cost of the other goods; an example of this is given in Chapter 9, where raw material costs are included in finished goods production cost.

If no new economic goods are obtained from the disposal of the single-period goods, then their acquisition cost is expensed in the period in which the goods are disposed of. An example of this is the expensing of expired rent on office premises.

(iii) *Multi-period goods.* These consist of economic goods with a limited useful life but yielding a service to more than one accounting period. Under the historic cost system the acquisition cost of multi-period assets must be allocated over a number of accounting periods, with any unallocated costs remaining at the end of each accounting period identified in that period's Balance Sheet as assets.

The allocation of the cost of acquisition of multi-period goods is justified on two counts:

(a) the need to avoid undue fluctuations in reported earnings from one year to the next;
(b) as an application of the matching concept, with expired costs, i.e. expenses, matched against the revenues which they have generated.

Without such allocations, acquisitions costs of multi-period goods would simply be expensed in the year of acquisition.

Although the above classification of non-monetary goods is a useful aid in identifying the area in which the allocation of cost is required, the classification has tended to be applied in an inconsistent manner in practice. Certain goods which may with some justification be regarded as multi-period goods are often treated as single-period goods, e.g., advertising costs promoting a brand image, research costs, staff recruitment and training costs. The reasons often advanced for this inconsistent treatment are the uncertainty attached to the future benefits from such expenditure, together with the overriding influence of the prudence concept.

The problems associated with the allocation of the acquisition cost of multi-period goods are not confined to fixed assets and depreciation. However, the nature of fixed assets tends to highlight these problems and to cast considerable doubts on the claims of the proponents of historic cost accounting of the objectivity of that approach to valuation and income determination.

Fixed or long-lived assets are those non-monetary assets which are not exhausted within one complete operating cycle or accounting year. They include both unlimited life goods and multi-period goods. Both accounting practice and company law recognise at least three categories of long-lived assets namely,

(i) tangible fixed assets;
(ii) intangible assets; and
(iii) investments.

As the accounting problems relating to each category differ, each will be considered in turn, beginning in this current chapter with tangible fixed assets.

7.3 Fixed assets and depreciation

Tangible fixed assets

Tangible fixed assets are those which have a defined physical existence, for example, plant and equipment or motor vehicles. These assets may have an unlimited useful life, as in the case of freehold land, or a more limited useful life, as in the case of leasehold land and buildings. The majority of fixed assets fall into the latter category of those possessing a limited useful life, but of an uncertain duration. As explained earlier in the chapter, the allocation problem involves the question of how to allocate acquisition cost of multi-period assets with a limited useful life over the duration of that useful life.

Allocations of fixed asset costs are made by means of the depreciation expense charged in the Income Statements. The expense should be calculated on a basis which attempts to measure the exhaustion of benefits or services obtained during the period in question, i.e., to match expenses with the revenues generated. By this allocation, the monetary value of ownership capital should be maintained over the life of the asset. If, however, the expense allocation does not exactly conform with the measure of exhaustion of benefits, i.e., if the allocation has been conducted on an arbitrary or otherwise incorrect basis, then maintenance of ownership capital may not be achieved on a period by period basis.

Illustration 1
Assume a firm acquires a single asset at a cost of £200. Annual benefits obtained from use of the asset amount to £100 per annum for each of four years. At the end of the fourth year the asset is scrapped at no further cost. Assume further that the firm distributes all income at the end of each year.

(a) Consider the situation where no depreciation expense is allocated by the firm. At the end of each of the four years net income will be identified as £100 and this amount will immediately be distributed. The Balance Sheet will also remain the same, showing

Fixed asset at cost	£200
Owner's interest	£200

The relationship Assets = Equities continues to hold, thus retaining the 'correctness' of the accounting equation. The above situation is misleading, however, as at the end of the fourth year the asset will be completely exhausted and its value will be zero. Owner's interest will be nominally shown as £200 in the books of accounts, but in practice, will have no value. Hence, in order to maintain the monetary value of the owner's interest, net income must be calculated after deducting a depreciation expense, which in total over the four years must equal £200.

(b) Suppose that the firm's accountant makes an annual allocation of depreciation expense of £50. Annual income will now be calculated at £50, i.e., £100 − £50. This amount will then be distributed and the remaining £50 is assumed to be placed in a bank account. As can be seen from the Balance Sheets summarised in Table 7.1(a), for each of the four years owner's interest will be represented by assets with total 'value' of £200. At the end of the fourth year £200 will be available either to replace the asset or to be used in whatever way the owner wishes. Notice that neither the historic cost system of valuation, nor any other system, will of itself provide liquid funds for replacement of the asset; it is for convenience in the illustration that the funds remaining after distribution of income are placed in the bank account. Similarly, the depreciation expense, in total, may not be sufficient to maintain the earnings capacity of the business if replacement cost of the asset is higher than £200.

TABLE 7.1 *Illustration of depreciation and capital maintenance*

	Year 1	Year 2	Year 3	Year 4
(a) *Accounting depreciation:*				
Fixed asset	£200	£200	£200	£200
less Accumulated depn	50	100	150	200
net book value	150	100	50	0
cash at bank	50	100	150	200
	£200	£200	£200	£200
Owner's interest	£200	£200	£200	£200
(b) *Actual depreciation:*				
Fixed asset	£200	£200	£200	£200
actual depreciation	80	140	180	200
	120	60	20	0
cash at bank	50	100	150	200
	£170	£160	£170	£200
'Shortfall'	£30	£40	£30	£0

(c) Assume that the actual measure of loss in benefits through ownership and use of the asset over the four years follows the following pattern;

Year 1	80
Year 2	60
Year 3	40
Year 4	20

If the depreciation expense continues to be allocated on the basis used in (b) i.e., equal annual amounts of £50, then owner's interest will not be maintained in terms of the monetary amount of capital invested in Years 1 to 3 although it will be by the end of Year 4 (see Table 7.1(b)). Hence, an arbitrary or incorrect allocation base will not even ensure maintenance of the money amount of owner's interest unless measured over the total life of the asset in question.

Depreciation

(a) Introduction

There are many different descriptions of the nature and causes of depreciation. Early attempts to record the value of assets and the allocation of depreciation related to the provision of funds for asset replacement.[3] Other descriptions include, a measure of physical deterioration of an asset either through use or through time; technological obsolescence, where more up to date equipment can perform the task required in a more economic manner than existing equipment; product obsolescence, where a fall in demand for the finished product has reduced the value of the asset in question.

Statement of Standard Accounting Practice (SSAP) 12, 'Accounting for Depreciation', defines depreciation as 'a measure of the wearing out, consumption or other loss of value of a fixed asset whether arising from use, effluxion of time or obsolescence through technology and market changes'.[4] This definition indicates that the cause of the depreciation is unimportant and that it is its effect which should be highlighted, namely the loss in value of the asset. It says nothing about the provision of funds for replacement of the asset, which is coincidental to the measurement of loss in value, nor in fact does it mention the allocation of acquisition cost. However, the Statement does indicate that depreciation should be based on asset cost (or valuation when the asset has been revalued in the financial statements) and that 'depreciation should be allocated to accounting periods so as to charge a fair proportion to each accounting period during the expected life of the asset'.[5]

(b) Market valuation basis

How should the depreciation expense be allocated to each period? One possible method is to ascertain the replacement cost of the asset at the end of each period, or more correctly the replacement cost of an asset with a similar unexpired service potential. If no suitable market price exists for such an asset then valuation might be obtained from independent professional valuers, or, as a last resort, from responsible, experienced employees of the business.

Illustration 2
Consider an asset which originally cost £4000 and has a four year useful life. Replacement cost of a 'second-hand equivalent asset' at appropriate stages in its life are given below, together with the depreciation expense for that year of the asset's life:

	'Second-hand equivalent asset'	
	Replacement cost	Depreciation expense
One year old	£2800	£1200
Two years old	1900	900
Three years old	700	1200
Four years old	0	700

Identification of the replacement cost of a similar asset will solve the problem of allocation of cost, provided, of course, that this particular basis of valuation is accepted as the most appropriate base, rather than any other basis, such as net realisable value. Unfortunately, the characteristics of many assets are sufficiently unique to reduce the likelihood that a replacement cost value exists for assets of similar unexpired service potential. Additionally, the use of independent valuers is an expensive matter and requires a valuer with an expert knowledge not only of the asset itself but also of the use to which the asset is being applied in that particular business. Such expert valuers are hard to find, if indeed they exist. The use of employees (or directors in the case of a company), in their place, reduces the objectivity, and perhaps the reliability, of the valuation.

(c) *Cost allocation basis*

Many businesses are either unable or unwilling to pay for the services of independent valuers or to use market based valuation data. Instead, depreciation is often calculated by means of an allocation of cost to different accounting periods, hopefully on a basis which attempts to match the depreciation expense with the benefits obtained. Less precise allocation methods are also adopted, including the choice of a more or less arbitrary basis of allocation, either deliberately or else because of insufficient thought for the principles involved.

In order to attempt the allocation of asset cost on a rational and systematic basis the following factors must first be identified or estimated;

(i) Acquisition cost (or revaluation, if this has taken place);
(ii) Useful life of the asset;
(iii) Pattern of expected benefits in each year of useful life; and
(iv) Estimated residual value.

The total amount to be depreciated, *the depreciable cost*, will be equal to acquisition cost less estimated residual value.

(i) *Acquisition cost* Not only must the acquisition cost include the invoice price of any fixed asset acquired, it must also include all those other costs incurred in placing fixed assets in the position where they can begin to provide benefits to the owners. As a general rule all those costs of a non-recurring nature, incurred as a direct consequence of the acquisition of a fixed asset, will be included in acquisition cost. For example, transportation costs to the point of use of the assets or to the owner's premises will be included, as will any installation costs (including wages paid to the acquiring organisation's own work-force for installation). Other costs incurred to replace damaged service potential, including costs incurred to repair damage to assets caused on shipment or installation, should not be included in asset cost but should be charged as an expense of the current accounting period. Expenditures, or costs, included in the acquisition price of a fixed asset are often described as *Capital Expenditures* while those which are expensed immediately are described somewhat confusingly as *Revenue Expenditures*.

Illustration 3
Bryant Traders recently acquired plant and machinery which was shipped from the manufacturers in Bristol to Bryant's business premises in Glasgow. The invoice price of the equipment amounted to £110 000 from which a discount of £10 000 was allowed for prompt settlement of the account. During transportation from Bristol, at the expense of the purchasers, the machinery was damaged and subsequently required repairs costing £3600. Costs of transportation amounted to £1150. During installation in the business premises, part of the factory had to be demolished in order to lay a concrete base for the new equipment. Cost of demolition and subsequent rebuilding amounted to £13 700 including the following:

Hire of equipment	£3 600
Materials used	2 900
Direct labour costs	7 200
	£13 700

The task of installation was performed by Bryant's own work-force. A training course was organised for those employees operating the new equipment at a cost of £2300, made up as follows:

Payment to outside demonstrators	£ 800
Loss of production during the course	1500
	£2300

Expenditures which will be capitalised in respect of the acquisition are:

	£
Invoice price	110 000
Transportation	1 150
Installation	13 700
Total asset cost	£124 850

The cash discount should not be deducted from the invoice price as this treatment would produce a different acquisition cost for the same asset; depending on the method of payment for the asset. In practice, however, many accountants may deduct the discount, particularly if the amount involved was not considered significant in relation to the asset cost.

Expenditures incurred in repairing damaged goods are revenue items and should be expensed in the period incurred.

The transportation and demolition costs were properly capitalised, as these were incurred in order to enable the asset to be placed in the position where it might begin to produce benefits, i.e., it was only as a result of these expenditures that future benefits or service potential might be obtained.

The cost of training staff should perhaps also be considered as capital expenditure as without such training the equipment would presumably lie idle. However, as the business retains no control over the future benefits available from the training (staff might leave) the expenditure is treated as a revenue item. The loss of production during training also involves an opportunity cost rather than a realised expenditure and, unfortunately or otherwise, current accounting practice tends to ignore opportunity costs.

Any annual, or otherwise recurrent, expenditure which must be incurred before an asset can be used is nevertheless treated as revenue expenditure, e.g., annual road tax on motor vehicles or insurance costs. In such cases the individual items of expenditure are matched with the periods to which they provide benefits; any time overlap between date of expenditure and period of benefit will be adjusted either by means of an accrual or a prepayment.

A number of businesses are able to manufacture or build fixed assets for their own personal use. The acquisition cost identified with these assets must include not only the materials and labour costs involved in their construction but also all other direct costs attributable, together with a reasonable proportion of indirect overheads incurred. This may also include 'interest on capital borrowed to finance the production of that asset to the extent that it accrues in respect of the period of production'.[6] The exercise of judgement required in the allocation of indirect overheads to the cost of 'homemade assets' introduces an additional element of subjectivity, this time into the identification of acquisition cost itself.

(ii) *Useful life* In order to ensure that each accounting period benefiting from the use of a fixed asset is allocated a proportion of the acquisition cost, some estimate will be necessary of the expected useful life. Useful life represents economic life and not technical life – many assets can be retained for a number of years beyond their economic life by unwise managers, sometimes at considerable maintenance or storage cost. In the case of major assets an estimate of expected useful life may have been made before deciding upon acquisition.

In many instances, revisions may be made to the earlier estimate of useful life, in which case the unallocated balance of cost must be charged to revenue over the revised, remaining useful life.

(iii) *Pattern of expected benefits* Before most fixed assets are acquired, an analysis will have been carried out on the relative worth of the proposed investment. This analysis will have included an estimate of the likely pattern of benefits to be obtained from use of the asset. Such an estimate, if available, will provide a guide for the allocation of the asset cost in accordance with the matching principle.

Allocation of cost on the above basis, even if the required information is available, is not without its critics. A. L. Thomas and others have suggested a number of criticisms of this approach including the following:

(a) revenues are a joint product of all the inputs of a firm and not normally specific to one particular input. Hence the assignment of revenues or benefits to each asset individually is not possible in an unambiguous manner;
(b) benefits received in different periods may not have an equal value. The practice sometimes adopted of applying the same implicit rate of return to all years of an asset's service life is itself arbitrary.

Again, the conclusion reached by A. L. Thomas is that 'insofar as cost-accumulation and matching involve allocations of nonmonetary goods, these allocations presently are almost always arbitrary; no general solution to this problem is possible within the framework of present allocation theory and present conventional rules'.[7] Thomas's comments, which apply not only to depreciation allocations but to all cost allocations, are worth remembering when students read comments concerning the objectivity of historic cost accounting.

(iv) *Residual value* Because estimates of residual values are necessarily based on factors relating to the physical condition of the asset and market prices for some future period, any estimate is likely to be a difficult task. In many situations, the estimated amount is likely to be small in relation to original cost and will be ignored for depreciation calculations; any eventual proceeds of disposal being reflected in the financial results of the year of disposal, as an offset against the depreciation charge of that year.

In summary, the calculation of total depreciable cost will be based on a relatively certain, but by no means unambiguous identification of asset acquisition cost, less an estimate of disposal proceeds. Depreciable cost will then be allocated over the estimated useful life of the asset in accordance with the estimated pattern of future benefits, if obtainable. In conclusion, the calculations of depreciation expense in a historic cost accounting system is likely to be a highly subjective process, based on uncertain estimates of future events. Indeed, the expense itself is normally described as a 'provision for depreciation', indicating that it is merely an estimation of a loss, the actual amount of which will only be ascertained at some future date, i.e., on disposal.

(d) *Depreciation techniques*

There are a number of methods available by which depreciable cost may be allocated to accounting periods. SSAP 12 lays down the requirement that the managers of a business 'have a duty to allocate depreciation as fairly as possible to the periods expected to benefit from the use of the asset and should select the method regarded as most appropriate to the type of asset and its use in the business'.[8]

Additionally, a change from one method of depreciation calculation to another is only allowed on the grounds 'that the new method will give a fairer presentation of the results and of the financial position'.[9] Further, the effect of the change should be disclosed in the year of change, if material.

Each method described in this section will be illustrated by means of a single asset, using the data given in Table 7.2.

Four methods are described for identifying annual depreciation allocations. They are not the only possible methods but represent the most commonly used ones.

TABLE 7.2 *Data used in depreciation illustration*

Asset cost	£5000
Estimated useful life	5 years
Residual value at end of Year 5	£500

(i) *Straight-line method* This is by far the most widely adopted method for the allocation of depreciable cost. Using this method, an equal amount of depreciable cost is allocated to each year of the asset's useful life.

$$\text{Annual depreciation expense} = \frac{\text{Acquisition cost} - \text{Residual value}}{\text{Useful life}}$$

In the case of the asset described in Table 7.2, the annual depreciation charge would be

$$\frac{£(5000-500)}{5} = £900 \text{ per annum for 5 years}$$

The expense will be recorded either by reducing the amount shown in the asset cost account, or else by crediting the amount to be accumulated depreciation account whilst retaining the amount on the asset account at original cost, the latter treatment being preferred. The debit entry will either be recorded initially in a depreciation expense account or else transferred directly to the Profit and Loss Account, i.e.

debit	Depreciation expense a/c	£900
credit	Accumulated depreciation a/c	£900

Being annual depreciation charge on fixed asset.

The Balance Sheet will report the net book value of the asset, i.e., the undepreciated balance of asset cost.

For example:

	£
End of Year 1 Balance Sheet will include;	
Fixed asset, at cost	5000
Less accumulated depreciation	900
net book value	£4100

The major justification offered for the adoption of the above method is its simplicity; only by chance will the pattern of expected benefits be the same each year. Uncertainty relating to the pattern of future benefits and estimated life of an asset have also been offered as possible justifications, but if the pattern of future benefits obtained from an asset was so uncertain, then an accelerated depreciation technique or even immediate 100 per cent write-off of depreciable cost would seem to possess a greater justification than the straight-line method.

(ii) *Reducing balance method* This method, together with the 'sum-of-the-years-digits' method, involves the allocation of a larger depreciation charge to earlier years of an asset's life than to later years, i.e., it is one of the so-called accelerated depreciation methods. Justifications for this treatment include an assumption either that:

(a) assets lose a greater value or generate higher benefits in the early years of usage than in the later years; or
(b) maintenance costs will rise as assets age, and that an appropriate allocation of depreciable cost should be made to equalise the total of depreciation plus maintenance costs in each year of an asset's life.

The reducing balance method, sometimes known as the double-declining balance method, involves calculating depreciation on the basis of a fixed percentage of the *net book value* of assets held. Theoretical calculation of the percentage rate to be applied is based on the following equation:

$$\text{Annual depreciation rate} = 1 - \sqrt[n]{\frac{\text{Residual value}}{\text{Acquisition cost}}}$$

where n = estimated useful life in years.

For the asset described in Table 7.2, the rate will be:

$$1 - \sqrt[5]{\frac{£500}{£5000}} = 1 - 0.63$$
$$= 0.37 \text{ or } 37\%$$

In fact, the actual rate used will normally be estimated by the use of double the straight-line rate, i.e., $2 \times 20\% = 40\%$, hence the alternative name used for this method.

Annual depreciation charge and net book values using the approximate rate of 40 per cent are applied to the asset example with the results shown in Table 7.3. Also provided are the results using the straight-line method. As the results demonstrate, use of the reducing balance method produce a relatively higher depreciation charge in the early years of the life of an asset but a lower charge in later years.

As can be seen in Table 7.3, application of the reducing balance method produces a sharp fall in the annual depreciation expense over the life of an asset. Because of the use of an approximate rate, the depreciation charge has been adjusted in Year 5 to produce a closing net book value equal to the estimated disposal value. With the uncertainty attached to estimates of ultimate disposal values, the depreciation charge in the final year of an asset's life often includes an adjustment to equate the closing net book value shown for the asset to the actual disposal proceeds. In principle though, the final

TABLE 7.3 *Comparison of the straight-line and reducing balance depreciation methods*

End of year	Depreciation expense	Accumulated depreciation	Net book value
	£	£	£
(i) *Straight-line*			
1	900	900	4100
2	900	1800	3200
3	900	2700	2300
4	900	3600	1400
5	900	4500	500
(ii) *Reducing balance*			
1	2000	2000	3000
2	1200	3200	1800
3	720	3920	1080
4	432	4352	648
5	148	4500	500

year's depreciation charge should be calculated in the same way as is used for other years, with any difference between estimated and actual disposal proceeds being separately identified, either as an adjustment to the depreciation charges of previous years, or else as a gain or loss on disposal.

Illustration 4
Assume that a business depreciates the asset described in Table 7.2 using the straight-line method and that actual disposal proceeds were (i) £800 and (ii) £300.

(i) Depreciation expense calculated in Year 5 according to original estimates should be £900 giving rise to a net book value at the end of Year 5 of £500. On disposal of the asset a 'gain' of £300 results, i.e.

	£
Disposal proceeds	800
Less net book value	500
'gain' on disposal	£300

The gain should be identified separately as a credit in the Profit and Loss Account, with a depreciation expense of £900 charged for the year as a debit to the Profit and Loss Account.

(ii) Again a depreciation expense of £900 should be charged in the Profit and Loss Account for Year 5, with an additional charge of £200, representing the 'loss' on disposal of the asset, i.e., an adjustment relating to under provision of depreciation expense over the life of the asset.

	£
Disposal proceeds	300
Less net book value	500
'loss' on disposal	£(200)

(iii) *Sum-of-years-digits method* An alternative to the above reducing balance technique, which involves a less rapid pattern of depreciation allocations, but retains the principle of higher depreciation charges in early years than in later years, is the 'sum-of-the-digits' method. This method, which is more widely adopted in the United States of America than in the United Kingdom, derives its name from the process by which the annual depreciation charge is calculated:

(a) Each year of an asset's life is assigned a number or digit in reverse order to the year of life. For example, for the asset in Table 7.2 the numbers assigned would be:

Year of life	Number assigned
1	5
2	4
3	3
4	2
5	1

Fixed asset measurement (I)

(b) Depreciable cost is then divided by the sum of the digits to obtain a depreciable cost per digit, i.e.

$$\frac{£4500}{(5+4+3+2+1)} = \frac{£4500}{15}$$

$$= \underline{\underline{£300}} \text{ per digit}$$

(c) Annual depreciation charge is calculated by multiplying the digit assigned to that year by the depreciable cost per digit, i.e.

Year	Depreciation expense
1	5 × £300 = £1500
2	4 × £300 = £1200
3	3 × £300 = £ 900
4	2 × £300 = £ 600
5	1 × £300 = £ 300

An alternative calculation of the annual depreciation charge involves:

$$\frac{\text{Number assigned}}{\text{Sum-of-digits}} \times \text{depreciable cost.}$$

Using the sum-of-the-years-digits method, the written down book value of the asset declines at a much less rapid rate than occurred using the reducing balance method, i.e.,

Year	Accumulated depreciation	Net book value
	£	£
1	1500	3500
2	2700	2300
3	3600	1400
4	4200	800
5	4500	500

The net book value of the asset at the end of Year 5 using this method, automatically adjusts to the estimated disposal value at the end of that year.

(iv) *Production (or usage) method* It may sometimes be possible to calculate annual depreciation expense based on estimated usage of the asset, e.g., units produced, hours worked, or mileage, in the case of a motor vehicle. Depreciation expense is calculated using this technique as a charge per unit of usage. This method assumes that the benefit obtained is the same for each unit of usage.

Illustration 5

Assume that expected output from the asset described in Table 7.2 is as follows:

Year	Expected output (units)
1	6 000
2	7 000
3	8 000
4	5 000
5	4 000
Total	30 000

$$\text{Depreciation expense per unit} = \frac{£(5000 - 500)}{30\,000}$$

$$= 15 \text{ pence}$$

Estimated depreciation expenses and net book values using the production basis over the life of the asset are shown in Table 7.4.

TABLE 7.4 *Production basis depreciation*

End of year	Cost	Depreciation expense	Accumulated depreciation	Net book value
	£	£	£	£
1	5000	900	900	4100
2	5000	1050	1950	3050
3	5000	1200	3150	1850
4	5000	750	3900	1100
5	5000	600	4500	500

7.4 Summary

Historic cost asset measurement is often justified on the basis of objectivity and prudent treatment. Uncertainties attached to estimates of useful asset life and likely pattern of future benefits, in addition to ambiguities about acquisition cost, make the claims of objectivity appear to be of rather doubtful validity. This claim is further reinforced when methods of depreciation allocation are considered. Additionally, the identification of depreciable cost based on original acquisition cost may result in accounting income being calculated without maintaining the earnings capacity of a business. Hence, the claim of prudent accounting treatment is also questionable.

Questions

1. To what extent do you agree with the view that the historic cost basis of asset valuation is more objective than other bases?

2. Explain the classification of economic goods used by A. L. Thomas, giving two examples of each type of good.
3. Why is the distinction between different categories of non-monetary goods so important to accounting income measurement?
4. 'Depreciation is a process of allocation not of valuation.' Explain whether you agree with the above statement.
5. Distinguish between the economic and the technical life of a fixed asset.
6. Draw up brief guidelines to distinguish between revenue and capital expenditures.

For each of the following questions **circle** the *letter* alongside the *best choice* from among the possible solutions presented.

7. A motor vehicle purchased at a cost of £6400 has an estimated useful life of 4 years and second-hand value at the end of that time of £1200. Depreciation is provided using the sum-of-the-years digits method. The depreciation charge in Year 2 is:

    (a) £1280;
    (b) £1040;
    (c) £1560;
    (d) £1920.

8. An asset bought at a cost of £24 000 is depreciated using the straight-line method over 6 years, assuming a resale value of £3000 at the end of that time. At the end of the third year of useful life of the asset the written down value is:

    (a) £13 500;
    (b) £12 000;
    (c) £11 000;
    (d) £10 500.

9. A caravan was acquired at a cost of £12 500 by a building firm for use as an on-site rest room. Cost of equipping the caravan with various fittings came to £1350, including an amount of £350 for freezer foods. Costs of transporting the caravan to building sites during the first year of useful life amounted to £1200. The total acquisition cost of the caravan to be shown in the Balance Sheet is:

    (a) £12 500;
    (b) £13 500;
    (c) £13 850;
    (d) £15 050;
    (e) none of these.

10. An asset was bought for £7500 in May 1982 with an estimated useful life of five years and salvage value of £1500 at the end of that time. Depreciation is to be allocated on the straight-line basis over the five years of useful life. The written-down value of the asset at the end of Year 3 is:

    (a) £3900;
    (b) £3000;
    (c) £3500;
    (d) £4300.

11. Equipment purchased on 1 January 1981 for £40 000 was sold on 31 December 1983 for £21 000. Depreciation had been charged on a double-declining balance basis, on the assumption of an estimated useful life of eight years. The total

depreciation expense for 1983, including any adjustment for the 'loss' or 'gain' on disposal of the equipment was:

(a) £1500 debit;
(b) £4000 debit;
(c) £1000 credit;
(d) £4125 credit.

12. Plant and equipment originally acquired at a cost of £80 000 had a written-down book value of £45 000 at the end of Year 2 using the reducing balance method. The equipment was estimated to have no salvage value at the end of its useful life. Using the straight-line depreciation method, the written-down value at the end of Year 2 would have been:

(a) £64 000;
(b) £48 000;
(c) £40 000;
(d) £60 000.

Problems

1. Bolderson Products have recently built an extension to their factory on waste ground which had cost £41 000. Old buildings standing on the waste ground were demolished at a cost of £5000. The company had employed direct labour to build the extension under the supervision of the factory manager. Costs involved included:

	£
Hire of labour force	24 000
Materials used	4 800
Allocation of factory manager's salary	1 500

In addition, disruptions caused by the building work meant that the factory workforce had been working additional overtime at a cost of £18 000. Overtime rates are 150 per cent of normal rates.

(a) Distinguish between the above costs according to whether each represents capital or revenue expenditure (or neither).
(b) Immediately after the extension had been built, it was sold to another manufacturer at a cost of £125 000. Explain whether the gain on disposal, if any, should be included in the profit for the year.
(c) Provide journal entries to record the transactions in (a) and (b) above.

2. A luxury villa has recently been acquired by Luxury Services for hire to holiday parties. The cost of acquisition was £110 000 and included £10 000 for 10 years use of private beach facilities and £40 000 for the land surrounding the villa. Costs of modernising and renovating the villa amounted to £40 000 including £15 000 paid for new furniture and £5000 on routine maintenance. By the end of the first year of rental the following additional costs had been incurred:

Rental of beach buggies for clients	£2400
Installation of security system in line with the requirements of the insurers	£4800
Purchase of beach furniture	£5500
Replacement of fittings which had been stolen, lost or damaged by clients	£7800

Fixed asset measurement (I)

Required
(a) Distinguish between all the above mentioned items according to whether each should be classified as a capital or a revenue expenditure. Give reasons for each classification.
(b) Explain whether the items identified as capital expenditures should be dealt with separately or jointly for depreciation purposes.

3. Plant and equipment which cost £16 000 has an estimated useful life of four years and salvage value of £1000 at the end of that time. Calculate the annual depreciation expense and Balance Sheet value at the end of each year of useful life using the following methods:

   (a) Straight-line;
   (b) Reducing balance (or double-declining balance);
   (c) Sum-of-the-years digits.

4. Production equipment bought at a cost of £37 000 has an estimated useful life of five years and a scrap value of £2000 at the end of that time. Estimated pattern of usage over the five years is as follows:

Year	Hours in use
1	4000
2	3500
3	2500
4	2000
5	2000

   The declining pattern of usage is expected to result from a higher level of maintenance work required in later years of life, and not from any decline in demand for the output.

   (a) Explain the depreciation method which you consider to be the most appropriate for this equipment.
   (b) Calculate the depreciation charge for each year of useful life using the depreciation method advocated in (a) and the resulting written-down book value of the asset at the end of each year.
   (c) Show journal entries to record the depreciation expense in Year 1.

5. Equipment purchased for £20 000 is to be depreciated using the double-declining balance method, assuming a useful life of five years and salvage value of £2000 at the end of that time.

   (a) Calculate the depreciation expense for each year of the estimated useful life.
   (b) Provide journal entries to record the depreciation expense in each year and the disposal of the equipment at the end of the useful life on the assumption that the actual salvage value was: (i) £2000, (ii) £5000.

6. An asset bought for £20 000 with an estimated useful life of four years and anticipated costs of disposal of £4000 at the end of that time, is depreciated on a straight line basis.

   (a) Calculate the annual depreciation expense.
   (b) Provide journal entries to record the disposal in Year 4.

Appendix Asset valuation and economic income
A The basic model explained

Consider the case of a '*single asset firm*' operating in an environment of certainty and where a perfect and complete market exists for the asset owned by the firm.

The assumption of a *complete market* implies that there will be a price available for the asset at all stages in its life-cycle, i.e., whatever its age. The assumption of *perfect market conditions* implies that the purchase and selling price of the asset will be equal at all times, as there will be no transaction costs involved in purchase or sale and all individuals operating within the market will have equal expectations of, and access to, the likely benefits obtainable from ownership of the asset. Finally, the assumption of *certainty* implies that the asset will be valued equally by all individuals and on the basis of the discounted present value of the future benefits obtainable from ownership and use of the asset. In the absence of risk, the relevant discount rate to be used will be the same for all individuals and equal to the time preference interest rate, i.e., the rate at which individuals will wish to be compensated for delay in receipt of funds.

Assume that the future benefits are all received at the end of the year to which they relate and are equal to:

Year 1	£100
Year 2	£200
Year 3	£100

The asset will be fully exhausted at the end of Year 3 with no disposal value at the end of that time. Also assume that the interest rate, representing the time preference of all individual investors, equals 10 per cent per annum. This rate will be the same for all investors in the conditions described above as they will all have equal expectations about future outcomes which are all known with certainty.

The value of the asset at time 0, and hence its cost to the firm will be equal to:

$$\frac{£100}{(1+0.10)} + \frac{£200}{(1+0.10)^2} + \frac{£100}{(1+0.10)^3}$$

$$= £100(0.909) + £200(0.826) + £100(0.751)$$

$$= £331.20$$

At the end of Year 1 the value of the asset will be equal to the present value, at that date, of the remaining stream of benefits available from the asset, i.e.,

$$\frac{£200}{(1+0.10)} + \frac{£100}{(1+0.10)^2}$$

$$= £200(0.909) + £100(0.826)$$

$$= £264.40$$

The fall in the value of the asset over the first year is equal to the amount which must be made good before the owner of the asset will be considered to

Fixed asset measurement (I)

be as well off at the end of the period as at the commencement of it, i.e., the amount which must be deducted from benefits before business income can be calculated. This fall in value is equal to:

£331.20 − £264.40 = £66.80

The fall in value of the asset may be described as depreciation in the value of the asset over the year and must be deducted from the benefits obtained before the income for the period can be calculated, i.e.,

Year 1 Benefits received	£100.00
Less depreciation incurred	66.80
Net income	£ 33.20

At the end of the second year of asset life, the remaining stream of benefits consists of:

Year 3: £100

The value of the above stream of benefits at the end of Year 2 equals:

$$\frac{£100}{(1+0.10)} = £100(0.909) = £90.90$$

Hence, the fall in value of the asset over the second year of its life, equal to the depreciation expense incurred during that year, is

£264.40 − £90.90 = £173.50

Net income for Year 2 is as follows:

Year 2 Benefits received	£200.00
Less depreciation incurred	173.50
Net income	£ 26.50

Finally, at the end of the third year of the asset's life the asset value is zero as there are no future benefits obtainable. The fall in value of the asset over Year 3 of its life is therefore £90.90. Net income for Year 3 is:

Year 3 Benefits received	£100.00
Less depreciation incurred	90.90
Net income	£ 9.10

Notice that the net income obtained from the asset each year is equal to a return of 10 per cent on its value at the commencement of that year (subject to slight rounding up adjustments), i.e.

	Year 1	Year 2	Year 3
Opening value	£331.20	£264.40	£90.90
Net income	£ 33.20	£26.50	£ 9.10

The depreciation expense calculated in the above illustration has been obtained as a result of the valuation process. It represents the loss in value of the asset over its useful life as a result of exhaustion of the benefits obtainable from owning and using the asset.

Another view of the nature of the depreciation expense is that it represents an allocation of the asset cost over its useful life, i.e.,

	£
Year 1 Depreciation expense =	66.80
Year 2 Depreciation expense =	173.50
Year 3 Depreciation expense =	90.90
Asset cost	£331.20

B Relaxation of assumptions

(a) Consider what would happen in the above illustration if the anticipated benefits had not been known for certain and that a revision had been made at the end of Year 1 to the estimated benefit obtainable at the end of the third year. Assume that the revised benefit expected at the end of Year 3 is £400 and that all other benefits are expected to remain the same as previously. Assume further that the revised benefits are subsequently obtained. The value of the asset at the end of Year 1 now becomes:

$$\frac{£200}{(1+0.10)} + \frac{£400}{(1+0.10)^2}$$

$$= £200(0.909) + £400(0.826)$$

$$= £512.20$$

Instead of depreciation, there is now an increase in the value of the asset amounting to £(512.20 − 331.20) = £181.00. An unexpected gain in value has arisen on the asset amounting to £(400 − 100) × 0.751, or £225.30 in present value terms at time 0. The amount of this gain can be verified by the following reconciliation:

Present value of revised estimate of benefits at time 0

$$= \frac{£100}{(1+0.1)} + \frac{£200}{(1+0.1)^2} + \frac{£400}{(1+0.1)^3}$$

$$= £100(0.909) + £200(0.826) + £400(0.751)$$

$$= £556.50$$

Present value of original estimate of benefits = £331.20

Unexpected gain = £556.50 − £331.20

= £225.30

Fixed asset measurement (I)

A number of alternative accounting treatments are available for recognising this unexpected gain:

(i) One possible treatment is to record the gain as income of the year in which the gain was identified, i.e., in this case Year 1. Depreciation expense for Year 1 will then be revised to £556.50 − £512.20 = £44.30. Revised asset value at the end of Year 2 becomes:

$$\frac{£400}{(1+0.1)} = £400(0.909) = £363.60$$

Fall in value of the asset over Year 2 is now:

£512.20 − £363.60 = £148.60 (as compared with £173.50 previously).

Asset value at the end of Year 3 is zero as before and the fall in value of the asset over Year 3 equals £363.60. The total depreciation expense is revised to:

	£
Year 1 Depreciation expense =	44.30
Year 2 Depreciation expense =	148.60
Year 3 Depreciation expense =	363.60
	£556.50

The revised depreciation total of £556.50 also includes depreciation on the revaluation of the asset. Hence, one of the surprising features of upward revaluation of assets is that it also leads to an increase in depreciation expense. Revised income figures are shown in Table A7.1.

Excluding the unexpected gain, annual net income is again shown by Table

TABLE A7.1 *Revised income figures: separating unexpected gain*

	Year 1	Year 2	Year 3
	£	£	£
Benefits received	100.00	200.00	400.00
Less depreciation incurred	44.30	148.60	363.60
	55.70	51.40	36.40
Add unexpected gain	225.30	—	—
	£281.00	£51.40	£36.40
Opening asset value	£556.50	£512.20	£363.60
Return (excluding unexpected gain)	10%	10%	10%

A7.1 to be equal to 10 per cent (but in this case of the revised asset values), after allowing for rounding adjustments on calculations.

(ii) A second alternative treatment of the unexpected gain is to recognise the gain as income in the year in which the benefit is actually received, i.e., in the year in which the benefit may be said to have been realised. If this treatment is adopted, then asset values at the end of Years 1 and 2 will remain at the amounts originally calculated as will the depreciation expense and net income for these years. Only the income figure for Year 3 will be revised as shown in Table A7.2.

By adopting the second alternative, the unexpected gain is included with other income in Year 3, rather than being identified separately. Under this treatment, total depreciation charge is £225.30 lower than under the first treatment as no asset revaluation has been recorded; since no gain on revaluation was recorded separately either, total income for the three years is the same under both treatments. The separation of the gain on revaluation made in the first alternative treatment has not been made in the second alternative.

TABLE A7.2 *Revised income figures: inclusive of unexpected gain*

	Year 1	Year 2	Year 3
	£	£	£
Benefits received	100.00	200.00	400.00
Less depreciation incurred	66.80	173.50	90.90
	£32.20	£26.50	£309.10
Opening asset value	£331.20	£264.40	£90.90
Return (inclusive of unexpected gain)	10%	10%	340%

One major criticism of both treatments (i) and (ii) above is that they result in a diminution of the future earnings capacity of the organisation. If it is assumed that the rise in market price for the asset reflects an expectation of increased benefits from ownership of the asset, then the inclusion of the unexpected gain as income will result in the owner's interest or owner's capital being reduced in terms of the future earnings capacity. There is, therefore, a very strong argument for excluding the gain on revaluation from business income and treating it as an adjustment to owner's capital.

A counter argument to the above is that there has been an actual increase in the money value of the owner's initial investment in the business and that this increase should be reflected in business income. This counter proposal implies that the existing asset might reasonably be replaced by one of smaller size with the same expectation of benefits as promised by the asset originally. Taken to its logical conclusion, if successive replacements all had to be made either at increased price, or at reduced scale, the business might ultimately become so small so as not to continue in existence. Hence, in order to maintain the earnings capacity and not invalidate the going-concern concept, gains on revaluation of assets should not be included in income but should be treated as adjustments to owner's capital.

(b) If the assumption regarding perfect capital markets was also relaxed, then buyers and sellers would place different values on the asset. The accountant would then be faced with two or more asset values to choose from at any one point in time. Use of economic values, i.e., present values, would be difficult because of uncertainty and a choice would be necessary based either on *entry prices*, i.e., current purchase or replacement price, or *exit prices*, i.e., current realisable or disposal values. Entry prices or exit prices are used therefore as surrogates for economic values.

A few commentators, including R. J. Chambers[1] advocate the use of exit prices, i.e., net realisable values, emphasising the identification of total resources available to a firm to redirect in whatever way it chooses. The majority of commentators who advocate adoption of current market prices for asset valuation, however, favour the adoption of an entry price, normally replacement cost. Exit prices are rejected by the latter group because:

(i) fixed assets are normally held for use rather than disposal and should therefore be assigned a value in use; and
(ii) the total of exit prices for individual assets is often much less than the total exit price obtainable for assets if sold as a group; hence exit prices do not measure resources available for redirection.

One advocate of entry prices, W. T. Baxter, suggests the use of what he describes as a 'deprival value' for asset measurement, representing 'the net outlay avoided by virtue of owning the asset'.[2] Deprival value should be calculated by reference to the loss which the firm would suffer if deprived of the asset, i.e., 'the lower of replacement cost or expected direct benefits (where) "expected direct benefits" means the higher of service in use and of scrap value'.[3] The concept of deprival value was adopted by the Sandilands Committee in its report on accounting for inflation[4] and subsequently by later pronouncements of the Accounting Standards Committee, including in principle at least, the latest statement on accounting for changes in asset values, SSAP 16.[5]

Acceptance of the deprival value concept implies use of replacement cost for asset valuation unless this is higher than the present value of the expected future stream of benefits from holding the asset. In the latter case, the higher of present value and net realisable value should be adopted; if replacement cost exceeded present value then loss of the asset would not be followed by replacement; similarly if net realisable value exceeded present value then the asset should be sold immediately and deprival value would be equal to net sale proceeds.

(c) If the assumption of complete markets is relaxed then a situation may arise where there will not be a ready price available for the asset, whatever its age. Advocates of the use of replacement cost are then faced with the dilemma of what to substitute for the replacement cost of an asset of similar age and service potential. One possible solution is to use the cost of a new asset performing a similar service, but to adjust this cost to take account of the remaining useful life of the existing asset. If this solution is accepted then the accountant must recognise the fact that comparison may not be made of 'like with like' and that the problem of lack of suitable data on replacement cost has now been replaced with the problem of arriving at a suitable adjustment to the price of a new asset for the depreciation which has taken place.

Another possible solution involves the adjustment of original asset cost by an index measuring the change in cost of similar types of asset since the acquisition date. Again the problem arises of adjusting the price of the asset for the annual depreciation charge over the asset's life.

In summary, relaxation of the assumptions under which economic income and depreciation are capable of being identified results in situations where:

(i) unexpected gains and losses may arise which if not separated from business income, result in a diminution of owner's capital and future earnings capacity;
(ii) a choice must be made between competing market prices, i.e., entry versus exit prices;
(iii) situations may arise where there is no relevant market price, whether entry or exit price.

As a result of the above factors and many others, there is a great deal of reluctance on the part of accountants to accept a system of asset measurement based on anything other than original acquisition cost, although historic cost accounting itself faces problems which are themselves only solved by reference to subjective judgement.

Appendix Questions

1. What are the characteristics of an asset market that is (a) complete and (b) perfect? To what extent do such markets require complete certainty about future events?
2. Define economic income. Explain why this concept is not used for the measurement of business income.
3. Explain the relative benefits that would accrue to external users of financial accounting statements by the use of each of the following assets bases? (a) replacement cost; (b) realisable value.
4. What is meant by the expression 'maintenance of owner's wealth'? Why is this considered to be an important element in the determination of business income?

8 Fixed Asset Measurement (II)

8.1 Introduction

In Chapter 7 the measurement of fixed assets under an historic cost basis of valuation was examined. The allocation of acquisition cost over the estimated useful life of finite life tangible assets was considered as part of the matching process in which revenues obtained are matched with the expenses incurred in earning these revenues.

The current chapter explores further issues relating to the accounting measurement of tangible fixed assets and also considers the treatment of intangible fixed assets and investments. A section is also included at the end of the chapter describing the system of UK tax allowances relating to finite life tangible fixed assets.

8.2 Tangible fixed assets

Revision to estimated useful life, etc.

Both estimated useful life and residual values are based on forecasts of the future, taking into account such factors as expectations of patterns of trade, levels of competition and technological innovations. It is highly likely, therefore, that the estimates made when an asset was first acquired will require subsequent revision in the light of experience. In some instances, later revision of the original estimates of useful life and salvage value will not have a significant effect on the calculation of the actual depreciation expense, and no adjustment will, therefore, be necessary. Where revision of the estimated useful life and/or disposal value is considered to have significant effect on the calculation of depreciation expense, then the remaining depreciable cost (i.e. net book value less residual value), should be written off over the revised useful life of the asset.

Illustration 1
An asset acquired for £10 000 with an estimated useful life of 10 years and zero disposal value, is re-evaluated at the end of the fourth year of useful life and given a revised estimate of remaining useful life of three years with a salvage value of £900 at the end of that time.

Assuming depreciation calculated on a straight-line basis, the net book value at the end of Year 4 is:

$$£10\,000 - (\frac{£10\,000}{10} \times 4) = £6000$$

Revised remaining depreciable cost becomes $£(6000 - 900) = £5100$

i.e., Revised annual depreciation $= \frac{£5100}{3} = £1700$

No charge is recommended under SSAP 12 for 'back-log' depreciation, i.e., a charge against retained earnings for under or over-allocations of previous years.

For all businesses, it is essential that a memorandum record be kept, not only of each fixed asset held but also of the estimates from which depreciable cost was calculated and the basis of allocation adopted. Periodic reviews should be undertaken of the assets held, to identify whether there is any need for revision to the depreciation charges. This memorandum record, known as a *Plant Register*, is also useful to both the internal and external auditors of a business, in pursuit of their tasks of verifying the accuracy of the accounting records and the control over the assets owned.

Asset revaluations

Many businesses have been criticised in the past for reporting Balance Sheet fixed asset values which are well below the current market values, whether based on replacement cost or disposal value. Such under-valuations distort the rate of return being earned by the business, and indeed the value of the organisation, as well as the level of security available to creditors. Significant Balance Sheet under-valuations by a number of companies in the 1950s and 1960s led to a rash of takeovers which were motivated mainly by the prospects of gains from 'asset stripping', i.e., the disposal of the assets of an acquired business in a piecemeal fashion, often for more than the original acquisition price of the business as a whole.

Revaluations of fixed assets are now much more common than before but give rise to two special accounting problems, namely;

(i) how to treat the gain or loss on revaluation; and
(ii) what adjustment if any, should be made to the annual depreciation expense on the revalued asset.

(a) *Gains and losses on revaluation*

(i) *Losses* Any loss on the revaluation of a limited life fixed asset represents an underprovision of depreciation expense over the life of that asset to date. A similar adjustment should therefore be made as was described earlier for the revision to estimates of useful life, or disposal value; i.e.

An additional expense should be charged in the Profit and Loss Account in the year of revaluation, sufficient to reduce the net book amount of the asset to the value indicated by the revaluation;
Depreciation expense in later years should be based on the revised book value of the asset after revaluation adjustment.

Fixed asset measurement (II)

SSAP 12 states that in the year of the revaluation 'there should be disclosed by way of note to the financial statements the subdivision of the [depreciation] charge between that applicable to original cost (or valuation, if previously revalued) and that applicable to the change in value on the current revaluation, if material'.[1]

Unlimited life assets, such as freehold land, are not normally expected to reduce in value. Occasionally, however, external factors may alter and lead to a reduction in asset values. For example, land may be acquired for a specific purpose, such as oil platform construction, but conditions may alter thereafter to render that purpose uneconomic (such as a fall in demand for oil). In these circumstances, the amount shown for the unlimited life asset should be reduced by means of a depreciation charge which should be identified, if considered significant, as an extraordinary item in the Profit and Loss Account.

(ii) *Gains on revaluation* Gains on revaluation of fixed assets will normally be recorded in the books of account of a business enterprise by the following entry:

    debit   Asset cost a/c

    credit   Revaluation (or Capital) Reserve a/c

with the excess of revaluation over the net book value of the asset revalued. The gains will not normally be transferred to the Profit and Loss Account. Because the revaluation will represent an upward reappraisal of benefits obtainable from future use of the asset, the Income Statements of future years will, however, gain to the extent that the higher benefits will then be included. Depreciation will be charged on the revalued asset net book value and allocated over the remaining useful life of the asset in the case of limited life assets. Hence, revaluations will give rise to an increase in depreciation expense in a similar manner to the unexpected gains identified in Section B of the Appendix to the previous chapter.

Because of the higher depreciation expense on revalued assets, some accountants make a transfer from the revaluation reserve to the credit of the Profit and Loss Account of an amount equal to the additional depreciation on the revaluation. This adjustment appears to accord with the principles of historic cost accounting, but not with those of maintenance of earnings capacity.

Illustration 2
An asset which originally cost £50 000 has been revalued at the beginning of Year 6 at £40 000. Depreciation is charged on a straight-line basis over 10 years with no salvage value anticipated at the end of that time. The revaluation did not affect the estimate of useful life. At the beginning of Year 6 the following journal entry is made:

    debit   Asset Account   £15 000
    credit   Revaluation Reserve   £15 000
Revaluation of asset from net book value of
£25 000

At the end of Year 6 the depreciation will be calculated on the revalued amount and recorded as follows;

debit	Depreciation expense a/c	£8000	
credit	Accumulation depreciation a/c		£8000

Depreciation for year ($\frac{£40\,000}{5}$)

The accountant also decides to make a transfer from the revaluation reserve to the credit of the Profit and Loss Account;

debit	Revaluation Reserve a/c	£3000	
credit	Profit and Loss a/c		£3000

Transfer from revaluation reserve ($\frac{£15\,000}{5}$)

As a result of the above entry the net charge to the Profit and Loss Account will be £5000, equal to depreciation on the unallocated balance of historic cost.

In the case of depreciation on revaluation (as with a revision to estimated useful life), a note must be shown in the Balance Sheet in the year of revaluation indicating the amount of the additional depreciation expense which is applicable to the increase in value of the asset.

Even when an asset increases in value over a number of years, it still is necessary to make an annual depreciation charge if that asset has a finite useful life. This requirement is particularly applicable in the case of buildings or leasehold land other than those held as investment properties. The justification for making a depreciation charge in such cases is that it is a necessary allocation of cost under the matching principle; this justification is, however, weaker if a replacement cost system of asset valuation is adopted instead of an historic cost system. Even in this latter case though depreciation allocation will ultimately be necessary.

Illustration 3
Highlife Properties own freehold land and buildings which they acquired originally at a cost of £1.2 millions, of which the cost of land was £200 000. As freehold land is an unlimited life good, no depreciation allocation will be necessary. Depreciation, which must be charged annually on the buildings, is calculated by means of the straight-line basis, assuming a useful life for the building of 50 years, with no disposal value.

At the end of five years of useful life the amount shown in the accounts relevant to the building will be:

	£
Building at cost	1 000 000
Accumulated depreciation	100 000
net book value	£900 000

At the beginning of the sixth year of operations the land and buildings are revalued by means of an independent valuation and found to be worth £1.9 millions, including £550 000 for the value of the land. The revaluation is incorporated into the books of account by means of the following journal entry

		£	£
debit	Land account	350 000	
debit	Buildings account	450 000	
credit	Revaluation Reserve a/c		800 000
	Being revaluation of assets held		

Revised net book value of buildings shown in the books of account are

Buildings at revaluation   £1 350 000

The depreciation expense to be charged in each remaining year of the buildings' life is equal to the remaining depreciable cost, i.e., the net book value, divided by the number of years of useful life remaining, i.e.,

$$\text{Revised depreciation expense} = \frac{£1\,350\,000}{45}$$

$$= £30\,000 \text{ per annum.}$$

Trade-in values and asset replacement

Existing assets are often allowed in part-exchange for newer replacements. This practice is particularly common in the case of motor vehicles. Although no definitive rules are available for such cases, the desirable criteria of comparability in financial statements suggests that assets acquired and disposed of should be treated for accounting purposes in exactly the same way as they would have been treated if no part-exchange had occurred. The disposal price of the old asset should be identified, if at all possible, by reference to its value if sold to a third party, i.e., an 'arms-length' value should be assigned. On many occasions the dealer from whom the replacement asset is acquired will provide information on the trade-in value, but care must be taken to ensure that this value has not been inflated in order to encourage the purchase. Any gain or loss on disposal of the old asset should be calculated in the same way as if the disposal had taken place without a part-exchange, but with the one difference that the 'arms length' value should be included as the disposal value. The acquisition cost of the replacement asset should include not only the amount paid for the asset but also the 'arms length' disposal value of the replaced asset.

Although the above treatment is suggested for accounting for trade-in values, it is not the only possible treatment as indicated by the following illustration.

Illustration 4

Hartley Transport have recently purchased a new vehicle recovery truck at a cost of £15 000 in cash plus a trade-in allowance on their old truck of £1500. The old truck had a written-down book value in the accounts of Hartley Transport of £300, although a customer had recently offered £850 for it.

There are a number of different ways in which the disposal of the old truck and subsequent acquisition of the replacement may be recorded. Table 8.1 identifies the journal entries relevant to four possible treatments.

Treatment (i) understates the cost of the new vehicle in relation to a similar asset

TABLE 8.1

Hartley Transport: JOURNAL

	£	£
Treatment (i)		
New motor vehicle account	15 000	
cash a/c		15 000
Cash paid to acquire new towing truck		
Profit and Loss Account	300	
Old motor vehicles account		300
'Loss' on disposal of old vehicle		
Treatment (ii)		
New motor vehicle account	15 300	
cash a/c		15 000
Old motor vehicle account		300
Cash paid in partial acquisition of new towing truck plus trade-in value of old truck		
Treatment (iii)		
New motor vehicle account	16 500	
cash a/c		15 000
Old motor vehicle account		300
Profit and Loss Account		1 200
Cost of new towing truck and profit on disposal of old truck		
Treatment (iv)		
New motor vehicle account	15 850	
cash a/c		15 000
Old motor vehicle account		300
Profit and Loss Account		550
Cost of new towing truck and profit on disposal of old truck		

acquired other than by means of a trade-in. Similarly, a loss has been recorded on the old asset which does not reflect the actual fall in value of that asset over its useful life. Accordingly, this treatment should not be adopted.

Treatment (ii) similarly understates the cost of the replacement asset, although in this case, no loss is recorded on the disposal of the old asset. Many accountants use this treatment especially when considering replacement of 'like with like'. However, as the cost of the replacement asset is understated, treatment (ii) should also be rejected.

Treatment (iii) recognises a gain on disposal of the old asset of £1200 but this is based on the supposed trade-in value offered by the dealer and not on an 'arms length' value. Acquisition cost of the replacement vehicle is overstated by this treatment as is the gain on disposal of the old vehicle.

Treatment (iv) records the disposal value of the old vehicle based on the 'arms length' price of £850. This treatment also records the cost of the replacement vehicle at an amount which includes the more realistic value of the replaced asset, and presumably at a price which the new replacement would have cost in the absence of any part-exchange. This final treatment also complies with the requirement in SSAP 12 that 'where fixed assets are disposed of for an amount which is greater or less than their book value, the surplus or deficiency should be reflected in the results of the year and disclosed separately if material'.[2]

Repairs and renewals

Expenditure on repairs and maintenance of fixed assets normally only provides benefits of limited duration and, in the normal course of events, will be repeated in future years. Such expenditure may, however, be considered to provide benefits in future accounting periods, as without the maintenance of fixed assets future use would be curtailed. Despite the obvious future benefits obtainable from maintenance of assets, the routine expenditure on repairs is normally considered to be a cost of ensuring that the asset provides the net benefits over its useful life as estimated when the decision was first taken to acquire the asset. As this expenditure is deemed to add nothing either to the useful life or to the service capacity of the asset over and above that expected when originally acquired, the expenditure is normally treated as a revenue item and expensed in the period in which it was incurred.

Occasionally, however, expenditures may be undertaken which have the effect of extending the useful life of the asset in question and/or the future benefits obtainable from use of the asset. In these circumstances, the expenditure on repairs and renewals would be treated as capital expenditure and depreciated over the remaining useful life of the asset in a manner commensurate with the revised pattern of benefits. Occasionally, the expenditure may result in the renewal of the earnings capacity of an asset, which had been exhausted in previous years.

Illustration 5
An aeroplane which originally cost £500 000 with an estimated useful life of 15 years and disposal value of £50 000 at the end of that time, is currently shown in the records of the owners, Tinpot Enterprises, at a net book value of £200 000. Depreciation is calculated on the straight line basis.

Recent expenditure of £180 000 incurred on an engine overhaul and general refit, is expected to increase the useful life of the aeroplane by an extra five years but reduce the eventual disposal value to £30 000.

The financial records of Tinpot Enterprises, after adjusting for the above expenditure, will give a net book value for the aeroplane of

	£
Original cost	500 000
plus renewal expenditure	180 000
	680 000
less accumulated depreciation	300 000
net book value	£380 000

Revised depreciation charge over the remaining ten years of useful life will be

$$\frac{£(380\,000 - 30\,000)}{10} = £35\,000 \text{ per annum}$$

Expenditure incurred on repairing assets without extending the benefits obtained from use of the asset, but which is of a sufficiently large and non-recurrent nature, may also be treated in the same manner as a prepaid expense (such as prepaid rent) and allocated over a number of accounting periods so as not to burden any one accounting period with the whole amount. This treatment is justifiable if the repairs undertaken in the one year have helped to avoid further expenditure on repairs in the subsequent accounting periods.

8.3 Intangible assets

Introduction

An intangible asset has been defined as 'a capital asset having no physical existence, its value being dependent on the rights that possession confers upon the owners'.[3] A variety of assets are described as intangible assets, including goodwill, research and development expenditure, patent or franchise rights. As with fixed assets of limited useful life, intangible assets give rise to benefits in more than one accounting period. The major difference between intangible and tangible fixed assets, apart from their lack of physical existence, is the greater degree of uncertainty surrounding the likely stream of future benefits obtainable from intangible assets. Because of this uncertainty, the allocation of the cost of intangibles over their useful life has at times been criticised as being out of step with the prudence concept. Instead of the provision of depreciation, or *amortisation*, it has been suggested that expenditure incurred on acquisition of intangibles should immediately be expensed as a revenue item.

In addition to the uncertainty surrounding the likelihood of future benefits, a further element of uncertainty attached to intangibles is their cost of acquisition. This uncertainty is particularly applicable to one intangible asset, namely research and development, where the cost of researching into and developing new ideas and products includes not only direct labour and material costs but also the allocation of overheads from other areas of the business. The increased uncertainty attached to the identification of costs involved adds weight to the argument for the treatment of expenditure on assets such as research and development as revenue items, i.e. expenses, rather than capital expenditure. On the other hand, it may be argued that the manufacture, or construction, of tangible long-lived assets for 'own-use' for example, also involves imprecise, or subjective, estimates of total cost.

Amortisation

Where an intangible asset has been acquired, either through external purchase or else through expenditures incurred internal to a business, the cost of acquisition should, in theory at least, be identified and allocated over the asset's useful life in the same way as with tangible fixed assets. As already stated, the identification of acquisition cost and the expected pattern of benefits is more difficult to identify for an intangible asset than for other assets. Three examples of intangible assets, namely goodwill, research and development, and patent rights, will be examined in turn and the recommended accounting treatment for each identified.

(a) *Goodwill*
Goodwill involves the receipt of a higher income from a business than would

normally be expected from a similar business with equivalent assets and liabilities. The value of goodwill is therefore related to the present value of the expected stream of higher income.

Purchased goodwill normally arises when a business has been acquired at a price which is greater than the sum of the prices which might have been paid for the assets individually. Non-purchased goodwill arises when a business builds up a reputation with its clients or customers over a number of years,[4] enabling it to achieve a pattern of benefits greater than would be obtainable without the goodwill. As the latter goodwill has not arisen in the books of account of a business enterprise as a result of a previously recorded event or transaction, it will have no value according to the accounting records, although it may have a very real value to the business itself. However, when goodwill has been purchased, usually by the acquisition of another business, it is often reported as an asset in the combined accounts of the acquiring and acquired business. The cost of purchased goodwill may arise partly out of goodwill built up in the acquired business over a number of years, as with non-purchased goodwill, and partly out of an excess of the cost of acquisition over the book value of the net assets acquired. In the case of purchased goodwill there are a number of possible accounting treatments, namely,

(i) to capitalise the cost of acquisition and subsequently amortise this cost over the period of years for which benefits are expected to accrue from the expenditure;
(ii) to write-off the cost of acquisition against the reserves, i.e., retained earnings, of the acquiring business;
(iii) to write-up the book values of the fixed assets acquired by an amount which in total represents the cost of the purchased goodwill;
(iv) to capitalise the cost and maintain this amount as an intangible asset indefinitely.

Of the four possible treatments (iii) is not recommended; although it will have the effect of allocating the cost of goodwill over a number of accounting periods by means of the depreciation subsequently charged on the revalued assets, the pattern of allocation may bear no resemblance to the pattern of benefits obtainable through the goodwill itself.

Treatment (iv) is rejected as it treats the intangible asset as an indefinite life asset which never loses its value. It is likely that even with the most prominent business, competitors will eventually rise to the challenge and draw away some, if not all, of the superior benefits previously obtainable. Of the remaining treatments (i) is favoured over (ii) as it recognises the multi-period nature of the acquired goodwill. Both treatments are, however, allowed by Exposure Draft 30, 'Accounting for Goodwill', provided that the period over which the purchased goodwill is amortised if treatment (i) is adopted, does not exceed twenty years.[5]

(b) *Research and development*
The principal difference between purchased goodwill and research and development expenditure seems to be the difficulty in identifying the relevant expenditure in the case of the latter. Both intangibles are associated with an uncertain pattern of future benefits with neither, on the face of it, any more

uncertain that the other. Nevertheless, a different accounting treatment is advocated, in SSAP 13, 'Accounting for Research and Development'[6] for research and development expenditure to that recommended for purchased goodwill, perhaps because of the experience of the former Rolls-Royce Ltd in the years preceding its demise in 1971.[7]

SSAP 13 categorises research and development expenditure into three forms; (i) pure research; (ii) applied research; (iii) development expenditure.

Pure research is considered to be research undertaken in pursuit of the advance of knowledge generally within a particular field as contrasted to applied research which is considered to be work directed towards the exploitation of pure research in a commercial manner. Both forms of research are considered by SSAP 13 as 'part of the continuing operation required to maintain a company's business and its competitive position'[8] and as such are recommended to be expensed as incurred.

Development expenditure is considered to be expenditure relating to the introduction, or improvement, of specific products or processes and as such is capable of closer identification with a stream of potential benefits, which are themselves regarded as more certain. In so far as there is:

(i) a clearly defined project with a reasonable chance of successful exploitation; and
(ii) the relevant development costs are separately identifiable,

SSAP 13 recommends that the development expenditure be capitalised as *deferred development expenditure* and allocated against the stream of benefits subsequently arising. The judgements required, firstly in the identification of development expenditure to be capitalised, and secondly in the pattern of amortisation, makes the accounting treatment of this item very subjective.

The accounting policy adopted by a business enterprise in respect of development expenditure should be clearly identified in the annual financial statements. Information should be provided on expenditure incurred during the year on development, together with any movements on the deferred expenditure account, including the opening and closing balances and the amount amortised during the year.

(c) *Patent rights, etc.*

A patent is a legal right granting the holder the exclusive right to the use or sale of a new process, product, or invention, for an initial period of time of 20 years which can be extended on application.

Patent rights have similar characteristics to other intangible assets which have defined maximum exclusive rights to ownership, including copyrights to literary, dramatic, or artistic works, and franchise rights to act as sole distributor of goods patented by another business.

For all the above intangible assets, the costs associated with their creation or acquisition should be capitalised and subsequently amortised over the legally defined life, or the economic life if shorter.

Ownership of trade names or trademarks differs from the above intangibles in that the legal rights of the registered owners are for an indefinite period. Hence, the asset may be deemed to be an unlimited life good and any cost associated with the creation or acquisition carried as an asset in the accounts of the business on an indefinite basis. As with purchased goodwill, however, it will normally be the case that competitors will eventually make sufficient inroads into the business, or else demand will alter so as to reduce the value of this asset. Hence, if a fall in value is anticipated or, indeed, identified it should be recognised by amortisation of the asset cost.

8.4 Investments

Introduction

The range of investments which a business may undertake is as wide as the range available to an individual. If the investment is intended to be made for other than temporary purposes it will be considered to be a long-lived asset. However, where the investment is held on a temporary basis, e.g., as a depository for a seasonal surplus of funds, it will be deemed to be a current asset and accounted for in the manner described in Chapter 10. Long-lived investments will not normally be expected (by the holder at least) to depreciate in value, but rather to increase in value. However, as the increase in value will not be expected to be realised in the short term, those accountants who follow a strict application of historic cost principles may not record any increases in value but merely credit the Profit and Loss Account with income received. Strict adherence to a principle of recording gains or increases in value of long-term investments only when these are realised will, however, create an understatement to the readers of financial statements both of the actual rate of return earned on the investment and the value of the asset itself. This understatement may influence decisions relating either to disposal of the investment, or to the availability of security for business debts. Additionally, the income earned during periods in which the investments are held will be understated by the unrealised gain in value and the income earned during the period in which disposal is made will be correspondingly overstated. The 1981 Companies Act requirements, relating to the disclosure of the market value of listed investments, are outlined in Chapter 13.

Investments in other companies

Where one company invests in another, the share of the voting power owned in the investee company may be sufficiently large as to warrant the investor treating the investment for accounting purposes, as an extension of its own business. In the case of an ownership of voting power in excess of 50 per cent, the investee company will normally be considered to be a subsidiary of the company owning the investment and what are described as *group, or consolidated, accounts* must normally be prepared. Consolidated accounts will replace the cost of investment in the Balance Sheet of the group with the underlying assets and liabilities of the subsidiary, together with an additional liability representing any interest of minority shareholders. Similarly, the investing company's share of profits in the subsidiary will normally be included in the group Profit and Loss Account rather than merely reporting income actually received.

In the case of investments held which amount to less than 50 per cent of the voting power in the investee company but more than 20 per cent, the investee is normally regarded as an associated company. An associated company is actually one in which a significant influence is said to be held by the investing company. As with investments in subsidiaries, the group accounts of the investing company will include the share of profits or losses of the associated company.

Where the investing company does not prepare groups accounts then the normal practice is to include in the investing company's own Profit and Loss Account only dividends received and receivable from the associated company.

The investing company's share of undistributed earnings of the associated company is not considered to be realised profits for the purposes of the Companies Act 1948 to 1981 (see Chapters 13 and 16). The amount of investment in the associated company will normally be shown in the investment company's Balance Sheet at cost less amounts written off, and in the consolidated Balance Sheet, if any, by reference to the group's share of the net assets of the associated company, rather than by replacing the cost of the investment with the amounts of the underlying assets and liabilities, as is the case with subsidiaries.

Finally, an investment made in another company representing less than 20 per cent of the voting power of the investee company will normally be recorded in the Balance Sheet of the investing company at cost, with a footnote referring to the market value of the investment if available. Only the actual income received (or receivable) for the period will be recorded in the Profit and Loss Account.

The above description of accounting for investments in other companies is not by any means intended to be exhaustive but is merely intended to identify the approach adopted in the accounting treatments of such investments. An introduction to the subject of accounting for groups of companies is provided in Chapter 16.

Investment in property

Investments in property may be undertaken by a business in order to obtain both a current income and also possible gain on eventual disposal. For such properties the systematic allocation of depreciable cost is not considered necessary, but rather the identification of current market values and changes in the current value are considered 'of prime importance'.[9] The recommended accounting treatment for investment properties is to include them in the Balance Sheet at open market values. These values would normally be obtained from independent valuers if the investments represented an important or substantial element of total assets, otherwise valuation may be undertaken by employees or officers of the investing company. Changes in the value of investment properties should not normally be taken to the Profit and Loss Account but should rather be recorded and disclosed as a movement on an investment revaluation reserve. Only when the asset was finally disposed of would the gain over original cost be recognised. If, however, a debit balance results on the revaluation reserve, i.e., if the market value falls below cost, and the fall is expected to be permanent, then the debit balance would normally be charged to the Profit and Loss Account in accordance with the prudence concept.

Although the Profit and Loss Account would normally only include income received on the investment during each period, disclosure of current market values plus any change in value over the accounting period will enable readers of the accounting reports to obtain the information necessary for their own purposes, whether this involves appraisal of profitability, security or whatever.

Other assets held as long term investments would fall into a similar category as investments in property and should therefore be treated in the accounting records in the same manner.

8.5 Capital allowances and investment grants

Capital allowances

By way of contrast to many other countries, taxation legislation in the United Kingdom precludes the deduction of depreciation expenses in the calculation of business profits subject to taxation. In place of the accounting expenses, a system of tax deductions known as *Capital Allowances* are granted. The capital allowances are approved by annual (and occasionally semi-annual) Finance Acts, details of which are announced on 'budget day' by the Chancellor of the Exchequer.

Two advantages of the use of allowances defined by legislation are that

(a) the accountant does not need to be influenced by taxation aspects when identifying the most suitable accounting depreciation method to use; and
(b) the government can, in theory at least, stimulate or otherwise control the level of fixed capital investment within the economy by judicious manipulation of the rates of allowance.

For users of accounting reports the capital allowance system may present one problem in that it is often difficult to estimate expected levels of future taxation for a business without receiving specific information in addition to that normally provided, e.g., in relation to capital allowances not yet claimed on assets currently held.

There are a number of different forms in which capital allowances may be granted, including:

(a) Initial, or first year, allowances;
(b) Writing-down allowances;
(c) Balancing allowance, or balancing charge.

(a) *Initial or first year allowances*
Since 1972, business enterprises have been permitted to claim an Initial Allowance amounting to 100 per cent of the acquisition cost of plant and machinery, to offset against taxable profits in the year of acquisition.[10] This

has resulted in a considerable benefit in cash flow terms for those businesses able to make use of the allowance. Initial Allowances granted on other assets, while not being quite so generous, have still helped reduce the effect of costs of additional assets, e.g., initial allowance on new industrial buildings is 75 per cent.[11]

In the case of those assets where a 100 per cent first year allowance is either not granted or else not claimed by the business, an annual writing-down allowance will be available. The writing-down allowance will be calculated on a straight-line basis on the acquisition cost of certain assets, e.g., in the case of industrial buildings a writing down allowance of 4 per cent per annum is available. For other assets, the writing-down allowance is calculated on a reducing balance basis, i.e., as a percentage on the written-down value of the asset at the beginning of the tax year.

Illustration 6
At the time of writing (August 1983) the writing-down allowance on motor vehicles is at the rate of 25 per cent per annum, subject to a maximum of £2000 in any one year. Writing-down allowances for the first two years on a motor vehicle costing £6400 would be calculated as follows:

Time		£
0	Motor vehicle cost	6400
1	Writing-down allowance 25%	1600
	Written-down value	4800
2	Writing-down allowance 25%	1200
	Written-down value	3600

(c) *Balancing allowances and balancing charges*
On disposal of assets other than 'pooled' assets (see below) it is often the case, as with the depreciation expense allocations, that the taxation allowances granted are not equal to the difference between acquisition cost and net disposal proceeds. An adjustment is therefore made in the year of disposal either for insufficient capital allowances previously granted, i.e., a *Balancing Allowance*, or else for excessive capital allowances previously granted, i.e., a *Balancing Charge*.

Illustration 7
Assume that the motor vehicle described in the previous illustration was sold at the end of Year 2 (i) for £4500; (ii) for £5000.

		£
(i)	Written-down value, beginning of Year 2	4800
	disposal proceeds	4500
	Balancing allowance	£300
(ii)	Written-down value, beginning of Year 2	4800
	disposal proceeds	5000
	Balancing charge	£200

Balancing allowances are deducted from profits subject to taxation in the same manner as other capital allowances, while balancing charges are added to taxable profits, thereby increasing the ultimate tax liability of the business. Generally the cost of plant and machinery is pooled with writing-down allowances calculated on the value of the pool. Disposal of assets which are treated for capital allowances in this way will not normally give rise to a balancing allowance or a balancing charge, unless the total pool of assets is sold at the same time.

Although the above section illustrates the way in which capital allowances may be claimed it does not attempt to explain the full complexities of the system. For example, it may not suit an accountant to claim all the capital allowances which a business is entitled to if by doing so other taxation allowances are forfeited; capital allowances underclaimed in one year will eventually be granted against future taxable profits when these arise. Additionally, capital allowances should not be viewed as a free gift granted to businesses except to the extent that they allow taxation liability to be postponed; instead, capital allowances are similar to the deductions for other expenses such as wages or rent and differ only in their timing and the attention paid to them by government legislation.

Investment grants

In addition to the above system of capital allowances, governments have also attempted to stimulate investment in specific regions by the payment of a cash grant. Such grants are calculated as a percentage of the acquisition cost of the asset and may differ from region to region. Again the receipt of a grant by a business may cause some difficulties for the analysis of the financial statements by users and for comparison of the results of businesses in different regions.

Three possible accounting treatments have at times been suggested for investment grants, namely,

(a) credit the total amount of the investment grant to the Profit and Loss Account immediately on receipt;
(b) credit the grant immediately to a non-distributable reserve;
(c) credit the grant to revenue over the useful life of the asset, either by
  (i) reducing the acquisition cost shown in the accounts by the amount of the grant and subsequently charging depreciation on the net amount; or
  (ii) treating the grant as a deferred credit balance and allocating a portion annually to the revenue side of the Profit and Loss Account.

Methods (a) and (b) above are now frowned upon as they produce inconsistent accounting treatments for the grant itself as compared to the expenditure to which the grant relates. Method (c) is recommended by SSAP 4 as it 'matches the application of the grant with the amortisation of the capital expenditure to which it relates'.[12]

Of the two possible forms of method (c), the advantage of the first is its simplicity while the advantage of the second is that it retains the comparability between accounts prepared for different businesses in different regions; both original acquisition cost and annual depreciation charges are identifiable under method (c(ii)), separately to the investment grant credit.

Illustration 8
An asset bought for £100 000 attracts an investment grant of 30 per cent, i.e., £30 000. The asset is depreciated on a straight line basis over 10 years, assuming no residual value. Depreciation expense and book value of the asset for its first year of life are given below using both variants of method (c);

Method (c(i))
Asset cost will be reduced in the accounting records by £30 000 to £70 000. Annual depreciation expense will be $\frac{£70\,000}{10}$, i.e., £7000 per annum.

At the end of Year 1, the net book value will be

	£
Asset cost (net)	70 000
Less accumulated depreciation	7000
net book value	£63 000

Method (c(ii))
Asset cost will be retained as £100 000. A deferred revenue account will be credited with £30 000. Annual depreciation expense will be $\frac{£100\,000}{10}$, i.e., £10 000 per annum.

Annual credit to the Profit and Loss Account, $\frac{£30\,000}{10} = £3000$

Net charge in Profit and Loss Account: £10 000 − £3000 = £7000
Net book value of asset at end of Year 1

	£
Asset cost	100 000
Less accumulated depreciation	10 000
net book value	£ 90 000

Deferred revenue balance shown in the Balance Sheet will be:

	£
Original grant	30 000
Less amounts recognised	3 000
balance	£27 000

Off-setting one against the other produces a net asset value of £90 000 − £27 000 = £63 000, which is equal to the net book value of the asset identified using treatment (c(i)).

8.6 Summary

Estimates of useful life or salvage value of tangible assets may require revisions from time to time in the light of new information. These revisions may also lead to adjustments in the pattern of allocation of the depreciable cost of the asset.

The useful life of an asset may similarly be altered by undertaking a

Fixed asset measurement (II)

programme of renewal of worn-out capacity. Where renewals increase either useful life or earnings capacity, the cost of renewals should be capitalised and allocated to Profit and Loss Accounts over the remaining useful life of the asset to which the renewal expenditures relate. When expenditure on repairs is of a recurrent nature then it is normally expensed as incurred, although major repairs may be allocated over a number of years if these provide benefits to more than one accounting period.

In the case of intangible assets, current accounting rules often suggest different accounting treatments depending on the uncertainty attached either to the cost of the asset or else to the stream of likely benefits obtainable.

Investments held as long-lived assets are likewise accorded different accounting treatments, this time dependent on the nature of the investment in question.

The system of taxation adopted in the United Kingdom substitutes capital allowances, determined according to legally defined rules, for depreciation expenses allocated according to accounting rules. Investment grants made available by government to stimulate investment should be accounted for in the accounts of the recipient company in a manner which will maintain comparability from one company to another.

Questions

1. Distinguish tangible from intangible assets.
2. To what extent do you agree with the different accounting treatments adopted for intangible as opposed to tangible fixed assets?
3. Describe the accounting treatment of gains and losses on revaluation of fixed assets.
4. Explain the arguments for and against making depreciation provisions on fixed assets which have risen in value.
5. Outline general guidelines for determining whether expenditure on repairs should be treated as capital rather than revenue expenditures.
6. Describe the different accounting treatments recommended for long-term investments and explain the relative merits of each.
7. Describe the possible accounting treatments of investment grants. Explain which method(s) satisfy: (a) the prudence concept; (b) the accruals concept.

For each of the following questions **circle** the *letter* alongside the *best choice* from among the possible solutions presented.

8. A fixed asset originally acquired at a cost of £48 000 is depreciated over eight years on a reducing (double-declining) balance basis. At the end of Year 3 the asset was revalued at £18 000. The depreciation expense for Year 3 including any loss or gain on revaluation of the asset, is
    (a) £1500 credit;
    (b) £6000 debit;
    (c) £9000 debit;
    (d) £2250 debit.
9. The summarised Balance Sheet of Midas Products at 30 June 1984 was as follows:

	£
Fixed assets	46 000
Goodwill	20 000
Current assets	18 500
	£84 500
Owners' interest	67 000
Current liabilities	17 500
	£84 500

Goodwill was originally acquired at a cost of £40 000 and is being expensed over a period of 20 years by equal annual instalments. If the company had written off the goodwill immediately on acquisition, the owners' interest would now stand at: (a) £27 000; (b) £47 000; (c) £49 000; (d) £67 000.

10. The cost of redecorating office premises, undertaken every four years, should be:

    (a) expensed in the period paid;
    (b) expensed in the period incurred;
    (c) added to the cost of premises and depreciated accordingly;
    (d) expensed equally over the four years.

11. An asset originally acquired on 1 January 1982 at a cost of £100 000 was depreciated on a straight-line basis over 10 years assuming a zero salvage value. An initial allowance of 100 per cent was given for tax purposes. On 31 December 1984 the assets were sold for £30 000 giving rise to

    (a) a balancing allowance of £70 000;
    (b) a balancing charge of £70 000;
    (c) a balancing allowance of £30 000;
    (d) a balancing charge of £30 000.

Problems

1. A fixed asset was originally bought for £22 000 and depreciated on a straight-line basis over five years, assuming a disposal value of £2000 for the asset at the end of that time. At the beginning of Year 3 a re-evaluation of the asset's usefulness produced a revised estimate of six years remaining useful life but with no disposal proceeds at the end of that time.

    (a) Calculate the depreciation expense for Year 3 and explain the basis of your calculation.
    (b) Describe any alternative way in which the depreciation expense for Year 3 and subsequent years may have been calculated.

2. The cost of a new delivery van acquired by a firm on 1 March 1984 was £5200, payable £1200 in cash, £400 on the trade-in of an old van, and £3600 by 12 monthly instalments beginning on 1 April 1984. The old van had originally cost £2400 but had a written-down book value at the date of disposal of £600.

    (a) Record in journal entry form the transactions dealing with the disposal of the old vehicle and acquisition of the new van.

Fixed asset measurement (II)

(b) Given that the new van is depreciated on the sum-of-the-years digits basis over four years, assuming a disposal value of £500 at the end of that time, prepare the ledger accounts relating to the acquisition of the van and the balances outstanding at the end of the accounting year to 31 December 1984.

3. The Balance Sheet of Dann Products at 31 December 1982 revealed the following information:

	£
Plant and equipment, at cost	103 000
Less accumulated depreciation	53 700
Net book value	49 300

The equipment is depreciated on the straight-line basis. During 1983 the following transactions took place:

(i) Equipment originally acquired at a cost of £15 000 was sold for £4200. The net book value of the equipment at the date of disposal was £6300.
(ii) Equipment which originally cost £64 000 on 1 January 1981 with an estimated useful life of four years and residual value of £8000 at the end of that time was re-evaluated and given a revised remaining useful life after 1983 of four years but with a salvage value of only £2000 at the end of that time.
(iii) Equipment was acquired on 1 July 1983 at a net cost of £46 000 after allowing a trade-in of £6000 on existing equipment which had originally cost £24 000 and had a net book value on 31 December 1982 of £7000. A reasonable second-hand disposal value of the old equipment on 1 July 1983 was £5000. The new equipment had an estimated useful life of six years and a salvage value of £3000 at the end of that time.

Required

(a) Prepare journal entries to record each of the above transactions and post these to the relevant ledger accounts.
(b) Identify the depreciation expense for 1983 and any loss or gain on disposal of fixed assets.
(c) Show the amount to be included in the Balance Sheet at 31 December 1983 for plant and equipment.

4. Identify which of the following items should be treated as revenue items and which should be capitalised. Give your reasons for each:

(a) Cost of a new shop sign;
(b) Respraying a delivery van;
(c) Expenditures incurred on an advertising campaign promoting a brand image;
(d) Repairs undertaken to office premises after a recent fire had destroyed the interior fittings;
(e) Replacement of asbestos insulation to factory pipes with alternative foil insulation in compliance with new health regulations;
(f) The cost of a spare wheel for a heavy goods vehicle.

5. On 30 June 1983 the accounting records of Adam Enterprises revealed the following:

	£000	£000
Long-term loan, 15%		80
Land, at cost	100	
Buildings, at cost	80	
Accumulated depreciation, buildings		40
Office equipment, at cost	62	
Accumulated depreciation, office equipment		32
Goods available for resale	146	
Office supplies inventory	11	
Trade debtors	75	
Trade and other creditors		125
Prepaid office expenses	16	
Accrued interest		3
Accrued wages		9
Cash at bank and in hand	17	
Owners' interest		218
	507	507

Transactions occurring, in summarised form, during the year to 30 June 1984 were as follows:

(i) Half-yearly interest on the loan was paid on the due dates of 30 September and 31 March.

(ii) Purchases on account:
  Goods for resale £495 000
  Office supplies £ 38 000

(iii) Sales during the year:
  Cash sales £117 000
  Sales on credit terms £1 042 000

(iv) Payments made to suppliers for goods and supplies received, £497 000;

(v) Cash received from credit customers £1 025 000;

(vi) Wages paid during the year amounted to £207 000. Accrued wages at 30 June 1984 were £7000;

(vii) Office expenses paid during the year amounted to £242 000. Further expenses outstanding at the year end amounted to £17 000.

(viii) Stocks at 30 June 1984 included:
  Goods available for resale £174 000
  Office supplies £ 19 000

(ix) Additional office equipment was acquired on 1 March 1984 at a cost of £30 000.

(x) Depreciation is to be charged on fixed assets on the following bases:

  Land: No depreciation
  Buildings: Straight-line over 20 years (assuming no salvage value)
  Equipment: Reducing balance, using 30 per cent rate.

Assets acquired during the year are to be depreciated for the fraction of the year for which they were owned by the business.

From the above information you are required to prepare:

(a) Ledger accounts recording the transactions undertaken.
(b) A Trading, Profit and Loss Account for Adam Enterprises for the year ended 30 June 1984.
(c) A Balance Sheet at 30 June 1984.

9 Current Assets (I)

9.1 Introduction

Current assets were described in an earlier chapter as those assets which are either expected to be held by an organisation for less than one year, or else those which are normally totally exhausted or consumed during one complete operating cycle of the business. The same asset may be considered to be a current asset in one business but a fixed asset in another; the categorisation will depend on the nature of the business and the purpose for which the asset is held. All businesses will, however, own current assets in some or all of the following categories:

(i) stocks and work-in-progress (or inventories);
(ii) trade debtors;
(iii) cash and liquid assets;
(iv) prepaid expenses.

The main focus of attention of this current chapter will be on category (i), stocks and work-in-progress. Chapter 10 will continue this examination and also consider category (iii) cash and liquid assets. Categories (ii), trade debtors and (iv), prepaid expenses have already been considered in Chapters 4 and 6.

9.2 Stocks and work-in-progress

Introduction

Examples of the application of the matching principle have been given in earlier chapters, including the accruing of expenditures arising in one period but paid in another, and the allocation of depreciable cost. However, for many businesses the major problem involved in matching, both because of the complexities involved and the size of the amounts involved, is the identification of the cost of goods sold, or of services rendered, to be charged against revenues received. There are, in fact, two complementary aspects of this problem; the first involves the identification of the cost of the goods sold during each accounting period; the second involves the identification of the value (or cost) of goods unsold at the end of a period. Cost of goods unsold at the end of one period must be carried forward and allocated as expenses in the future period(s) in which revenues will be received from the ultimate sale of the goods.

In some forms of business enterprise, principally retailing organisations, unsold stocks, or inventories, will consist entirely of goods bought in from suppliers. In manufacturing enterprises, however, there will be a number of categories of stock on hand:

(a) raw materials not yet introduced into the manufacturing process;
(b) work-in-progress, i.e., in a semi-complete state;
(c) finished goods, complete and available for sale.

In addition, in businesses contracting to build or manufacture major assets, e.g., a motorway or a ship, over more than one accounting period, there will normally be a considerable volume of work in a semi-complete stage at the end of each accounting period. This work is also categorised as closing stock, but of '*contract work-in-progress*'.

Manufactured goods and stock valuation

(a) *Introduction*

An application of the principles of historic cost accounting requires the cost of goods sold and the value of closing stocks to be determined by reference to acquisition cost, or cost of manufacture. In certain situations, a value lower than cost may have to be adopted in anticipation of potential future losses, e.g., if net realisable proceeds from disposal are expected to be lower than cost. Only rarely will closing stocks be valued at higher than cost, for example, in the case of long-term contract work-in-progress which will be considered later. Gains on assets will not normally be recognised until they are realised, in accordance with the prudence concept and this practice will normally be applied even to those situations where it is relatively certain that goods produced will eventually be sold at a profit, or where the major task performed by the organisation is the production rather than the sale of the product.

Limiting the value at which closing stocks are to be recorded to cost might appear to make the task of the accountant a relatively simple one. After all, most costs should be capable of objective verification either from invoices received or from payments made. The task is not, however, as straightforward as it seems, as will be explained in the current and the following sections.

For a manufacturing organisation, 'cost' must include not only the price of raw materials used in production but also all other costs or expenditures which have been incurred in 'bringing the product or service to its present location and condition'.[1]

The accounting standard concerned with the treatment of stocks and work-in-progress, SSAP 9, defines cost as including:

(i) Cost of purchase, including purchase price, import duties, transport and handling cost and any other directly attributable cost, less trade discounts, rebates and subsidies;

Current Assets (I)

(ii) Cost of conversion, including those direct costs specifically attributable to units of production, production overheads, and any other overheads attributable to bringing the product or service to its present location and condition.

Hence, for a manufacturing business, inventory cost will include an allocation of various overhead costs. Additionally, as will be demonstrated later, where input costs change during a period, a further problem arises as to the order in which the costs should be recognised.

(b) *Cost allocations and unit cost*

The identification of unit cost is important for a number of purposes, including pricing and production decisions. Although the primary emphasis in this chapter is given to the calculation of the cost of goods produced and stock valuation for purposes of profit determination, the use of cost information in internal management decision-making will also be considered.

The process of cost allocation and cost determination will be demonstrated using the information identified in Table 9.1 for the ABC Company, the manufacturer of two products, X and Y.

A distinction is drawn between *directly attributable* and *non-directly attributable* costs shown in Table 9.1. Directly attributable costs are, as the name suggests, those costs which can be identified directly with a product or service, while non-directly attributable costs are those incapable of direct identification with products or services and which must be applied to these in some indirect manner. The actual separation of the two categories of cost is a major task in itself and one which is beyond the scope of this current text.

It has been assumed for purposes of illustration in Table 9.1 that the directly attributable costs include direct labour and direct material costs and that each of these are also variable costs. Variable overheads are likewise considered to be directly attributable costs.

Variable costs will alter in total amount depending on the level of

TABLE 9.1 *ABC Company, production cost data*

(i) *Inputs per unit*		
Product:	X	Y
Direct labour	4 hr	2 hr
Direct materials	1 lb	4 lb
Machine hours	1	2

(ii) *Input costs:*
- Labour rate — £1.00 per hour
- Materials — £3.00 per lb
- Variable overheads — £0.50 per machine hour
- Fixed factory overheads (including power, supervision) — £1500 per period

(iii) *Anticipated normal production*
100 units of each product

production achieved, as distinct from fixed costs which will remain at a constant level irrespective of the level of output, for the short-term at least.

For the purpose of the current demonstration, variable cost per unit of production is assumed to be constant, i.e., the variable cost of producing 20 units will be exactly two times that of producing 10 units.

By making the above assumptions, many of the technical problems of cost identification have been avoided in this illustration. One major problem does still face the accountant of ABC Company however, namely the allocation of fixed production costs to the two different products. Total variable cost for the expected levels of production are shown in Table 9.2.

TABLE 9.2 *ABC Company, attributable costs of production of 100 units of each product*

	Product X	Product Y	Total
Direct labour	£400	£200	£600
Direct materials	300	1200	1500
Prime cost	700	1400	2100
Variable production overheads	50	100	150
Total attributable cost	£750	£1500	£2250

There are a number of possible bases for allocating the fixed overheads to the two products including the following:

Direct labour cost;
Direct material cost;
Prime cost, i.e., direct labour and direct material cost;
Labour hours;
Total variable cost.

The above list is not an exhaustive one and, in fact, the basis of allocation may include a combination of more than one of the methods listed. The chosen method of allocation should be that which the accountant believes relates cost most closely to the activity or product which gives rise to them. Adoption of one particular allocation base may result in a different figure being calculated for total product cost than that produced by another, perhaps equally appropriate, allocation base.

Illustration 1

(a) If 'machine hours' was selected as the basis of allocation for the ABC Company, then fixed overhead costs will be allocated to the product as follows:

Product X $£1500 \times \frac{100}{300} = £500$

Product Y $£1500 \times \frac{200}{300} = £1000$

(b) Suppose instead total labour cost had been selected as the allocation basis then the allocation of fixed overheads to the products becomes

$$\text{Product } X \quad £1500 \times \frac{£400}{£600} = £1000$$
$$\text{Product } Y \quad £1500 \times \frac{£200}{£600} = £500$$

As fixed overheads have been identified as those costs not directly attributable to any one product, then whatever allocation is finally chosen, must be accepted as having some degree of imprecision attached to it. This fact must be borne in mind by managers when decisions are made based on the resulting total manufacturing cost data.

(c) *Production costs and selling price*

Assume for the purpose of further analysis that *total attributable cost* has been chosen as the basis of allocation of fixed overheads to products, and that the product selling price is '*cost determined*' and calculated on the basis of 'total production cost plus 20 per cent mark-up', i.e., selling price equals cost price × 120 per cent. The calculation of selling price for products X and Y of ABC Company is shown in Table 9.3.

TABLE 9.3 *ABC Company, selling price calculation*

	Product X	Product Y
Total attributable costs	£750	£1500
Allocated production overheads (1:2)	500	1000
	£1250	£2500
Unit cost	12.50	25.00
'Mark up' (20%)	2.50	5.00
Selling price	£15.00	£30.00

Cost based product pricing is not always possible. It assumes that the business is able to set its own price and that it is not in the position of a 'price-taker' where the market will set the price for the product. Cost-based pricing will result in a dependence between the method of overhead allocation and the choice of selling price. Indeed, the method of overhead allocation may have a considerable influence on the level of profits as most firms will be faced with some degree of elasticity of demand for their products, i.e., the likely demand for products will be inversely related to the selling price. It is important for firms in such circumstances to remember the somewhat arbitrary nature of certain cost allocations and indeed the imprecise nature of all allocations of non-directly attributable overheads. Consider for example, the following illustration relating to the proposed closure of unprofitable operations.

Illustration 2

Closem Ltd produce two distinct products. Most costs, including certain fixed overheads, are directly attributable to each product; a significant proportion, however, fall within the category of non-attributable fixed overheads. Non-attributable overheads have been allocated to production on the basis of 50 per cent of direct labour cost. Management is concerned with the estimated level of profitability for Product A in the coming period as highlighted in the Income Statement shown in Table 9.4.

It is assumed for purposes of this illustration that selling prices for Products A and B cannot be increased nor can costs be reduced other than through the termination of production of Product A.

Should the management decide to end production of A, however, they will not save £1000. Even assuming that all direct costs, including attributable fixed overheads, can be saved by stopping production of A, the business will be in a worse position than previously. As Table 9.5 shows, profits will actually fall to £2000 if production of A is ended, as non-attributable fixed overheads would in future all have to be expensed against the revenues generated by Product B alone.

Only if either

(i) non-attributable costs are reduced by at least £1500; or
(ii) additional production of B or some other product is substituted and could subsequently generate an excess of revenues over additional costs of £1500,

TABLE 9.4 *Closem Ltd, Forecast Income Statement*

	Product A	Product B	Total
Sales revenue	£12 000	£18 000	£30 000
Direct materials cost	4 000	3 000	7 000
Direct labour cost	5 000	6 000	11 000
Variable overheads	1 000	800	1 800
Fixed overheads:			
attributable	500	700	1 200
non-attributable	2 500	3 000	5 500
	13 000	13 500	26 500
Net profit (loss)	£(1 000)	£4 500	£3 500

TABLE 9.5 *Calculation of net profit excluding product A*

	Product B
Sales revenue	£18 000
Direct material	3 000
Direct labour	6 000
Variable overheads	800
Fixed overheads: attributable	700
non-attributable	5 500
	16 000
Net profit	£2 000

Current assets (I)

would termination of production of A be justified. A decision based solely on the allocated costs shown in Table 9.4 would not in this case be in the interests of the company, or improve profitability.

Break-Even analysis

It is often useful for the managers of a business to know the number of units of a product which must be sold for that business to achieve a position of *break-even*, i.e., 'no profit, no loss'. This level of sales may act as a guide in investment decisions, particularly, where the demand for a product is a relatively unknown quantity.

In a multi-product company such as ABC, the determination of break-even points depends very much on the expected ratio of sales of product X to product Y. Assume:

(i) All units produced will be sold.
(ii) The same number of units of X and Y will be produced.

The unit cost and sales revenue from a batch consisting of one unit each of X and Y are shown in Table 9.6.

The difference between selling price and variable cost is described as the 'contribution' towards fixed costs and profit.

TABLE 9.6 *Calculation of contribution on batch*

	Product X	Product Y	Total
Selling price	15.00	30.00	45.00
Direct materials	3.00	12.00	15.00
Direct labour	4.00	2.00	6.00
Variable overheads	0.50	1.00	1.50
Total variable cost	7.50	15.00	22.50
Contribution	£7.50	£15.00	£22.50

As the fixed overheads were previously identified at £1500, then the required level of sales to break-even (in batches of X and Y) is given by:

$$\text{Break-even Sales (units)} = \frac{\text{Fixed overheads}}{\text{Contribution per batch}}$$

$$= \frac{£1500}{£22.50}$$

$$= 66\tfrac{2}{3} \text{ batches}$$

Production and sales levels would have to achieve at least $66\tfrac{2}{3}$ units of each of X and Y before the ABC Company began to make a profit. The result is illustrated graphically in Figure 9.1 and also demonstrated in the summarised Income Statement shown in Table 9.7. Although in practice the

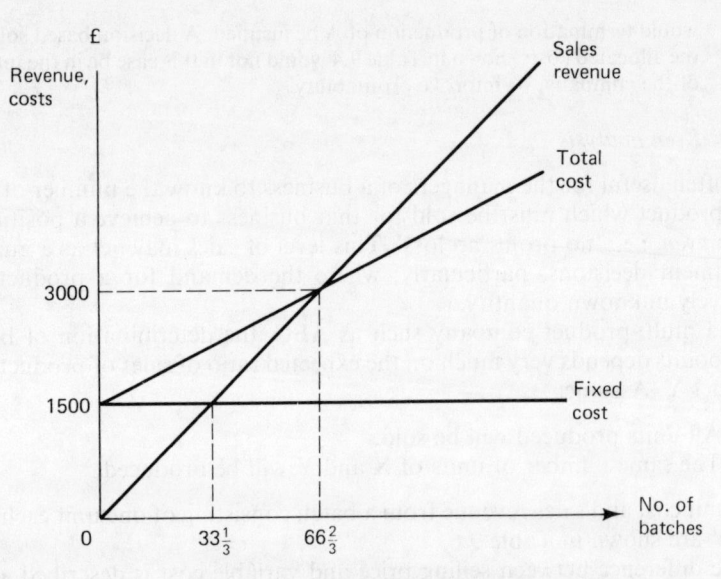

FIGURE 9.1 *Break-even analysis*

TABLE 9.7 *ABC Company, Income Statement*
Production = Sales = $66\frac{2}{3}$ batches of X and Y

	Product X	Product Y	Total
Sales revenue	£1000	£2000	£3000
Variable production costs	500	1000	1500
Contribution	£500	£1000	£1500
Less Fixed production overheads			1500
Gross profit (loss)			£ 0

company will not be able to produce or sell two-thirds of one unit, the calculation of break-even point is useful as a minimum level to exceed not a target for the company to aim for.

The calculation of break-even point was based on an assumption that the level of production and sales were equal during the accounting period. If this assumption is not valid, then the result shown in Table 9.7 will no longer hold unless the company valued the closing stocks at variable, or marginal cost. For purposes of income determination and external profit reporting, businesses are required to calculate cost of closing stock on a 'full cost basis', including an allocation of fixed overheads.

Table 9.8 illustrates the effect of adoption of a full cost stock valuation method by the ABC Company in a situation where production of Products X

TABLE 9.8 *Income Statement for ABC Company, production not equal to sales*

Production (units)	100	100	
Sales (units)	66⅔	66⅔	
	Product X	*Product Y*	*Total*
Sales revenue	£1000	£2000	£3000
Variable production costs	750	1500	2250
Fixed production overheads	500	1000	1500
Cost of goods produced	1250	2500	3750
Less closing stock	417	833	1250
Cost of goods sold	833	1667	2500
Gross profit	£167	£333	£500

and Y was 100 units but sales were only 66⅔ units. Fixed costs are allocated to the products on the basis of total variable costs.

As Table 9.8 demonstrates, the company has made a reported profit of £500 despite having achieved sales of only 66⅔ batches. The reported profit has arisen in this case because of the allocation of fixed production overheads to the units of closing stock as follows;

    To Product X: 33⅓ units at £5 = £167
    To Product Y: 33⅓ units at £10 = 333
                                          £500

In the earlier example, where the numbers of units produced and sold were equal, there was no closing stock to bear an allocation of fixed overheads. All the overheads would have been allocated to goods sold with the consequence that the cost of goods sold was £500 higher than in the current example and hence no profit was achieved.

The adoption of the full cost, or absorption costing, method of stock valuation, as recommended in SSAP 9, can lead to some confusing results and may even suggest actions that are the exact opposite of that which prudent business management might be expected to take. It also contradicts the principle laid down in SSAP 2 that where the prudence concept conflicts with the accruals concept, the former prevails.

Illustration 3
Watson Industries manufacture and distribute a single product for which production cost and selling price are as follows;

Unit selling price	£10
Unit variable cost	£3
Total fixed production overheads	£500

Under normal conditions the company expects to manufacture and sell 100 units of the product each period, providing £200 gross profit as shown in the summarised Income Statement.

Watson Industries
Income Statement

	£
Sales revenue	1000
Variable production costs	300
Fixed production costs	500
Costs of goods purchased and sold	800
Gross profit	£200

Because of a slump in demand for the product, the company only expects to sell 60 units in the next accounting period. Sales demand beyond the following year is at present unknown, although the future outlook is more likely to be for reduced rather than increased or maintained product demand.

Table 9.9 shows the projected results for Watson Industries for the coming period under two different scenarios. The first, situation A, shows an expected gross loss if production was reduced to meet the lower expected sales level, while situation B shows the expected gross profit if production is maintained at the current level. Watson Industries adopts an absorption costing basis of stock valuation.

As can be seen from Table 9.9 reported profits of Watson Industries are maintained at a reasonable level if production is maintained rather than being curtailed during the period of falling demand. This result is due solely to the allocation of fixed overheads to the closing stock of goods unsold at the end of the accounting period, i.e., closing stock includes fixed overheads amounting to:

$$\frac{40}{100} \times £500 = £200$$

Opponents of the absorption cost system of stock valuation point to this conflict, in that management reporting results under such a system are encouraged to take the opposite action to that which a change in demand would suggest. An alternative system of stock valuation is suggested instead which operates on a variable, or marginal, cost basis and results in a calculation for the gross income of a period which is independent of the level of closing stock.

The results for Watson Industries if 100 units were to be produced but only 60 sold, are given in Table 9.10 using the marginal costing method. The Income Statement in Table 9.10 shows a loss of £80 equal to that achieved when

TABLE 9.9 *Watson Industries, projected Income Statements (absorption basis)*

	Situation A £	Situation B £
Sales revenue	600	600
Variable production costs	180	300
Fixed production costs	500	500
Cost of goods produced	680	800
Less closing stock	—	320
Cost of goods sold	680	480
Gross profit (loss)	(80)	120

TABLE 9.10 *Watson Industries, Income Statement (marginal cost basis)*

	£
Sales revenue	600
Variable production costs	300
Less closing stock	120
Cost of goods sold	180
Gross contribution	420
Less Fixed production overheads	500
Net contribution	(80)

production and sales were both at 60 units. In fact, as storage costs and financing charges would be likely to rise because of the higher levels of stock, management would be encouraged to cut production if demand fell.

Marginal versus absorption cost

Illustration 3 demonstrated that the method of stock costing, whether full or variable cost, can have a considerable effect on the reported profits of an organisation. The fear has been expressed that the use of an absorption costing basis of stock valuation may encourage some managers to maintain production at levels greater than that justified by expected sales demand, in order to boost profits artificially or perhaps to hide a deteriorating profit situation.

Which of the two methods of stock costing is most in accord with the fundamental accounting concepts?

The accruals concept may be claimed as an argument in favour of the full cost method of stock valuation as the costs incurred in production are only expensed when the goods produced are actually sold. An alternative viewpoint is that as fixed costs are, by definition, fixed regardless of the level of production (in the short term at least), then the fixed overheads are a time period cost and not a cost to be allocated to production. This second argument favours marginal costing, and replaces the idea of matching revenues with expenses, with an idea of matching expenses with time periods, a principle which appears to have little or no justification on the basis of fundamental accounting principles.

Support for the use of a marginal cost basis of stock valuation may be claimed, however, from the prudence concept as it may be deemed to be imprudent to carry forward to future accounting periods the fixed costs of producing goods which were not sold during the current period. If this argument was accepted, however, all costs of producing unsold goods should be expensed in the period incurred, and not merely fixed production overheads.

For many years, business managers were free to choose whichever method of stock valuation they preferred. Both SSAP 9 and the 1981 Companies Act now require stock to be valued on a full cost basis with the inclusion of 'all related production overheads, even though these may accrue on a time basis'.[2]

Net realisable value

One exception to the use of the full cost stock valuation base occurs when the net realisable value of the stock is expected to be lower than cost. In this situation net realisable value will replace full cost as the basis of stock valuation.

Calculation of net realisable value of stock involves estimating the following;

(i) All future costs of completion;
(ii) All costs incurred in the marketing, selling, and distribution of units of stock.

Net realisable value will be equal to the estimated selling price, less (i) plus (ii) above.

Comparison of cost and net realisable value is required to be made separately in respect of each item of stock whenever possible. If this is not possible then 'groups or categories of stock items which are similar'[3] may be considered together. However, such groupings are to be avoided wherever possible as it may lead to situations where net realisable value is used, when it is in fact higher than absorption cost.

Illustration 4

Included in the closing stock of Holden Products are the following items:

Product A	
5 units, total cost to date	£120
Estimated (i) costs to completion	50
(ii) sales revenue	160
(iii) selling and distribution expenses	30
Product B	
10 units, total cost to date	£190
Estimated (i) costs to completion	40
(ii) sales revenue	280
(iii) selling and distribution expenses	20

(i) Valuing the products individually gives a net realisable value of:

	£	£
Product A		
Estimated sales revenue		160
Less costs to completion	50	
selling and distribution	30	80
Net realisable value		£80

: *adopted*, as lower than total cost of £120

	£	£
Product B		
Estimated sales revenue		280
Less costs to completion	40	
selling and distribution	20	60
Net realisable value		£220

: *not adopted*, as total cost is lower, i.e., £190

(ii) Valuing the two products as a group:

	£
Total costs to date:	
Product A	120
Product B	190
	£310

versus net realisable value:	£	£
Estimated sales revenue		440
Less costs to completion	90	
selling and distribution	50	140
		£300

Net realisable value of £300 will be adopted in this instance as it is lower than total costs to date of £310. A loss of £10 would therefore need to be expensed in the Profit and Loss Account and subsequently disclosed as a separate item in the published income statement. Notice that the stock valuation given by separate identification of individual product net realisable values is £80 + £190 = £270. The latter valuation is, in fact, the one which should be adopted, giving rise to a loss to date of £40 on the stock.

Although some countries also allow stock valuation to be based on current replacement cost if this latter figure is lower than the full cost recorded, this practice is not normally allowed in the United Kingdom. The use of a rule involving 'lower of cost or replacement cost' would allow a loss to be recorded which may never be incurred, and which is, in fact, an opportunity cost. Replacement cost is only recommended by SSAP 9 in those exceptional circumstances where it is considered to be the best measure of net realisable value.[4]

Work-in-progress

Issues examined so far in this chapter have related to a single production process and apart from the last section, stocks of completed goods. In many manufacturing organisations, however, the finished product of one process becomes the raw materials input of the next process. Additionally, closing stocks will often consist of unused raw materials, together with work-in-progress which has not been completed by the end of an accounting period. The allocation of total costs across both finished goods and work-in-progress is required in these circumstances, involving

(i) Assignment of costs to the individual processes;
(ii) Absorption of cost across goods produced.

Assignment of costs to individual processes takes place in a similar manner to that of assignment of costs to different products in a single process firm, as described in Section 9.2(b) above. Directly attributable costs will be assigned directly, after which indirect costs will be allocated by reference to one or more factors, e.g., direct labour cost, labour hours worked or even floor space. Whichever method is chosen for the allocation procedure, it should attempt to relate the indirect costs as precisely as possible to the process which has given rise to them.

Absorption of costs by products within a period will follow a similar pattern. Directly attributable costs will first be identified for each product and then indirect costs will be apportioned on a basis which again attempts to charge each product with an equitable proportion of these costs.

Problems arise over the decision whether to assign costs and allocate overheads on an actual basis, i.e., using actual expenditures incurred, or on some predetermined basis, i.e., based on normal or standard costs. If the latter basis is adopted, as it often is, there is also the question of what level of production to use in the predetermination of standards. Finally, a problem arises relating to the valuation of semi-complete production remaining at the end of an accounting period.

The valuation of closing work-in-progress is normally undertaken by reference to the number of completed units of output which the work-in-progress is equivalent to, either in work effort or in costs incurred. The responsibility for this task will often fall to a process engineer or a manager with technical knowledge of the product, rather than the accountant. Total costs assigned to the process will then be averaged across *the total equivalent whole units of production.*

Illustration 5
Parkinson Products manufacture a single product in two stages, the finished product S of the first process being one of the raw materials of the second process.
(i) *Process A.* Production takes place evenly in Process A with labour and material inputs continually introduced. Direct costs are assigned directly to production while fixed overheads are allocated to the process at the rate of 200 per cent on direct labour cost. Costs relating to a production period in which 25 labour hours were worked are given below.

	£
Labour: 25 hours at £1 per hour	25.00
Materials, R: 35 lbs at £1.50	52.50
Variable overheads: 25 hours at £0.50 per hour	12.50
	90.00
Fixed overheads allocated	50.00
Total costs for period	£140.00

10 lbs of raw materials, although included in the above costs, remained unused at the end of the period. At the end of the period the process manager estimated that the equivalent of 12½ units of S had been completed, with 12 fully completed. Production cost per unit of output of S can now be calculated as follows:

		£
Direct labour: £25 ÷ 12.5	=	2.00
Direct materials, R: £(52.50 − 15.00) ÷ 12.5	=	3.00
Variable overheads: £12.50 ÷ 12.5	=	1.00
Fixed overheads: £50 ÷ 12.5	=	4.00
Cost of producing one unit of S		£10.00

In the above calculation of unit cost, £15 was deducted from the direct material cost, representing the cost of unused raw materials i.e., 10 lbs at £1.50 each. The total assignment of costs to the completed products and to work-in-progress is given in Table 9.11.

(ii) *Process B.* During the same accounting period, 43 labour hours were worked in process B. Costs identified for the period were:

TABLE 9.11

Parkinson Products
Process A Cost Assignment

	£
Completed units of S, transferred to Process B: 12 units at £10.00 each	120.00
Work-in-progress: 1 unit of S 50 per cent complete	5.00
Raw materials: 10 lbs of R, at £1.50 each	15.00
	£140.00

	£
Transfers-in from Process A, material S	120.00
Additional costs:	
Direct labour: 43 hours at £1.25	53.75
Direct materials, T: 48 lbs at £1.00	48.00
Variable overheads: 43 hours at £0.80 per hour	34.40
Fixed overheads allocated	107.50
	£363.65

Output of Process B during the period amounted to 10 units of finished product Z, plus one unit which was estimated at 75 per cent complete. In addition, one unit of S and 5 lbs of material T had not yet entered the production process. Fixed overheads were again allocated to this process on the basis of 200 per cent of direct labour cost.

As output of Process B is $10\frac{3}{4}$ units, in equivalent numbers of whole units of production, then cost per unit of Z may be calculated as follows:

	£
Direct labour: £53.75 ÷ 10.75	5.00
Direct materials, T: £(48 − 5) ÷ 10.75	4.00
Variable overheads: £34.40 ÷ 10.75	3.20
Fixed overheads: £107.50 ÷ 10.75	10.00
	22.20
Plus one unit of S	10.00
Cost of producing one unit of Z	£32.20

The total costs for Process B are assigned as shown in Table 9.12. Note that the incomplete unit of Z will nevertheless be assigned with the full unit cost of material S; the finished product of Process A is assumed, in this case at least,

TABLE 9.12

Parkinson Products
Process B Cost Assignment

	£
Completed unit of Z: 10 units at £32.20 each	322.00
Work-in-progress: 1 unit of Z, 75 per cent complete	26.65
Raw materials: 1 unit of S, at £10.00	10.00
5 lbs of T, at £1.00 each	5.00
	£363.65

to be included immediately into Process B and not gradually throughout production, as was the case with other raw materials. Hence, the calculation of the cost of work-in-progress is given by $(£22.20 \times \frac{3}{4}) + £10 = £26.65$.

A sub-classification of stocks must be given in the Balance Sheet or in a note annexed to it, with the figures shown in Table 9.13.

TABLE 9.13

Parkinson Products
Stocks to be included in Balance Sheet

Raw materials	£20.00
Work-in-progress	41.65
Finished goods	322.00
	£383.65

The figures shown in Table 9.13 were calculated as follows:

Raw materials: 10 lbs (R) at £1.50	£15.00
5 lbs (T) at £1.00	5.00
	20.00
Work-in-progress S 1 unit 50% complete	5.00
1 unit 100% complete	10.00
Z 1 unit 75% complete	26.65
	£41.65
Finished goods: Z 10 units	£322.00

It is assumed in Table 9.13 that none of the finished product of Process B have been sold by the Balance Sheet date.

9.3 Flow of costs

At this point a break will be made from the problems relating to the measurement of stock cost, in order to identify the accounting entries which must be made to record the flow of costs through a manufacturing organisation. To aid in the illustration of the accounting entries the data used in the above section relating to Parkinson Products will be used.

The flow of costs records the physical process which is taking place as illustrated in Figure 9.2. Raw material and other inputs are introduced into various processes where production is in progress. The finished product will be transferred either to a warehouse for eventual shipment to customers, or else reintroduced into work-in-progress as a materials input to later stages in the production cycle.

Journal entries to record the accounting transactions undertaken by Parkinson Products in Illustration 5 are as shown in Table 9.14.

The relevant T accounts including the above Journal Entries are shown in

Current assets (I)

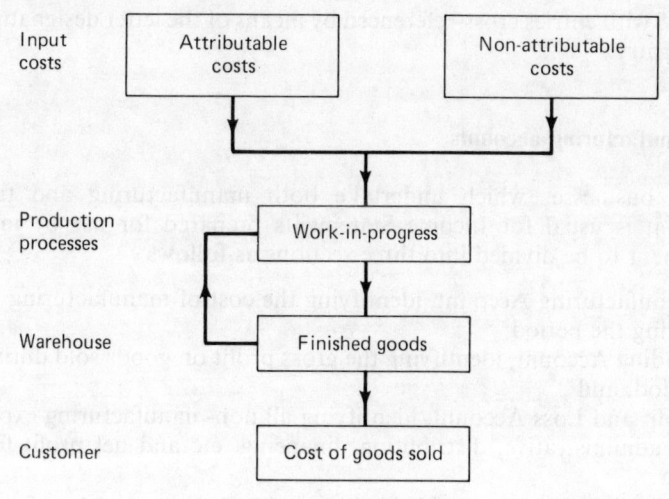

Figure 9.2 Flow of costs

- Input costs → Attributable costs, Non-attributable costs
- Production processes: Work-in-progress
- Warehouse: Finished goods
- Customer: Cost of goods sold

TABLE 9.14

Parkinson Products
JOURNAL ENTRIES

			£	£
(a)	debit	Material R, stores a/c	52.50	
	credit	Trade creditors a/c		52.50
		Being goods purchased from suppliers		
(b)	debit	Process A, work-in-progress a/c	125.00	
	credit	Wages a/c		25.00
		Material R, stores a/c		37.50
		Variable overheads a/c		12.50
		Fixed overheads a/c		50.00
		Being cost inputs into Process A		
(c)	debit	Materials S, stores a/c	120.00	
	credit	Process A, work-in-progress a/c		120.00
		Being goods completed during period		
(d)	debit	Materials T, stores a/c	48.00	
	credit	Trade creditors a/c		48.00
		Being goods purchased from suppliers		
(e)	debit	Process B, work-in-progress a/c	348.65	
	credit	Materials S, stores a/c		110.00
		Materials T, stores a/c		43.00
		Wages a/c		53.75
		Variable overheads a/c		34.40
		Fixed overheads a/c		107.50
		Being cost inputs into Process B		
(f)	debit	Materials Z, stores a/c	322.00	
	credit	Process B, work-in-progress a/c		322.00
		Being the cost of goods completed during the period		

Table 9.15 with entries cross-referenced by means of the letter designating the Journal Entry.

9.4 Manufacturing accounts

In those businesses which undertake both manufacturing and trading activities it is usual for Income Statements prepared for use by internal management to be divided into three sections as follows:

(i) Manufacturing Account, identifying the cost of manufacturing goods during the period;
(ii) Trading Account, identifying the gross profit on goods sold during the period; and
(iii) Profit and Loss Account, identifying all non-manufacturing expenses, i.e. administrative, distribution, financing, etc and net profit for the year.

Using the information provided in illustration 5 above the Manufacturing, Trading and Profit and Loss Account will be prepared for Parkinson Products.

Manufacturing Accounts include the total of materials, wages and other costs associated with the production of goods during the period. For Parkinson Products the amounts involved are as follows:

		£	£
(i)	*Materials consumed*		
	Opening stock		—
	Purchases:		
	Materials R		52.50
	Materials T		48.00
			100.50
	Less Closing stock:		
	Materials R	15.00	
	Materials T	5.00	20.00
			80.50
(ii)	*Direct labour*		
	Process A		25.00
	Process B		53.75
			78.75
(iii)	*Variable overheads*		
	Process A		12.50
	Process B		34.40
			46.90
(iv)	*Fixed overheads*		
	Process A		50.00
	Process B		107.50
			157.50

TABLE 9.15

Parkinson Products
LEDGER ACCOUNTS

Materials R, Stores a/c

		£			£
(a)		52.50	(b)		37.50
				Balance c/d	15.00
		£52.50			£52.50
Balance b/d		15.00			

Variable overheads a/c

	£			£
		(b)		12.50
		(e)		34.40
				46.90

Process A Work-in-progress a/c

		£			£
(b)		120.00	(c)		120.00
				Balance c/d	5.00
		£125.00			£125.00
Balance b/d		5.00			

Process B Work-in-progress a/c

	£			£
(e)	322.00	(f)		322.00
	26.65		Balance c/d	26.65
	£348.65			£348.65
Balance b/d	26.65			

Creditors Control a/c

			£
		(a)	52.50
		(d)	48.00
			100.50

Wages a/c

			£
		(b)	25.00
		(e)	53.75
			78.75

Fixed overheads a/c

			£
		(b)	50.00
		(e)	107.50
			157.50

Materials S, Stores a/c

		£			£
		120.00	(e)		110.00
				Balance c/d	10.00
		£120.00			£120.00
(c) Balance b/d		10.00			

Materials T, Stores a/c

		£			£
		48.00	(e)		43.00
				Balance c/d	5.00
		£48.00			£48.00
(d) Balance b/d		5.00			

Materials Z, Stores a/c

(f)	322.00

(v) *Factory cost of goods produced*

Materials consumed		80.50
Direct labour		78.75
Variable overheads		46.90
Fixed overheads		157.50
		363.65
Add opening work-in-progress		—
		363.65
Less closing work-in-progress		
Process A	5.00	
Process B	36.65	
		41.65
Cost of goods produced		£322.00

The amount identified as cost of goods produced is then transferred to the trading account and, after adjustment for opening and closing stocks of unsold goods, is deducted from the sales revenue for the period. The Manufacturing and Trading Account of Parkinson Products is shown in Table 9.16, in horizontal format, assuming no opening stocks of unsold goods and that 8 units of Z are sold at a price of £50 each.

9.5 Departmental accounts

Introduction

In some businesses goods may be transferred from one department to another on the basis of 'cost plus a mark-up'. For example, in the illustration above, the manufacturing department may have been credited with an amount in excess of £322.00 in recognition of the 'profit' earned by itself on goods produced.

The crediting of some notional profit to the manufacturing department may be used if, for example, the business management wished to assess the profitability of different sections of the business. An appropriate price at which to transfer goods under such circumstances would be the cost of buying-in the manufactured goods from an external supplier. If no external price is available then the business may adopt the practice of adding a fixed percentage on to manufacturing cost. The use of a percentage addition to manufacturing cost does, however, reduce the effectiveness of the analysis of departmental profitability as the percentage rate adopted must of necessity be an arbitrary one.

If a business adopts the practice of transferring goods between departments at a price in excess of cost, then a note must be kept of the amount of mark-up in order to eliminate any 'unrealised' profit from the closing stock of unsold goods at the end of each accounting period.

TABLE 9.16

Parkinson Products
Manufacturing and Trading Account

	£		£
Materials consumed:		Transferred to	
Opening stock	—	Trading Account	322.00
Purchases	100.50		
	100.50		
Less closing stock	20.00		
	80.50		
Direct labour	78.75		
Prime cost of production	159.25		
Variable overheads	46.90		
Fixed overheads	157.50		
Factory cost of production	363.65		
Add Opening work-in-progress	—		
	363.65		
Less Closing work-in-progress	41.65		
Factory cost of goods produced	£322.00		£322.00
Finished goods:		Sales	400.00
Opening stock			
Cost of goods produced	322.00		
	322.00		
Less closing stock	64.40		
Cost of goods sold	257.60		
Gross profit – transferred to Profit and Loss Account	142.40		
	£400.00		£400.00

Accounting procedures

One of the most common examples of the use of departmental accounts is in the control systems of large retailing organisations.

For each department within the organisation two new accounts are normally opened.

(i) A Stock Account in which goods transferred into the department are debited at their selling price; and
(ii) A mark-up, or gross profit, account into which the difference between selling price and original cost will be credited.

When goods are sold the sale proceeds will be credited to the departmental Stock Account. At the end of each accounting period the amount of stock on hand, at selling price, should be equal to the balance on the Stock Account.

Thus the use of the Stock Account will allow some measure of control to be exercised over the physical resources available for sale.

If any goods are sold at a price lower than the anticipated selling price, then the difference must be credited to the Stock Account and debited to the Mark-up Account. Any increase in selling price will be debited to the Stock Account and credited to the Mark-up Account.

Similarly the selling price of any goods which have been lost or destroyed during the year will be credited to the Stock Account. The Mark-up Account will be debited with the gross profit on such goods and a Cost of Goods Mislaid Expense Account (or Cost of Goods Sold Account) debited with the original cost of the goods lost or destroyed.

At the end of each accounting period the amount of the mark-up on the closing stocks of unsold goods will be calculated and transferred to the next accounting period by the following Journal entry:

> Credit Mark-up Account Old period
>
> Debit Mark-up Account New period

Illustration 6

Bradshaw Retailers Ltd operate a departmental accounting system with a Stock Account and a Mark-up Account maintained for each department as an integral part of the overall accounting system.

The following information relates to the accounting records of the footwear department for the accounting year ended 31 March 1985:

	£
Stock 1 April 1984	24 000
Footwear purchases at cost	156 000
Sales for the year (including January 'sales')	289 000

Standard mark-up on footwear – 100% on cost

In the January 1985 sales, shoes which had cost £32 500 were sold for £46 800. Stock at 31 March 1985 was valued, on a selling price basis, at £28 500. Any difference between the physical stock count and the accounting records is to be charged initially to a Mislaid Stock Account. Transfers from the latter account will involve debiting a Cost of Missing Goods Expense Account with the cost price of such goods and crediting the Mark-up Account with the gross profit thereon. The relevant departmental accounts are as follows:

Footwear Stock Account

1984			£	1985		£
April 1	Balance b/f		24 000	March 31	Sales	289 000
	Purchases – cost		156 000	Jan. 31	Mark-down	18 200
		– mark-up	156 000	March 31	Mislaid Stock	300
				March 31	Balance c/f	28 500
			336 000			336 000
April 1	Balance b/f		28 500			

Footwear Mark-up Account

1985		£	1984		£
Jan. 31	Mark-down	18 200	April 1	Balance b/f	12 000
March 31	Mislaid goods	150		Stock Account	156 000
	Balance c/f	14 250			
	Gross profit for year	135 400			
		£168 000			£168 000
			1985		
			April 1	Balance b/f	14 250

Footwear Mislaid Stock Account

1985		£	1985		£
March 31	Stock Account	300	March 31	Mark-up Account	150
				Cost of missing goods	150
		£300			£300

Note. The mark-down on the 'January Sales' is as follows:

	£
Original cost	32 500
Normal mark-up: 100%	32 500
	65 000
Less: actual selling price	46 800
Mark-down	£18 200

Allocation of overheads

Before completing departmental income statements it will be necessary to allocate to each department a 'fair' proportion of all overheads incurred. Certain costs may be capable of direct allocation to departments concerned, e.g. sales persons' salaries, but most will need to be allocated on the basis of one or more of the overhead methods described earlier. As the overhead allocations are based on relatively subjective judgements, then the reported results for each individual department must be treated with some caution. Management must be careful not to read too much into such results and to remember the possible arbitrary nature of certain overhead allocations. It may be necessary, when considering internal decisions, to pay more attention to the contribution achieved by a department, rather than the net profit, after deducting overhead allocations.

9.6 Summary

In the previous sections, the nature of inventory cost of a manufacturing organisation has been defined and explained. An outline has also been given of the way in which inventory cost is measured and this outline has shown that the following steps are required,

(i) Identification of costs directly attributable to products;
(ii) Assignment of non-attributable costs to production processes;
(iii) Absorption of attributable and non-attributable costs by units of production.

Calculation of unit cost has been demonstrated to be fraught with difficulties and is often an exercise in judgement, which however expert, is essentially subjective in nature. For example, the separation of attributable and non-attributable costs, the basis for allocation of costs to production centres, the level of activity for which standard costs are calculated, the measurement of the degree of completion of work-in-progress – all these decisions involve an element of judgement, and the resulting costs will only be as accurate as the judgements on which they are based. Indeed, as the illustrations used in this chapter have been presented in a simplified form, without for example joint-products produced in a single process, the problems involved in inventory costing for a manufacturing organisation have been understated.

As the next chapter demonstrates not all the fundamental inventory measurement problems have yet been considered. One problem in particular remains to be considered which is not peculiar to manufacturing organisations only but also to trading organisations, the problem of 'cost recognition'.

Questions

1. Explain the following terms:
    (a) Attributable costs;
    (b) Contribution;
    (c) Break-even point;
    (d) Net realisable value.
2. Distinguish absorption from marginal cost. Explain the relative merits of these two bases of stock valuation.
3. Identify the relevant costs involved in a decision as to whether a journey from London to Edinburgh and return should be undertaken by car or train.
4. Describe the problems involved in the identification of unit cost for a firm which manufactures a number of products each of which must pass through more than one production process.
5. Explain the arguments for and against the use of current replacement cost as a basis for stock valuation.

For each of the following **circle** the *letter* alongside the *best choice* from among the possible solutions presented.

6. Semi-complete goods on which costs to date amount to £100 per unit, will require a further £60 per unit to complete, plus £15 selling expenses per unit. Estimated unit selling price is £140. These goods should each be included in the closing Balance Sheet at: (a) £100; (b) £125; (c) £140; (d) £65.
7. Year end stock sheets had been incorrectly added resulting in the closing stock at 31 December 1983 being recorded as £12 864 rather than £21 864. The effect of the error would be:
    (a) overstate profit for 1983 and 1984 by £9000;
    (b) understate profit for 1983 and 1984 by £9000;

Current assets (I) 191

   (c) overstate profit for 1983 by £9000 and understate profit for 1984 by the same amount;
   (d) understate profit for 1983 by £9000 and overstate profit for 1984 by the same amount.
8. Malcolm Products manufacture widgits. The selling price of a widgit is £12 while the variable cost is £7 per unit. Fixed costs of production amount to £6000. The number of units which need to be produced and sold each period to earn a profit of £2000 are (a) 400; (b) 800; (c) 1200; (d) 1600.
9. Using the data provided for Malcolm Products in Question 8, with the exception that 2000 units are produced each period but only 1200 units are sold in the first period of operations, the reported profit for the first period, using an absorption cost basis of stock valuation, is: (a) £2400; (b) £4000; (c) £8000; (d) £6400.
10. During the second period of operations for Malcolm Products production was again 2000 units. Sales during the second period amounted to 1500 units. Assuming all costs remained constant, the closing stock at the end of period 2 amounted to: (a) £13 000; (b) £5000; (c) £3500; (d) £8100.

Problems

1. The following information was extracted from the accounting records of Concordia Stores:

	1981 £	1982 £	1983 £
Sales to customers	20 000	25 000	30 000
Purchases at cost	15 000	22 000	19 000
Operating expenses	3 000	3 500	5 000

   Closing stocks were valued as follows:
1980	£9 000
1981	£11 000
1982	£14 000
1983	£12 000

   (a) Prepare summarised annual income statements for 1981, 1982 and 1983.
   (b) In 1984 it was discovered that the following errors had occurred in the 1981 and 1982 stock counts:

   1981 closing stock should have been £12 500
   1982 closing stock should have been £13 500

   Prepare adjustments in the form of journal entries to revise the annual profits calculated in (a) above to the correct figures.

2. The following information relates to the production and assembly departments of the Popcorn Manufacturing Company for 1983.

	Production	Assembly
Direct labour	£60 000	£45 000
Direct materials	£90 000	£15 000
Machine hours worked	15 000 hr	9000 hr
Labour hours worked	12 000 hr	8000 hr
Floor space occupied	1 600 sq ft	900 sq ft
Number of employees	160	140

   Indirect overheads incurred:

	£
Power for equipment	36 000
Supervisors salaries	9 000
Heat and light	6 000
Indirect materials	3 000
Miscellaneous production overheads	6 000
Depreciation on equipment	10 800

   (a) Identify four different bases for the allocation of indirect overheads to the two departments and explain the relative merits of each base.
   (b) Calculate the overheads for each department using each of the four bases identified in (a).

3. The Popcorn Manufacturing Company introduced in Problem 2 have decided to allocate overheads on the basis of labour hours worked. During 1983 the following levels of production were achieved (in units):

	Production	Assembly
Opening stock	0	0
Goods manufactured	10 000	8 000
Closing stock	2 000	1 000

The closing stock of 2000 units remaining in the production process represented fully completed goods that had not yet been transferred to the assembly process, while the closing stock in the assembly process represented fully completed goods which were unsold at the end of the year.

All production costs are absorbed on the basis of the actual levels of production achieved.

   (a) Prepare the ledger accounts to illustrate the flow of costs for 1983.
   (b) Assuming that the selling price of the finished product was £65 per unit, prepare an Income Statement on an absorption cost basis for 1983.

4. Lanark Enterprises began operations on 1 January 1982. The accounting records for the first two years of operations revealed the following:

	1982	1983
Sales revenues	£54 000	£48 000
Variable manufacturing costs	£30 000	£27 000
Fixed manufacturing costs	£20 000	£20 000
Selling and administrative expenses	£16 000	£25 000
Opening stock	0	1 000
Units produced	10 000	10 000
Units sold	9 000	8 000

There were no semi-complete units in closing stocks at the end of either year.

Prepare separate income statements for 1982 and 1983 under each of the following basis of stock valuation:

   (a) Absorption, or full-cost, basis;
   (b) Marginal, or variable, cost basis.

5. The Scrimgeour Company manufactures and sells flag-poles. The unit selling price is fixed at £20 with variable costs of production of £8 per unit. Fixed production costs per period are £16 000, and non-production overheads amount to a further £8000. Assuming a marginal cost basis of stock valuation calculate:

   (a) the number of units which need to be sold to breakeven;
   (b) the number of units which need to be sold to earn a profit of £6000 per period.

6. The following information relates to the manufacture of widgits by Reliant Products in 1983:

Opening stock: 600 units valued at £1200
   Degree of completion, 40 per cent
Production costs incurred: £54 300
Goods produced and fully completed: 10 000 units
Closing stock: 1000 units, 50 per cent complete

(a) Calculate the cost of the closing stock of semi-complete goods and the cost of the fully completed goods;
(b) Prepare the relevant ledger accounts to record the cost flows.

7. The following information relates to the second and final stage in the production process for Cawdor Engineering for 1983.

Opening stock: 1000 units valued at £5000
   Degree of completion:
   Materials   50%
   Labour   20%
   Overheads   10%
Transfers from previous process: 12 000 units at £2 each
Additional production costs:
   Direct materials   £60 000
   Direct labour   £18 000
   Production overheads   £23 000
Closing stock: 2000 units
   Degree of completion:
   Materials   75%
   Labour   60%
   Overheads   30%

Assume that the transfers from the previous process are introduced immediately into the current process and that no closing stock of unutilised transfers remained.

(a) Calculate the cost of completed goods and the value of work-in-progress at the end of the year.
(b) Prepare the ledger accounts to record the flow of accounting information through the final production process.

10 Current Assets (II)

10.1 Introduction

In Chapter 9 a description was given of the procedures involved in the determination of stock cost for manufacturing organisations. In the current chapter one further problem involved with the identification of the cost of goods sold expense and closing stock values will be considered. This problem, involving the determination of the order in which stock costs are to be recognised, is present for trading, as well as manufacturing organisations.

Also considered in this current chapter is (i) the valuation of work-in-progress on long-term contracts; and (ii) those accounting problems relating to cash and near-cash assets which have not previously been examined.

10.2 Inventory cost recognition

Cost recognition methods

When goods bought by a trader for resale or the finished goods produced by a manufacturer, are indistinguishable from one another, and input costs have altered over an accounting period, the accountant is faced with a problem of cost recognition. In such circumstances, where it is physically impossible to identify which units were purchased or manufactured at which price, or cost, it is necessary to introduce a systematic method of cost recognition which will identify the order in which costs are to be allocated or expensed. Without such a system the accountant is faced with a bewildering array of potential cost of goods sold figures, and values for closing stock, as the following simple illustration demonstrates.

Illustration 1
Solo Retailing Stores sell a single product line. Purchases and sales during the month of May 1984 were as follows;

Opening stock	Nil
Purchases: (i) 10 units @ £5 each	£ 50
(ii) 25 units @ £6 each	150
	£200
Sales: 25 units at a price of £10 each	£250

Current assets (II)

The retailer is faced with the problem of identifying which costs to set against revenues for the month of May, and which to assign to the closing stock of unsold goods. The method which appeals intuitively to many observers, is to recognise costs in the order in which they occur, i.e., the cost of goods acquired first should be expensed first, or *'first-in-first-out'* (Fifo method). Calculation of gross profit for Solo Retailing using the Fifo basis of cost recognition is as follows:

	£
Sales revenue	250
Cost of goods sold:	
10 units @ £5	50
15 units @ £6	90
	140
Gross profit	£110

Closing stock of unsold goods consists of 10 units at a cost of £6 each, i.e., £60.

An alternative approach, is to recognise costs in the order of *'last-in-first-out'* (Lifo method), i.e., the last costs incurred will be recognised first. One justification for this method is the argument that in times of rising prices the Lifo method produces a cost of goods sold figure which reflects a close approximation to replacement cost, while still retaining the historic cost system of valuation. However, it is quite possible for a business with stock levels which fluctuate from period to period, for the cost of goods sold figure to be lower under Lifo than under Fifo, even when prices are continually rising. In any event, it would be better to adopt a complete replacement cost system than a piecemeal system if inflation adjustments were considered to be necessary, particularly as a relatively higher Lifo cost of goods sold figure will automatically produce a relatively lower closing stock figure. The Lifo method of stock valuation, although widely adopted elsewhere, has never gained much support in the United Kingdom and is not a method recommended by SSAP 9, as it is not considered 'to bear a reasonable relationship to actual costs obtained'[1] during an accounting period.

Calculation of gross profit for Solo Retailing using the Lifo system of cost recognition is as follows:

	£
Sales revenue	250
Cost of goods sold:	
25 units at £6	150
Gross profit	£100

Closing stock of unsold goods consists of 10 units at a cost of £5 each, i.e., £50

One further method of cost recognition which is allowed and used in the UK is that of *average cost*, or more commonly, weighted average cost. Weighted average unit cost is calculated by dividing the total cost of units acquired during an accounting period by the number of units acquired.

For example, the weighted average cost of goods purchased by Solo Retailing for the month of May 1984 is $\frac{£200}{35 \text{ units}} = £5.71$. Calculation of the gross profit for Solo Retailing using a weighted average system of cost recognition is as follows:

	£
Sales revenue	250.00
Cost of goods sold:	
25 units at £5.71	142.90
Gross profit	£107.10

Closing stock would consist of 10 units at a cost of £5.71 each, i.e., £57.10.

Perpetual and periodic stock valuation

As demonstrated in the previous illustration, in periods of changing input prices, the method chosen for cost recognition will affect the cost of goods sold and the value of the closing stock. In addition, the timing of the identification of cost of goods sold expense may also affect the allocation of costs between goods sold and closing stocks. Cost of goods sold and inventories may be valued *periodically* as in the previous illustration, i.e., at the end of each time period, or *perpetually*, that is, after each new purchase or sale.

Periodic valuation of stock involves a transfer at the end of a particular time period, from the stock account either to a cost of goods sold expense account, or else directly to the Profit and Loss Account.

The summarised journal entries required to record cost of purchases and goods sold identified in Illustration 1, using the Fifo periodic method of cost recognition, are as follows:

		£	£
debit	Stock a/c	200	
credit	Trade creditors a/c		200
Being goods purchased during May 1984.			

		£	£
debit	Cost of goods sold expense a/c	140	
credit	Stock a/c		140
Being cost of goods sold during May 1984			

With the perpetual method of cost recognition and stock valuation on the other hand, cost of goods sold will be identified immediately each sale has been made. Transfers from the stock account to cost of goods sold expense a/c will be made immediately following a sale with the result that the stock account will be continuously adjusted to the actual level of stocks held.

Illustration 2

Purchases and sales made by Cooper Stores for the first seven days of June 1984 are as follows:

Day 1	Purchases	20 units @ £5 each
3	Sales	15 units
5	Purchases	30 units @ £6 each
7	Sales	10 units

The effect of using different approaches to cost recognition is demonstrated in Tables 10.1 and 10.2. Table 10.1 demonstrates the application of three methods of cost recognition Fifo, Lifo and weighted average, but applied on a periodic basis. Table 10.2 demonstrates the application of the same three methods, but this time on a perpetual basis.

The results shown in the two tables demonstrate that the Fifo method of cost recognition will produce the same figures for cost of goods sold and closing stock whether calculated on a periodic or a perpetual basis. Lifo and weighted average methods, however, produce different results according to whether they are applied on a perpetual or a periodic basis.

10.3 Long-term contracts and work-in-progress

As a general rule, the valuation of stocks under an historic cost system does not allow recognition of potential gains on eventual disposal of the stocks. One exception is allowed, however, in the case of manufacturing or construction contracts entered into in which 'a substantial proportion of all such contract work will extend for a period exceeding one year'.[2] SSAP 9 permits the amount of work-in-progress on long-term contracts to be calculated on the basis of cost 'plus any attributable profits, less any foreseeable losses'.[3] If firms engaged in long-term contracts were unable to recognise profits until after a contract was completed, they would be placed in a situation in which reported profits might be subject to wide fluctuations from year to year; reported profits would depend on the value of contracts actually completed during a particular time period, which may bear no relation to the level of activity of the organisation. Indeed, without recognition of attributable profit, it is possible to envisage situations where a highly profitable firm is

TABLE 10.1

Cooper Stores
Periodic Stock Valuation

Cost of Goods Sold		Closing Stock	
Fifo			
20 units at £5	100		
5 units at £6	30	25 units at £6	150
	£130		£150
Lifo			
25 units at £6	150	20 units at £5	100
		5 units at £6	30
	£150		£130
Weighted average			
25 units at £5.60*	£140	25 units at £5.60*	£140

*Weighted average cost $= \dfrac{£280}{50} = £5.60$ per unit.

TABLE 10.2

Cooper Stores
Perpetual Stock Valuation

	Day	Units	Unit price £		Stock balance £		Cost of Goods sold £
Fifo							
Goods in	1	20	5		100		
Goods out	3	15	5		75	@£5	75
		5			25		
Goods in	5	30	6		180		
		35			205		
Goods out	7	10			55	5@£5	25
						5@£6	30
Balance		25	6		£150		£130
Lifo							
Goods in	1	20	5		100		
Goods out	3	15	5		75	@£5	75
		5			25		
Goods in	5	30	6		180		
		35			205		
Goods out	7	10			60	@£6	60
Balance		25		5@£5	£145		£135
				20@£6			
Weighted average							
Goods in	1	20	5		100		
Goods out	3	15	5		75	@£5	75
		5			25		
Goods in	5	30	6		180		
		35	5.86		205		
Goods out	7	10			58.6	@£5.86	58.60
Balance		25	5.86		£146.40		£133.60

engaged in a small number of major contracts and yet appears to make heavy losses for a number of years followed by huge profits in the years in which the contracts terminate. Recognition of profit on work-in-progress is one of the few allowable methods of 'income smoothing'.

A number of contracting firms choose not to recognise profits before completion of contracts because of the uncertainty attached to the final level of costs and the eventual profit on the contract. Most firms, however, will allocate a proportion of the estimated total profit on their contracts to the accounting periods in which the work is carried out, but normally with the deduction of a provision to cover unforeseen events such as the cost of remedial work.

The amount of any profit (or loss) attributed to contract work-in-progress should reflect the proportion of the contract completed during the accounting period, together with any known inequalities in the profitability of various stages of a contract. Often the estimation of profit earned to date will depend on certificates of work completed or on the advice of contract engineers. In the absence of more precise information it may be feasible to apportion revenues on the basis of 'cost incurred to date in proportion to total expected contract costs'.

Illustration 3
Bricks Ltd have entered into a contract to build a dam for the Republic of Monrovia. The contract is expected to cost £8 million and yield revenues of £10 million. (All costs and revenues have been converted to their sterling equivalent.)

At the end of the last accounting year, the contract records show that costs incurred to date amounted to £3 million. The contracts manager of Bricks Ltd therefore feels justified in attributing to the last accounting period a profit of £2million $\times \dfrac{\text{£3 million}}{\text{£8 million}} =$ £750 000. Contract work-in-progress, at the end of the year will then be valued at £3.75 million, with this amount shown in the Balance Sheet, less any progress payments received from the government of Monrovia.

The apportionment of profit in the above illustration assumed that the actual costs would be equal to the budgeted costs, and that no unforeseen expenses are likely to arise in the future relating to work already completed or work not yet begun. Neither assumption will necessarily be realised in practice.

An alternative basis for attributing profit to contract work-in-progress is possible for those contracts on which separate stages are identifiable. On such contracts, the amount of work completed at each stage is normally certified by an agent of the contractee before payment is made for the work certified. With such contracts each stage may be considered to be a separate contract with revenues identified as either the amount certified to date, or the payment received for work completed. In either of these possible treatments, a deduction will normally be made from the gross figure as a provision against unforeseen future expenses. The agent for the contractee may even withhold a fixed percentage of the amount certified before making payment to the contractor, again as a provision for contingencies.

There will be an element of subjectivity whichever method is adopted for recognising revenues and attributable profits on long-term contract work-in-progress. The overriding principle stressed in SSAP 9 appears to be one of prudence: 'there can be no attributable profit until the outcome of a contract can reasonably be foreseen'.[4] Additionally, the calculation of *total* estimated profit on a contract should be revised before determining attributable profit on each stage, taking into account not only the total costs to date and total estimated future costs, but also any possible costs of rectifying inadequate work or any guarantee work. Whichever method is chosen for recognising attributable profit, it should be applied consistently from year to year and from contract to contract, in so far as the circumstances of each contract permit.

Illustration 4
Apex Construction have entered into a contract worth £2 million, with work to be completed in three stages. Estimated costs and profits for each stage are as follows:

Stage	Estimated costs £000	Value of work completed £000	Anticipated profits £000
1	400	500	100
2	560	800	240
3	620	700	80

As these figures indicate, the profitability of each stage is expected to differ, with the second stage anticipated to be the most profitable. An apportionment of profit to each stage on the basis of costs incurred would therefore be inappropriate for this contract.

Payments on the above contract will be received after each stage has been certified as complete. Payment is made on the basis of 75 per cent of the value of work completed, with a retention of 25 per cent being made by the contractee until six months after completion of the contract. Cash receipts and retentions will be as follows:

Stage	Value of work completed £000	25% retention £000	Cash payment received £000
1	500	125	375
2	800	200	600
3	700	175	525
	£2000	£500	£1500

(a) If actual costs were equal to expected costs, then, after each stage had been certified and cash payment received, the value of work-in-progress and the amount shown in the Balance Sheet would be as shown in Table 10.3.

TABLE 10.3

Apex Construction
Contract work-in-progress

STAGE	1 £000	2 £000	3 £000
Costs incurred	400	560	620
Add Attributable profit	100	240	80
Value of work-in-progress	500	800	700
Cumulative work-in-progress (a)	500	1300	2000
Payment received on account	375	600	525
Cumulative payments received (b)	375	975	1500
Work-in-progress included in Balance Sheet [(a) − (b)]	125	325	500

(b) If, as is likely, actual costs differed from initial estimates, then attributable profit would need to be revised to adjust for the revised level of profits earned to date plus any adjustment to future attributable profits. For example, if Apex Construction reached the end of the second stage of the contract with actual costs equal to estimates but with a revised estimate of costs for the third and final stage of £720 000, attributable profits of the second stage must be revised for the foreseeable loss estimated during the third stage:

i.e.
		£000
Third stage		
	Estimated costs	720
	Value of work to complete	700
	Foreseeable loss	(20)

Adjustment to work-in-progress and attributable profits for the second stage would be as follows:

	£000
Second stage	
Costs incurred to date	960
Attributable profit to date	340
	1300
Less foreseeable loss	20
Value of work-in-progress	1280
Attributable profits on stage 2	240
Less foreseeable loss	20
Adjusted profits	220
Add attributable profits, stage 1	100
Adjusted attributable profits to date	320

Given the likelihood that actual cost will differ from estimates, it is possible that Apex may wish to provide for this eventuality by setting aside a provision at each stage in the contract against which unexpected costs may be charged. This provision may be calculated in a number of different ways depending on the degree of certainty attached to the cost estimates, and the risks of the particular contract. Some firms may choose to recognise attributable profits only to the extent that payment has been received for work certified, while others may provide a fixed percentage of work certified to date. Since an element of subjectivity will once again be attached to the estimates made, however expertly calculated, the requirement to apply the chosen method of determining attributable profit in as consistent a manner as possible is important if users of the final accounting statements are to place any credibility on them.

10.4 Cash and other liquid assets

Cash

(a) *Introduction*

Cash is one asset for which there should be no ambiguity about its measurement. The purchasing power of money does, however, alter from period to period as a result of either a rise or fall in the price of goods and services. Accounting for changes in the purchasing power of money is a subject which will be considered in Chapter 15 along with other approaches to accounting for the effects of inflation (or deflation). In the following sections, three other cash-related topics will be considered, as follows:

(i) the separation of cash from bank transactions;
(ii) the reconciliation of bank statement balances with balances shown in the accounting records; and
(iii) the control of cash.

(b) *Cash and bank transactions*

The cash book was introduced in Chapter 5 as one of the books of prime entry. The accounting treatment of cash and bank related payments and receipts was also identified but without any distinction being made between the two. In order to achieve some measure of control over liquid resources and indeed to ascertain balances of cash-in-hand and cash-at-bank at any point in time it is necessary to prepare separate accounts for each. As many businesses operate with more than one bank current account, it will also be necessary to maintain a separate accounting record for each bank current account.

Maintenance of the separation between cash and bank accounting records is achieved by recording transactions in the exact manner in which they are undertaken, i.e., bank receipts and payments will be recorded in the accounting record for the bank account, while cash receipts and payments will be recorded in the cash account. Although most cash receipts will ultimately be banked, it is important for control purposes to record these receipts initially in the cash account, even if they are in the form of cheques received. When the cash is subsequently banked, the resulting accounting entry is:

debit   Bank account
credit Cash account

With the total amount banked, including cheques.

Similarly, funds may sometimes be withdrawn from a bank account to finance cash payments. The amount withdrawn will be recorded as follows:

debit   Cash account
credit Bank account

With the total amount withdrawn.

Cash payments will subsequently be recorded in the cash account by means of a credit entry in the cash account and a debit entry in the appropriate expense, or other, account.

Many businesses combine both the cash account and the bank current account (or No. 1 bank current account if more than one is operated) into one cash book. Transfers from bank account to cash account and vice versa are then recorded by means of what are described as bank-cash, or cash-bank, contra's.

Illustration 5

The cash book of North Fisheries for May 1984 is shown in Table 10.4. Two columns of figures are included on each side of the cash book, one for cash transactions, the other for bank transactions. Additional columns are also included

TABLE 10.4 North Fisheries Cash Book

Date		Folio No.	Bank Account	Cash Account	Date		Cheque No.	Folio No.	Bank Account	Cash Account
			£	£					£	£
1984					1984					
May 1	Balance	b/d	—	820	May 1	Balance	—	b/d	246	600
1	Cash	¢	600		1	Bank	—	¢		
3	H. Jones	SL/17		274	2	Electricity	73	NL/8	85	210
6	D. Hogg	SL/14	86		7	Wages	—	NL/10		24
7	Cash sales	NL/2		412	9	Stationery	—	NL/11		210
14	Cash sales	NL/2		536	14	Wages	—	NL/10		
15	B. Miles	SL/23		981	15	C. Watt	74	PL/6	380	
16	Cash	¢	1530		16	Bank	—	¢		1530
21	Cash sales	NL/2		505	20	A. Round	75	PL/11	576	
24	L. Davies	SL/4	324		21	Wages	—	NL/10		210
28	Cash sales	NL/2		740	28	Wages	—	NL/10		210
30	Cash	¢	960		30	S. Teel	76	PL/14	423	
					30	Bank	—	¢		960
					31	Balances		c/d	1790	314
			£3500	£4268					£3500	£4268
June 1	Balances	c/d	1790	314						

203

to record cheque numbers and folio numbers of accounts in which the accounting entries will be completed.

The credit balance of £246 on the bank account at 1 May 1984 indicates that the account was overdrawn.

£600 in cash has been banked on day 1 with the accounting transaction recorded by:

debit	Bank account	£600	
credit	Cash account		£600

The folio column shows the figure ¢ alongside the above entries indicating a contra item.

Similar bankings of cash have taken place on 16 May and 30 May, for £1530 and £960 respectively.

Two customers D. Hogg and L. Davies pay their accounts by means of credit-transfers which are recorded as direct receipts in the bank account. Receipts from other customers, whether cheques or cash, are first recorded in the cash book before they are banked.

At the end of May both the cash account and the bank account show balances of cash on hand amounting to £314 and £1790 respectively. These amounts are carried down as debit balances in the cash book at the beginning of June.

(c) *Bank reconciliation statements*

It is a constant source of irritation to many individuals that the balance of cash at bank, recorded either on cheque counterfoils in the case of personal accounts, or in accounting records in the case of business accounts, frequently differs from the balance shown on the statements received from the bank.

The differences between the balances may arise from the following:

(i) Direct banking receipts not recorded in the cash book;
(ii) Bank charges, dishonoured cheques, or other bank payments not recorded in the cash book;
(iii) Cash banked at the end of the month but not yet included on the bank statement;
(iv) Cheques paid and recorded in the cash book but not yet presented to the bank.

A reconciliation of the balance in the cash book with the balance shown on the bank statement may be undertaken by first recording the missing item, i.e., (i) and (ii) above, in the cash book in order to identify the correct balance of cash at bank, and then by adjusting the balance shown on the bank statement for items (iii) and (iv) above.

Illustration 6
Suppose the bank statement received by North Fisheries at the end of May 1984 showed a balance on hand of £1656. Subsequent examination reveals the following:

(i) a receipt of £147 from D. Hogg, paid directly to the bank by credit transfer, has not yet been recorded in the cash book;
(ii) an amount of £14 was included on the bank statement for bank charges; also a cheque for £110, received in payment on a cash sale to A. Bent and subsequently banked, has not been honoured by Bent's own bank;

Current assets (II)

(iii) the banking of £960 on 30 May has not been included on the bank statement;
(iv) cheques sent to C. Watt and S. Teel during May have not yet been presented to the bank for payment.

Journal entries showing the required adjustments to the bank account for amounts included in (i) and (ii) above are as follows:

			£	£
(i)	debit	Bank account	147	
	credit	D. Hogg account		147

Being payment received from customer

			£	£
(ii)	debit	Bank charges expense account	14	
	credit	Bank account		14

Being bank charges to date

			£	£
	debit	A. Bent account	110	
	credit	Bank account		110

Being dishonoured cheque

The effect of the above transactions will be to adjust the bank balance in the cash book to £1813:

		£
Balance per cash book		1790
Add payment received		147
		1937
Less bank charges	14	
dishonoured cheque	110	124
Adjusted bank balance 31.5.84		£1813

A bank reconciliation statement may now be prepared to reconcile the balance shown on the bank statement at 31.5.84 to the corrected bank balance of £1813 shown in the cash book. The bank reconciliation statement is given in Table 10.5.

(d) *Control of cash*

Apart from the recording of cash transactions one other important aspect of cash accounting is the control aspect. There are two elements to the control

TABLE 10.5

North Fisheries Bank Reconciliation Statement at 31 May 1984

		£
Balance per bank statement		1656
Add deposit not yet recorded		960
		2616
Less cheques unrepresented:		
No. 74	380	
No. 76	423	803
Balance per cash book 31.5.84		1813

of cash; the first involves the maintenance of the most effective level of cash balances, while the second involves the prevention of misappropriation.

There are three important motives for holding cash as follows:

(i) *Transactions motive* Cash balances must be available to meet the necessary payments in the ordinary course of business. These balances may fluctuate from period to period, depending on seasonal trade patterns.

(ii) *Precautionary motive* Cash balances may sometimes be required to meet unforeseen events, such as major repairs on buildings, etc. The need to hold precautionary balances will vary according to the degree of certainty with which cash receipts and payments may be predicted and also the extent to which a business can borrow additional funds at short notice. Overdraft facilities available from a bank are a useful help here, as is the practice of holding 'near cash' assets such as short-term government securities, or cash on deposit with savings institutions.

(iii) *Speculative motive* This involves the holding of a balance of cash resources in order to be ready to exploit profitable situations as they are identified. Although this is not a common motive in business enterprises, a few maintain cash reserves for this purpose; in particular, merger intensive companies may hold large cash balances in anticipation of potential takeover victims.

In the main, most businesses will seek to hold the minimum cash balance which is compatible with the above motives. Cash on hand or in a bank current account does not earn any income and even cash held on deposit would normally be expected to earn a lower return than funds reinvested within a business, e.g., for expansion of production capacity. A major part of the function of the treasurer of a business is to manage cash resources and ensure that funds are available to meet payments when required, but with excess funds reinvested in the most profitable investments available. Cash budgets are an important aid in these tasks as are Funds Flow Statements, which are described in Chapter 14.

The second aspect of control over cash, namely prevention of misappropriation, is also an important part of the accounting function. There are a number of ways in which such control can be exercised including the following:

(i) Separation of financial duties, in particular:
cash collection and subsequent recording;
recording of cash and maintenance of customers' records;
control over stocks and ordering and maintenance of suppliers records;
(ii) Independent verification of accounting records including spot-checks of cash-in-hand and stocks and periodic confirmation with customers and suppliers of balances outstanding;

Current assets (II)

(iii) Minimisation of the amount of cash-on-hand held for day-to-day transactions, with immediate banking of receipts and introduction of a petty cash imprest system i.e., the advance of a small amount of funds to a petty cashier to meet specified payments.

re (i) Separation of recording duties may not always be possible in smaller firms but it is a desirable practice wherever possible. Examples of possible misappropriations include setting up fictitious creditors accounts and subsequently pocketing the supposed payment; pocketing receipts from customer A then crediting the account of customer A with a receipt from customer B, etc.; misappropriation of goods received either for personal use or for resale privately.

re (ii) Internal checking by following up goods requisitions to sales delivery notes and subsequently to customers' invoices, statements and payments, will also help to deter or identify, if not eliminate, systematic fraud.

re (iii) Many businesses allow only a limited amount of payments and receipts to be made in cash, with the majority transacted through a bank account. In such businesses it is normal to operate what is known as a petty cash system.

The cashier responsible for petty cash payments and receipts will receive a small amount of cash to meet day-to-day business obligations. Payments will be recorded initially only in the petty cash book and a limit will normally be placed on the maximum permitted payment, together with restrictions on the type of expenditures permissible. The cash balance will be replenished either at periodic intervals or else when it is exhausted, at which time the cashier would normally be expected to provide receipts for all expenditures made. At the same time as the cashier receives reimbursement for payments made, the dual aspect of the expenditures i.e., the relevant debit entries, will be completed.

Illustration 7
The petty cashier of Bowser Products receives a £50 float to meet incidental payments. The following authorised expenditures were made by the petty cashier during January and the relevant receipts were retained:

	£
Cash purchases	15.00
Travelling expenses	3.50
Stationery	7.30
Light bulbs	1.60
General expenses	2.45
	£29.85

At the end of January the petty cashier presented the receipts to the cashier and received reimbursement of £29.85 for the expenditures made. Relevant journal entries to record the transactions undertaken during January are as follows:

		£	£
debit	Petty cash account	50.00	
credit	Bank account		50.00
Being recording of petty cash float received.			

		£	£
debit	Stock a/c	15.00	
	Travelling expenses	3.50	
	Stationery	7.30	
	Heat and light	1.60	
	General expenses	2.45	
credit	Petty cash account		29.85
Being expenditures incurred during January			

		£	£
debit	Petty cash	29.85	
credit	Bank account		29.85
Being reimbursement to petty cashier for expenditures incurred			

Other liquid assets

When a business has a temporary surplus of cash resources the funds may often be invested in securities which will earn a higher return than bank deposit accounts, while providing ease of access to the funds, should this be required.

Although temporary investments come in a variety of forms they may be grouped under two main headings, namely *listed securities* and *unlisted securities*.

(a) *Listed securities*

Listed securities include those securities which are either quoted on the United Kingdom Stock Exchange or on a recognised overseas Stock Exchange. These securities come in a variety of forms, and include investments in Public Quoted Companies, British Government Securities, and local authority securities.

The principal feature of listed securities is that they possess a quoted price which is readily available and verifiable. The normal rule for valuation of these securities at Balance Sheet date is the 'lower of cost or market value rule' which was adopted for stock valuation earlier. Hence, these investments will be shown in the Balance Sheet at cost price where this is lower than market value, but at market value where this is lower than cost. This seemingly illogical rule is perhaps only understandable within an accounting system in which conservatism is a dominant principle. After all, these investments are readily realisable and assets with market value higher than cost are as liquid as those with market values less than cost. However, the generally adopted rule recognises only a loss in value from original cost by means of a charge to the Profit and Loss Account and ignores unrealised gains. Income received on these investments will be the only revenues recorded until disposal, at which time any gain on disposal may be recorded as an extraordinary item, i.e., separate from normal operating profits in the Profit and Loss Account.

A note should be appended to the Balance Sheet of all businesses holding listed investments, stating their aggregate market value where this differs from cost.

Cost for listed securities includes any transaction costs involved in acquisition, while market value is normally taken as the average of the closing selling and purchasing price of the listed investment (rather than selling price itself), on the Balance Sheet date.

(b) *Unlisted securities*

Unlisted securities are those for which an actively traded market may not exist and hence no independently verifiable market price may be available. Shares quoted on the unlisted securities markets of either Granville & Co.[5] or the Stock Exchange are also classified as unlisted securities, perhaps because of the relative infrequency at which these are traded. The difficulty in identifying up-to-date market values for unlisted securities makes the operation of the 'lower of cost or market value' rule more difficult to apply. However, where the owners or managers of a business have valued unlisted securities, or when an independent valuation has been obtained, then the above-mentioned rule must be applied.

10.5 Summary

Current assets are those resources owned by an organisation which are expected to be consumed or otherwise exhausted during one complete operating cycle. Valuation of current assets under the historic cost accounting system is made on the basis of lower of cost or market value, where market value represents net realisable value after deducting costs of disposal.

The determination of stock cost was identified as a highly complex process even for the most simple forms of manufacturing organisation. Cost includes not only those expenditures directly attributable to the product or manufacturing process but also indirectly attributable production overheads. Cost is defined by SSAP 9 to include fixed as well as variable production costs, i.e., an absorption basis is recommended.

Even when the cost of goods produced is identifiable the problem of the order of recognition of the cost of goods subsequently sold remains. This problem of cost recognition applies both to the raw materials and finished goods of a manufacturing enterprise, and also to those goods bought for resale by a trading organisation. Various conventions for recognising the order of cost recognition are available, including Fifo, Lifo and weighted average methods, with Fifo being the method most widely adopted in the United Kingdom.

Work-in-progress on long-term contracts forms one exception to the general rule of not recognising profits until realised. Normally an allocation will be made of attributable profit to work undertaken on such contracts in the accounting period in which the work is undertaken.[5]

Cash accounting problems are primarily involved with control rather than measurement, although a bank reconciliation statement is often required to ascertain the balance of cash held in business bank account(s) at the end of each accounting period. Control over cash and other business resources is helped by

(i) Separation of recording duties;
(ii) independent verification of balances held;
(iii) operation of a petty cash system.

Near-cash assets, including quoted investments and others, are included in financial statements at lower of cost or current market valuation. Any loss in value of investments is recorded in the accounting period in which it is identified, but gains in value are not normally recorded in Profit Statements until the gains have been realised through disposal of the investment.

Questions

1. Explain in which of the following types of business stocks might be capable of valuation on an individual basis:

    (a) Furniture retailer;
    (b) Motor-car assembly plant;
    (c) Jewellers' store;
    (d) Perfumery.

2. Describe the following:

    (a) Fifo stock valuation;
    (b) Lifo stock valuation;
    (c) Periodic versus perpetual stock valuation.

3. Compare the relative merits of the Fifo and Lifo systems of stock valuation. Explain the expected effects of each method on stock values and profits during periods in which prices are (a) rising and (b) falling, but where physical stock levels are constant.

4. Do you agree that recognition of attributable profit on long-term contracts appears to contradict the prudence concept? Identify other examples of accepted accounting treatments which appear to contradict this concept.

5. The lower of cost or market value rule is applied to short-term investments. Stocks are not, however, valued on a lower of cost or current replacement price. Explain why these two treatments are recommended for the valuation of the respective current assets and also whether there appears to be any contradiction in the treatments.

6. Outline the major business motives for holding cash resources and the dangers in holding excessive cash balances.

7. (a) Identify four possible forms in which misappropriation of business resources may occur either because of inadequate control, or lack of separation of accounting duties; (b) Explain procedures which may be adopted to eliminate or minimise the possibility of the misappropriations identified in (a) above.

For each of the following **circle** the *letter* of *best choice* among the possible solutions presented

Current assets (II)

8. When goods are purchased on credit terms rather than for cash, the appropriate entry is:

    (a) none;
    (b) debit stock, credit cash;
    (c) debit cost of goods sold, credit cash;
    (d) debit stock, credit trade creditors.

9. Stamp Traders adopt a periodic basis of stock valuation. Opening stocks plus purchases are recorded in a stock account at a figure of £110 000. Closing stocks are valued at a cost of £15 000. The appropriate journal entry to record the closing stocks is:

    (a) debit cost of goods sold, credit stock account, £95 000;
    (b) debit stock account old period, credit stock account new period, £15 000;
    (c) credit stock account old period, debit stock account new period, £15 000;
    (d) credit stock account old period, debit stock account new period, £95 000.

10. The following information relates to Nibor Products for May 1984:

    Opening stocks consisted of 25 units at a cost of £5 each. Goods purchased during the month amounted to:
    40 units at £6 on 7 May,
    55 units at £7 on 21 May,
    100 units were sold during the month at £10 each.

    The cost of goods sold for May using a Fifo stock valuation base is:

    (a) £750;
    (b) £1000;
    (c) £650;
    (d) £610.

11. The bank statement for Dale Traders at the end of June 1984 showed a balance on hand of £1650, while the business accounting records show a balance at bank of £1960. Further examination reveals deposits not yet recorded by the bank of £570 and unpresented cheques amounting to £295. In addition, bank charges for the month of June, amounting to £35, had not been entered in the business accounting records. The adjusted balance of cash at bank at the end of June 1984 is:

    (a) £1685;
    (b) £2210;
    (c) £2260;
    (d) £1925.

12. Securities were acquired as a short-term investment at a cost of £1200 on 1 May 1983. Investment income of £150 was received on the securities in December 1983. At the Balance Sheet date of 31 December 1983 the securities had a quoted market value of £1100. The total net income from the securities during the year to 31 December 1983 and Balance Sheet value at that date was:

    (a) £150 net income, Balance Sheet value £1200;
    (b) £50 net income, Balance Sheet value £1100;
    (c) £150 net income, Balance Sheet value £1100;
    (d) £50 net income, Balance Sheet value £1200.

Problems

1. Argyle Factors is a wholesaler of engine lubricants. On 1 June 1984, it had a stock of 20 000 litres of lubricant valued at 25 pence per litre. The following movements in lubricant stocks were recorded during the month of June 1984:

June	3	sold	14 000 litres
	10	purchased	50 000 litres at 28 pence per litre
	13	sold	30 000 litres
	15	sold	12 000 litres
	20	purchased	30 000 litres at 30 pence per litre
	27	sold	34 000 litres.

The company operates a perpetual method of stock valuation and stock control.

(a) Calculate the value of closing stocks and cost of goods sold using each of the following methods:

    (i) First in, first out (Fifo);
    (ii) Last in, last out (Lifo);
    (iii) Weighted average.

(b) Prepare journal entries to record all movements in the stock account for June 1984 and show the stock ledger account for the month using the Fifo method of cost recognition, i.e. (i) above.

2. Using the information provided in Question 1 and assuming a periodic method of stock valuation and stock control,

(a) calculate the value of closing stock and cost of goods sold using each of the following methods:

    (i) First in, first out (Fifo);
    (ii) Last in, last out (Lifo);
    (iii) Weighted average.

(b) Prepare journal entries to record the cost of goods sold and value of closing stock using the Lifo method of cost recognition, i.e. (ii) above.

3. The Everlasting Company act as wholesale distributors of Vitrim, a raw ingredient for a variety of rubberised compounds. Opening stock of Vitrim on 1 January 1983 was 25 000 litres at a cost of £1.20 each. Purchases during the year amounted to 100 000 litres at a cost per litre of £1.25 followed by 95 000 litres at a cost per litre of £1.15. Sales of 200 000 litres of Vitrim took place during the year. The company operates a periodic basis of stock valuation and stock control.

(a) Calculate the value of the closing stock at 31 December 1983 and the cost of goods sold during the year using the following bases of cost recognition:
    (i) Fifo;
    (ii) Lifo.

(b) Compare the relative merits of the two approaches to stock cost recognition using the information obtained in (a).

4. The following information has been extracted from the records of Aragon Products:

Bank Account

1984 March			£	1984 March			Cheque no.	£
	1	Balance b/f	1150		3	Wages	212	345
	3	James Co	720		7	Mason Co	213	212
	10	Falcon Products	500		10	Brentford Co	214	126
	10	A. Jones	600		17	Wages	215	330
	20	R. Davies	500		20	British Traders	216	297
	31	Bryant Products	440		29	Belling Co	217	1618
					31	Wages	218	340
					31	Electricty	219	290
					31	Delve Ltd	220	333

Aragon Products—in Account with the Royal Hibernian Bank
Statement of Current Account

Date		Description	Debits £	Credits £	Balance £
1984 March	1	Brought forward			1233
		206	27		1206
		Counter credit		380	1586
	3	212	345		1241
		Counter credit		720	1961
	5	209	436		1525
	10	Counter credit		500	2025
	10	Counter credit		600	2625
	12	214	126		2499
	15	Bank charges	25		2474
	17	215	330		2144
	20	Counter credit		500	2644
		B.P. – Dividend		32	2676
	21	213	212		2464
	31	218	340		2124
		Cheque returned unpaid – B. Lewis	138		1986
		Cannonby – Standing order	200		1786
		216	297		1489

(a) Prepare a Bank Reconciliation Statement at 31 March 1984.
(b) Present in journal entry form, the required adjustments to the bank account in the books of Aragon Products.
(c) Post the journal entries to the bank account and bring down the balance of cash at bank at 31 March 1984.

5. Collingwood Enterprises operate a petty cash imprest system, with an initial advance of £100 being made to the petty cashier to meet incidental expenses. Petty cash expenditures are reimbursed to the petty cashier on the Friday of each week, after a summary of petty cash expenses and accompanying vouchers have been presented to the general cashier. The following expenditures were recorded by the petty cashier during the first two weeks of May 1984:

	Week 1	Week 2
	£	£
Stationery	10	5
Casual wages	8	13
Goods for resale	25	8
General expenses	7	11
	50	37

(a) Prepare a petty cash memorandum account for the first two weeks of May 1984.

(b) Present journal entries recording all transactions relating to petty cash for the first two weeks of May 1984.

11 Forms of Business Organisation (I): Sole Traders and Partnerships

11.1 Introduction

There are three major forms of business organisation operating within the private sector, namely, sole trader, partnership, and limited companies.[1] Of the three, limited companies are by far the most important in terms of share of total output and employment. There are, however, many more unincorporated than incorporated businesses operating in the United Kingdom. Sole traders and partnerships are normally much smaller in scale of operations than incorporated businesses, although many of the latter also qualify under almost any definition of small business. Specific financial problems of small businesses have been studied by a number of government committees, including in recent years the Bolton Committee[2] and the Wilson Committee.[3] The subject of this current chapter are those accounting issues which relate specifically to unincorporated businesses. Accounting for Value Added Tax is also considered in this chapter although the procedures explained apply equally to incorporated businesses.

11.2 Sole traders

Introduction

A sole trading organisation is a business owned by one individual. Accounting reports will be provided primarily for use by the owner, and occasionally for inspection by third parties at the discretion of the owner. For example, the owner may be requested to provide a copy of the most recent business financial statements before a bank loan is granted. Unlike other forms of business organisation, there is no need to provide reports which satisfy a stewardship role, as the owner will normally be in close contact with all aspects of the business operations.

Any accounting problems occurring in the sole trader form of business organisation will normally result from the limited attention which the owner will be willing, or able, to devote to the maintenance of adequate accounting records. This problem is not by any means unique to sole traders, nor is it found in all such organisations, but it is more common in this form of business than in any other. In the next section the problem of incomplete records will be considered and a comprehensive system for the preparation of final accounts from incomplete records will be explained.

Incomplete records

The description 'incomplete records' involves the state of affairs which exists when 'some or all of the prime accounting information from which the normal way [sic] the books of a business are written up and final accounts prepared'[4] are lacking. The vast majority of businesses with incomplete accounting records will be trading organisations rather than manufacturing concerns, as the latter will not normally be able to make routine decisions without detailed accounting records.

The steps involved in the preparation of accounts for a trading enterprise from incomplete records were identified in guidelines issued in 1965 by the Institute of Chartered Accountants in England and Wales[5] as follows:

(a) drawing up the opening Balance Sheet where one is not available;
(b) preparing a summary of the cash and bank accounts;
(c) preparing a schedule of debtors and creditors;
(d) determining, in consultation with the trader, the value to be attached to closing inventories;
(e) making year-end adjusting entries;
(f) preparing the final accounts from the information obtained.

(a) *Opening Balance Sheet*

Assuming that no opening Balance Sheet is available the accountant commissioned by the owner of the business will need to prepare a schedule listing all the assets and liabilities of the business at the beginning of the accounting year. Most of the problems encountered in the preparation of the opening Balance Sheet will be similar to the problems encountered in later stages of the process, and hence only a brief preview is given here.

From discussions with the trader and examination of the business premises themselves, it should be possible to provide a list of the fixed assets owned. Original cost of fixed assets should then be identified or, if not known, an estimate should be made of current value, i.e., replacement cost of similar assets.

All business bank accounts should similarly be identified together with an estimate of opening cash in hand. Opening balances on bank statements should be adjusted for any cheques outstanding, identified from an examination of the previous year's cheque stubs and bank statements. A similar adjustment must be made for any deposits not yet credited by the bank.

Identification of the opening value of stock on hand may prove to be difficult if the accounting records are in a very poor state. As a last resort, it may be necessary to make an estimate based on gross profit percentages, as explained later under (d).

Opening creditors may be identified by reference to statements received

Forms of business organisation (I): sole traders and partnerships 217

from suppliers relating to the last months of the previous year, and to payments made to suppliers in the first months of the current year. Opening debtors may be less easy to identify if no statements are sent out, but normally copy invoices are available and these should be capable of being matched with cheques received in the first months of the current year. A reasonable guide to the completeness of the list of creditors and debtors will also be available by comparison with the schedules drawn up at the end of the year.

Once the above information, or as much as is possible, is ascertained, a Balance Sheet may be drawn up with owner's interest identified by reference to total net assets.

Illustration 1
Errant Traders have not maintained a comprehensive set of accounting records for a number of years nor have annual financial statements been prepared. Pressure from the Inland Revenue has led to the appointment of an accountant by the owner of the business to prepare a Balance Sheet at 1 January 1983 and subsequently to prepare annual accounts. An exhaustive interview conducted by the accountant with the owner revealed the following information:

(i) One bank current account; balance shown in bank statement at 31 December 1982, £1957; cheques outstanding identified as £48 and £391.
(ii) One bank deposit account; balance shown in pass book, £2400; interest for 1982 notified but not yet included in pass book, £168.
(iii) Estimated cash in hand amounts to £375. This amount is partly confirmed by reference to a banking of £240 made on 2 January 1983, and cash payments of £80 made on the same day, the first day of the business in 1983.
(iv) Business premises, acquired freehold in 1960 at a cost of £3500. A revaluation of the premises has been undertaken recently (in December 1983) by a firm of property valuers. The valuation of £24 600 was incorporated into the opening Balance Sheet and subsequently in the closing Balance Sheet at 31 December 1983.
(v) A motor vehicle was bought in June 1981 at a cost of £4175. It was decided to charge depreciation on the sum-of-the-years-digits method over 4 years, assuming a resale value of £675 at the end of that time. An estimate was made of notional depreciation to 1 January 1983, but with six months depreciation only to be charged for the first year of ownership.

i.e. $\dfrac{\text{Depreciable cost}}{\text{Sum-of-years-digits}} = \dfrac{£(4175-675)}{4+3+2+1}$

= Depreciation per 'digit' = $\dfrac{£3500}{10}$ = £350

1981 Depreciation = $4 \times £350 \times \tfrac{1}{2}$ = £700

1982 Depreciation = $4 \times £350 \times \tfrac{1}{2}$ = £700
              + $3 \times £350 \times \tfrac{1}{2}$ = £525
                                          £1225

Total notional depreciation   £1925

Written down value 31 December 1982   £2250

(vi) Shop furnishings and fittings were estimated to be worth £1900 on 31 December 1982.
(vii) Stock of goods for resale were estimated at £14 250.
(viii) Examination of purchase invoices and statements, together with payments made, produced a list of creditors totalling £5706. A similar examination of sales invoices and subsequent receipts produced an estimate of trade debtors at 1 January 1983 amounting to £7340.
(ix) Finally, an examination of expense invoices revealed that (a) a payment of £360 had been made in February 1983 in respect of electricity for the three months to 31 January 1983; and (b) a payment of property and contents insurance of £708 made in October 1982 related to insurance for the 12 months ended 30 September 1983. From the above two payments, amounts were included in the Balance Sheet at 1 January 1983 as follows:

Accured heating and lighting expense:
$\frac{2}{3} \times £360 = £240$
Prepaid insurance expense:
$\frac{9}{12} \times £708 = £531$

A Balance Sheet was drawn up on the basis of the information provided as illustrated in Table 11.1.

(b) *Summary of bank and cash accounts*

When there are incomplete records available, often the only reliable record available to the accountant will be the bank statements. Even here there may

TABLE 11.1

Errant Traders
Summarised Balance Sheet at 1 January 1983

	£	£
Fixed assets		
Freehold premises at valuation		24 600
Furnishings and fittings		1 900
Motor vehicle		2 250
		28 750
Current assets		
Stock	14 250	
Debtors	7 340	
Prepayments	531	
Cash on hand	375	
Bank deposit account	2 568	
Bank current account	1 518	
	26 582	
Current liabilities		
Trade creditors	5 706	
Accrued expense	240	
	5 946	
Net current assets		20 636
Total net assets		£49 386
Owner's interest		£49 386

be difficulties; cheque stubs may not have been completed, returned cheques and paying-in slips may not have been retained; there may even be additional bank accounts which have not been disclosed to the accountant.

Perhaps the best approach available is to begin by attempting to reconstruct the transactions which have passed through the business bank account(s), by reference to the bank statements. Payments made are identifiable from returned cheques or cheque stubs, and can be verified by reference to the invoices if these are available. Cheques written but unpresented at the year end should be identified for bank reconciliation purposes, as should deposits not yet recorded. Any unusual payments should be noted and the owner subsequently questioned as to their nature in order to identify, for example, fixed asset acquisitions or private payments. Receipts should similarly be examined to identify unusual items, relating perhaps to the disposal of fixed assets, payments into the business by the owner, or even transfers from previously unknown business bank accounts.

An attempt should also be made to identify those receipts and payments which might be expected to appear on the bank statements but which do not, for example, quarterly expense bills, or the proceeds of known disposal of fixed assets.

Once the bank account has been reconstructed, attention can then be turned to cash receipts and payments.

The opening and closing cash balances should be verified by a physical count wherever possible, even if the count is made a few days before, or after, the year end; suitable adjustments can be made for subsequent, or earlier, receipts and payments. If a count is impossible then an estimate will be required from the owner, verifiable by reference to bankings and cash payments made in the first days of the following accounting year.

An examination of any receipts which are available will help in the identification of cash payments made. Further payments may be identified from any list of essential payments which ought to have been made through the bank account but which were not, for example, annual road tax payment on motor vehicles.

From discussions with the owner it should be possible to obtain an estimate of personal drawings. It may, however, be necessary, in extreme situations, to identify the total private expenditures of the owner, less any other known sources of income, before drawings can be identified.

Specific cash receipts should be identified wherever possible, including for example the proceeds of the sale of fixed assets. Receipts from customers will then be identified as a balancing item on the cash account identifiable after all bankings, payments and specific receipts have been ascertained.

Illustration 2
After a detailed examination of those records and invoices which were available for Errant Traders for 1983, a summary was obtained for receipts and payments transacted through the bank current account as shown in Table 11.2. It was also possible to identify the following cash payments after discussion with the owner and examination of cash receipt vouchers:

TABLE 11.2

Errant Traders
Summarised Bank Account for year ended 31 December 1983

	£		£
Opening balance	1 518	Payment to suppliers	41 463
Cash banked	59 139	Expenses paid (incl.	
Sale of motor vehicle	1 760	bank charges)	9 724
		Personal drawings	3 125
		Fixtures and fittings	526
		Motor vehicle	6 400
		Balance c/d	1 179
	£62 417		£62 417
Balance b/d	1 179		

	£
Wages paid to part-time employees	4 160
Personal withdrawals: £100 per week	5 200
Owner's national insurance payments	676
Cash purchases	839
Electricity bill paid in cash	417
Petrol and oil	2 153
Repairs to premises	196
	£13 641

A balance of £1170 cash-on-hand at the end of the year was identified. This balance was partly confirmed by reference to the amount of the first banking made on 3 January 1984 of £980.

From the above figures the summarised cash account of Errant Traders for 1983 was reconstructed as follows:

	£		£
Opening balance	375	Payments (listed above)	13 641
Difference: Revenues		Cash banked	59 139
received	73 575	Closing balance c/d	1 170
	£73 950		£73 950
Balance b/d	1 170		

(c) *Scheduling debtors and creditors*

(i) *Debtors* Most sole traders will have only a limited number of customers who buy goods on credit terms. There will normally be a list available of such customers and an up-to-date record of customers' indebtedness. Without any record of debts outstanding at the year end, however, it may be possible to identify any debtors outstanding from sales invoices issued in the closing months of the year, if available, together with the record of receipts in the first months of the new year, particularly cheque receipts.

Forms of business organisation (I): sole traders and partnerships

(ii) *Creditors* Suppliers will normally issue statements of account at periodic intervals, usually monthly, providing a record of goods received on credit terms and amounts outstanding. By matching the record of payments made with the monthly statements, it should be possible to identify any amounts outstanding at the end of a year. Comparison of the closing schedule of trade creditors with the schedule for the previous year may help to highlight any obvious omissions, as may the record of payments made in the first few months of the following year.

Expense payments outstanding at the end of the year should be identifiable in respect of those expenses paid at regular intervals, for example, quarterly telephone bills. Outstanding bills relating to any expenses paid at irregular intervals are more difficult to identify, and again reference should be made to any payments made in the first months of the following year.

(d) *Closing stock*

Wherever possible the owner should undertake a physical count of the inventory of closing stocks of unsold goods at the end of each accounting year, or preferably obtain the services of an independent stock valuer. The basis on which stock should be valued is, as mentioned in Chapter 9, lower of cost or net realisable value. Cost price must be identified net of value added tax (see later). Where no stock count has been made, it may be possible in certain businesses to match units purchased with units sold; in businesses selling a wide variety of goods at relatively low prices, however, this will not normally be possible.

If all else fails, it may be necessary to identify the closing stock figure by reference to the expected level of gross profit on the sales achieved. Gross profit percentages for similar types of business are applied to the sales revenue for the year in question in order to obtain an estimate of cost of goods sold. Using the figures available for the opening stock and purchases made during the year, combined with the estimated costs of goods sold figure, the value of the closing stock may then be estimated. Any figure so estimated will be the subject of careful scrutiny by third parties (in particular the Inland Revenue). If the estimation exercise produces a stock figure way out of line with expectations, then a re-evaluation of all the above stages of analysis must be undertaken to ascertain whether any omissions have occurred.

Illustration 3

The owner of Errant Traders failed to take a stock count at 31 December 1983, the end of the accounting year. From an examination of the results of similar businesses and the mark-up applied by Errant to various products, it was estimated that the level of gross profit on sales should be of the order of 40 per cent. Schedules of closing debtors and creditors at 31 December 1983 totalled £5764 and £8340 respectively. Using this information together with that provided earlier in Illustrations 2 and 3, an estimate of the value of the closing stock at 31 December 1983 was made as follows:

Sales

Revenues received	73 575
Add closing debtors	5 764
	79 339
Less opening debtors	7 340
1983 Sales	£71 999

Cost of goods sold: £71 999 × 60/100 = £43 199

Purchases

Cash payments	839
Bank payments	41 463
Add closing creditors	8 340
	50 642
Less opening creditors	5 706
1983 Purchases	44 936
Add opening stock 1.1.83	14 250
	59 186
Less cost of goods sold	43 199
Closing stock 31.12.83	£15 987

(e) *Adjusting entries*

The adjusting entries made before the preparation of final accounts from incomplete records will be similar to those made with complete accounting records. Special attention will be focused on withdrawals made by the owner, either of goods or of cash, together with any payments made on behalf of the owner through the business bank account. Certain expenditures, identifiable as business expenses if made on behalf of employers, are not so treated if made on behalf of the owner. Payments made on behalf of, or to, owners are considered to be either distribution of profits or withdrawals of capital and not business expenses. This principle applies equally whether the payment is in the form of a salary paid to the owner, goods withdrawn for personal use, or even national insurance stamps bought on behalf of the owner.

Illustration 4

On the basis of data presented in Illustrations 1 to 3 together with the following additional information, the adjusting entries for Errant Traders at 31 December 1983 and entries reversing adjustments made in the previous years are provided in journal entry form in Table 11.3.

Additional data:

(i) Bank deposit interest for the year to 31st December 1983 amounted to £215.

(ii) Depreciation is to be charged on the new motor vehicle for the whole year using the sum-of-the-years digits basis and assuming a useful life of five years and residual value of £400 at the end of that time.

(iii) Depreciation is to be charged on fixtures and fittings on a reducing balance basis at 10 per cent per annum.

(iv) An electricity bill amounting to £420 was paid in February 1984 for the three months ended 31 January 1984.

(v) Property and contents insurance of £960 was paid in August 1983 for the year to 30 September 1984.

Forms of business organisation (I): sole traders and partnerships 223

The journal entries identified in Table 11.3 are recorded in the work-sheet illustrated in Table 11.4. The work-sheet provides a vital summary of all the data obtained through the stages identified earlier, in Sections (a) to (e).

(f) *Preparation of final accounts*

From the adjusted trial balance in Table 11.4, final accounts may be prepared for Errant Traders for the year ended 31 December 1983. The summarised Trading and Profit and Loss Account is shown in Table 11.5 and the Balance Sheet in Table 11.6.

One final act is necessary before the preparation of accounts from incomplete records is regarded as complete. The inadequacy of the prime data sources for the preparation of final accounts introduces an additional

TABLE 11.3

Errant Traders
Adjusting Entries – Journal Form

		£	£
debit	Bank deposit account	215	
credit	Profit and Loss account		215
Being interest earned on bank deposit account in 1983			
debit	Profit and Loss account	490	
credit	old motor vehicle account		490
Being loss on disposal: (£2250 − £1760)			
debit	Accumulated depreciation: motor	1925	
credit	Motor vehicle account		1925
Being accumulated depreciation of old vehicle			
debit	Profit and Loss Account	2000	
credit	Accumulated depreciation: motor		2000
Being depreciation on new motor for the year: $\frac{£(6400-400)}{15} \times 5$			
debit	Profit and Loss account	243	
credit	Accumulated depreciation: fixtures		243
Being depreciation for the year: £(1900 + 526) × 10%			
debit	Heat and Light expense a/c	280	
credit	Accrued expenses		280
Being accrued electricity at 31 December 1983: £420 × $\frac{2}{3}$			
debit	Prepaid expense	720	
credit	Insurance expense		720
Being insurance prepaid at 31 December 1983 £960 × $\frac{9}{12}$			
debit	Stock account	44 936	
credit	Trade creditors		44 936
Being goods purchased during 1983			

TABLE 11.4
Errant Traders
Work Sheet for the year ended 31 December 1983

	Opening Balance £	Bank Accounts £	Cash Account £	Adjusting Entries £	Adjusted Trial Balance £
Freehold premises	24 600				24 600
Furnishings and fittings	1 900	526			2 426
accumulated depreciation				243	243
Motor vehicle	4 175	6 400		490	6 400
accumulated depreciation	1 925			1 925	
				2 000	2 000
Stock	14 250			44 936 43 199	15 987
Trade debtors	7 340		73 575	71 999	5 764
Prepaid expenses	531			720 531	720
Cash on hand	375		73 575 72 780		1 170
Bank deposit account	2 568			215	2 783
Bank current account	1 518	60 899 61 238			1 179

	Dr	Cr	Dr	Cr	Dr	Cr	Dr	Cr	Dr	Cr
Trade creditors	5 706	41 463			839		44 936			8 340
Accrued expenses	240							280		280
Sales			9 724				71 999	240		71 999
Trade expenses				417		531		720	9 992	
Cost of goods sold						43 199			43 199	
Motor expenses					2 153				2 153	
Depreciation of motor						2 000			2 000	
Depreciation of fixtures						243			243	
Loss on disposal						490			490	
Repairs					196				196	
Wages					4 160				4 160	
Bank deposit interest						215				215
Owner's interest	49 386									49 386
Drawings			3 125		5 876			9 001		
Cash–bank–contra			59 139	59 139						
	£57 257	£57 257	£122 137	£122 137	£146 355	£146 355	£166 778	£166 778	£132 463	£132 463

TABLE 11.5

Errant Traders
Trading and Profit and Loss Account for the year ended 31 December 1983

	£	£
Sales:		71 999
Less cost of goods sold		43 199
Gross profit		28 800
Less		
Trade expenses	9992	
Motor expenses	2153	
Wages	4160	
Repairs	196	
Depreciation: motor vehicle	2000	
fixtures	243	
Loss on disposal of motor	490	19 234
Operating profit		9 566
Add Bank interest received		215
Net profit for year		£9 781

TABLE 11.6

Errant Traders
Balance Sheet at 31 December 1983

	£	£
Fixed assets		
Freehold premises at valuation		24 600
Fixtures and fittings	2 426	
Less accumulated depreciation	243	2 183
Motor vehicle	6 400	
Less accumulated depreciation	2 000	4 400
		31 183
Current assets		
Stock	15 987	
Debtors	5 764	
Prepayments	720	
Cash on hand	1 170	
Bank deposit account	2 783	
Bank current account	1 179	
	27 603	
Current liabilities		
Trade creditors	8 340	
Accrued expenses	280	
	8 620	
Net current assets		18 983
Total net assets		£50 166
Owner's interest		
Balance 1.1.83		49 386
Add net profit for year		9 781
		59 167
Less drawings		18 983
Balance 31.12.83		£50 166

degree of uncertainty to the results obtained. The accountant responsible for their production should therefore conduct a critical review of all the figures included in the final accounts to ascertain whether these appear to be reasonable, given the nature of the business and the owner's expectations. The review should involve comparison of the current year's results with those obtained in previous years, and wherever possible, with the results of similar businesses. Percentage relationships or ratios are often calculated to help the comparison (see Chapter 14). The accountant responsible for the accounts must exercise judgement in determining whether the amounts arrived in the final statements appear reasonable given the available accounting records and explanations. Where any doubt remains the owner should be questioned again, and the available accounting records re-examined, before the accountant approves the final accounts.

11.3 Value added tax

Introduction

Value added tax (VAT) is a tax on all taxable supplies of goods and services made in the United Kingdom by a taxable person in the course of any business which that person carries on. As such, VAT is an indirect form of taxation, with the ultimate burden of the tax falling on the eventual consumer of the goods and services taxed, and not on the business on which the impact of the tax initially falls. VAT is collected at each stage in the process of production and distribution of goods and services by taxable persons.

Any person who carries on a business which has a taxable turnover in excess of a prescribed minimum, currently £18 000, is a taxable person. The amount of VAT charged is calculated by the addition of a fixed percentage on to the cost of goods or services provided by the taxable person to customers. The total of VAT collected by the taxable person is described as *output tax* while the total tax borne by the taxable person on goods and services received is known as *input tax*. Each taxable person is liable to account to the Customs and Excise authorities for the excess of output over input tax, calculated on a three-monthly basis. If an excess of input tax over output tax occurs, then a repayment will be receivable from the Customs and Excise authorities.

There are currently two rates of VAT, a 'standard rate' and a 'zero rate'. The standard rate of VAT is currently fixed at 15 per cent although the Chancellor of the Exchequer has discretionary power to alter this rate by up to 10 per cent, i.e., up to 25 per cent or down to 5 per cent. Although it may seem strange to describe goods as 'zero rated' for tax purposes, the introduction of this category of goods as distinct from goods which are exempt from tax is an important one. *Zero rated goods* are technically taxable goods, and if a taxable body distributes zero rated goods then a claim may be made for repayment of all input tax incurred. However, if the taxable body distributes *exempt goods* then input tax must normally be apportioned between taxable and exempt outputs, with only the proportion of input tax relating to taxable outputs allowed as a deduction; a person cannot be registered for VAT if all outputs are exempt. Examples of goods and services falling within the various categories for VAT purposes are as follows:

Zero rated goods Basic foodstuffs, other than that supplied in the course of catering; books, newspapers, and periodicals; fuel and power, other than road fuel;

Standard rated goods Alcoholic and mineral drinks; petrol and diesel road and aviation fuel; letting of accommodation in hotels and similar establishments;

Exempt goods Insurance; postal services; finance services; education and health services.

The above examples of the tax categories are indicative of their general nature only. As with other aspects of taxation in the United Kingdom, there are many anomalies and students requiring information on the tax position of specific goods or services are recommended to obtain a copy of Guidance Note number 701 produced by the Customs and Excise authorities.[6]

Accounting for VAT

(a) *Introduction*

Each taxable person or business must prepare a summary of VAT transactions in a VAT account. The taxable persons will not themselves bear the direct cost of VAT except on non-deductible expenditures mentioned later. Indirect burdens are, however, faced by many businesses including the increased difficulty in raising prices, reduced demand on higher priced goods, and increased administration costs involved in acting as a 'collector of taxes'.

For a business which is accountable for VAT the cost of goods and services incurred and provided should be included in the accounting records 'net' of VAT. The amount of tax added to customers' invoices for goods sold or services rendered will be debited along with the cost of these goods and services to the individual customer's accounts or to cash, but the credit entry for the tax element will be to a Value Added Tax Account rather than to sales revenue.

Illustration 5

(a) The relevant accounting entry for goods sold for cash by Albert Products at a price of £115, including VAT at 15 per cent, will be:

		£	£
debit	Cash a/c	115	
credit	Sales revenue a/c		100
	VAT a/c		15

Being recording of cash sale and VAT thereon.

(b) Assuming that the above goods had been sold on credit terms to B. May, accounting entries relating to the sale of goods and ultimate payment by May are:

		£	£
debit	B. May a/c	115	
credit	Sales revenue a/c		100
	VAT a/c		15

Being recording of credit sale and VAT thereon

		£	£
debit	Cash a/c	115	
credit	B. May a/c		115

Being payment received from trade debtor

Similarly, the cost of goods and services acquired will be credited to cash or the relevant creditors account in total, but the debit entry will be partly to the Value Added Tax Account for the tax borne, if recoverable, and partly to the relevant asset or expense account.

Illustration 6
Raw materials were acquired by Albert Products at a cost of £230, including VAT at 15 per cent.
(a) Assuming that the goods were bought for cash, the relevant accounting entry to record the acquisition will be:

		£	£
debit	Stock a/c	200	
	VAT a/c	30	
credit	Cash a/c		230
Being cost of goods acquired, including VAT			

(b) Assuming that the above goods were purchased on credit terms, the relevant accounting entries including eventual payment are:

		£	£
debit	Stock a/c	200	
	VAT a/c	30	
credit	Trade creditor a/c		230
Being cost of goods acquired on credit terms			
debit	Trade creditor a/c	230	
credit	Cash a/c		230
Being payment made to trade creditor			

From the above illustrations, it may be observed that expense and revenue amounts will be included in the Income Statement *net* of VAT and stocks will also be included in the Balance Sheet *net* of VAT, but trade debtors and trade creditors will be included *gross* of VAT. The net amount of VAT due to, or from, the Customs and Excise will be included in the Balance Sheet 'as part of debtors and creditors'.[7]

(b) *Non-deductible VAT*
VAT is charged on certain expenditures for which no right of offset is available against VAT on outputs. The VAT charged on these expenditures must therefore be included as part of the cost of acquisition in the case of an asset, or as part of the expense incurred in other cases.

In the case of assets such as motor cars, on which no right of VAT offset is available, the depreciation expense and also the capital allowances will be calculated on the total cost inclusive of VAT.

In addition to the above, businesses which are not registered for VAT will bear VAT on purchases and other inputs but have no right to charge VAT on sales or other outputs. Hence, the cost of acquiring the inputs will be shown inclusive of the VAT for these businesses.

(c) *VAT and the recording process*
The system of accounting using day books, journals, etc., as described in

Chapters 5 and 6, requires only slight modification in order to account for VAT.

In the sales day book the total column will include the gross amount of sales including VAT, with the amount of each sale being posted individually from this column to the debit of the relevant debtors' account. An additional column will, however, be introduced in the day book to record the amount of VAT included in each sale with the periodic total of this column posted to the credit of the VAT account. Sales revenue, net of VAT, will be included in another day book column, or columns, according to whether the business wishes to sub-classify sales or not. The total of the net sales columns will be posted to the credit of the Sales Revenue account.

The purchases day book will similarly include a total column in which the gross cost of expenditures, or costs will continue to be shown. From the total column, individual amounts will be posted to the credit of the relevant creditor's accounts. An additional column will be included in the day book to record the VAT borne on purchases, with the periodic total of that column posted to the debit of the VAT account. Other columns categorising the type of purchase may be included, with the amount shown in these columns net of VAT. From these latter columns postings will be made to the debit of the relevant expense and/or asset accounts.

At the end of the quarterly tax period, a payment will be made to the Customs and Excise authorities, or received from them, depending on whether there is a credit or a debit balance on the VAT account.

If the accounting year end does not correspond to the date of settlement of the VAT account, an amount must be included in the Balance Sheet, either as a creditor for VAT payable, or as a debtor for VAT recoverable.

Illustration 7

The summarised totals of purchase and sales day books for Linden Industries are given below for their first three months of operations.

Purchase Day Book

	Total £	VAT £	Goods Purchased £	Operating Expenses £
Totals for three months	13 760	1748	9650	2362

Total VAT borne is not equal to 15 per cent of total (net) purchases and expenses as certain expenses will be zero rated, e.g., wages and power costs.

Sales Day Book

	Total £	VAT £	Sales £
Total for three months	16 330	2130	14 200

All sales for this company bear VAT at the rate of 15 per cent.

Accounting entries required to post the totals shown in the day books are as follows:

		£	£
debit	VAT a/c	1748	
	Stock a/c	9650	
	Operating expense a/c	2362	
credit	Trade creditors a/c		13 760

Being transfer of purchases made and VAT thereon

debit	Trade debtors a/c	16 330	
credit	Sales revenue a/c		14 200
	VAT a/c		2 130

Being transfer of sales made and VAT thereon

Assuming that no other VAT related transactions occur during the three months of operations and that the quarterly VAT account period corresponds with the end of the first three months of operations, a payment will be due to the Customs and Excise of

	£
VAT charged on outputs	2130
Less VAT borne on inputs	1748
Amount payable	£ 382

11.4 Partnerships

Introduction

(a) *The nature of a partnership*

A partnership is defined according to the 1890 Partnership Act as 'the relation which subsists between persons carrying on a business in common with a view of profit'.[8] Three essential elements have been identified to every partnership enterprise, namely, (i) a business; (ii) two or more persons carrying on that business in common; and (iii) a profit motive on the part of those persons.[9] Joint ownership or control of resources does not of itself constitute a partnership, nor does the operation of a business on behalf of others by an agent. An individual may be a partner in a business without sharing the profits other than by receipt of a fixed salary; in this case the individual would be described as a salaried partner.

The importance of identifying who is and who is not a partner in a particular business relates partly to the liability of the partnership as a whole, and partly to the actions of a partner as an agent binding the other partners to any obligations or transactions entered into.

Individuals enter into business partnerships with others for many diverse reasons, although most do so in order to pool individual resources, both financial and other, e.g., business or technical abilities and experiences.

(b) *The partnership agreement*

It is recommended that an agreement is drawn up before commencement of a partnership, to provide a yardstick for resolving any future conflicts which may arise. The partnership agreement will normally cover the following:

(i) the amount of permanent capital to be contributed by each partner;
(ii) the amount of interest, if any, to be paid on capital contributed, including any interest payable on capital contributed in excess of the amount agreed in (i), or the interest charged on the shortfall;
(iii) the maximum level of drawings allowed by each partner;
(iv) the basis of calculation of profits, e.g., whether extra-ordinary items are to be excluded or not, whether any partner's salary is to be deducted first, etc.;
(v) the amount of any salaries paid to partners;
(vi) the share of profits which each partner is entitled to;
(vii) the duties, powers and obligations of each partner;
(viii) the procedure for dissolution of partnership and admission of new partners.

Partnership accounts

(a) Introduction

Accounting records maintained by partnerships and the financial statements prepared will be based on the accounting principles outlined in earlier chapters, together with any further requirements laid down in the partnership agreement, or Section 24 of the 1890 Act. The major areas of difference between the financial accounts of partnerships and those of sole traders will be in relation to the division of profits and losses and the financial standing of individual partners in relation to the firm as a whole.

The books of account of a partnership are required to be maintained in good order at the place of business and to be available for inspection by any of the partners. A common practice in 'partnership accounting' is to maintain two separate ledger accounts for each partner; one to record the amount of capital which the partner has provided in accordance with any agreement made, the other to record any additional amounts contributed, together with all shares of profits less withdrawals from the business. The latter account is often described as a partner's current account, with the former described as the capital account of each partner.

(b) Division of profits

If a partnership agreement exists then this will normally state the basis for the division of profits and losses. Although there are many different bases possible, the most common appears to be a division in proportion to the amount of capital which each partner has agreed to contribute.

Division of profits and payment of agreed interest and/or salaries to partners normally takes place through an Appropriation Account, rather than the Profit and Loss Account.

Illustration 8

Faith, Hope and Charity, trading in partnership, have agreed to the division of profits in proportion to the capital contributed, after paying a salary to Faith of £3000, and interest of 10 per cent on closing balances on current accounts before apportionment of profits. The profit for the year to 31 December 1983 was £36 241. Additional information relating to capital and current accounts is as follows:

Capital Account balances, 31 December 1983:

	£
Faith	15 000
Hope	10 000
Charity	25 000
	£50 000

Current Account balances, 1 January 1983:

	£
Faith	9 390
Hope	10 210
Charity	7 390
	£26 990

Drawings for year to 31 December 1983:

	£
Faith	6 290
Hope	7 460
Charity	4 830
	£18 580

The appropriation account is given in Table 11.7 in vertical form.
The 1983 current accounts for each partner are shown in Table 11.8.

(c) *Changes in partnership*

Changes in partnership may come about by the retirement or death of an existing partner or admission of a new partner. Unless agreed otherwise by the remaining partners, retirement or death will lead to dissolution of the existing partnership, and subsequent creation of a new partnership by the remaining partners, if so desired. The retiring partner, or the estate if deceased, will be entitled to withdraw the agreed share of the assets of the old business and will be accountable for a share of debts and liabilities of the old partnership incurred up to the date of dissolution. There will often be a

TABLE 11.7

Faith, Hope and Charity
Appropriation Account
for the year ended 31 December 1983

	£	£
Profit for the year		36 241
Less Salary to Faith		3 000
		33 241
Interest on current accounts:		
Faith	310	
Hope	275	
Charity	256	841
		32 400
Share of profits:		
Faith (3/10)	9 720	
Hope (2/10)	6 480	
Charity (5/10)	16 200	32 400

TABLE 11.8

Faith Hope and Charity
Current Account

1983	Faith £	Hope £	Charity £	1983	Faith £	Hope £	Charity £
Drawings	6 290	7 460	4 830	Balances b/d	9 390	10 210	7 390
Balances c/d	16 130	9 505	19 016	Salary	3 000		
				Interest	310	275	256
				Share of profits	9 720	6 480	16 200
	£22 420	£16 965	£23 846		£22 420	£16 965	£23 846
				1984 Balance b/d	16 130	9 505	19 016

revaluation of the assets and liabilities after a change in a partnership in order to credit the old partners with their share of any goodwill which may have arisen, i.e., the excess of the value of the business as a going concern over the book value of the net assets. Any goodwill arising on revaluation, will be shared by the old partners in proportion to their profit sharing ratio.

A revaluation may also take place on the admission of a new partner, even if the existing partners continue in business, in order to credit the existing partners with their due share of any goodwill. If partners do not wish to retain goodwill in the books of account, then the goodwill will be removed by debiting the new partners current accounts in proportion to the revised profit-sharing ratio.

Illustration 9

Bushey, Bagot and Green have been in partnership for many years sharing profits equally. A new partner, Todd, will replace Green who is due to retire on 30 July 1984, the end of the partnership accounting year. Revaluation of net assets on 30 July 1984 gives rise to goodwill of £30 000. Goodwill is not to be retained in the books of account but to be written off in the new partner's current accounts, in proportion to their profit sharing ratios.

Toad has contributed £20 000 to be divided equally between capital and current accounts; he will receive a share of profits equal to half the amount received by Bushey and Bagot, i.e., the new profit sharing ratio is 4:4:2. Accounting entries relating to the goodwill are shown in Table 11.9 in the current accounts of the old and new partners.

Green, the retiring partner, will either immediately withdraw the amount of the balance on current account, together with the amount shown on capital account, or else retain a balance as a loan to the new partners, with interest payable at some agreed rate.

Other aspects of partnerships

(a) *Change in profit-sharing ratios*

When partners agree to change the way in which profits and losses are divided, then revaluation of the net assets of the business will normally be necessary. Any increase or reduction in valuation arising will be credited to partners in accordance with their old profit-sharing ratios. If revalued amounts are not subsequently to be retained in the accounting records, then any gain or loss arising on revaluation will be written off to the partners' accounts in accordance with their new profit-sharing ratios.

If a change in profit-sharing ratios takes place during an accounting year,

TABLE 11.9

Partnership Current Accounts

	Bushey £	Bagot £	Green £	Toad £		Bushey £	Bagot £	Green £	Toad £
Goodwill written off	12 000	12 000	—	6 000	Balances b/d	7 150	8 360	7 940	—
Cash withdrawn	—	—	17 940	—	Share of goodwill	10 000	10 000	10 000	—
Balances c/d	5 150	6 360	—	4 000	Cash introduced	—	—	—	10 000
	£17 150	£18 360	£17 940	£10 000		£17 150	£18 360	£17 940	£10 000
					Balances b/d	5 150	6 360	—	4 000

the profit or loss for the year must be apportioned on a time basis, unless separate profit statements are prepared for each part of the year.

Illustration 10
Cook and Parsons are in partnership, sharing profits in the proportion 1 to 2, after providing for a salary of £8000 for Cook. At 31 March 1984 the partnership agreement was changed to allow for an equal share of profits and losses, but with no salary in future payable to Cook. Net profits before partners' salary for the accounting year ended 30 June 1984 amounted to £40 000. Partnership assets were revalued at 31 March 1984 at £62 000, as compared to the book value of £47 000. The revaluation is not to be retained in the partnership books but should be dealt with through the partners' current accounts.

Apportionment of profits for the year to 30 June 1984 is as follows:

	£	£
(i) *9 months to 31 March 1984:*		
$\frac{3}{4} \times £40\,000$		30 000
Cook's salary: $\frac{3}{4} \times £8000$		6 000
		24 000
Share of profits: Cook	8 000	
Parsons	16 000	24 000
(ii) *3 months to 30 June 1984:*		
$\frac{1}{4} \times £40\,000$		10 000
Share of profits: Cook	5000	
Parsons	5000	10 000

Table 11.10 illustrates the partners' current accounts including allocation of profits, together with the adjustments arising on the revaluation of assets.

TABLE 11.10

Cook and Parsons: Current Accounts

	Cook £	Parsons £		Cook £	Parsons £
			Salary	6000	—
Revaluation of assets	7 500	7 500	Share of profits (i)	8 000	16 000
Balance c/d	16 500	23 500	Revaluation of assets	5 000	10 000
			Share of profits (ii)	5 000	5 000
	£24 000	£31 000		£24 000	£31 000
			Balance b/d	16 500	23 500

(b) *Conversion into Limited Company*

In order to achieve limited liability for the debts and obligations of the business without giving up control over day to day management, the partners may decide to convert the status of the business to that of a limited liability company.[10] The accounting entries relevant to the conversion will be similar to the adjustments explained earlier for changes in partnership, but with any revaluations on dissolution remaining in the partners' current accounts. The entries relevant to the formation of the limited liability company are the same as those which would be required for the formation of any limited liability company except that the payment for the share capital in the new company will partly be effected by transferring into the company certain assets (and liabilities) of the old partnership. An example of the accounting entries relating to formation of incorporated business is given in the following chapter.

Forms of business organisation (I): sole traders and partnerships 237

11.5 Summary

The current chapter has examined specific accounting matters relating to unincorporated businesses. In the main the accounting principles used in sole traders and partnerships will be the same as those adopted by incorporated businesses. Any differences which may exist normally relate to responsibilities to report to third parties. The owners of unincorporated businesses will normally have no general responsibilities to report to third parties and will themselves be in day-to-day contact with the business operations.

One of the major accounting problems facing sole traders is the inadequate maintenance of accounting records.

The introduction of VAT in 1973 placed obligations on registered businesses to maintain additional accounting records, including a VAT Account in which input tax and output tax are both recorded, together with any amounts owed to or by the Customs and Excise authorities.

Accounting for partnerships involves the added feature of apportionment of business profits and losses amongst the partners. A partnership agreement should be drawn up by the partners to deal with transactions taking place between them, including share of profits or losses, changes in partnership, revaluation of assets and dissolution of partnership.

Questions

1. Identify the accounting records which should ideally be maintained by the sole owner and manager of a small grocery shop, operating with a turnover of around £60 000 per annum.
2. Explain the purposes for which a sole trader may wish to prepare annual financial statements.
3. List the points which should ideally be included in a partnership agreement.

For each of the following **circle** the *letter* of the *best choice* from among the possible solutions presented.

4. 100 units of merchandise were acquired during 1983 by Douglas Traders at a total cost of £3910 (including VAT at 15 per cent). 50 units were subsequently sold at a price of £57.50 each, including VAT. The profit (or loss) on the sale of the 50 units was:

    (a) £1035 loss;
    (b) £920 profit;
    (c) £1175 profit;
    (d) £800 profit.

5. The totals of input and output taxes of Mordred Products for their first three months of trading were £11 600 and £12 400 respectively. As a result the VAT account will show:

    (a) a debit balance of £800 representing tax due to the Customs and Excise;
    (b) a credit balance of £800 representing tax recoverable;
    (c) a debit balance of £800 representing tax recoverable;
    (d) a credit balance of £800 representing tax due to the Customs and Excise.

6. Goods bought for resale at the end of the 1983 accounting year cost £2300 including VAT. The invoice for these goods remained outstanding at the Balance Sheet date and the goods were included in closing stock. The effect of the

purchase on net current assets (i.e., current assets less current liabilities) is as follows:

(a) £2300 increase;
(b) £300 increase;
(c) £300 decrease;
(d) no effect.

7. James and Andrew trade in partnership and share profits in the proportion 3 to 2 after deducting salaries of £6000 for James and £8000 for Andrew. Net profit for the year to 31 May 1984 was £30 000. The division of profits between the partners is:

(a) £15 600 James and £14 400 Andrew;
(b) £18 000 James and £12 000 Andrew;
(c) £17 600 James and £12 400 Andrew;
(d) £12 400 James and £17 600 Andrew.

Use the following information to answer Questions 8 to 10

Bill, Benn and Brown trade in partnership sharing profits in the proportion 3:2:1. In addition, Benn receives a salary of £3000 per annum. Net profits for 1981, 1982 and 1983 were £24 000, £27 300 and £28 500, respectively.

8. Benn's share of the total profits for the three years is:

(a) £26 600;
(b) £32 600;
(c) £35 600;
(d) £29 600.

9. If Brown had been guaranteed a minimum share of profits of £4000 per annum, Bill's share would have fallen, in total over the three years by:

(a) £300;
(b) £333;
(c) £120;
(d) £133.

10. Assume that a new partner was introduced at the commencement of the 1984 accounting year with profits subsequently shared equally by all partners and no salaries or guaranteed shares payable. 1984 profits were provisionally fixed at £42 000 but further examination revealed that the closing stock for 1983 had been understated by £6000. Adjustment for this error would require the following adjustment to Brown's share of profits for the four years:

(a) £500 reduction;
(b) £1250 increase;
(c) £1500 increase;
(d) £1000 reduction.

Problems

1. The Trial Balance of T. Randolph as on 31 December 1983 was as follows:

	£	£
Capital on 1 January 1983		40 000
Capital introduced on 1 July 1983		10 000
Drawings	3 780	
Plant and machinery	28 420	

	£	£
Motor vehicles	6 500	
Furniture and fittings	1 600	
Accumulated depreciation:		
Plant and machinery		9 420
Motor vehicles		2 500
Furniture and fittings		700
Debtors and creditors	13 200	16 400
Bank overdraft		3 490
Bank interest	250	
Stock on 1 January 1983	11 470	
Purchases and sales	88 490	141 200
Discounts	1 070	950
Office salaries	17 200	
Rent, rates and insurance	6 420	
Wages	39 410	
Advertising	5 830	
Bad debts written off	650	
Cash in hand	370	
	£224 660	£224 660

Additional information:
 (i) Stock on 31 December 1983 was valued at £12 690.
 (ii) Randolph drew a salary of £200 per month throughout the year, payments being debited to office salaries.
 (iii) No record has been made of a disposal of a motor vehicle that had originally cost £2500 and whose book value at 1 January was £1200. It was sold on credit for £1000 on 31 December 1983. A full year's depreciation should be provided at 20 per cent of book value on all motor vehicles held at the year end.
 (iv) Create a provision for bad debts of 1½ per cent of outstanding debtors.
 (v) Provide 10 per cent depreciation on the book value of plant and machinery and 15 per cent on the cost of furniture and fittings.
 (vi) Rent due but unpaid at 31 December 1983 is £810. Insurance premiums paid in March 1983 for the year to 30 April 1984 amounted to £690.

Prepare a Trading and Profit and Loss Account for T. Randolph for the year ended 31 December 1983 and a Balance Sheet as that date.

2. J. Maxwell, the owner of a retail shop, maintains very elementary business accounting records. From an analysis of bank statements for the year ended 30 April 1983 the following summary of bank receipts and payments was prepared:

Receipts	£
Takings banked	119 500
Sale of motor car	2 400
Additional capital introduced	10 000
	£131 900

Payments	
Purchase of motor vehicle	7 600
Trade creditors for goods	34 300
Operating expenses	27 900
Wages to employees	31 600
Private payments	6 300
	£107 700

Business assets and liabilities at 1 May 1982 and 30 April 1983 were identified as follows:

	1.5.82	30.4.83
Trade debtors	34 600	41 800
Accrued expenses	490	370
Trade creditors	16 950	18 960
Bank overdraft	2 730	—
Shop premises, at cost	30 000	30 000
Stock of goods for resale	21 480	23 140
Cash in hand	350	460

In addition the following information was obtained:

(i) Cheques paid to suppliers and amounting to £1150, had not yet been presented at the bank at the year end, although the list of trade creditors had been drawn up after allowing for these payments.

(ii) Summarised cash payments made during the year were:

	£
Payments to owner	7480
Casual wages to part-time employees	1150
Purchases	375
General expenses	865

All cash receipts were from customers.

(iii) The motor vehicle sold during the year was valued on 1 May 1982 at £4200. The new motor vehicle was acquired on 1 August 1982 and is to be depreciated on a reducing balance basis at 25 per cent per annum. Depreciation for the first year of ownership is to be apportioned on a time basis.

(iv) Shop fittings and furnishings at 1 May 1982 were valued at £8500. These are to be depreciated on a straight-line basis over 10 years assuming zero salvage value.

(v) No depreciation is to be charged on the shop premises.

Prepare the following:

(a) A statement identifying owner's interest at 1 May 1982;
(b) Ledger accounts to record the transactions which have taken place during the year to 30 April 1983;
(c) Trading, Profit and Loss Account for the year ended 30 April 1983 and a Balance Sheet on that date.

3. The following information was extracted from the accounting records of Higham Products for the three-month VAT period ending on 31 March 1984.

(i) Balances at:

	1.1.84	31.3.84
Trade debtors	34 500	32 200
Trade creditors	19 550	24 500
Accrued expenses	8 050	7 590
Stocks	46 000	55 200

(ii) Receipts from customers £88 895;
(iii) Payments to suppliers £43 700;
(iv) Payments for operating expenses £24 380;
(v) VAT payable 1 January 1984, £180.

All goods bought and sold are subject to VAT at the standard rate, as are all expenses, apart from £3200 relating to exempt goods.

Prepare the following for the first three months of 1984:

(a) a VAT account;
(b) a summarised Income Statement.

12 Forms of Business Organisation (II): Incorporated Businesses

12.1 Introduction

The need to produce financial accounting reports is greater for incorporated businesses than for unincorporated businesses for a number of reasons including:

(i) the separation of ownership from control, giving rise to the need to provide stewardship reports;
(ii) the privilege of limited liability status, requiring some counter-measures to protect creditors' interests and to ensure their continued co-operation;
(iii) the size and influence of the corporate sector, requiring some degree of accountability to the public at large.

Although reporting requirements may be placed on individual companies by the shareholders and even at times by the creditors, specific reporting requirements are placed on all companies by company legislation. In addition, the recommendations made in Statements of Standard Accounting Practices (SSAPs) are generally more likely to be followed by the corporate sector, not least because of the need for auditors to report on compliance with the SSAPs.

In the current chapter the general features of incorporated businesses will be examined, whilst the following chapter will consider the specific accounting problems and reporting requirements of this category of business.

12.2 Features of incorporated businesses

Categories of corporate status

An incorporated business may be formed by two or more individuals 'subscribing their names to a memorandum of association and otherwise complying with the requirements of the Companies Acts 1948–81 in respect of registration'.[1]

Three categories of corporate status are recognised in law, namely:

(i) Companies having the liability of members limited by the memorandum to the amount, if any, unpaid on the shares held by them, i.e., *a company limited by shares*. The majority of companies fall within this category.
(ii) Companies having the liability of members limited by the memorandum to the amount which the members have undertaken to contribute in the event of the company being wound-up, i.e., *a company limited by guarantee*.
(iii) Companies not having any limit on the liability of the members, i.e., *an unlimited company*.

Companies may also be categorised as either public or private. A *public company* is one in which members' liability is limited either by shares or by guarantee (but having a share capital) and which is stated to be a public company in the memorandum of association and is registered as such under the provisions of the Companies Acts. A private company is defined in law as one which is not a public company.

The major feature distinguishing a private company from a public company is that a private company is not allowed to offer either shares or debentures in the company to the general public.

Company registration

After the passing of the 1844 Joint Stock Companies Act it became possible to form a company merely by registering with the relevant authority, i.e., the Registrar of Companies. On registration, the following documents have to be delivered to the Registrar:

(i) the memorandum of association;
(ii) the articles of association;
(iii) a list of the names of individuals who have agreed to act as directors, with a minimum of two in the case of a public company and one in the case of a private company;[2]
(iv) a statement of the authorised nominal share capital;
(v) a statement giving the intended situation of the company's registered office;
(vi) a statutory declaration that the requirements of the Companies Acts 1948–81 have been complied with.

Memorandum and articles of association

The memorandum of association describes and governs the relationship between the company and the outside world.

The memorandum states:

(i) the name of the company, including the ending 'limited' in the case of private companies and 'public limited company' (PLC) in the case of public companies;

(ii) the country in which the registered office is to be situated, i.e., England, Scotland or Wales;
(iii) a statement that the liability of the members is limited, if this is indeed the case;
(iv) for a company limited by guarantee, a statement regarding each member's guarantee and the maximum amount thereof;
(v) for a company limited by shares, the nominal value of proposed share capital and the number of shares;
(vi) a statement defining the objects of the company, often in fairly wide terms;
(vii) a list of the subscribers to the share capital, with a minimum of two persons both for public and for private companies (Companies Act 1980, S.2(1)), together with their addresses and descriptions, plus the number of shares which each subscriber will take up.

The articles of association govern the internal regulations for the management of the company and also relations with, and among, shareholders. Many companies adopt, with minor amendments, the regulations included in Schedule 1, Table A of the 1948 Companies Act. These regulations deal with the following matters:

(i) the rights attached to the different categories of shareholders;
(ii) transfer of shares;
(iii) alteration of share capital;
(iv) general and special meetings; including the required length of notice to be given, timing, proceedings and voting;
(v) directors; their appointment and removal, remuneration powers and duties;
(vi) maintenance of accounting records and right of inspection by members;
(vii) capitalisation of profits; procedures and limitations;
(viii) notices to members; form, timing, right to receive;
(ix) appointment of auditors; duties and means of appointment;
(x) winding-up; division of property.

Directors

The first directors are appointed by the original subscribers to the company. At the first annual general meeting all these directors will retire from office but may offer themselves for re-election by the shareholders. At the end of each subsequent annual general meeting one-third of the directors (or as close an approximation as is possible) will retire from office, with the longest serving directors retiring first.

Directors' remuneration will be fixed by the company in general meeting. In effect, the shareholders are presented with annual accounts which include provisional figures for the remuneration of the directors for the past accounting year. If, and when, the shareholders approve the annual accounts, they are effectively approving directors' remuneration also. The annual accounts must therefore provide detailed information relating to directors' remuneration.[3]

The operations of the company are managed by the directors and it is they who are ultimately responsible for any breaches of law by the company or its employees, acting on their instructions.

Authorised share capital

The amount of share capital which the directors of a company are authorised to issue is stated in the memorandum of association together with the number of shares which this represents; for example, £500 000 authorised share capital divided into two million shares each with a nominal value of 25 pence.

The amount of the authorised share capital may be altered, subject to the approval of the ordinary shareholders in the manner laid down in the articles.

Increases in share capital will require the approval of shareholders, by means of an ordinary resolution requiring 21 days' notice, while reductions require both a special resolution with 28 days' notice, and subsequently formal confirmation by the courts. The additional requirements placed on resolutions to reduce authorised share capital exist in order to provide safeguards to the creditors of the company who might otherwise lose some of their security for money owed to them.

Despite the recommendations of a number of influential committees, including the Wilson Committee,[4] companies are not allowed to issue shares at a discount below the nominal share price (or *par value*). The inability to issue shares at a discount means that it will not normally be possible for a company to issue additional share capital when the market value is below the nominal value.

Although the opportunity to repurchase redeemable shares (see later) has been available for many years, it was not until after the 1981 Companies Act[5] that a company was given the legal right to repurchase its own ordinary shares. The legal right to repurchase shares must in addition be given in the articles of association, and must also be authorised by the shareholders, normally by means of a general resolution. One of the main advantages which the above right confers on a company is the opportunity to fight off an unwelcome takeover bid by purchasing the shares of dissatisfied shareholders.

Separate legal entity

One of the major advantages of corporate status over other forms of business organisation, is that a company is regarded as a legal person in its own right, with an existence separate from that of its members. This separate legal identity ensures continuation of the company after the death or retirement of the original members or directors in contrast to the position of unincorporated businesses which are normally deemed to be dissolved on the death or retirement of the owners.

The ownership of a company is transferable by means of the sale of the ordinary shares. Shares in a public company will normally be easier to dispose of than those of a private company, particularly if the former are quoted on a recognised security exchange, such as the United Kingdom Stock Exchange.

A company with a separate legal status may enter into debts and contracts

Forms of business organisation (II): incorporated businesses

in its own right through agents, and will be personally liable on these. In the case of companies in which liability is limited by shares, the liability of the members will be restricted to the amount, if any, unpaid on the shares which they have contracted for. Investing in a company therefore places less of the property of an owner at risk than investing in a partnership or sole trading entity.

One final feature of corporate status is that the company will be liable to corporation tax on profits earned while the shareholders themselves will only be liable to income tax on any profits distributed to them in the form of dividends.[6]

12.3 Forms of share capital

Introduction

There are two major categories of share capital, namely ordinary shares and preference shares, each of which exists in a variety of forms. Not all companies have an authorised preference share capital, but all public companies limited by shares must have an authorised ordinary share capital of at least £50 000. There is no legally defined minimum share capital for private companies, only a requirement to state the authorised amount in the memorandum of association.

The rights of the different classes of shareholders, laid down in the articles of association, may only be varied with the consent of the holders of three-quarters of the nominal values of that class of shares, by means of an extraordinary resolution passed at a special meeting of that class of shareholders.

Ordinary Share Capital

(a) *Introduction*

Ordinary shareholders are the ultimate owners of a company, possessing the right to share in the profits (and losses) of the company and ultimate disposal proceeds on dissolution, in proportion to the number of shares which they hold. Ordinary shareholders are, however, residual claimants and are therefore the major risk holders in a company as their claims can only be met after all other prior claims have been satisfied.

Ordinary shares may be issued *fully paid* or *partly paid*. In the latter case the holder will be liable to any further calls which the company may wish to make up to the value of the amount unpaid.

(b) *Dividend entitlements*

As residual claimants to profits, etc., ordinary shareholders face the greatest risks of all investors in a business but in return they also expect to receive the greatest benefits. A general rule applicable to all investments is that the greater the risk on the investment, the greater will be the expected benefits. Note that there is a difference between benefits expected and benefits achieved; the presence of risk by implication involves the possibility that expected returns will not be achieved.

Ordinary shareholders receive a return on their investment either through their share of profits distributed through dividends, or else by means of a capital gain on ultimate disposal of the shareholding. There is no legal obligation placed on a company to declare dividends, although most, if not all, profitable companies will eventually do so. Indeed, the eventual price obtained on disposal of a shareholding will be based on the future dividend stream expected from the shares by the new owner.

Dividends are paid net of income tax to shareholders, with an imputed tax credit attached. Shareholders not liable to income tax will be able to recover an amount equal to the imputed credit from the Inland Revenue authorities. Only those individuals who are liable to income tax at a higher rate than base rate, or who receive more than £6250 dividend income[7] (including the imputed tax credit) from UK companies, will be required to pay additional income tax.

Illustration 1
J. Whyte owns 1000 shares in Dornan Products Ltd on which a dividend of 70 pence per share is declared. Base rate of income tax currently stands at 30 per cent.
The total dividend received by J. Whyte is £700, equivalent to a gross dividend of £700 × 100/30 = £1000, including the imputed tax credit of £300.

The directors recommend the level of dividends to be paid, subject to the approval of the shareholders in general meeting. Shareholders have a right to reduce the dividend below the level proposed by the directors, but not to increase the level. Interim dividends may also be declared by the directors from time to time, out of distributable profits.

(c) *Voting rights*
Although there are other varieties of ordinary shares possessing different entitlements, most ordinary shares will entitle the holder to the possession of one vote for every share held. Other voting entitlements range from no votes under ordinary circumstances on 'A' ordinary shares, to the multiple votes of deferred or founders' shares.

Proxy votes may be given to nominees on behalf of shareholders unable, or unwilling, to attend meetings. The proxy vote must be made in writing by the shareholder or an attorney duly authorised by the shareholder, and may be granted to a nominee who is not personally a member of the company.

Preference share capital
(a) *Introduction*
Preferences share capital is equity capital containing some of the characteristics of debt capital (see later). Rights as to voting entitlements, dividends and repayment, may vary from company to company and depending on the terms of each share issue. As a general rule, however, preference shareholders rank before ordinary shareholders with regard to dividends and repayment of capital but after interest bearing, and other, creditors.

(b) *Dividend entitlement*
Preference shares are normally issued with a stated rate of dividend (net of tax) payable on the nominal amount of the preference capital. In addition *participating preference shares* may also be issued which confer upon the

Forms of business organisation (II): incorporated businesses

holder the right to a further dividend once the ordinary share dividend has exceeded a specified amount.

Although the holders of preference shares are not automatically entitled to receive a dividend, most issues of preference capital are normally in the form of *cumulative preference shares*. With cumulative preference shares the holder will be assured that even if no dividend was paid on preference shares for a number of years, the arrears would eventually have to be paid before the ordinary shareholders become entitled to receive any dividend.

Illustration 2
The Balance Sheet for Wilson Fabrics Ltd shows the following issued share capital:

	£
10 000 £1 ordinary shares, fully paid	10 000
5 000 £1 cumulative preference shares, 7%	5 000
5 000 £1 non-cumulative preference shares, 8.4%	5 000
	£20 000

According to the articles of association of Wilson Fabrics, the non-cumulative preference shares rank for dividend before the cumulative preference shares.

The directors of Wilson Fabrics decide to pay no dividends for Years 1 and 2 but wish to pay a dividend to ordinary shareholders in Year 3. Before paying the ordinary dividend in Year 3 preference dividends must be paid as follows:

	£
Non-cumulative preference dividend:	
one year: £5000 × 8.4%	420
Cumulative preference dividend:	
three years: £5000 × 7% × 3	1050
	£1470

(c) *Other features*

Redeemable preference shares may be issued, with an obligation on the part of the issuing company to repay the preference capital at some future date, or within some period of time, either at par or at a premium over the nominal value.

Convertible preference shares may also be issued which offer the holder the right to convert to ordinary shares at some future time, in accordance with some predetermined formula.

Preference shares have been an unpopular form of long-term finance for companies since the mid-1960s because dividends are not a deductible expense for corporation tax purposes, unlike interest on borrowed funds. A slight renewal in popularity has occurred over the last few years, however, because of the relatively high level of interest rates on borrowed funds.

12.4 Debenture capital

Introduction

Unlike other forms of business organisation, companies may borrow funds through the issue of securities known as *debenture stock*. Debenture stock is transferable to new holders, with all the rights attached, in the same way in which equity capital is transferable. Unlike equity capital, however, debenture stock is not part of ownership capital and no voting rights are attached to the stock, unless the company defaults on its obligations under the debenture trust deed.

Debenture capital is normally issued in amounts of £100 nominal value, offering interest at a fixed rate, although a few issues have been made recently at variable rates of interest as hedges against inflation. As debenture interest is not considered to be a distribution of income to the owners, it is included as a financial expense in Income Statements (and is also an allowable deduction from profits for corporation tax purposes).

Trustees are normally appointed to look after the interests of the debenture holders under the terms of a trust deed which will be drawn up specifying various rights attached to the debentures, including:

(i) the rate and date of interest payments;
(ii) action available in respect of any interest arrears;
(iii) security available on the loan;
(iv) redemption and conversion rights, if any.

Security offered

Debenture capital is often held by investors who are unwilling to hold more risky investments, such as equity capital. In order to ensure the success of a debenture issue, a company will therefore normally feel obliged to offer some form of security to guarantee the repayment of loans advanced. If no security is advanced then the debenture will be described as an *unsecured debenture*.

Security for debentures may come in the form of a *fixed charge* on specific assets of the company, i.e., a mortgage debenture, or as a *floating charge* over all the assets of the company. The advantage to the debenture holder of a fixed charge security, is that this will involve readily identifiable assets, often with known values. Debenture issues possessing a floating charge will allow the directors of a company to proceed with disposal and renewals of fixed assets, normally without being in default of trust deeds. A floating charge becomes fixed, only if the company defaults on any of its obligations under the debenture trust agreement.

Debentures are normally redeemable at the end of a fixed period of time, specified in the trust deed. Only in very exceptional cases will an irredeemable debenture be issued, as the risks attached, both in terms of future levels of interest rates and security available on the loan, will be too high for most potential debenture holders.

Convertible debentures have been a feature of the last twenty years or so, with loan capital issued at rates slightly lower than the market would normally dictate but with the added attraction that the debentures may be converted into ordinary shares at some future period of time and in accordance with some predetermined formula, at the option of the debenture holder. If conversion rights are not exercised at the end of the agreed time period then the trust deed will normally provide for the convertible debenture to be redeemed.

Debenture versus equity issues

The decision by a company as to whether additional long-term capital should be raised through an issue of debentures or an issue of ordinary shares (or preference shares) will depend on a number of factors, including the following:

(i) the current level of gearing, i.e., the level of debenture capital to equity capital in the company's financial structure;
(ii) the expected variability of future income and cash flow streams, together with the amount of the possible interest payments to be made;
(iii) current commitments for other fixed payments, including payments for leased assets;
(iv) current interest rates and the expected trend in future long-term interest rates;
(v) security available both for the proposed loan, and for any prior ranking debentures issued by the company;
(vi) recent capital market reaction to issues of ordinary shares and debentures either by the company itself or by companies with similar business and financial characteristics;
(vii) willingness, or otherwise, of existing shareholders to dilute control, i.e., reduce their proportion of total shares issued;
(viii) likelihood that sufficient taxable profits will be generated in the near future to take advantage of the deductibility of interest payments.

On the final note, readers are reminded that private companies are not allowed by law to offer debentures for sale to the general public.

12.5 Security issues

Marketability

(a) *Introduction*
There are a number of different ways in which securities may be issued, some of which are restricted to public companies. The different methods for issuing securities have been designed to try and ensure the greatest likelihood that an issue will be successful, whatever the status of the company or the prevailing economic climate.

The more marketable a security is, the greater will be the likelihood that the response to a new issue will be favourable. Marketability is greatly improved by having the security quoted, or listed, on a recognised stock exchange. The United Kingdom Stock Exchange lists around 5000 company securities, of which about 1000 are preference shares and the remainder are divided fairly evenly between ordinary shares and debentures.[8]

In addition to the listed market, the Stock Exchange has operated, since 1980, a smaller Unlisted Securities Market (USM). The USM was formed to help small companies and those unwilling to have a high proportion of their equity capital in the hands of the investing public at large: 25 per cent is required in the case of a full listing but only 10 per cent in the case of the USM. One hundred and seventy-one companies were admitted to listing on the USM during the first thirty months of trading.[9]

A smaller, but earlier, version of the USM was founded by a licensed firm of security dealers and named the Over-the-Counter Market. This market now deals in the securities of approximately twenty companies, under the direction of Granville & Co. Ltd (formerly M. J. H. Nightingale & Co. Ltd).

(b) *Stock Exchange Introduction*

One way a public company may obtain a Stock Exchange listing for its ordinary shares without actually issuing additional shares is by means of a Stock Exchange Introduction.

Before obtaining a listing the company concerned must first obtain the permission of various sub-committees of the Council of the Stock Exchange, together with the support of at least two jobbers (dealers in securities). Advertisements will then be placed in two leading London (or national) daily newspapers and information provided to various statistical services. A limited number of shares, sufficient to ensure that a free market has been created for the securities in question will then be offered for sale via the supporting jobbers.

One recent example of a Stock Exchange Introduction was that of the ordinary shares of Bespak plc in August 1983. The ordinary shares of the company had previously been listed on the USM. The aims of the switch to full listing in this case appeared to be the widening of the share ownership base and the additional stability and prestige accorded to companies listed on the full market.[10]

(c) *Underwriting*

In order to insure a security issue against possible lack of demand by investors, companies may obtain the services of underwriters who will undertake to purchase any securities not taken up by the general public. The underwriters will obtain a fee for this service, normally amounting to around $1\frac{1}{4}$ per cent of the proceeds of the issue and payable whether the issue was a success or not. The principal underwriter will normally be a specialist issuing house who will often arrange for the issue to be sub-underwritten by other financial institutions.

Obtaining the services of an underwriter will produce benefits in two ways: first, the issuing company is guaranteed receipt of the funds required; second, the demand for the company's shares, and subsequent share price, will often be enhanced by the knowedge that a specialist issuing house is willing to be recognised with the issuing company.

Methods of issue

Table 12.1 identifies the major sources of finance for UK industrial and commercial companies in recent years and contrasts the amount of capital raised through new issues with the amount provided through retained earnings. As the table demonstrates, retained earnings are by far the major source of additional finance to these companies. However, the new issues

TABLE 12.1 Sources of finance: industrial and commercial companies (£ billion)

	Internal* funds	Bank borrowing	Other loans and mortgages	UK capital issues	Other sources
1978	16.2	3.0	0.5	0.8	1.2
1979	17.5	4.8	0.7	0.9	2.1
1980	13.7	7.2	0.3	1.3	1.8
1981	15.5	7.1	1.1	1.7	1.9
1982	13.4	7.3	0.9	0.9	1.7

*Retained profits after providing for stock appreciation.
SOURCE: *Bank of England Quarterly Bulletin*, vol. 23, no. 2, June 1983, p. 236.

market is also important as it often provides capital to the more profitable and faster growing areas of the economy.

(a) *Rights issue*
Using this method, a company offers existing shareholders the right to subscribe cash for additional shares in proportion to their existing shareholdings. The subscription price will normally be at a discount below the currently quoted market price (but above nominal price). If shareholders are unwilling, or unable, to take up their right then they have the opportunity to sell the rights on the Stock Exchange. The essential feature of a rights issue is that the shareholder should be no worse off after the issue than before, whether their entitlement is taken up in full, in part, or not at all.

Rights issues have provided most of the new external funds for companies in recent years. This result is due in part to the Stock Exchange requirement that a listed company must issue new shares to existing shareholders, unless the prior approval of these shareholders had been obtained at a general meeting.

A recent example of a rights issue is the one made by Midland Bank plc in August 1983 which raised £155 million by means of one new share for every four held at a subscription price of £3.50 per share.[11]

(b) *Prospectus issue*
A Prospectus issue, or public issue, involves an offer direct to the public by the company of a fixed number of shares at a fixed price. A financial institution, known as an Issuing House, specialising in share issues will normally be employed as agents for the company and act as advisers to the issue. The issuing house will also normally arrange for the issue to be underwritten.

One of the main features of the prospectus issue is the amount of detail which the issuing company must provide to prospective shareholders, both in public advertisements and also in a comprehensive prospectus.

Companies making prospectus issues must obtain the permission of the Stock Exchange before dealings can commence in the shares issued. Additionally, in the case of a company already listed, prior agreement of the existing shareholders must be obtained. The method is normally only used for exceptionally large issues, and has rarely been used in the last few years, partly because of the reduced number of companies applying for Stock Exchange listing in recent years, and partly because of the lower cost of the offer for sale method.

(c) *Offer for sale*

As with the prospectus issue, an offer for sale involves an issue of shares to the public at large. Unlike a prospectus issue, however, the issue is first sold by the company to the issuing house at an agreed price. The issuing house will then offer the shares for sale to the general public, normally at a slightly higher price to cover fees and costs involved. The issuing house may also underwrite the issue and will be obliged to advertise the offer by means of a prospectus document and similar advertisements to those required for the prospectus method of issue.

As with the prospectus issue, an offer for sale can only be made by a public company, and will normally be made on behalf of a previously unlisted company.

The offer for sale method has been used more frequently in recent years than the prospectus issue. Issuing houses using this method have come in for some degree of criticism for underestimating the demand for shares issued by this method, i.e., undervaluing the shares. One outstanding example of this was the offer for sale of shares in Eurotherm Ltd in 1978 when the demand for shares was 85 times greater than the number of shares on offer.[12] On the other hand, other isues have suffered from an overestimation of demand and share value, as for example, in the recent offer of shares in Technology For Business plc which was 34 per cent undersubscribed.[13] Using the offer for sale method, the company is at least guaranteed the receipt of the required funds from the issuing house, whatever the eventual public demand for the issue.

(d) *Placement*

Placements may be made privately by unlisted companies, or by listed companies with the permission of the Stock Exchange.

Using this method, shares are sold to clients of an issuing house (or broker) which acts as the agent for the issuing company. The issue may be undertaken to obtain additional finance for the company or merely to allow existing shareholders to dispose of a portion of their holdings. Placements may also be undertaken together with a Stock Exchange introduction in order to obtain a listing for the securities issued.

The method is normally only allowed for the shares of listed companies if there is likely to be a limited demand for the shares issued, or if the amount involved is relatively small compared to the costs which would be incurred using other methods of issue.

A recent placement made by Oceonics plc in August 1983, involving 1.75 million new ordinary shares at a price of £2.85 each and 3 million 10.75 per cent cumulative redeemable preference shares, raised £8 million. At the same time the company, which was previously listed on the USM, gained a full Stock Exchange listing.[14]

(e) *Tender Issue*
One method which has gained some notoriety recently but which has otherwise been used relatively infrequently is the tender method. This method is similar to that of an auction for shares, with a stated number of shares being put on offer to the general public and only a minimum offer price stated in the prospectus. Investors are then invited to subscribe for shares at a price chosen by themselves but above the minimum stated price. Once all the bids are received shares will be allocated to subscribing investors at one price only, which is set sufficiently low to ensure that the maximum amount of capital is raised. The tender method is useful for those issues for which no accurate estimate of likely demand is available (see the Eurotherm issue earlier). The issue of shares in Britoil plc made on 19 November 1982 was an illustration of a relatively unsuccessful use of the tender method. The lack of success of that particular issue may be blamed partly on the uncertainty attached to the price of oil at that time, and perhaps also on the use, as sub-underwriters, of a substantial number of institutional investors who might otherwise have been expected to tender for the issue themselves; there was no incentive for the latter to subscribe for the shares at a price above the minimum subscription price.

A tender offer that was successful was made by SR Gent plc in June 1983 when the minimum tender price for 9 million shares on offer was set at £1.60 but the striking price was eventually set at £1.90 after the offer was oversubscribed.[15]

12.6 Accounting for security issues

Forming a company

(a) *Preliminary expenses*
When a company is founded, either by conversion of an unincorporated business, or from first beginnings, expenses will be incurred by the founders. These expenses include:

(i) Stamp duties and fees on the nominal amounts of authorised share capital and on any contracts drawn up to transfer assets into the ownership of the company;
(ii) Legal and accounting costs of preparing the memorandum and articles of association and other related matters.

The above expenses, together with any other preliminary or formation expenses, will be charged to a Preliminary expenses account, and should in theory, subsequently be amortised over the life of the company. The 1981 Companies Act, however, prohibits formation expenses from being treated as an asset, with a similar prohibition applying to expenses and commissions involved with the issue of securities. Instead, these items must all be written off through the Profit and Loss Account of the year in which they were incurred.[16]

(b) *Conversion to incorporated status*
Many companies are formed by the conversion of previously unincorporated businesses, whose owners wish to obtain the advantages of corporate status.

In order to record the cessation of the old business, a Realisation Account must be opened in the books of account into which the balances on asset and liability accounts will be transferred. The transfer may be accompanied by a general revaluation of the assets of the old business. Any gain or loss on revaluation of the assets will be transferred to the owner's account in the case of a sole trader, or to partners' accounts in proportion to their profit-sharing ratios in the case of partnerships.

An account will also be opened in the name of the new company which will be debited with the value assigned to the net assets taken over by the new company, the corresponding credit being made in the Realisation Account.

The account in the name of the new company will then be credited with the agreed value of shares and other consideration offered to the owner(s) of the unincorporated business, with the corresponding debit made in the relevant owner(s) capital accounts.

Illustration 3
The United Company Limited was formed to purchase the business of L. Andrew and H. David who share profits equally, and whose summarised closing Balance Sheet was as shown in Table 12.2.

TABLE 12.2

Andrew and David
Balance Sheet

	£	£
Fixed assets		42 500
Current assets	17 600	
Less current liabilities	6 400	
		11 200
Total net assets		£53 700
Capital accounts:		
L. Andrew		30 150
H. David		23 550
		£53 700

The new company is to take over the total net assets of the old business at a valuation of £60 000. The purchase consideration consists of 40 000 £1 ordinary shares and £20 000 10 per cent debenture stock, both issued at par. Each of the old partners will receive 20 000 shares in the new company and any remaining balance due to them will be settled using the debenture stock.

Journal entries to record the transfer in the books of the old business are:

		£	£
debit	United Co. Ltd account	60 000	
credit	Realisation account		60 000
	Being agreed purchase consideration		

Forms of business organisation (II): incorporated businesses

debit	Realisation account	53 700	
	Current liabilities accounts	6 400	
credit	Fixed asset accounts		42 500
	Current asset accounts		17 600
Being transfer of net assets.			

debit	Realisation account	6 300	
credit	L. Andrew, Capital account		3 150
	H. David, Capital account		3 150
Being gain on revaluation of old business assets, shared equally.			

debit	Ordinary shares (in United Co. Ltd) account	40 000	
	Debentures (in United Co. Ltd) account	20 000	
credit	United Co. Ltd account		60 000
Being satisfaction of purchase consideration			

debit	L. Andrew account	33 300	
credit	Ordinary Shares (in United Co. Ltd) account		20 000
	Debentures (in United Co. Ltd) account		13 300
Being transfer of securities to L. Andrew			

debit	H. David account	26 700	
credit	Ordinary shares (in United Co. Ltd) account		20 000
	Debentures (in United Co. Ltd) account		6 700
Being transfer of securities to H. David			

Assuming that the gain on revaluation of the net assets of the old business will be recorded as Goodwill, journal entries opening the accounts of the new company will be as follows:

		£	£
debit	Fixed assets accounts	42 500	
	Goodwill account	6 300	
	Current assets accounts	17 600	
credit	Current liabilities accounts		6 400
	Ordinary share capital		40 000
	10 per cent debentures		20 000
Being net assets acquired and securities issued as purchase consideration			

New Issues

(a) *Share premium account*

When a company issues shares, either for cash or other consideration, at a value in excess of the nominal value then the excess must be transferred to a Share Premium Account. The balance on the Share Premium Account is treated as being equivalent to the paid-up share capital of the company, which is what it effectively is, and is not available for distribution as dividends to the members of the company. The balance on the share premium account may only be utilised for certain specified purposes, e.g., in writing-off the following:

(i) preliminary expenses of the company;
(ii) expenses paid on the issue of shares or debentures;
(iii) premium payable on redemption of debentures.

Illustration 4
The Angelica Co. Ltd made an issue of one million £1 ordinary shares for cash, at a price of £1.50 per share. Costs of the issue amounted to £75 000. The Journal entries recording the issue and subsequently writing-off issue costs to share premium account are:

		£	£
debit	Cash account	1 425 000	
	Issue expenses account	75 000	
credit	Ordinary share capital account		1 000 000
	Share premium account		500 000

Being the net proceeds of an issue of one million £1 shares at £1.50 each, less issue expenses

debit	Share premium account	75 000	
credit	Issue expenses account		75 000

Being cost of share issue, written-off against share premium

(b) *Application and allotment*

When a public issue of securities is made, there will normally be a time delay between the date of receipt of applications from potential investors and the date of allotment of shares to successful applicants. This delay will be caused partly by the administrative difficulties associated with new issues, particularly when the issue is oversubscribed, and partly because many issues are dependent on approval for listing being obtained for the security from the Stock Exchange.

The amount of money received from applicants will be credited to an Application Account and debited to an account representing the bank account in which the application money has been lodged. When letters of allotment are sent to the successful subscribers and money returned to any unsuccessful applicants, the appropriate entries will be as follows:

debit   Application account with the total value of the securities issued and the cash returned to unsuccessful applicants, thus clearing the Application account;
credit   Bank account with the amount returned, the Security account with the nominal values of securities issued, and the share premium account with any excess over the nominal value.

The basis on which shares will be allotted, in the case of public issues which are over-subscribed, will normally be stated in the prospectus document, and will vary from company to company. A minimum level of subscriptions will also be stated below which the issue will lapse.

Illustration 5
Macdonald plc made an offer for sale of one million £1 ordinary shares at a price of £1.30 each by means of a prospectus issue. The full amount of the share price was to be paid on application. Applications were received for four million shares and allotments were subsequently made on the basis of one share for every four applied for. Journal entries to record applications received and subsequent allotments are as follows:

		£000	£000
debit	Bank account	5200	
credit	Application account		5200

Being money received for four million shares at £1.30 each

		£000	£000
debit	Application account	5200	
credit	Bank account		3900
	Ordinary share capital a/c		1000
	Share premium account		300

Being allotment of shares and return of cash in respect of unsuccessful applicants

(c) *Partly paid shares*

Partly paid shares are those on which the issue price has not yet been completely paid by the subscriber. Although it is uncommon for issues of partly paid shares to be made nowadays, two recent large issues have involved such shares:

(i) the sale of shares in BP plc made in November 1979 involved a payment of £1.50 per share on application followed by subsequent final payment of £2.13 per share in February 1980.
(ii) the sale of Britoil shares referred to earlier involved the payment of £1 share on application after 19 November 1982, followed by a subsequent final payment of £1.15 per share on 6 April 1983.

Both of these issues involved the sale of securities previously held by the government.

Section 22 of the 1980 Companies Act requires that 25 per cent of the nominal value and 100 per cent of the share premium must be received on any share issue by a public company before any shares can be allotted.

Partly paid shares must be identified as such in the company's Balance Sheet, or in a note annexed to it.

12.7 Summary

The current chapter has described the major characteristics of incorporated businesses, particularly companies limited by shares. The particular characteristics of such companies give rise to additional reporting obligations which will be examined more fully in the following chapter.

Various categories of investors provide finance to companies in exchange for expected returns which may be in the form of interest receipts, in the case of debenture holders, or dividends, in the case of ordinary and preference shareholders. The owners of limited liability companies are the members, who are the ordinary shareholders in the case of companies limited by shares, and guarantors in the case of companies limited by guarantee.

Questions

1. Compare the relative merits to an owner of the following forms of business enterprise: (a) sole-trader; (b) partnership; (c) limited liability company.
2. Describe the main features of the following methods of raising equity capital: (a) Rights issue; (b) Offer for sale; (c) Tender issue; (d) Placement.
3. What are the advantages and disadvantages to a company of obtaining a quotation on a recognised stock exchange?
4. Describe the relative merits to a potential investor of investing in the following types of security: (a) ordinary shares; (b) preference shares; (c) debentures.
5. Explain in which of the following types of business you would expect to find relatively high levels of gearing and in which you would expect to see relatively low levels of gearing. (a) retail trading; (b) building constructors; (c) brewers and distillers; (d) property company.
6. (a) Explain the functions of underwriters.
   (b) Does the presence of underwriters for a new issue indicate that risk averse investors should beware of the issue?

Problems

1. Kippen Products plc made an offer for sale of 1 million ordinary shares during May 1984 at a price of £2.50 payable on application. Applications were subsequently received for 2.4 million shares, allotments made to successful applicants and money returned to unsuccessful applicants. Costs of making the issue, including underwriting commission amounting to £150 000, were written-off against the Share Premium Account. You are required to prepare journal entries to record the transactions relating to the above issue of shares.
2. Ross plc has operated since the business was founded with the following capital structure:

	£000
2 million, 50 pence Ordinary Shares, fully paid	1000
8 per cent Cumulative Preference Shares	500
10 per cent Non-cumulative Preference Shares	500
	£2000

Earnings after tax for the first four years of operations are:

	£000
Year 1	50
Year 2	80
Year 3	140
Year 4	520

You are required to show dividends on each class of shares, assuming:

(a) The directors of the company have agreed to pay no dividend unless ordinary shareholders can be guaranteed a dividend of 10 pence per share, in which case retained earnings will amount to 50 per cent of the earnings available to ordinary shareholders, after first providing for the 10 pence dividend;

(b) All profits are to be paid out as dividends with non-cumulative preference shareholders ranking first in order of priority for dividends.

3. Ewen and Stephen Watt are in partnership sharing profits equally. The latest Balance Sheet, in summarised form, is as follows:

Balance Sheet at 30 June 1984

		£000
Fixed assets		174
Current assets	98	
Less current liabilities	46	52
		£226
Partnership Capital Accounts:		
E. Watt		50
S. Watt		50
Current Accounts:		
E. Watt		72
S. Watt		54
		£226

The partnership is to be converted to a limited liability company, Watt Brothers Ltd. All the existing assets and liabilities are to be transferred, at Balance Sheet values. The partners are each to receive as part of the purchase consideration 60 000 £1 ordinary shares in the new company valued at a premium of 25 pence per share. Any additional funds due to the partners are to be paid to them out of the proceeds of a loan of £200 000 made available to the new company by a private investor who will also subscribe for 40 000 shares in the new company at a price of £1.25 per share.

Required:
(a) Prepare journal entries to record the cessation of the partnership in the books of the old business.
(b) Show the amount of cash received by each of the old partners.
(c) Prepare journal entries to record the formation of the new company and post the entries to the relevant ledger accounts.
(d) Prepare the opening Balance Sheet of the new company.

13 Corporate Financial Reporting Requirements

13.1 Introduction

A brief outline of the history of financial disclosure requirements placed on companies by corporate legislation was given in Chapter 1. No attempt will be made in this current chapter to re-examine that history in detail although the following points are worth reconsidering:

(i) The information needs of shareholders, creditors and other potential external users of financial statements were largely ignored in the nineteenth century. Both the courts and legislators preferred to allow a relatively free hand to businessmen. Other parties were judged to have the freedom to enter into contracts with companies, or not, as they wished and were not protected against their own possible bad judgement by company legislation.
(ii) A requirement for companies, to provide a Balance Sheet to shareholders was not reintroduced following its deletion in the 1856 Act, until 1900 in the case of public companies, and 1948 in the case of private companies.
(iii) Public companies were not required to provide shareholders with a copy of the Profit and Loss Account until after the passing of the 1929 Companies Act while private companies were not required to do so until after the 1948 Companies Act.
(iv) The type of information to be disclosed in the reported Profit and Loss Account and Balance Sheet was not specified in any detail until the 1948 Companies Act. Successive legislation has increased the disclosure requirements considerably, culminating in the detailed requirements of the 1981 Act.
(v) Independent verification of annual accounts by professionally qualified auditors was not required until the 1948 Companies Act which also specified the duties and powers of auditors.

In summary, the above points indicate that the detailed disclosure of financial information has not been a required feature of corporate reporting until relatively recently. Legislators and the courts tended rather to restrict their attention to specific areas such as the definition of profits available for distribution to shareholder.

13.2 Financial disclosure requirements

Introduction

The 1981 Companies Act introduced major changes to the law affecting companies registered in the United Kingdom. Of particular significance in the context of the present textbook are those changes which have been introduced into company reporting requirements.

The major impetus for the 1981 Act appears to have been the move towards harmonisation of company law within the EEC and the requirement to implement the EEC Fourth Directive in UK Company law. There are close similarities between the 1981 Act and the EEC Fourth Directive which deals with the form and content of company accounts and also lays down detailed accounting rules. The 1981 Companies Act, in following the lead of the Fourth Directive by detailing the accounting principles and rules which should be followed in the preparation and presentation of corporate financial statements, has gone well beyond previous company legislation. Both parliament and the courts have in the past been reluctant to provide a lead in this area, preferring rather to rely on the professional judgement of accountants and the pronouncements and standards issued by recognised accountancy bodies.

Accounting principles and rules

The accounting principles upon which corporate financial statements are to be prepared are in the main those outlined in SSAP 2, i.e., going-concern, consistency, prudence, accruals.[1] The overriding requirement for corporate financial statements is to provide what is described as a 'true and fair view'. If the adoption of any of the above accounting principles were to lead to such a view not being presented, then the directors are permitted to depart from that principle in preparation of the annual accounts. When, however, the directors have departed from the application of any basic accounting principle, then the particulars of the departure, the reason for it, and its effects should be disclosed by way of a note to the accounts.

One further principle also laid down by the 1981 Companies Act was the requirement that 'in determining the aggregate amount of any item the amount of each individual asset or liability that falls to be taken into account shall be determined separately'.[2]

The 1981 Act requires annual accounts to be prepared either on the basis of historic cost accounting rules detailed in the Act, or else on the basis of selected alternative accounting rules. The alternative accounting rules allow companies to revalue certain fixed and current assets and to base annual charges on these revalued amounts. If the alternative accounting rules are adopted for the financial accounts, then notes must be appended to the accounts showing for each item separately (except stocks) the corresponding amount determined under historic cost rules.

Format of annual accounts

The 1981 Act laid down for the first time required formats for annual accounting statements. Alternative formats are available but once one particular format has been chosen this may be replaced by an alternative only if there are special reasons for the change, which must be given by the directors in a note to the accounts. The adoption of prescribed formats, although a break from the previous tradition of optional formats, seems to be part of the trend towards improved information content for external users particularly in relation to comparability.

Although two prescribed formats are given for the Balance Sheet, the information to be provided in each is identical, with the first format essentially coinciding with the vertical method of Balance Sheet presentation, and the second format with the horizontal method. Both formats are reproduced in their entirety in Appendix A to this chapter.

The vertical format is illustrated for a fictional company, Octagon plc, in Table 13.1.

Four alternative formats are available for the Profit and Loss Account, although these include the vertical and horizontal forms of two distinct presentations only. The 1981 Act requires greater disclosure of information relating to the operating expenses of companies and further requires the expense information disclosed to be grouped either according to type of expense (as in Formats 2 and 4), or else according to the function of the expense (as in Formats 1 and 3). All four formats are reproduced in Appendix A at the end of the chapter, while Format 1 is illustrated for Octagon plc in Table 13.2 and Format 2 is illustrated in Table 13.3.

In addition to the information included in the prescribed formats, each Profit and Loss Account must show the following:

(i) any amount set aside or proposed to be set aside to, or withdrawn or proposed to be withdrawn from, reserves;
(ii) the aggregate amount of any dividends paid and proposed.

Additional information requirements

(a) *General*

The accounting policies adopted by a company in determining the amount to be included in respect of items shown in the Balance Sheet and in determining the profit or loss of the company must be stated by way of a note to the accounts. This requirement is similar to that identified in SSAP 2, which also requires disclosure of accounting policies but in relation to material or significant items only.

The corresponding figures for the previous financial year must be provided both for information included on the face of the accounts, and for information provided by way of notes.

Additional information is required to be disclosed by means of notes to the accounts if not already included on the actual face of the accounts. The use of notes allows a greater detail of information to be given than would otherwise be possible, although various commentators have suggested that important information useful to users may be 'hidden' in notes.

TABLE 13.1

Octagon plc
Balance Sheet as at 31 July 1984
(Format 1)

1983 £000		1984 £000	1984 £000
	Fixed assets		
84	Intangible assets (note 11)		171
1157	Tangible assets (note 12)		1223
51	Investments (note 13)		67
1292			1461
	Current assets		
649	Stocks (note 15)	784	
586	Debtors (note 16)	496	
17	Investments (note 17)	524	
19	Cash in bank and in hand	17	
1271		1821	
995	Creditors: Amounts falling due within one year (note 18)	1246	
276	Net current assets		575
1568	Total assets less current liabilities		2036
(642)	Creditors: Amounts falling due after more than one year (note 19)		(768)
(61)	Provisions for liabilities and charges (note 20)		(103)
£865	Total net assets		£1165
	Capital and Reserves		
400	Called up share capital (note 21)		450
50	Share premium account (note 21)		200
100	Revaluation reserve		100
125	Other reserves		125
190	Profit and Loss Account		290
£865			£1165

A. Campbell
D. Watt   Directors

1 September, 1984.

(b) *Supplementary Balance Sheet Information*[3]
The following information must be shown by way of note, if not included in the accounts.

(i) *Share capital* The amount of the authorised share capital and its division, if any, into different classes of shares; earliest and latest redemption dates of any redeemable shares and any premium payable on redemption together with a statement as to whether redemption is at the option of the company or not.

The number, nominal value and classes of any shares allotted during the

TABLE 13.2

Octagon plc
Profit and Loss Account for the year ended 31 July 1984
(Format 1)

1983 £000		1984 £000
6145	Turnover (note 2)	8172
(3712)	Cost of sales	(4538)
2433	Gross profit	3634
(709)	Distribution expenses	(947)
(1613)	Administrative expenses	(2483)
111		204
5	Income from shares in related companies	7
6	Income from other fixed asset investments	9
122		220
(74)	Interest payable (note 6)	(56)
48	Profit on ordinary activities before taxation (note 3)	164
(12)	Corporation tax on profit on ordinary activities (note 7)	(67)
36	Profit on ordinary activities after tax	97
—	Extraordinary profit (note 8)	34
—	Corporation tax on extraordinary profit	(17)
36	Profit for the financial year	114
(12)	Dividends paid and proposed (note 9)	(14)
24		100
166	Retained profit brought forward	190
190	Retained profit carried forward	290
8 pence	Earnings per share (note 10): before extraordinary item	22.8 pence
8 pence	after extraordinary item	26.8 pence

year, together with the reason for the allotment and the value of the consideration received by the company; details of any options to subscribe for shares which are outstanding, including the amount and type of option, the period during which the option is exercisable and the price to be paid for the shares.

(ii) *Debentures* The reason for any debenture issue made during the year, together with the amount and class of debentures issued and the consideration received; particulars of any redeemed debentures which the company has power to reissue and the nominal value of any debentures in the company held by a nominee or trustee for the company itself.

(iii) *Fixed assets* Movements in both gross and net amounts for each category of fixed asset; opening and closing balances on asset cost and accumulated provisions, together with any amounts provided during the year and any other adjustments made. Where assets have been revalued, the year

TABLE 13.3

Octagon plc
Profit and Loss Account for the year ended 31 July 1984
(Format 2)

1983			1984	
£000	£000		£000	£000
6145		Turnover (note 2)		8172
	117	Increase in stocks of finished goods and work in progress	58	
	2016	Raw materials and consumables	3317	
	1788	Other external charges	2109	
	1937	Staff costs (note 5)	2249	
	176	Depreciation and other amounts written off tangible and intangible fixed assets	235	
6034				7968
111				204
5		Income from shares in related companies		7
6		Income from other fixed asset investments		9
122				220
(74)		Interest payable (note 6)		(56)
48		Profit on ordinary activities before taxation (note 3)		164
(12)		Corporation tax on profit on ordinary activities (note 7)		(67)
36		Profit on ordinary activities after tax		97
—		Extraordinary profit (note 8)		34
—		Corporation tax on extraordinary profit		(17)
36		Profit for the financial year		114
(12)		Dividends paid and proposed (note 9)		(14)
24				100
166		Retained profit brought forward		190
190		Retained profit carried forward		290
8 pence		Earnings per share (note 10): before extraordinary item		22.8 pence
8 pence		after extraordinary item		26.8 pence

of revaluation and the names of valuers together with the basis of valuation. In relation to the above, separate amounts must be disclosed relating to freehold, long leasehold and short leasehold land.

(iv) *Investments* All investments must be included under a heading of either fixed or current assets, thus allowing external readers to identify their intended use. For each category of current or fixed asset, the amount of listed investments must be identified together with the division between securities listed on the UK Stock Exchange and those listed on other recognised exchanges. The aggregate market value of the listed securities must also be disclosed.

(v) *Reserves and provisions* Reserves normally arise either as appropriations out of profits, on revaluation of assets, or else by the issue of share capital at amounts in excess of their nominal value.

Provisions, on the other hand, arise out of the setting aside of charges against the revenues of a business, i.e., as expenses in the Profit and Loss Account. Provisions are made in anticipation of likely future losses occurring as a result of events which have taken place by the Balance Sheet date, the amounts of which are not known with certainty at the time of making the provision. Doubtful debts and estimates of diminution in the value of fixed assets i.e., depreciation, are two areas in which provisions are made.

Any movement which takes place during the year together with the opening and closing balance on each reserve or provision, must be disclosed; separate identification of any provision which relates to taxation other than deferred taxation. (In practice any such amounts will normally be shown as a current liability rather than a provision.)

(vi) *Details of indebtedness* The 1981 Act requires a considerable amount of additional information to be disclosed relating to a company's indebtedness. For each category of long-term creditor, the amount that is payable or repayable more than five years after the Balance Sheet date must be disclosed distinguishing those repayable by instalment from other long-term creditors; the terms of repayment of each long-term liability including the interest rate payable, if any; if any liability is secured, the aggregate amount of secured liabilities together with an indication of the nature of the security provided; the amount of any arrears of fixed cumulative dividends on the company's shares together with the period for which the dividends are in arrears for each class of shares involved.

(vii) *Guarantees and other financial commitments* In addition to liabilities actually incurred, companies may from time to time enter into obligations which are contingent upon the happening of particular future events. As these obligations may result in future liabilities, the amounts involved, or estimated to be involved, must be disclosed. In particular, the following information must be shown by way of note to the Balance Sheet:

(a) particulars of any charge on the assets of a company to secure the liabilities of a third party including where practicable, the amount secured;
(b) the estimated amount of any contingent liability not provided for, its legal nature and the nature of any security which may have been provided by the company in connection with that liability;
(c) any commitment for pensions, disclosing any commitments for which no provision has yet been made with any amounts relating to directors disclosed separately;
(d) the amount of any contracts entered into for capital expenditures which have not yet been provided for and the estimated aggregate amount of capital expenditure authorised by the directors which has not yet been contracted for;
(e) any other financial commitments which have not yet been provided for but which are relevant in assessing the company's state of affairs.

Disclosure of all the above categories is also required for any commitments entered into by the company on behalf of, or for the benefit of:

(a) any holding company or fellow subsidiary
(b) any subsidiary of the company, with the information relating to each of (a) and (b) shown separately.

The disclosure requirements for contingencies and commitments as outlined above are comprehensive, including not only items which will definitely become liabilities in the future but also those which may with a reasonable degree of certainty be expected to be incurred. The requirements of the 1981 Act are in this respect broadly in line with the requirements of SSAP 18 'Accounting for Contingencies'.[4]

(viii) *Miscellaneous matters* The following information, not identifiable under any of the categories (i) to (vii) above, is also required to be disclosed:

(a) the aggregate amount of proposed dividends;
(b) the amount of any loans extended for purchase of a company's own shares including separately, amounts loaned to employees and others;
(c) any amounts shown for the first time in respect of fixed assets for which the purchase price or production cost cannot be identified.

(c) *Supplementary Profit and Loss Account information*[5]

(i) Separate disclosure of specified income and expenditure is required by way of a note, if not identified in the Profit and Loss Account itself, i.e.,

(a) interest and other similar charges on loans repayable within five years of the Balance Sheet date and interest on other loans;
(b) the amount set aside for redemption of share capital and redemption of loans;
(c) the amount of income from listed investments;
(d) the amount of income, net of expenses, from rent of land and buildings (if a substantial part of the company's income);
(e) charges in respect of hire of plant and machinery (including leases not capitalised);
(f) the auditor's remuneration, including expenses;
(g) the aggregate amount of provisions for depreciation and amortisation where formats 1 and 3 are adopted.

(ii) *Particulars of tax* The following must be disclosed:

(a) the basis on which the charge for United Kingdom corporation tax and income tax has been computed;
(b) the particulars of any special circumstances which have affected the company's liability for tax either in the current year or in any future years;
(c) the amount of the charge for United Kingdom corporation tax;
(d) the amount which the charge for corporation tax would have been but for double taxation relief, if any;
(e) the charge for United Kingdom income tax;

(f) any charge for taxation imposed outside the United Kingdom on profits, income and capital gains (so far as charged to revenue).

Each of the above amounts of tax must be separated between that arising on ordinary activities of the company and that arising on extraordinary items. This requirement is in line with SSAP 6 'Extraordinary Items and Prior Year Adjustments'.[6]

(iii) *Particulars of turnover* Disaggregated information on classes of business must now be disclosed by way of a note to the Profit and Loss Account, where previously it was included in the directors' report. If the amount involved in different classes of business undertaken is deemed by the directors to be substantial, then the following information must be stated for each class:

(a) a description of the class;
(b) the amount of the turnover;
(c) the amount of the profit or loss before taxation.

If substantially different geographical markets have also been served during the year, then the turnover attributable to each market must also be shown.

The 1981 Act also allows that where the interests of the company might be prejudiced by the disclosure of disaggregated data then none need be shown, although the fact of the omission must be given.

(iv) *Particulars of staff* Disclosure requirements include:

(a) the average number of employees of the company together with a division of employees into categories of employment, as determined by the directors;
(b) the aggregate amounts of wages and salaries paid or payable;
(c) social security costs incurred;
(d) other pension costs.

(v) *Directors emoluments* Amounts received distinguishing between:

(a) directors emoluments;
(b) pensions, including those for past directors;
(c) compensation in respect of loss of office.

In addition a distinction should be made between those emoluments received in respect of services as a director and those received in respect of other offices:

(d) the chairman's emoluments and those of the highest paid director if not the chairman;
(e) the number of directors whose emoluments fall into brackets on a scale rising in multiples of £5000, i.e., 0–£5000, £5001–£10 000, etc.;
(f) the number of directors who have waived rights to receive emoluments during the year and the aggregate amount thereof.

(vi) *Miscellaneous matters* Particulars must be given of those items which would not normally have occurred during the year, i.e., extraordinary items including those relating to previous accounting years. In addition, particulars must be disclosed of any items which would normally be included as revenues or expenses but which, in the current year, are exceptional by virtue of size or incidence.

Notes annexed to the accounts of the fictional company Octagon plc introduced earlier, are given in Appendix B at the end of this chapter.

Directors' report

(a) *Introduction*

A report by the directors of a company must be annexed to every Balance Sheet, providing statutory information in addition to that which is required to be disclosed in the annual accounts. Although the 1981 Companies Act introduced several important new requirements to the report, it also withdrew a provision of previous company law which had allowed certain information to be included in the directors' report instead of in notes to the accounts. Most of the information previously included in the directors' report is now required to be shown in the notes to the accounts.

(b) *Disclosure requirements*
  (i) A review of the development of the business of the company and its subsidiaries over the past financial year;
  (ii) Details of any important events affecting the company or any of its subsidiaries after the Balance Sheet date. These items are identified in SSAP 17 'Accounting for post Balance Sheet Events'[7] as being either adjusting or non-adjusting events. Adjusting events will require changes in the amounts to be disclosed in the financial statements, while non-adjusting amounts will merely require disclosure. The first category of events are those which provide additional evidence of conditions existing at the Balance Sheet date while the second category concerns conditions which did not exist at the Balance Sheet date.
  (iii) An indication of the likely future developments in the business of the company and its subsidiaries, if any;
  There is, however, no requirement as to the form which the 'indication' should take, nor does there seem to be any requirement to provide quantifiable data.
  (iv) An indication of the activities if any, of the company and its subsidiaries in the field of research and development;
  Again no quantifiable data is specified but the amount of research expense written off during the year and any balances and movements on deferred development expenditure will have been disclosed in the accounts.
  (v) Information relating to any purchase by the company of its own shares;
  This information was previously provided in the notes to the accounts.
  (vi) The names of directors together with details of beneficial interests in

shares and debentures of the company, both at the beginning and the end of the financial year;
(vii) Any significant changes in the fixed assets of the company or any of its subsidiaries, together with any difference between the market value of any land and buildings held and the book value of these assets as disclosed in the Balance Sheet;
(viii) Proposed dividends;
(ix) Proposed transfers to reserves;
(x) The total of any money given for charitable or political purposes if greater than £200, together with the names of the individuals or political parties in receipt of any political contribution over £200;
(xi) Where the average number of employees exceeds 250, a statement relating to the company's policy as to the employment of disabled people, the continued employment and training of persons who became disabled while in the company's employment, and the training, career development and promotion of disabled people.

On a final note, the auditors are required to check the consistency of the directors' report with the accounts. Although many auditors would have carried out this task prior to the 1981 Act, it is now a statutory requirement for all company audits. If the auditors are of the opinion that the information given in the directors' report is not consistent with that provided in the company's accounts, then they must state that fact in their report.

Illustration 1
The directors' report of Octagon plc for the year ended 31 July 1984 will include information along the following lines.

Octagon plc

Report of the Directors

The directors present their annual report and audited accounts for the year end 31 July 1984.

Business Review
The principal activities of the company during the year consisted of:

the sale of timber and timber related products:
the manufacture and sale of wood pulp products.

There has been no significant change in the activities of the company during the year although a major expansion of the manufacture of timber-related products is planned during the coming year.

Summarised results for the year are as follows:

	1984 £000	1983 £000
Turnover	8172	6145
Profit before taxation	164	48
Taxation	67	12
	97	36
Extraordinary item (net)	17	—
Profit for the year	114	36

An analysis of turnover and profit by activity and of turnover by geographical region is given in notes 2 and 3 to the accounts.

Sales have increased significantly over the year, especially those made to other EEC countries. The increase of sales in timber products has outstripped those of wood pulp, due mainly to the shortage of spare production capacity for the latter. The additional investments planned in the coming year are expected to allow production of wood pulp products to increase substantially to meet the expected higher demand.

Share Capital
50 000 £1 ordinary shares were issued on 31 January 1984 at a premium of £3 per share, in order to raise finance for planned expansion. No shares were repurchased or charged by the company during the year.

Dividend
The directors propose a final dividend of 2 pence per share (1983 2 pence) which together with the interim dividend of 1.25 pence (1983, 1 pence) on shares in existence at the start of the year, involves a total payment of £14 000 (1983, £12 000).

Research and Development
Additional expenditure was incurred during the current year on the development of interrelated products.

Directors
Directors during the past financial year, together with their shareholdings at the beginning and end of the year were:

	Shareholdings at 1.8.83	at 31.7.84
A. Campbell (Chairman)	1200	1400
C. Brady (Managing Director)	2000	3500
L. Wright	900	1800
D. Watt	1500	2000

No director held any beneficial interests in shares other than those identified above.

L. Wright retires by rotation and, being eligible, offers himself for re-election.

Significant Shareholdings
The directors are not aware of any shareholder with a holding of 5 per cent or more of the shares of the company.

Political and Charitable Contributions
During the year the company made charitable contributions of £1500. No political contributions were made.

Employees
The company operates a policy of employment and promotion of disabled persons in those areas of the business which their abilities permit. Rigid safety rules and health precautions are enforced throughout. Where employees have become temporarily or permanently disabled during the year it is company policy to offer continued employment, either in the same job or in such other occupations as the disability permits, after suitable retraining.

In addition to the directors' report a chairman's report will normally be annexed to the accounts. There is, however, no statutory requirement to produce the report, nor will the contents be audited. The form of each chairman's report varies from company to company but normally includes a comprehensive, although general, review of the activities of the company over the previous year.

Auditors

(a) Introduction

Auditors are appointed by the members at the annual general meeting and may only be removed by resolution of the members. Remuneration of the auditors is also approved by the members. Auditors are therefore considered to act as agents of the members and not of the directors, reporting to the members on those matters which statute require and any additional matters which the members may from time to time require. Any auditor resigning office must deposit at the time of resignation, a notice in writing stating either:

(i) that there are no circumstances concerning the resignation which should be brought to the notice of the members or creditors of the company; or
(ii) the circumstances as aforesaid.

If the resignation of the auditor requires a statement as in (ii) above, then they may require the directors of the company to call an extraordinary general meeting in order to explain the circumstances leading to the resignation.

Only those individuals recognised by the Companies Act 1976, Section 13 as qualified to do so, may act as auditors of United Kingdom registered companies.[8]

(b) Auditors' report

The auditors of a company are required to examine the accounts of the company and the underlying books and accounting records and subsequently to make a report on every Profit and Loss Account and Balance Sheet, directors' report and set of group accounts laid before the members in general meeting.

The report must be read before the company at the annual general meeting and must be open to inspection by the members. A copy of the report must also be annexed to every set of full individual accounts.

The following matters must be included in the auditors' report:

a statement, whether in the auditors' opinion, the company's Balance Sheet and Profit and Loss Account have been prepared in accordance with the provisions of the Companies Acts 1948–81 and whether in their opinion a true and fair view is given:

(i) in the case of the Balance Sheet, of the state of the company's affairs at the end of its financial year;
(ii) in the case of the Profit and Loss Account, of the company's profit or loss for its financial year;[9]

(iii) a similar requirement to the above is made in respect of any group accounts presented.

In preparing their report, the auditors should carry out sufficient investigations to ascertain whether proper accounting records have been kept and whether these are in agreement with the company's Balance Sheet and Profit and Loss Account. If the investigation produces negative findings in respect of the above, then this fact should be stated in their report.

In addition to the statutory requirements placed on auditors, they must also ensure that any significant departures from statements of standard accounting practice are disclosed by the directors in the accounts, together with the reasons for the departure. The auditors must also comment on any such significant departure and to the extent that they concur with these, provide justification for the departure.

13.3 Distributable profits

Introduction

Although the nature of profits available for distribution as dividends has been the subject of many court cases since 1844, it was not until the 1980 Companies Act that any clear definition of distributable profits appeared. In the 1980 Act, distributable profits were defined for a company, as 'accumulated, realisable profits, so far as not previously utilised by distribution or capitalisation, less its accumulated realised losses, so far as not previously written off'.[10]

Realised profits are those which are 'required by statements of standard accounting practice to be recognised in the Profit and Loss Account',[11] and those which SSAPs do not specifically identify as unrealised. Gains on revaluations of fixed assets will not be included as distributable profits.

Depreciation charged on any revalued amount in excess of historic cost depreciation must be added back to accounting profits, in order to identify distributable profits. However, any loss arising on the revaluation of a fixed asset is considered to be a realised loss, unless it arises on a revaluation of all the assets.

Attributable profit included in long-term work-in-progress is considered to be realised profit, as this will have been calculated on the basis of 'reasonable certainty of realisation'.[12]

A further restriction placed on distributions by a public company, is that the net assets must be 'not less than the amount of the company's called-up share capital and its non-distributable reserves',[13] both before and after the distribution. This means that a public company must deduct all net unrealised losses from accumulated net realised profits before identifying distributable profits. No such obligation is placed on private companies.

Bonus issues

As an alternative to the payment of a cash dividend, companies may from time to time make what is described as a capital or bonus issue. Before making such an issue, permission must be obtained from shareholders, usually by ordinary resolution in general meeting. No such issue is possible, however, unless the articles of association include a provision for capital issues.

In order to make a bonus issue, an amount must be transferred from undistributed profits to share capital account, equal to the nominal value of the shares issued, i.e.,

debit   Undistributed profit (Retained Earnings)
credit Ordinary share capital
         with the nominal value of shares issued.

Bonus issues may be made out of unrealised profits if the articles of association of the company permit this. In fact, many financial commentators argue that a bonus issue is a distribution on paper only and provides no real benefit to shareholders; the number of shares held will increase but their individual value will fall, leaving the total market value of the shareholding unchanged.[14]

13.4 Company taxation

Introduction

Corporation tax was introduced as a distinct tax on corporate bodies by the 1965 Finance Act. Prior to that, the profits of companies had been subject to income tax and profits tax. The system of corporation tax introduced in 1965 required dividends to be declared out of after-tax profits with income tax subsequently deducted from the dividends. Dividends were therefore subject to two levels of taxation before reaching shareholders.

With the move into the EEC, a more 'tax neutral' system was introduced in respect of dividend payments. The 1972 Finance Act introduced an imputation system of taxation in which dividends are paid out of profits after corporation tax but with an imputed tax credit attached to the dividend which is equal to income tax at the base rate. Hence, within limits imposed by the 1972 Act, the level of dividend payments will have no effect on the total tax liability of the company.

Tax liability

The corporation tax liability of a company is calculated by applying a percentage rate to taxable profits. The percentage rate will be announced for a particular financial year in the annual Budget which will take place at the end of the financial year. The financial year runs from 1 April to the following 31 March. It is therefore quite possible for a company not to know with certainty its ultimate corporation tax liability until well after the end of its accounting year. Hence, corporation tax liability will normally be described as a provision in the annual accounts.

If an accounting period overlaps two financial years, each with different corporation tax rates applying, the taxable profits will have to be apportioned on a time basis over the two years and each portion charged to tax at the appropriate rate.

Payment of Tax

Corporation tax will be payable to the Inland Revenue in two ways as follows:

(i) If any dividend, or other qualifying distribution, is paid during the chargeable accounting period then an Advance Corporation Tax (ACT) payment must also be made. The ACT payment is equal to an imputed tax credit on the dividend received equivalent to the base rate of income tax.

For example, if a dividend of £70 was paid and the base rate of tax at the date of payment was 30 per cent, then an imputed tax credit of $\frac{3}{7} \times £70 = £30$ would be available to the shareholder. The company must pay the £30 as an advance payment of ultimate gross corporation tax liability on the taxable profits of that accounting year.

(ii) Mainstream corporation tax is equal to the gross corporation tax liability less any ACT payments made during the accounting year. Mainstream tax is payable either nine months after the end of the company's accounting year, or thirty days after the issue of the tax assessment, if later. In the case of those companies assessed to tax before 1965/66, the mainstream tax will normally be due for payment on 1 January following the end of the financial year in which the company's accounting year ended. For example, with an accounting year ended on 30 June 1984, a company which had been in existence before 1965 would not be required to pay its mainstream corporation tax liability until 1 January 1986.

Because of the way in which tax is now payable, companies which may not have a gross liability for corporation tax (because, for example, of a large amount of capital allowances), may none the less have made ACT payments in respect of dividends paid during the accounting year. In such cases, there may be an amount of recoverable ACT shown as a debit balance in the accounts of the company. To the extent that the directors believe that the amount of ACT is not recoverable in the near future, it should be 'written off in the Profit and Loss Account in which the related dividend is shown'.[15] Any ACT payment which is deemed to be recoverable will be included as a current asset in the Balance Sheet.

Deferred tax

For most companies, there will be a difference between accounting profits and taxable profits. The difference will be due either to permanent or to temporary factors.

Permanent factors include items which are not allowable expenses for corporation tax purposes, such as entertainment expenses, and income which is not subject to the full rate of corporation tax, including gains on disposal of non-current assets. Temporary factors include additional tax allowances over and above accounting expenses, the effect of which will eventually be reversed, e.g., capital allowances are normally much greater than depreciation charges in early years of an asset's life, but much less in later years.

In order to equalise the tax charge from year to year an additional provision for corporation tax is normally made in those accounting periods in which the tax liability is lower than 'normal'. In later years, when tax allowances become exhausted, credits will be transferred from the corporation tax provision to reduce the tax charge in the Profit and Loss Account. The additional corporation tax provision over the amount actually payable is known as a deferred tax provision and is required to be made on all temporary timing differences[16] to the extent that it is likely that a liability will crystallise.[17]

Deferred tax balances must be shown separately in the Balance Sheet, or in a note thereto. In Appendix B deferred tax is shown by way of note 20 and included with Provisions. Deferred tax is described in note 1 of Appendix B as being provided using the *liability method*. Using the liability method, the deferred tax liability will be adjusted if, and when, the corporation tax rate alters. The alternative, *deferral method* computes the deferred tax liability at the rate applying when the provision was calculated. Although both methods are allowed, most companies choose to use the liability method.

13.5 Summary

Company legislation has identified specific information disclosure requirements for limited companies and has also detailed the duties and responsibilities of the directors and auditors of the company. These requirements are specified in order to achieve equity in relations both between the company and outside parties, and within the company between various interest groups, including different classes of security holders.

The 1981 Act continued the trend towards additional information disclosure requirements and introduced for the first time in the United Kingdom, a requirement to follow prescribed formats in the preparation of published financial statements. The accounting principles on which the calculation of profits available for distribution are based, were also laid down in the 1981 Act with the reinforcement of historic cost accounting as the valuation base to be used.

Appendix A Format of financial statements

Prescribed formats for company accounts, as laid down in the 1981 Companies Act, pp. 129–139, are reproduced in full in this appendix.

(The following is reproduced with the permission of the Controller of Her Majesty's Stationery Office.)

Letters and numerals assigned to each item in the prescribed formats do not have to be reproduced in practice. The arrangement, headings, subheadings in the formats must, however, be complied with. Those items to which an arabic number has been assigned may be combined if either the amounts are not material or the combination facilitates the assessment of the company's state of affairs. In the case of any combined amounts on the face of the accounts, detailed disclosure must be provided in the notes thereto.

Companies Act 1981 c. 62

Balance Sheet Formats Sch.1
Format 1 Part I

A. Called up share capital not paid (*1*)

B. Fixed assets
   I Intangible assets
      1. Development costs
      2. Concessions, patents, licences, trade marks and similar rights and assets (*2*)
      3. Goodwill (*3*)
      4. Payments on account

   II Tangible assets
      1. Land and buildings
      2. Plant and machinery
      3. Fixtures, fittings, tools and equipment
      4. Payments on account and assets in course of construction

   III Investments
      1. Shares in group companies
      2. Loans to group companies
      3. Shares in related companies
      4. Loans to related companies
      5. Other investments other than loans
      6. Other loans
      7. Own shares (*4*)

C. Current assets
   I Stocks
      1. Raw materials and consumables
      2. Work in progress
      3. Finished goods and goods for resale
      4. Payments on account

   II Debtors (*5*)
      1. Trade debtors
      2. Amounts owed by group companies
      3. Amounts owed by related companies
      4. Other debtors

C.62 *Companies Act 1981*

   5. Called up share capital not paid (*1*)
   6. Prepayments and accrued income (*6*)
 III Investments
   1. Shares in group companies
   2. Own shares (*4*)
   3. Other investments
 IV Cash at bank and in hand

D. Prepayments and accrued income (*6*)

E. Creditors: amounts falling due within one year
   1. Debenture loans (*7*)
   2. Bank loans and overdrafts
   3. Payments received on account (*8*)
   4. Trade creditors
   5. Bills of exchange payable
   6. Amounts owed to group companies
   7. Amounts owed to related companies
   8. Other creditors including taxation and social security (*9*)
   9. Accruals and deferred income (*10*)

F. Net current assets (liabilities) (*11*)

G. Total assets less current liabilities

H. Creditors: amounts falling due after more than one year
   1. Debenture loans (*7*)
   2. Bank loans and overdrafts
   3. Payments received on account (*8*)
   4. Trade creditors
   5. Bills of exchange payable
   6. Amounts owed to group companies
   7. Amounts owed to related companies
   8. Other creditors including taxation and social security (*9*)
   9. Accruals and deferred income (*10*)

I. Provisions for liabilities and charges
   1. Pensions and similar obligations
   2. Taxation, including deferred taxation
   3. Other provisions

J. Accruals and deferred income (*10*)

K. Capital and reserves
 I Called up share capital (*12*)

II   Share premium account
III Revaluation reserve
IV   Other reserves
    1. Capital redemption reserve
    2. Reserve for own shares
    3. Reserves provided for by the articles of association
    4. Other reserves
V   Profit and loss account

SCH. 1
PART I

Balance Sheet Formats

Format 2

ASSETS

A. Called up share capital not paid (*1*)

B. Fixed assets
    I   Intangible assets
        1. Development costs
        2. Concessions, patents, licences trade marks and similar rights and assets (*2*)
        3. Goodwill (*3*)
        4. Payments on account
    II Tangible assets
        1. Land and buildings
        2. Plant and machinery
        3. Fixtures, fittings, tools and equipment
        4. Payments on account and assets in course of construction
    III Investments
        1. Shares in group companies
        2. Loans to group companies
        3. Shares in related companies
        4. Loans to related companies
        5. Other investments other than loans
        6. Other loans
        7. Own shares (*4*)

C. Current assets
    I   Stocks
        1. Raw materials and consumables
        2. Work in progress
        3. Finished goods and goods for resale
        4. Payments on account

II Debtors (5)
  1. Trade debtors
  2. Amounts owed by group companies
  3. Amounts owed by related companies
  4. Other debtors
  5. Called up share capital not paid (1)
  6. Prepayments and accrued income (6)

III Investments
  1. Shares in group companies
  2. Own shares (4)
  3. Other investments

IV Cash at bank and in hand

D. Prepayments and accrued income (6)

LIABILITIES

A. Capital and reserves
  I Called up share capital (12)
  II Share premium account
  III Revaluation reserve
  IV Other reserves
   1. Capital redemption reserve
   2. Reserve for own shares
   3. Reserves provided for by the articles of association
   4. Other reserves
  V Profit and loss account

B. Provisions for liabilities and charges
  1. Pensions and similar obligations
  2. Taxation including deferred taxation
  3. Other provisions

C. Creditors (13)
  1. Debenture loans (7)
  2. Bank loans and overdrafts
  3. Payments received on account (8)
  4. Trade creditors
  5. Bills of exchange payable
  6. Amounts owed to group companies
  7. Amounts owed to related companies
  8. Other creditors including taxation and social security (9)
  9. Accruals and deferred income (10)

D. Accruals and deferred income (10)

Notes on the balance sheet formats SCH. 1
PART I

(1) Called up share capital not paid

(Formats 1 and 2, items A and C.II.5.)

This item may be shown in either of the two positions given in Formats 1 and 2.

(2) Concessions, patents, licences, trade marks and similar rights and assets

(Formats 1 and 2, item B.I.2.)

Amounts in respect of assets shall only be included in a company's balance sheet under this item if either—
- (a) the assets were acquired for valuable consideration and are not required to be shown under goodwill; or
- (b) the assets in question were created by the company itself.

(3) Goodwill

(Formats 1 and 2, item B.I.3.)

Amounts representing goodwill shall only be included to the extent that the goodwill was acquired for valuable consideration.

(4) Own shares

(Formats 1 and 2, items B.III.7 and C.III.2.)

The nominal value of the shares held shall be shown separately.

(5) Debtors

(Formats 1 and 2, items C.II.1 to 6.)

The amount falling due after more than one year shall be shown separately for each item included under debtors.

(6) Prepayments and accrued income

(Formats 1 and 2, items C.II.6 and D.)

This item may be shown in either of the two positions given in Formats 1 and 2.

(7) Debenture loans

(Formats 1, items E.1 and H.1 and Format 2, item C.1.)

The amount of any convertible loans shall be shown separately.

(8) Payments received on account

(Format 1, items E.3 and H.3 and Format 2, item C.3.)

Payments received on account of orders shall be shown

for each of these items in so far as they are not shown as deductions from stocks.

(9) *Other creditors including taxation and social security*

(Format 1, items E.8 and H.8 and Format 2, item C.8.)

The amount for creditors in respect of taxation and social security shall be shown separately from the amount for other creditors.

(10) *Accruals and deferred income*

(Format 1, items E.9, H.9 and J and Format 2, items C.9 and D.)

The two positions given for this item in Format 1 at E.9 and H.9 are an alternative to the position at J, but if the item is not shown in a position corresponding to that at J it may be shown in either or both of the other two positions (as the case may require).

The two positions given for this item in Format 2 are alternatives.

(11) *Net current assets (liabilities)*

(Format 1, item F.)

In determining the amount to be shown for this item any amounts shown under 'prepayments and accrued income' shall be taken into account wherever shown.

(12) *Called up share capital*

(Format 1, item K.I and Format 2, item A.I.)

The amount of allotted share capital and the amount of called up share capital which has been paid up shall be shown separately.

(13) *Creditors*

(Format 2, items C.1 to 9.)

Amounts falling due within one year and after one year shall be shown separately for each of these items and their aggregate shall be shown separately for all of these items.

Corporate financial reporting requirements 283

Profit and loss account formats Sch. 1
Format 1 Part I
(see note (*17*) below)

1. Turnover
2. Cost of sales (*14*)
3. Gross profit or loss
4. Distribution costs (*14*)
5. Administrative expenses (*14*)
6. Other operating income
7. Income from shares in group companies
8. Income from shares in related companies
9. Income from other fixed asset investments (*15*)
10. Other interest receivable and similar income (*15*)
11. Amounts written off investments
12. Interest payable and similar charges (*16*)
13. Tax on profit or loss on ordinary activities
14. Profit or loss on ordinary activities after taxation
15. Extraordinary income
16. Extraordinary charges
17. Extraordinary profit or loss
18. Tax on extraordinary profit or loss
19. Other taxes not shown under the above items
20. Profit or loss for the financial year

Profit and loss account formats

Format 2

1. Turnover
2. Change in stocks of finished goods and in work progress
3. Own work capitalised
4. Other operating income
5. (*a*) Raw materials and consumables
   (*b*) Other external charges
6. Staff costs:
   (*a*) wages and salaries
   (*b*) social security costs
   (*c*) other pension costs
7. (*a*) Depreciation and other amounts written off tangible and intangible fixed assets
   (*b*) Exceptional amounts written off current assets
8. Other operating charges
9. Income from shares in group companies
10. Income from shares in related companies
11. Income from other fixed asset investments (*15*)
12. Other interest receivable and similar income (*15*)
13. Amounts written off investments
14. Interest payable and similar charges (*16*)
15. Tax on profit or loss on ordinary activities
16. Profit or loss on ordinary activities after taxation
17. Extraordinary income
18. Extraordinary charges
19. Extraordinary profit or loss
20. Tax on extraordinary profit or loss
21. Other taxes not shown under the above items
22. Profit or loss for the financial year

Profit and loss account formats

Format 3

(see note (*17*) below)

SCH. 1
PART I

A. Charges
 1. Cost of sales (*14*)
 2. Distribution costs (*14*)
 3. Administrative expenses (*14*)
 4. Amounts written off investments
 5. Interest payable and similar charges (*16*)
 6. Tax on profit or loss on ordinary activities
 7. Profit or loss on ordinary activities after taxation
 8. Extraordinary charges
 9. Tax on extraordinary profit or loss
 10. Other taxes not shown under the above items
 11. Profit or loss for the financial year

B. Income
 1. Turnover
 2. Other operating income
 3. Income from shares in group companies
 4. Income from shares in related companies
 5. Income from other fixed asset investments (*15*)
 6. Other interest receivable and similar income (*15*)
 7. Profit or loss on ordinary activities after taxation
 8. Extraordinary income
 9. Profit or loss for the financial year

Profit and loss account formats

Format 4

A. Charges
1. Reduction in stocks of finished goods and in work in progress
2. (*a*) Raw materials and consumables
   (*b*) Other external charges
3. Staff costs:
   (*a*) wages and salaries
   (*b*) social security costs
   (*c*) other pension costs
4. (*a*) Depreciation and other amounts written off tangible and intangible fixed assets
   (*b*) Exceptional amounts written off current assets
5. Other operating charges
6. Amounts written off investments
7. Interest payable and similar charges (*16*)
8. Tax on profit or loss on ordinary activities
9. Profit or loss on ordinary activities after taxation
10. Extraordinary charges
11. Tax on extraordinary profit or loss
12. Other taxes not shown under the above items
13. Profit or loss for the financial year

B. Income
1. Turnover
2. Increase in stocks of finished goods and in work in progress
3. Own work capitalised
4. Other operating income
5. Income from shares in group companies
6. Income from shares in related companies
7. Income from other fixed asset investments (*15*)
8. Other interest receivable and similar income (*15*)
9. Profit or loss on ordinary activities after taxation
10. Extraordinary income
11. Profit or loss for the financial year

Notes on the profit and loss account formats

(14) Cost of sales: distribution costs: administrative expenses

(Format 1, items 2, 4 and 5 and Format 3, items A.1, 2 and 3.)

These items shall be stated after taking into account any necessary provisions for depreciation or diminution in value of assets.

(15) Income from other fixed asset investments: other interest receivable and similar income

(Format 1, items 9 and 10: Format 2, items 11 and 12: Format 3, items B.5 and 6: Format 4, items B.7 and 8.)

Income and interest derived from group companies shall be shown separately from income and interest derived from other sources.

(16) Interest payable and similar charges

(Format 1, item 12: Format 2, item 14: Format 3, item A.5: Format 4, item A.7.)

The amount payable to group companies shall be shown separately.

(17) Formats 1 and 3

The amount of any provisions for depreciation and diminution in value of tangible and intangible fixed assets falling to be shown under items 7(*a*) and A.4(*a*) respectively in Formats 2 and 4 shall be disclosed in a note to the accounts in any case where the profit and loss account is prepared by reference to Format 1 or Format 3.

Appendix B   Octagon plc: notes to the accounts

1. *Accounting policies*

The following accounting policies have been followed consistently in dealing with items which are considered to be material in determining the profit for the year and in stating the financial position:

(a) *Basis of accounting*

The accounts have been prepared under alternative accounting rules set out in the 8th Schedule to the Companies Act 1948. Freehold land is stated in the accounts at revalued amounts, while all other items are stated in accordance with the historic cost accounting rules.

(b) *Depreciation and amortisation*

Depreciation is calculated on the straight-line basis so as to write off the cost of tangible fixed assets over their estimated useful lives as follows:

Freehold buildings   40 years
Plant and machinery   5–10 years
Furniture and fittings   8 years

Development expenditure is amortised over a period of 10 years, representing in the opinion of the directors, a prudent estimate of the period over which benefits will be obtained from the expenditure.

Patent rights are amortised over their expected useful lives, ranging from 5 to 15 years.

(c) *Stocks and work in progress*

These are valued on the basis of lower of cost and net realisable value. Cost is determined on a 'first-in, first-out' basis in accordance with the guidelines laid down in SSAP 9.

(d) *Deferred taxation*

Deferred taxation is provided using the liability method.

(e) *Pensions*

The company operates a contributory pension scheme covering the majority of employees. The scheme is independently administered by trustees who are also responsible for administration of the pension funds. Company contributions are charged against profits in the year in which the contributions are made. In the opinion of independent actuaries, the value of the scheme's assets equals the liability which is expected to arise.

2. *Turnover*

Turnover represents the amount of sales invoiced by the company over the year, net of value added tax. The analyses of turnover by geographical region and type of business is as follows:

	1983 £000	1984 £000
Timber sales	3582	4976
Wood pulp products	2563	3196
	£6145	£8172
United Kingdom	4861	5328
Other EEC countries	747	1915
Rest of Europe	308	471
Africa	146	329
Other	83	129
	£6145	£8172

3. *Profit before taxation*

(a) The analysis of profit on ordinary activities, before taxation, by activity is as follows:

	1983	1984
	£000	£000
Timber sales	17	65
Wood pulp products	20	83
Income from shares in related companies	5	7
Income from other investments	6	9
	£48	£164

(b) Profit on ordinary activities has been calculated after charging the following:

	1983	1984
	£000	£000
Depreciation:		
Freehold buildings	10	10
Plant and machinery	134	168
Furniture and fittings	19	24
Amortisation:		
Development expenditure	17	29
Patent rights	3	4
Auditors' remuneration	18	24
Hire of plant and equipment	6	22
Directors' emoluments: (see note 4)		
Fees as directors	26	28
Other emoluments	30	40
Income from investments	4	7

4. Directors' emoluments

The chairman's emoluments amounted to £15 000 (1983, £12 500) excluding pension contributions. Emoluments of the highest paid director were £22 000 (1983, £17 500). Emoluments of all directors, including the above, but excluding pension contributions were within the following categories:

	1983	1984
£10 001–£15 000	2	1
£15 001–£20 000	2	2
£20 001–£25 000	—	1

5. Employment

(a) The average number of persons employed during the year was as follows:

	1983	1984
Production	177	189
Selling	27	31
Administration	46	60
Managment	11	13
	261	293

(b) Total payments made in respect of employment were as follows:

	1983 £000	1984 £000
Wages and salaries	1796	2074
Social security costs	82	103
Other pension costs	59	72
	1937	2249

(c) No employee other than a director of the company received emoluments of £20 000 or over, excluding pension contributions.

6. *Interest payable*

	1983 £000	1984 £000
On bank overdrafts and loans repayable within five years	11	9
On other loans	63	47
	74	56

7. *Taxation*

	1983 £000	1984 £000
(a) Taxation based on profit for the year:		
Corporation tax @ 50 per cent	9	46
Deferred taxation	3	21
	12	67
(b) The corporation tax for the year has been reduced by:		
Stock relief	14	16
Capital allowances	17	43
	31	59

8. *Extraordinary Item*

Recovery of bad debts previously written off, £34 000 (1983, nil), less corporation tax of £17 000.

9. *Proposed dividend*

	1983 £000	1984 £000
Interim 1.25p per share (1983 1p per share)	4	5
Proposed final 2p per share (1983 2p per share)	8	9
	12	14

Corporate financial reporting requirements

10. Earnings per share

Earnings per share is calculated on earnings of £97 000 (1983, £36 000) before extraordinary items and on the weighted average of 425 000 ordinary shares in existence over the year (1983, 400 000).

11. Intangible fixed assets

	Deferred Development Expenditure £000	Patents £000	Total £000
Cost:			
at 1.8.83	121	41	162
Additions	106	14	120
at 31.7.84	227	55	282
Amortisation			
at 1.8.83	52	26	78
Charged in year	29	4	33
at 31.7.84	81	30	111
Net book value			
at 31.7.83	69	15	84
at 31.7.84	146	25	171

12. Tangible fixed assets

	Freehold land at valuation £000	Freehold buildings £000	Plant and machinery £000	Furniture and fittings £000	Total £000
Cost or valuation					
at 1.8.83	346	400	931	146	1823
Additions	—	—	226	63	289
Disposals	—	—	(58)	(17)	(75)
at 31.7.84	346	400	1099	192	2037
Depreciation					
at 1.8.83	—	120	471	75	666
Charged in year	—	10	168	24	202
On disposals	—	—	(46)	(8)	(54)
at 31.8.84	—	130	593	91	814
Net book value					
at 31.7.83	346	280	460	71	1157
at 31.7.84	346	270	506	101	1223

The amount of freehold land included above at valuation includes a revaluation of £100 000 over historic cost.

13. *Fixed asset investments*

	Listed £000	Unlisted £000	Related company £000	Total £000
Cost or value at 1.8.83	20	7	24	51
Additions	22	–	4	26
Disposals	(10)	–	–	(10)
Cost or value at 31.7.84	32	7	28	67

The market value of the listed investments (all of which are listed on the Stock Exchange) at 31.7.84 was £47 350 (1983, £29 800).

14. *Related investment*

The related investment represents a 30 per cent interest in the ordinary share capital of Wellington plc (1983, 22 per cent).

15. *Stocks and work in progress*

	1983 £000	1984 £000
Raw materials	162	239
Work in progress	311	347
Finished goods	176	198
	649	784

16. *Debtors and prepayments*
    (all due within one year)

	1983 £000	1983 £000
Trade debtors	381	291
Other debtors	56	32
Prepaid expenses	149	173
	586	496

17. *Current asset investments*

All these investments are unlisted securities

18. *Creditors: amounts falling due within one year*

	1983 £000	1984 £000
Debentures	120	90
Bank loans and overdrafts	106	75
Payments received on account	–	–
Trade creditors	667	821
Bills of exchange payable	–	–
Dividends payable	8	9
Taxation payable	17	24
Social security payable	5	11
Accrued expenses	72	216
	995	1246

19. *Creditors: amounts falling due after more than one year*

	1983 £000	1984 £000
Debentures		
10% mortgage debenture 1999, secured on land and buildings, repayable at par 31 July 1999	300	300
12% unsecured loan stock 1992/96, repayable at par by equal annual instalments from 1 January 1992	—	200
Corporation tax, payable 15 January 1986	19	43
Bank loans:		
at 13% per annum, secured by a floating charge on the assets of the company and repayable by equal annual instalments from 1 January 1990	200	200
Unsecured loan at 14% repayable within next five years	123	25
	642	768

20. *Provisions for liabilities and charges*

	Deferred taxation £000	Other provisions £000	Total £000
At 1.8.83	46	15	61
Transfer from Profit and Loss a/c	21	31	52
Utilised during the year	—	(10)	(10)
at 31.7.84	67	36	103

The 'other provisions' relate to costs involved in a legal action over patent rights. No further costs are likely to be incurred in addition to the provisions already made at 31 July 1984.

21. *Share capital and share premium*

	1983 £000	1984 £000
(a) *Share Capital*		
Authorised: 500 000 ordinary shares of £1 each	500	500
Allotted, issued and fully paid: 450 000 ordinary shares of £1 each (1983 400 000 shares)	400	450

An issue of 50 000 £1 ordinary shares was made on 31 January 1984 by private placement, at a price of £4 per share. The issue was made to provide finance for future expansion.

	£000
(b) *Share premium account*	
Balance 1.8.83	50
Premium on issue made during year	150
Balance 31.7.84	200

22. *Capital commitments*

	1983 £000	1984 £000
Authorised and contracted for	56	275
Authorised but not contracted for	—	148

No provision has been made in respect of any of the above amounts.

23. *Contingent liabilities*

The company has guaranteed certain loans of its related company, Wellington plc, up to an amount of £120 000. No liability is expected to materialise in respect of this guarantee.

Questions

1. Explain why United Kingdom legislation places requirements on companies to disclose financial accounting information to the public at large, when no such requirements are placed on unincorporated businesses.
2. Explain the advantages and disadvantages to the directors, and ultimately the owners, of a company of public disclosure of financial accounting information.
3. What do you understand by the term 'accounting policies'? Why is disclosure of accounting policies considered desirable?
4. Explain whether you believe that the introduction by the 1981 Companies Act of required formats for financial statements was a progressive or retrogressive step.
5. What information does the 1981 Companies Act require companies to provide in financial statements (including the Directors' Report) relating to future events?
6. Give reasons why companies are required to disclose information relating to
    (a) political and charitable contributions;
    (b) directors' emoluments;
    (c) auditors' fees;
    (d) loans to employees;
    (e) particulars of staff.
7. Distinguish between exceptional and extra-ordinary items and explain why the distinction is important.
8. (a) What disclosure requirements are placed on companies relating to: (i) turnover; (ii) profit before taxation?
   (b) Why are the disclosure requirements identified in (a) above considered to be important?
9. What information must a company disclose relating to the amount of indebtedness?
10. (a) Briefly outline the categories of information currently disclosed in company accounts which would be of interest to the following groups: (i) investors; (ii) creditors (excluding suppliers); (iii) competitors; (iv) suppliers; (v) employees.
    (b) Identify any additional information which would be of value to the above groups.
    (c) What conflicts of interest arise in the provision of company reports to the public at large?

Problems

1. The balances on the plant and machinery accounts of Sparkling Traders plc at 1 January 1983 were:

	£000
Plant and machinery at cost	9850
accumulated depreciation	4760

Depreciation is charged on a reducing balance basis assuming a ten year useful life on fixed assets unless otherwise indicated. Depreciation is also charged for a full year in the year of acquisition of any asset.

During 1983 the following asset movements took place:

(i) Plant and machinery which had originally cost £800 000 in 1978 was disposed of for £34 650.
(ii) Machinery acquired in 1981 at a cost of £1.2 million was revalued at £550 000 at the end of 1983. Any gain or loss on revaluation is to be disclosed separately to the depreciation charge for 1983. Depreciation in subsequent years, however, is to be computed on the revalued amounts.
(iii) New machinery was acquired in 1983 at a total cost of £2.5 millions. Included in the total was special machinery acquired at a cost of £500 000 for a short term project. The short term project will run for only five years, beginning in 1983 and the special machinery is therefore to be depreciated over this period using the reducing balance method.

You are required

(a) To prepare journal entries to record the above transactions in the books of Sparkling Traders for 1983.
(b) To show how the above information may be included in the final accounts of Sparkling Traders plc for 1983, published according to the requirements of the 1948–81 Companies Act.

2. The trial balance of Faroe plc at 30 June 1984 was as follows:

	£000	£000
Ordinary share capital account		10 500
Share premium account		4 300
Preference share capital account		5 000
General reserve		7 340
Freehold land and buildings	24 200	
accumulated depreciation, buildings		3 860
Plant and equipment, at cost	9 580	
accumulated depreciation, plant and equipment		3 190
12% Debenture stock		4 000
Cash at bank	111	
Sales		64 538
Cost of sales	43 720	
Administrative expenses	11 946	
Distribution expenses	7 835	
Stocks at 30 June 1984	4 209	
Trade debtors and creditors	11 423	8 769
Debenture interest for the year	480	
Prepaid expenses and accrued charges	1 747	4 650
Directors' fees	146	
ACT recoverable	225	
Interim dividend, preference shares	175	
ordinary shares	350	
	£116 147	£116 147

The following additional adjustments are required:

(i) A provision is to be made for an estimated liability for United Kingdom corporation tax on the profits for the year of £276 000.

(ii) Additional dividends are payable as follows:

On preference shares £175 000 net

On ordinary shares £315 000 net

Income tax at the basic rate of 30 per cent is deducted from all dividends paid by the company.

Required

Prepare a Profit and Loss Account for the year ended 30 June 1984 and a Balance Sheet at that date for publication by Faroe plc in accordance with the requirements of the Companies Acts 1948–81.

3. Thomas plc is a recently established company which manufactures and sells car accessories. The preliminary trial balance for the company at 31 December 1983, the end of the first year of operations is as follows:

	£000	£000
Freehold land and buildings at cost	12 000	
Leasehold property at cost	2 400	
Preliminary and formation expenses	1 560	
Plant and equipment, at cost	8 750	
Balance at bank	83	
10% Debenture		4 000
Office equipment at cost	105	
Sales		43 812
Ordinary share capital		12 000
Share premium		6 000
Manufacturing cost, excluding depreciation and wages	18 567	
Salaries and wages	12 480	
Distribution expenses	4 930	
Administrative expenses	3 196	
Debenture interest paid	200	
Trade debtors and prepayments	6 380	
Trade creditors and accruals		4 935
Directors' emoluments	96	
	£70 747	£70 747

The following additional information is relevant:

(i) The authorised share capital of the company is £30 million, divided into 20 million ordinary shares of £1 each and £10 million 7 per cent preference shares. The issued share capital is 12 million £1 ordinary shares, fully paid.

(ii) The issue of debenture stock was made on 1 April 1983. The debentures are secured by a fixed charge on the freehold property and are redeemable at par in 2008.

(iii) The cost of the freehold land and buildings should be apportioned £4 million to the land and £8 million to the buildings. All these buildings are used in the manufacturing side of the operations. The buildings have an estimated useful life of 50 years.

(iv) The leasehold property includes warehouses which cost £800 000 and office premises which cost £1.6 million. All leases are for 25 years duration.

(v) Depreciation on fixed assets is to be provided on the following bases:

Freehold buildings	straight-line
Leasehold property	straight-line
Plant and equipment	reducing balance over 10 years
Office equipment	straight-line over 7 years

(vi) Salaries and wages are to be apportioned as follows:

to manufacturing	50 per cent
to distribution	20 per cent
to general administration	30 per cent

(viii) Closing stocks were valued as follows:

raw materials	£173 000
work-in-progress	£946 000
finished goods	£1 150 000

(viii) An ordinary dividend of 6 pence per share has been proposed.

(ix) Directors' emoluments include:

Chairman's salary	£28 000
Managing director's salary	£24 000
Finance director's salary	£20 000

Three other directors received salaries of £8000 each.

Required

(a) Prepare the final accounts of Thomas plc for publication in accordance with the requirements of the Companies Acts 1948–81, using recommended format 1 for the Profit and Loss Account.

In order to calculate the company's liability for corporation tax for the year you may assume that accounting profits are equal to taxable profits and that the appropriate corporation tax rate is 50 per cent.

(b) Identify those factors which are likely to cause a difference for Thomas plc between accounting profits and taxable profits.

(c) What tax, if any, would you expect Thomas plc to pay in respect of profits earned in 1983?

(d) Explain, with reasons, whether the company should make a provision for any future tax liability arising in respect of the 1983 accounting profits.

4. The following trial balance was prepared for Banyan plc at the close of the accounting year ended 31 May 1984:

	£000	£000
Ordinary share capital		24 850
Share premium account		4 320
General reserve		8 186
Freehold land and buildings	17 940	
accumulated depreciation, buildings		3 280
Motor vehicles	14 840	
accumulated depreciation, motors		6 945
Plant and machinery	19 680	
accumulated depreciation		3 180
Trade debtors and creditors	13 067	14 484
Prepayments and accrued expenses	990	2 450
Distribution expenses	14 020	
Administrative expenses	9 035	
Sales		57 395
Cost of sales	27 847	
Stocks, 31 May 1984	6 110	
Directors' fees	600	
Dividends payable	2 380	
Bank loan		1 750
Cash at bank	331	
	£126 840	£126 840

(a) From the information provided, prepare final accounts for Banyan plc for 1984 in accordance with the requirements of the Companies Acts 1948–81.
(b) Describe briefly any additional accounting information which the company should disclose in the financial statements for 1984, or in the Notes thereto, in order to comply fully with the requirements of corporate legislation.

14 Analysis of Accounting Statements

14.1 Introduction

In Chapter 2, recognition was given to the fact that financial accounting reports are not produced as an end in themselves, but merely as means to an end. Financial accounting information is provided both to internal and external users with the objective of improving their decision-making. Indeed, an overall objective for financial reporting was identified as the provision of information about business enterprises that is useful in making economic decisions.

Whilst accepting the overall objective, it was also recognised that different user groups will have different information needs. Internal user groups may have their specific needs satisfied by the production of 'tailor made' financial reports, using data prepared on agreed bases, e.g., budget forecasts based on future estimated costs rather than on past, historic costs. External user groups, on the other hand, have no right to obtain any information other than that required by statute, or recommended in Statements of Standard Accounting Practice; these users are therefore normally obliged to obtain their particular information requirements from general purpose financial statements.

External users will also face further problems when attempting to use the financial information extracted from general purpose reports. Analysis and interpretation of financial information is helped greatly if comparison is possible with a suitable standard. Comparability will be enhanced if the accounting data for different firms are produced using the same accounting policies for similar transactions, with suitable adjustments made for the different dates at which transactions are undertaken. Similarly, comparability will be enhanced if the firms being compared are of a similar size or if the accounting information can be adjusted to take account of the different sizes of the business enterprises being compared.

Accounting policy differences

When the Accounting Standards Committee (ASC) was first formed (as the Accounting Standards Steering Committee) one of the stated objectives was to reduce the range of acceptable accounting practices.[1] The ASC has succeeded to a large extent in achieving this objective although there is still, and will probably always continue to be, considerable scope for different firms to apply different accounting policies, e.g., one firm may use straight-line depreciation on its plant and equipment while another may use the reducing balance basis. From evidence provided by empirical studies undertaken in the United States and elsewhere,[2] it does, however, appear that the use of different accounting policies by different businesses does not mislead the investor user group as a whole, provided that the accounting policy adopted by each business is disclosed; this does not mean that individual investors may not be misled, however.

Timing differences

If the same transaction is undertaken by two businesses at different dates and the cost of the transaction alters over the time interval between the two transaction dates then comparability may be reduced.

Illustration 1
Assume business A acquires premises on 1 January 1930 at a cost of £10 000 while business B acquires identical premises on 1 January 1980 at a cost of £100 000. Both premises are rented out to tenants at an annual rent of £5000.

Assuming no other assets for either business and no costs, the annual financial results for each will be as follows (ignoring depreciation on the premises):

	Business A £	Business B £
Fixed asset, at cost	10 000	100 000
Rental revenues	5 000	5 000
Profit on investment	50%	5%

Although both businesses are carrying out the same activities, business A appears to be carrying out the activities more efficiently and effectively. The only real difference between the two in fact is that premises acquired in 1930 had a much lower historic cost than the premises acquired in 1980.

The simple illustration given above perhaps exaggerates the effects of movements in cost over time and the subsequent effect on financial reporting. However, the problems caused by changing costs over time are sufficiently important to have warranted a considerable amount of attention by accountants over the last ten years or so and will be considered separately in Chapter 15.

Size differences

The third way in which comparability of financial results may be improved, namely, the elimination of size differences, is perhaps the easiest to solve. A variety of techniques are available for eliminating size differences, including the standardisation of accounting figures to a uniform scale (e.g., percentage figures), and the calculation of ratios of related accounting numbers. The first technique, involving standardisation of accounting data, requires all accounting figures in an accounting statement to be restated as a percentage

Analysis of accounting statements

of an agreed base, i.e., using one of the other figures included in the statement.

Illustration 2

The following Profit and Loss Account was produced for SD Enterprises for the year ended 31 December 1983:

	£000
Sales	800
Cost of sales	600
Gross margin	200
Operating expenses	160
Profit before tax	40
Taxation	15
Profit after tax	25

Restatement of all figures in the Profit and Loss Account as a percentage of sales produces the following statement:

	%
Sales	100
Cost of sales	75
Gross margin	25
Operating expenses	20
Profit before tax	5
Taxation	2
Profit after tax	3

The use of such standardised reports enables the relationship between the agreed base and other factors to be identified, but not other relationships. To allow the relationship between, say, operating expenses and cost of sales to be identified, either a new standardised Profit and Loss Account must be prepared with one of these as the agreed base, or else the ratio of the two figures must be calculated. Hence, the use of standardised reports is limited and is inferior to the use of the second technique for eliminating size differences, namely, ratio analysis.

14.2 Ratio analysis

Bases for comparison

As indicated in the previous section the interpretation of financial accounting information is often helped by comparison with suitable standards. A number of possible standards for comparison exist including:

(a) Past results of the same firm;
(b) Industry average results;
(c) Industry sub-group results.

All three possible standards for comparison have their merits and all suffer from potential disadvantages.

The choice of past results of the firm in question has the merit of comparison of 'like with like' both with respect to business characteristics and also with respect to the accounting policies adopted. The major disadvantage of this choice of standard for comparison is that it is an internally generated standard and one which may not reflect the current potential of the business in question. Also business conditions may have altered to invalidate comparison with the past.

Comparison with industry average results provides a standard that is based on currently attainable performance. This standard may not, however, be valid unless the firm under analysis contains characteristics which are similar to those of the 'average firm' in the industry, e.g., in relation to age, size, geographical location, product range and accounting policies.

The use of an industry sub-group for comparison of results is perhaps the most valid standard but will probably be the most difficult to obtain as the industry sub-group should contain firms with similar characteristics as the firm under analysis.

The use of ratio analysis as described in the following section will help to minimise the lack of comparability of businesses of different sizes. There will still, however, be some areas where comparisons may not be valid. Larger scale of operations will introduce economies in many areas which smaller firms cannot achieve except through growth. Hence, measures involving the efficiency of the utilisation of resources, for example, are not strictly comparable between firms of different size. The use of such ratios may well indicate the benefits (or otherwise) of greater size but may not be able to identify how efficient the current management team have actually been with the resources at their disposal.

The use of ratios and other tools of financial analysis will not provide definitive answers to questions posed by analysts. Rather, the ratios will help to support, or refute, impressions formed on the basis of other qualitative, and perhaps more subjective, information, including the external analysts' judgement of the abilities of the business's management team.

Accounting ratios

(a) *Introduction*
It is possible to calculate so many different accounting ratios that the analyst may become blinded to the essential information conveyed in financial statements. A system should therefore be adopted by each analyst in order to help concentrate on the important features of the business under examination, with a limit placed on the number of ratios prepared initially. Further ratios may then be computed and analysed should a particular aspect of business operations call for more detailed analysis.

One possible approach to analysis is to concentrate on growth elements, including rates of growth in sales and earnings. Following on from the preliminary analysis, the key factors involved in past growth may be identified including the level of asset utilisation, profit margin on sales and financing policies.

An alternative approach is to use a pyramidal structure of ratios, such as is used in the Du-pont system[3] beginning with a general analysis of overall

Analysis of accounting statements

profitability and moving to more specific examination of particular areas. This second approach will be adopted in this section in an analysis of the financial statements of a fictitious company, Bailey plc, shown in Tables 14.1, 14.2 and 14.3.

(b) Overall profitability

The overall profitability of a business may be defined and calculated in a variety of ways, depending on the particular needs of each analyst. Each calculation will, however, involve a statement of profit in relation to capital employed.

Profits may be calculated on the following bases:

(a) before, or after, tax;
(b) before, or after, financial charges;
(c) before, or after, depreciation and amortisation charges;
(d) combinations of the above.

TABLE 14.1

Bailey plc
Balance Sheet as at 31 December 1984

1983 £000			£000	1984 £000
	Fixed assets			
100	Land (see Note 1)			100
80	Buildings (see Note 2)			76
35	Plant and machinery (see Note 3)			44
28	Motor vehicles (see Note 4)			18
243				238
20	Research and development (see Note 5)			24
	Current assets			
		Stock	84	
117		Debtors and prepayments	67	
86		Cash on hand	9	
203				160
£466				£422
	Shareholders' funds			
200	Ordinary share capital:			
	£1 ordinary shares (see Note 7)			240
—	Share premium (see Note 7)			20
17	Retained earnings			43
217				303
	Long-term liabilities			
140	Mortgage debenture (see Note 6)			60
	Current liabilities			
	20	Taxation payable	13	
	—	Dividends payable	6	
	82	Trade creditors and accrued expenses	40	
109	7	Bank overdraft	—	59
£466				£422

TABLE 14.2

Bailey plc
Trading, Profit and Loss Account for the year ended 31 December 1984

1983 £000			£000	1984 £000
792		Sales		863
414		Cost of goods sold		475
378				388
351		Operating expenses (including depreciation)		304
27		Operating income		84
	24	Interest expenses	13	
	2	Research and development amortisation	6	
26	—	Losses on disposal of fixed assets (see Note 8)	7	26
1		Net income for year before taxes		58
20		Corporation tax		26
(19)		Net income after taxes		32
36		*Add* Retained earnings b/f		17
17				49
—		*Less* Dividends proposed		6
17		Retained earnings c/f		43

(i) Profit before tax may be chosen as an appropriate measure if the analyst is interested in performance controllable by general management and if taxation payable is considered to be dependent on factors which are to a large extent outside of the control of general management.

(ii) Profit before finance charges may be chosen as an appropriate measure if the intention is to identify a measurement of profitability independent of the way in which the business operations are financed. The appropriate capital base would in this case be total assets (or total capital employed, including loan capital).

Wherever possible the amount of capital employed should be calculated as the average of opening and closing figures. As this is not possible for Bailey plc, the closing figures have been used.

Application of the above definitions of profit and capital employed to the results of Bailey plc provides the following measure of profitability:

$$\frac{\text{Net income before interest expenses}}{\text{Total assets}} \times 100\%$$

For 1983: Profitability = $\frac{25}{466} \times 100\% = \underline{5.4\%}$

For 1984: Profitability = $\frac{71}{422} \times 100\% = \underline{16.8\%}$

Analysis of accounting statements

TABLE 14.3
Bailey plc
Notes to the Accounts

1. *Land.* No additions or disposals took place during the year.
2. *Buildings.* Depreciation of £4000 was charged as an expense for the year.
3. *Plant and Equipment*

	Gross cost	Accum. depn	Net book value
Balance 1.1.84	84	(49)	35
Additions	31	—	31
	115	(49)	66
Depreciation expense		(18)	(18)
Disposals	(28)	24	(4)
Balance 31.12.84	87	(43)	44

4. *Motor vehicles*

Balance 1.1.84	70	(42)	28
Additions	26	—	26
	96	(42)	54
Depreciation expense		(18)	(18)
Disposals	(48)	30	(18)
Balance 31.12.84	48	(30)	18

5. *Research and Development*

Balance 1.1.84	20
Additional expenditure	10
	30
Amortisation expense	6
Balance 31.12.84	24

6. Redemption of Debentures amounting to £80 000 took place during the year.
7. There was a Rights Issue of Ordinary Shares on a 1 for 5 basis at £1.50 during the year.
8. Loss on the disposal of fixed assets shown in the Profit and Loss Account includes the following:

Gain on disposal of Plant and Machinery	£ 9 000
Loss on disposal of Motor Vehicles	£16 000

(iii) An alternative choice of profits after interest expense and tax may be made if the analyst is interested in the returns available to ordinary shareholders. If this is the case, then the appropriate capital base will be total shareholders' funds.

Return to shareholders in Bailey plc is:

For 1983: $\frac{(19)}{217} \times 100\% = \underline{-8.8\%}$

For 1984: $\frac{32}{303} \times 100\% = \underline{+10.6\%}$

(iv) Finally, a choice of operating profit before depreciation, interest charges, and taxation, may be adopted if it is felt necessary to eliminate from an analysis of overall profitability the effect of alternative depreciation (and amortisation) methods on profits and fixed asset values. Operating profits will similarly be calculated before adjusting for depreciation, amortisation, and for any gains or losses on the disposal of fixed assets. Fixed assets will be included in the computation of capital employed on the basis of gross asset cost (i.e., before deducting accumulated depreciation).

For Bailey plc this last definition of overall profitability, assuming depreciation expense for 1983 of £30 000, produces the following results:

	1983	1984
Capital employed:	£000	£000
Fixed assets (net)	243	238
Add accumulated depreciation	91	77
	334	315
Research and development*	20	24
Current assets	203	160
	557	499

*Included net.

Operating profitability:

$$1983 = \frac{(27+30)}{557} \times 100\% = \underline{10.2\%}$$

$$1983 \quad \frac{(84+40)}{499} \times 100\% = \underline{24.8\%}$$

No matter which of the above methods for measuring profitability is chosen, it is apparent that the company has achieved an improvement in performance in 1984.

Achievement of a satisfactory level of operating performance is dependent on two broad factors which work together, i.e., the profit margin on sales and the rate of asset turnover (sales per unit of assets). Improvements in profitability may be obtained as a result of improvements in one or the other of these two factors. Indeed, it is possible to improve overall profitability by increasing one factor at the expense of the other, i.e., lower selling prices leading to an increase in assets turnover, or vice versa.

The two broad factors relating to the achievement of the level of operating profitability (before depreciation) identified in (iv) are as follows:

Operating profitability
= Operating profit on sales × Total asset turnover

i.e., $\dfrac{\text{Operating profit}}{\text{Total assets}} = \dfrac{\text{Operating profit}}{\text{Sales}} \times \dfrac{\text{Sales}}{\text{Total assets}}$

Analysis of accounting statements

Operating profit on sales for Bailey plc was:

$$1983 \quad \frac{(27+30)}{792} \times 100\% = \underline{\underline{7.2\%}}$$

$$1984 \quad \frac{(84+40)}{863} \times 100\% = \underline{\underline{14.37\%}}$$

Total asset turnover was:

$$1983 \quad \frac{792}{557} = \underline{\underline{1.42 \text{ times}}}$$

$$1984 \quad \frac{863}{499} = \underline{\underline{1.73 \text{ times}}}$$

The improvement in overall profitability in the year ended 31 December 1984 has therefore come about both by an increase in profit margins and also by an improvement in asset turnover ratios, i.e.,

$$1983 \quad 7.2\% \times 1.42 = \underline{\underline{10.2\%}}$$

$$1984 \quad 14.37\% \times 1.73 = \underline{\underline{24.8\%}}$$

Possible reasons for the increase in each of the two broad factors will now be examined in detail by analysing two broad categories of ratios, namely, operating ratios; and asset utilisation ratios.

(c) *Operating ratios*

There are a number of possible reasons for the increase in profit margin in 1984 including:

(a) a change in pricing strategy: from low profit margin plus high turnover to higher profit margin plus lower turnover;
(b) a change in product mix;
(c) an improvement in internal efficiency, or a change in the product cost structure;
(d) a combination of some or all of the above.

Possible evidence of changes in pricing strategy may be confirmed by analysis of turnover ratios (see later).

Changes in product mix may be identifiable from an analysis of turnover by product range, if provided, or from government statistics relating to the business's share of product markets.

Improvements in internal efficiency, changes in cost structure and indeed changes in pricing strategy, may be identifiable through the calculation of specific expense-related ratios. For example, the ratio of cost of goods sold to sales, or alternatively gross profit to sales, may be calculated.

Gross profit margins are as follows:

$$1983 \left(\frac{378}{792}\right) \times 100\% = \underline{47.7\%}$$

$$1984 \left(\frac{388}{863}\right) \times 100\% = \underline{45.0\%}$$

The cause of the increase in profit margin does not appear to lie with a change in pricing strategy, as a reduction in the gross profit margin has taken place, so other ratios of expenses to sales should be examined.

The overall ratio of operating expenses to sales are:

$$1983 \left(\frac{351}{792}\right) \times 100\% = \underline{44.3\%}$$

$$1984 \left(\frac{304}{863}\right) \times 100\% = \underline{35.2\%}$$

The improvement in internal efficiency appears to be directly attributable to a reduction in the relative level of operating expenses. With more detailed information about the nature of the operating expenses it will be possible, using additional ratios, to pinpoint the actual factors leading to the improvement and perhaps to their degree of permanence.

(d) *Asset utilisation ratio*

The amount of sales generated per £1 invested in assets has increased from £1.7 in 1983 to £2.05 in 1984. The causes of the apparent improvement may be identified by the calculation of ratios relating to sub-groupings of assets or even individual assets as follows:

(i) *Sales to fixed assets* The amount of sales generated per £1 of net book value of fixed assets was as follows:

$$1983 \left(\frac{792}{243}\right) = \underline{£3.26}$$

i.e. Fixed asset turnover = 3.26 times.

$$1984 \left(\frac{863}{238}\right) = \underline{£3.63}$$

i.e. Fixed asset turnover = 3.63 times.

The apparent increase in utilisation of fixed assets may be an accounting phenomenon only, as it may have arisen because of the reduction in the net book value of assets held after charging the 1984 depreciation expense. The ratio should therefore be recalculated using gross cost of assets as the denominator.

Using year end figures:

$$1983 \left(\frac{792}{100+80+84+70} \right) = \underline{\underline{2.37 \text{ times}}}$$

$$1984 \left(\frac{863}{100+80+87+48} \right) = \underline{\underline{2.74 \text{ times}}}$$

i.e., an increase in fixed asset turnover has occurred, however measured.

Note that an increase in fixed asset utilisation may not necessarily be beneficial as it may indicate an insufficient fixed asset base, with existing assets being over-utilised. Comparison of turnover rates with similar sized firms in the relevant industry sub-group may provide additional evidence on this.

(ii) *Sales to stocks* The rate of turnover of stocks will provide an indication of whether a business maintains insufficient levels to meet sales demand, or excessive levels, giving rise to unnecessary storage and financing cost. Optimal stock levels will vary from business to business, depending on the proximity to suppliers, the length of the manufacturing process, and storage and ordering costs.

Mathematical models are available to help identify optimal stock levels for businesses. One significant feature of these mathematical models is that the optimal stock level increases in proportion to the square root of any increase in sales and not in a linear relationship. Hence, stock turnover ratios are only really comparable between businesses of similar size.

Turnover ratios should be calculated wherever possible for each category of stock as follows:

$$\text{Raw materials turnover} = \frac{\text{Cost of goods produced}}{\text{Average raw materials stock}}$$

$$\text{Work-in-progress turnover} = \frac{\text{Cost of goods produced}}{\text{Average work-in-progress stock}}$$

$$\text{Finished goods turnover} = \frac{\text{Cost of goods sold}}{\text{Average finished goods stock}}$$

From the figures available for Bailey plc the average finished goods turnover for 1984 may be calculated (assuming all stocks represent finished goods) as follows:

$$\left[\frac{475}{(117+84)/2} \right] = \left(\frac{475}{100.5} \right) = \underline{\underline{4.73 \text{ times}}}$$

(iii) *Average collection period* An overall view of the average time taken by credit customers to pay outstanding accounts may be identified using this ratio. Comparison can then be made with the stated terms of credit of the company, or with the normal period of credit granted in the relevant industry sub-grouping, in order to identify whether credit management is too lax or indeed too rigid.

A credit policy which is too lax will, at the very least, result in higher financial costs than would otherwise be necessary, and may even give rise to a higher volume of bad debts; extended credit policies that are more generous than those of competitors often attract customers who are less willing or less able to pay their debts on time.

A credit policy which is too rigid, on the other hand, may discourage potential customers. A balance must be struck between the two, sufficient to ensure that any increased profit from higher sales will more than outweigh the cost of any increase in bad debts.

Assuming that all sales made by Bailey plc are on credit terms, and that there are no prepaid expenses at the end of the 1983 and 1984 accounting years, the average collection period for 1984 may be calculated as:

$$\left(\frac{\text{Average debtors}}{\text{Total credit sales}}\right) \times 365 \text{ days}$$

$$= \left[\frac{(86+67)/2}{863}\right] \times 365 \text{ days}$$

$$= \underline{\underline{32.3 \text{ days}}}$$

An additional help for internal management in the examination of credit control is the compilation of an *age profile* of debtors, i.e., the identification of the number and value of debtors accounts outstanding on a time-denominated scale as follows:

$$\frac{\text{Days outstanding}}{XX} : \frac{\text{Number of accounts}}{YY} : \frac{\text{Amount outstanding}}{ZZ}$$

(e) *Financing and liquidity ratios*

Shareholders returns may be improved not only by increasing overall operating profitability but also by financing operations partly from borrowed funds. The use of borrowed funds is not without its risks, however, ranging from the risk that there may be insufficient cash flow to meet financing charges and also ordinary dividends in the short term, to the ever present possibility that the business may not be able to meet its liabilities and obligations when these fall due for repayment. This may result in a business being wound up, often with insufficient resources to repay any funds to the members. Financial management should therefore ensure that the level of external financing is not too great to put the survival of the company at risk.

The management must also identify the optimal proportion of long-term to current borrowings. Long-term borrowing is generally more expensive, while short-term borrowing is subject to more frequent risk i.e., the chance that replacement loans may not be available after old ones are repaid. Short-term loans are, however, more flexible than long-term loans and may be made available to cover temporary or seasonal needs.

As a general rule, businesses tend to finance all fixed assets and a proportion of current assets (a so-called 'permanent' level) out of long-term capital sources, including debentures and shareholders funds. Non-permanent levels of current assets tend to be financed out of current liabilities, including short-term loans.

Analysis of accounting statements

(i) *Gearing ratio* The proportion of finance provided by long-term loans is known as the gearing ratio (or leverage ratio) of a business. There are a number of ways of defining the ratio including: Long-term Debt to Total Assets; and Long-term Debt to Shareholders' Funds.

It does not appear to matter which definition an analyst chooses to use, provided the chosen definition is applied consistently. Applying a definition of gearing as 'Long-term Debt to Total Assets' the ratios for 1983 and 1984 for Bailey plc are:

$$1983 \quad \left(\frac{140}{466}\right) \times 100\% = \underline{30\%}$$

$$1984 \quad \left(\frac{60}{422}\right) \times 100\% = \underline{14.2\%}$$

The higher the level of gearing, the higher the potential returns to shareholders *and* the higher the level of risks. Bailey has reduced its level of debt but perhaps has the opportunity to raise additional debt finance in the future to finance any investment plans.

(ii) *Total debt to total assets* Certain businesses will be able to rely on short-term borrowings, including credit extended by suppliers, without having any need to make recourse to long-term borrowings. A more suitable measure of the reliance on external funds for such companies would involve an examination of a total debt ratio, i.e., 'long-term plus short-term liabilities'. For Bailey plc the relevant ratios are:

$$1983 \quad \left(\frac{249}{466}\right) \times 100\% = \underline{\underline{53.4\%}}$$

$$1984 \quad \left(\frac{119}{422}\right) \times 100\% = \underline{\underline{28.2\%}}$$

As can be seen, borrowing ratios for the company have dropped considerably over the year. The possibility that the directors may shortly wish to raise additional debt capital should be considered. However, at present there appears to be sufficient 'slack' to meet future financial requirements.

(iii) *Current ratio* The ratio of current assets to current liabilities provides a rough guide to the liquidity position of a business, i.e., the ability to meet maturing obligations. The relevant ratios for Bailey plc are:

$$1983 \quad \left(\frac{203}{109}\right) \times 100\% = \underline{186\%}$$

$$1984 \quad \left(\frac{160}{59}\right) \times 100\% = \underline{271\%}$$

Bailey appears to have increased its liquidity position significantly over the past year.

A commonly quoted standard for the current ratio is 200 per cent (or 2:1).

There is, however, little justification for this standard as opposed to any other, apart from the fact that a large proportion of current assets are normally tied up in relatively illiquid stocks. Whether the current level of the ratio is appropriate for the company may be determined partly by reference to industry standards and also to the ratios identified earlier relating to current asset utilisation.

On the face of it, it appears that the company is making insufficient use of trade credit. Financial management may, however, be adopting a deliberate policy of taking advantage of cash discounts, thus reducing the net cost of goods purchased. If this is the case, then a comparison of the annual equivalent of the cash discount rate with the likely interest rate which the company would have to pay on borrowed funds should identify whether the chosen course of action is the current one.

(iv) *Quick ratio* The quick ratio or 'acid test' is an alternative measure of liquidity which excludes stocks from the numerator, on the grounds that they are a relatively illiquid asset, i.e.

$$\frac{\text{Current assets} - \text{stocks}}{\text{Current liabilities}}$$

Using the average of opening and closing Balance Sheet figures the ratio for 1984 was:

$$\left[\frac{(86+76)}{2} \Big/ \frac{(109+59)}{2}\right]$$

$$= \left(\frac{81}{84}\right)$$

$$= \underline{0.96}$$

(v) *Cash flow ratios* One of the major disadvantages of the use of liquidity ratios is that they measure relationships which may only be of temporary duration, i.e., for the Balance Sheet date only. The use of average figures only partly overcomes this deficiency. An alternative form of ratio, based on cash flows generated from operations has been found to have a high degree of explanatory power in a number of studies including those investigating the determinants of corporate bankruptcy.[4] Liquidity measures, based on operating cash flows, might include for example:

'Operating cash flow to fixed charges' (including loan interest)

'Operating cash flow to current liabilities.'

The calculation of operating cash flows would involve the adjustment of operating profit from an accruals basis to a cash basis and is partly the subject of the following sections of the current chapter.

Analysis of accounting statements 313

14.3 Funds flow analysis

Introduction

SSAP 10 lays down a requirement for Funds Flow Statements, or *Statements of Sources and Applications of Funds*, to be presented with the audited financial statements of all enterprises, other than those with a turnover of less than £25 000 per annum.[5] Although there is no legal requirement to comply with SSAPs, nor any requirement laid down by statute to produce Funds Flow Statements, the vast majority of companies publish an annual statement which is broadly in line with the requirements of SSAP 10.

The same basic information is used in the preparation of Funds Flow Statements as in the preparation of Income Statements and Balance Sheets. Differences do exist, however, in the aims of the Funds Flow Statement, with attention focused not on the level of profits or the current financial position, but on the investing and financing activities which have led to these.

Objectives of funds statements

The objectives of the Funds Flow Statement are not easily identifiable from official publications of accountancy bodies although the following objectives have been suggested:

(i) To identify the extent to which the enterprise has generated funds (a) internally from operations and (b) from external sources;
(ii) To summarise the utilisation of funds over the period, in investments and other activities, including distributions to owners;[6]
(iii) To provide information about the flow of funds and changes in financial resources that is not available in the Profit and Loss Account or Balance Sheet;
(iv) To identify gross investment strategies and gross funding strategies adopted by a firm.

In addition to the above, the Funds Statement may give the answer to specific questions such as the following:

'What has happened to the increase in profits? Why hasn't it resulted in a larger cash balance?'
'Why weren't dividends increased?'
'What happened to the funds from the issue of shares?'
'How has working capital increased while profits fell?'
'Can maturing debt obligations be met without further borrowing?'[7]

Definition of Funds

Although many readers will automatically equate the notion of 'funds' with cash, this is in fact only one of a number of possible interpretations of the concept. There are, in fact, three possible accounting interpretations as follows:

(i) The term may be used to refer to cash or near cash resources, e.g., short-term investments. Adoption of this definition should lead to the preparation of a Funds Statement either as a summary of Receipts and Payments, or at least in a form which emphasised the effect of the various transactions analysed on the cash position of the enterprise.

(ii) The term may be applied to the Net Working Capital of an enterprise, i.e., current assets minus current liabilities. Adoption of this definition of funds recognises movements in the individual components of the current assets and current liabilities of the enterprise. These movements lead to continual changes in the cash balance and turns the identification of those factors causing a change in the cash balance alone into a relatively meaningless exercise.

(iii) The third possible interpretation of Funds recognises what is known as the 'total funds' concept, and considers all the financing and investment aspects of financial transactions undertaken by an enterprise.[8] Adoption of this definition would allow transactions to be reported which would not by themselves affect either the cash or the net working capital position of an enterprise; for example, the purchase of a fixed asset by the issue of securities, or the exchange of one fixed asset for another without any cash movements. This broad concept of funds is adopted by the American Institute of Certified Public Accountants but is not the concept formally adopted in SSAP 10.

Requirements of SSAP 10

The definition of funds adopted by SSAP 10 is described as 'Net Liquid Funds', i.e.,

> cash at bank and in hand and cash equivalents (e.g. investments held as current assets), less bank overdrafts and other borrowings repayable within one year of the accounting date.[9]

On the face of it, this definition appears to be the narrow one of cash or cash equivalent. However, closer examination of the statement reveals a more confusing situation which has led more than one writer to describe the funds statement as a hybrid.

For example, SSAP 10 requires the Statement to show 'the increase or decrease in working capital sub-divided into its components'. This requirement is further demonstrated in the examples provided in the Appendix to SSAP 10. Also, Part 4 of the explanatory note requires a minimum of 'netting off' thus ensuring that significant sources and applications should be separately identified, an example being given of the sale of one asset and purchase of another, reminiscent of the total funds concept.

Finally, SSAP 10 requires dividends paid and taxation paid to be identified as applications of funds, whereas adherence to a working capital definition would require dividends payable and tax payable to be shown as the applications.

Specific requirements for information to be disclosed in the Funds Statement are as follows:

(a) The profit or loss for the period, together with the adjustments required for any items not involving the movement of funds;

(b) Dividends (and tax) paid during the period;
(c) Acquisitions and disposals of fixed and other non-current assets;
(d) Funds raised by increasing, or expended in repaying or redeeming, medium or long-term loans or the issued capital of the company;
(e) Increases or decreases in working capital sub-divided into its components and movements in net liquid funds;
(f) Comparative figures for the corresponding previous period.

14.4 Preparation of a statement of sources and applications of funds (as per SSAP 10)

Introduction

The 'fund' may be compared with a reservoir (Figure 14.1) which rises or falls over a period, with the Funds Statement explaining the amount of the rise or fall by measuring the difference between the inflows (the Sources) and the outflows (the Applications).

In the case of a statement which is based on the concept of a fund as working capital, changes within the component elements of working capital have no effect on the total level of the fund, e.g., the purchase of goods on credit terms will have no effect on working capital as the increase in current assets will be offset by the increase in current liabilities. Using the above illustration of the fund as a reservoir, movements within the reservoir itself have no effect on the level of the fund, changes in the level will be affected by the sources and the applications moving in and out of the reservoir.

The first stage in the preparation of the type of Funds Flow Statement required by SSAP 10 involves the identification of the sources and applications (uses) of working capital. After this is achieved, movements in the individual components of working capital should be analysed in order to identify the movement in 'net liquid funds'.

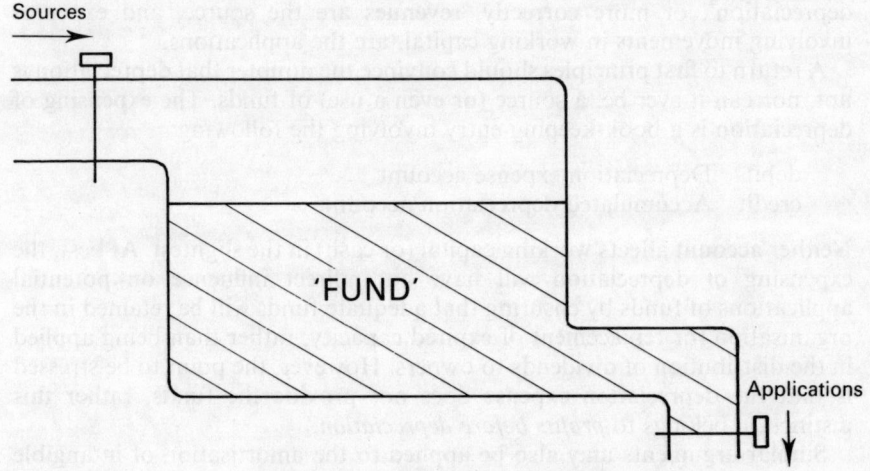

FIGURE 14.1 *The fund as a reservoir*

Sources of working capital

Potential sources of working capital are as follows:

(i) Retained profits from operations;
(ii) Proceeds of an issue of share capital, net of issue costs;
(iii) Proceeds of an issue of long-term loan stock, or medium-term borrowings;
(iv) Proceeds from the sale, or other disposal, of fixed and other non-current assets.

SSAP 10 requires a minimum amount of disclosure of net amounts, e.g., 'additions net of disposals', as otherwise the investing and financing strategies of the reporting entity would tend to be distorted. For example, when one asset is acquired partly for cash and partly in exchange for another asset, the gross (arms length) disposal proceeds of the old asset should be included as a source, while the gross cost of the new asset should be included as an application.

One error frequently made by accountancy students, and even by financial journalists, is to describe depreciation as a source of funds. This error is perhaps caused by the practice adopted in many companies of calculating 'funds from operations' using the so-called 'bottom-up' method. This method is illustrated in SSAP 10 by the following example taken from Appendix A:[10]

	£000
Profits before tax	1430
Adjustments for items not involving the movement of funds:	
Depreciation	380
Total generated from operations	1810

The impression which may be given by the above is that depreciation is indeed a source of funds when, in fact, the source is 'profits before tax and depreciation', or more correctly, revenues are the source, and expenses involving movements in working capital, are the applications.

A return to first principles should convince the doubter that depreciation is not, nor can it ever be, a source (or even a use) of funds. The expensing of depreciation is a book-keeping entry involving the following:

debit Depreciation expense account
credit Accumulated depreciation account.

Neither account affects working capital (or cash) in the slightest. At best, the expensing of depreciation will have an indirect influence on potential applications of funds by ensuring that adequate funds will be retained in the organisation for replacement of expired capacity, rather than being applied in the distribution of dividends to owners. However, the point to be stressed is that the depreciation expense does not provide the funds, rather this distinction belongs to *profits before depreciation*.

Similar arguments may also be applied to the amortisation of intangible assets, e.g., of Research and Development expenditure or of patents, and also to losses or gains on the disposal of non-current assets.

Analysis of accounting statements

Applications (uses) of Working Capital

Most of the potential applications of funds actually involve the reverse of one of the sources, as follows:

(i) Net loss from operations before tax and depreciation;
(ii) Redemption, or repayment, of share capital;
(iii) Redemption, or repayment, of long-term or medium-term loans;
(iv) Acquisition cost of fixed and other non-current assets;

Both (ii) and (iii) above should be shown when, for example, the redemption of one class of security is made possible through funds raised from the issue of another class of securities.

In addition, the following applications are also identified in SSAP 10 but are allowed to be netted against funds from operations:

(v) Dividends paid during the year;
(vi) Tax paid during the year.

For these last two applications it should be noted that it is the amounts *actually paid* during the year and not the amounts *payable* which are required to be shown as applications. Hence, the movement in working capital disclosed by the Funds Statement is not directly reconcilable with the change reflected in successive Balance Sheets, without first excluding tax payable and dividends payable from current liabilities shown in the Balance Sheets.

Preparation of the statement

There are essentially four steps involved in the preparation of the first part of the Funds Statement up to the point of identification of the net change in Working Capital. These four steps are as follows:

(i) Analysis of changes in fixed and other non-current assets;
(ii) Analysis of changes in owner's interest;
(iii) Analysis of changes in medium-term and long-term liabilities;
(iv) Reconciliation of (i), (ii), (iii) above.

The changes referred to in each of the above steps are those changes occurring between successive Balance Sheet dates. After following through each step in a methodical manner, the preparer of the Fund Statement should find that every item, other than working capital items, will have been analysed and the effect on working capital calculated.

An illustration of the preparation of the Funds Statement follows, using the information presented earlier in Tables 14.1, 14.2, and 14.3. At each step, journal entries are given to recreate the effect, if any, the changes analysed would have had on working capital.

Step 1. Analysis of changes in fixed and other non-current assets

(a) *Land* No changes are shown in the Balance Sheets or recorded in the notes to the accounts.

(b) *Buildings* The Balance Sheet value has fallen by £4000 over the year. This fall corresponds to the depreciation expense shown in Note 2.

Journal entry	£000	£000
debit Depreciation expense	4	
credit Accumulated depreciation		4
Being depreciation expense on buildings for the year, with no effect on working capital.		

(c) *Plant and Machinery* The Balance Sheets reveal an increase of £9000 over the year. Reference, to Note 3 reveals that the increase is the result of both purchases and disposals of plant and machinery, both of which should be shown in the Funds Statement, as follows:

Journal entries:	£000	£000
debit Plant and machinery	31	
credit 'Working capital'		31
Being acquisition of Plant and Machinery over the year, and reduction in working capital.		

The gain on disposal of Plant and machinery was £9000 and the book value was £4000. Hence proceeds of disposal amounted to £13 000 (as shown in Note 8). Gain on disposal and disposal proceeds are journalised as follows:

	£000	£000
debit Plant and Machinery accumulated depreciation	9	
credit Profit and Loss Account		9
Gain on disposal of Plant and machinery		

	£000	£000
debit 'Working Capital'	13	
credit Plant and Machinery		13
Source of Working Capital		

Finally the depreciation expense for the year is as follows:

	£000	£000
debit Profit and Loss Account	18	
credit Plant and Machinery accumulated depreciation		18
Depreciation expense for the year, not involving any movement in Working Capital.		

(d) *Motor Vehicles* As with Plant and Machinery, the change shown from one Balance Sheet date to the other, of £10 000, reveals only part of the picture. Note 4 explains that both purchases and disposals of motor vehicles have taken place. The effect of the acquisition on working capital is as follows:

Analysis of accounting statements

		£000	£000
debit	Motor vehicles	26	
credit	'Working Capital'		26

Acquisition of Motor Vehicles and application of Working Capital.

To record the disposal, the Motor Vehicles account must first be adjusted to record the loss on disposal:

		£000	£000
debit	Profit and Loss Account	16	
credit	Motor Vehicles account		16

Loss on disposal of Motor Vehicles.

The proceeds of disposal is shown as:

		£000	£000
debit	'Working Capital'	2	
credit	Motor Vehicles		2

Proceeds of disposal and source of Working Capital

Depreciation on motor vehicles held during the year is recorded as:

		£000	£000
debit	Profit and Loss Account	18	
credit	Motor Vehicles accumulated depreciation		18

Depreciation expense for the year, not involving any movement in Working Capital.

(e) *Research and Development* The net increase of £4000 shown in the Balance Sheet is a result both of additional expenditure of £10 000 and the amortisation expense of £6000 as shown by Note 5.

		£000	£000
debit	Research and development expenditure	10	
credit	'Working capital'		10

Being additional R & D expenditure incurred

		£000	£000
debit	Profit and Loss account	6	
credit	Research and development expenditure		6

Being amortisation of Research and development during the year

Step 2. Analysis of changes in owner's interest

(a) *Ordinary Share Capital and Share Premium Account* Note 6 refers to a

Rights Issue during the year, which is reflected in the increases in Ordinary Share Capital and Share Premium.

		£000	£000
debit	'Working capital'	60	
credit	Ordinary Share capital		40
	Share Premium account		20

Being increase in Working Capital through proceeds of share issue.

(b) *Retained Earnings* From a comparison of successive Balance Sheets it may be observed that retained earnings have increased over the year by £26 000. Analysis of the Profit and Loss Account reveals that the Source of Funds from operations is as follows:

	£000
Sales	863
Cost of goods sold	475
	388
Operating expenses (excluding depreciation etc)	264
	124
Interest expense	13
Funds from operations	111

Journalising this source of funds:

		£000	£000
debit	'Working capital'	111	
credit	Retained Earnings		111

Being source of funds from operations.

In order to reconcile the above figure with the increase in Retained Earnings of £26 000, further adjustments involving expenses not involving movement in funds are summarised in the two journal entries below:

		£000	£000
debit	Retained Earnings	53	
credit	Depreciation: buildings		4
	plant and machinery		18
	motor vehicles		18
	Loss on disposal of fixed assets		7
	Research and development amortisation		6

The items included in the last journal entry have already been adjusted in previously reported journal entries. Further adjustments which have not yet been included, however, are as follows:

		£000	£000
debit	Retained earnings	32	
credit	Tax payable		26
	Dividends payable		6

Analysis of accounting statements

Neither tax payable nor dividends payable are recorded as movements in working capital for the purposes of SSAP 10, although they are both included in current liabilities and, hence, working capital in the Balance Sheet.

The net increase in retained earnings of £26 has now been explained by the last three journal entries i.e.:

£111 − £(53 + 32) = £26

An alternative method for arriving at the figure for Funds from Operations is the method illustrated in SSAP 10 and described as a 'bottom up' approach as compared to the 'top down' approach just explained. The 'bottom up' approach recognises that all the information available to internal management will not be made available to external users of financial accounts and therefore bases calculation of Funds from operations on the information provided in the published Financial Accounts. One possible effect of this approach, as mentioned earlier, is to offer unintentional support for the error of describing depreciation as a source of funds. Calculation based on a 'bottom up' approach is as follows:

	£000	£000
Net income for the year before taxes		58
Adjustments for items not involving the movement of funds:		
Depreciation	40	
Amortisation of Research and development	6	
Loss on disposal of fixed assets	7	53
Funds from operations		111

While taxation payable is ignored in the calculation of funds from operations, tax actually paid during the year involves an application of funds. Tax actually paid is calculated as follows:

	£000
Balance outstanding 1.1.84	20
Tax liability for year, from Profit and Loss account	26
	46
Balance outstanding 31.12.84	13
Tax paid during the year	33

Journalising the above application,	£000	£000
debit Taxation account	33	
credit 'Working capital'		33
Being the tax paid during the year and decrease in working capital		

No dividends were paid during the year and so no adjustment is necessary for these.

Step 3. Analysis of changes in medium and long term liabilities
Loans outstanding have decreased by £80 000. While Note 6 reveals that

certain loans have been repaid during the year no mention is made of any additional loans raised. The overall effect on working capital is therefore:

		£000	£000
debit	Mortgage debenture	80	
credit	'Working capital'		80

Being repayment of mortgage debenture and application of working capital

Step 4. Reconciliation of changes identified in Steps 1, 2 and 3

In summary, the above analysis reveals the following sources and applications of working capital:

		£000
Sources		
From operations	(2b)	111
Issue of ordinary shares	(2a)	60
Disposals of: Plant and machinery	(1c)	13
Motor vehicles	(1d)	2
		186
Applications		
Taxation paid	(2b)	33
Redemption of debentures	(3)	80
Investment in non-current assets:		
Plant and machinery	(1c)	31
Motor vehicles	(1d)	26
Research and development	(1c)	10
		180

The increase in working capital over the year is calculated as the excess of Sources over Applications, £6000.

In order to produce the statement required by SSAP 10, movements in the component elements of working capital and the resultant effect on net liquid assets must also be shown. Movements in the component elements of Working capital may be calculated as follows:

	Working Capital		Change Increase/ Decrease
	1.1.84	31.12.84	
	£000	£000	£000
Decrease in stocks	117	84	(33)
Decrease in debtors and prepayments	86	67	(19)
Decrease in Trade creditors and accruals	(82)	(40)	42
Increase in cash balance	(7)	9	16
	£114	£120	£6

Analysis of accounting statements

The complete statement can now be prepared to comply with the requirements of SSAP 10 (apart from the inclusion of comparative figures) and is shown in Table 14.4.

14.5 Cash flow statements

Introduction

The Funds Flow Statement required by SSAP 10 is not based on a concept of cash as the definition of funds. In order to prepare a statement from published financial statements, based on a 'cash' definition of funds, items included in the Income Statement on an accruals basis must be adjusted to a cash basis.

Preparation of a Funds Statement on a cash basis is demonstrated in the following section using the information provided earlier for Bailey plc together with the following additional information:

(i) Total debtors consists of:

	1984 £000	1983 £000
Trade debtors	62	79
Prepaid expenses	5	7
	67	86

(ii) Current liabilities includes:

Trade creditors	31	65
Interest payable	1	3
Accrued expenses	8	14
	£40	£82

Preparation of Cash Flow Statement

The statement of sources and applications of funds illustrated in Table 14.4 identifies all sources and applications of funds on a cash basis, except for 'funds from operations'. Funds from operations were calculated as follows:

	£000
Sales	863
Cost of goods sold	475
	388
Operating expenses (excluding depreciation etc.)	264
	124
Interest expense	13
Funds from operations	111

As this calculation involves figures calculated on an accruals basis, these must be adjusted to identify cash movements, as follows:

TABLE 14.4

Bailey plc
Statement of Sources and Applications of Funds
For The Year Ended 31 December 1984

	£000	£000
Sources of funds from operations		
Profits before depreciation and tax		111
Other sources:		
Issue of Ordinary Shares		60
Disposal of fixed assets:		
Plant and machinery	13	
Motor vehicles	2	15
		186
Applications of funds		
Taxation paid	33	
Redemption of debentures	80	
Investments in non-current assets:		
Plant and machinery	31	
Motor vehicles	26	
Research and development	10	180
Increase in Working Capital		6
Decrease in Stocks	(33)	
Decrease in Debtors and Prepayments	(19)	
Decrease in Creditors (excluding taxation and proposed dividends)	42	
Movement in net liquid funds:		
Increase in Cash balances	16	
		6

		£000
(i)	*Receipts from customers*	
	Sales revenue	863
	Add trade debtors 1.1.84	79
		942
	Less trade debtors 31.12.84	62
	Cash received from customers	880
(ii)	*Payments to suppliers*	
	Cost of goods sold	475
	Add stock 31.12.84	84
		559
	Less stock 1.1.84	117
	Goods purchased	442
	Add trade creditors 1.1.84	65
		507
	Less trade creditors 31.12.84	31
	Payments to suppliers	476

Analysis of accounting statements

(iii) *Operating expenditures* £000
    Operating expenses   264
    Add accrued expenses 1.1.84   14
        prepaid expenses 31.12.84   5
            283
    Less accrued expenses 31.12.84   (8)
        prepaid expenses 1.1.84   (7)
    Expenditures incurred   268

(iv) *Interest payments*
    Interest expense   13
    Add interest payable 1.1.84   3
            16
    Less interest payable 31.12.84   1
    Payments made   15

Summarising (i) to (iv) above:
    Receipts from customers   880
    Less payments:
        to suppliers   476
        expenses paid   268
        interest paid   15   759
    Funds from operations   121

A Funds Flow Statement for Bailey plc, prepared on a cash basis is shown in Table 14.5.

TABLE 14.5

Bailey plc
Statement of Sources and Applications of Funds (Cash Basis) for the year ended 31 December 1984

	£000	£000	£000
Source of Funds			
From operations			121
Proceeds of Issue of Ordinary Shares			60
Proceeds of Disposal of Fixed Assets:			
Plant and machinery		13	
Motor vehicles		2	15
			196
Applications			
Taxation paid		33	
Redemption of debentures		80	
Investments in non-current assets:			
Plant and machinery	31		
Motor vehicles	26		
Research and development	10	67	180
Increase in Cash Balance			16

14.6 Summary

The external users of financial accounting statements may use a variety of techniques to extract information in a form suitable for specific needs. One of the most common techniques is the compilation of accounting ratios to explain relationships within a firm. Accounting ratios may also be used for comparison either with ratios produced for other businesses, or with those of the same firm for previous years. The use of ratio analysis is limited to a certain extent by the lack of comparability of accounting practices between firms, despite the activities of the Accounting Standards Committee and the requirements of corporate legislation.

The statement of sources and applications of funds provided in accordance with SSAP 10 provides information on financing and investment policies adopted by a business. The statement may also be modified to a cash flow basis by adjustment to the figure of 'funds from operations'.

Questions

1. Identify the major advantages and limitations involved in the use of accounting ratios in the analysis of accounting information.
2. Describe the merits and deficiencies of the following bases of comparison of financial ratios:
   (a) past performance;
   (b) industry average performance.
3. Explain under what circumstances each of the following concepts of capital might be chosen as the denominator of a ratio measuring overall profitability. For each of the concepts of capital, identify the appropriate definition of profit to be used as numerator:

   (a) total assets, including fixed assets at gross cost;
   (b) total assets, including fixed assets at net cost;
   (c) total net assets, i.e., total assets less total liabilities.
4. What are the alternative concepts of 'funds'? Explain which concepts the following groups would be most interested in: (a) trade creditors; (b) investors; (c) competitors.
5. Identify industries in which you would expect to observe the following characteristics:

   (a) low profit margins with high sales turnover ratios;
   (b) low sales turnover ratios with high profit margins;
   (c) high stock levels;
   (d) low stock levels.
6. Explain the significance of the current ratio. Is it possible for this ratio to be too high?

For each of the following **circle** the *letter* alongside the *best choice* from among the possible solutions presented.

7. For the XYZ Company, the ratio of sales to total assets in 1983 was 2.4 while operating profit on total assets was 6 per cent. Sales for 1983 totalled £120 000. Operating profit for 1983 was:

   (a) £7200;
   (b) £17 280;
   (c) £2500;
   (d) £3000.

8. The following information is available from the financial statements of ABC Enterprises at the end of the 1984 accounting year:

Sales	£480 000
Gross profit margin	20 per cent
Stock turnover	12 times
Debtors' turnover	8 times
Cash in hand	£6500
Current ratio	2.5

   Current liabilities at the end of the 1984 accounting year totalled:

   (a) £42 600;
   (b) £39 400;
   (c) £246 250;
   (d) £31 933.

9. The following information was extracted from the Balance Sheet of PQR Products at 31 December 1983:

Total debt to total assets	50 per cent
Current ratio	1.25
Fixed assets	£160 000
Current liabilities	£64 000

   Shareholders' funds at 31 December 1983 were:

   (a) £240 000;
   (b) £120 000;
   (c) £104 000;
   (d) £180 000.

10. Notes to the accounts of MNO Electronics for 1984 revealed the following information:

	Cost £000	Accum. depn £000
Plant and equipment 1.7.83	167	94
Plant and equipment 30.6.84	175	93

    Depreciation on plant and equipment of £33 000 was charged in 1984, and included a loss on disposal of plant and equipment amounting to £4000. New equipment, costing £46 000 was acquired during 1984. Proceeds of disposal of plant and equipment amounted to:

    (a) £4000;
    (b) £8000;
    (c) nil;
    (d) £12 000.

11. Retained profits of Smith plc for the year ended 31 May 1984 amounted to £176 000 after adjusting for the following:

Depreciation	£110 000
Amortisation of development expenditure	£36 000
Interest payable	£34 000
Gain on disposal of fixed assets	£17 000
Directors' fees	£24 000
Proposed dividends	£20 000
Corporation tax payable	£84 000

The source of funds from operations applicable to the funds flow statement prepared in accordance with SSAP 10 is:

(a) £409 000;
(b) £467 000;
(c) £443 000;
(d) £305 000.

12. The summarised Profit and Loss Account of Baird Products for the year ended 31 March 1984 is as follows:

	£000
Sales	864
Cost of sales	709
	155
Operating expenses	84
Profit before tax	71

The operating expenses included depreciation of £9000. The following additional

	1.4.83	31.3.84
	£000	£000
Trade debtors	94	111
Prepaid expenses	7	4
Trade creditors	86	91
Accrued expenses	13	19
Stock of goods for resale	124	136

Total funds from operations for 1984, calculated on a cash basis, is:

(a) £81 000;
(b) £73 000;
(c) £59 000;
(d) £65 000.

Problems

1. The summarised Balance Sheet and Profit and Loss Accounts of Norse plc at 31 December 1983 and 1984 are given below:

Balance sheet	1983		1984	
	£000	£000	£000	£000
Freehold premises at cost		90		90
Plant and equipment	120		160	
Less accumulated depreciation	50	70	70	90
Stocks	45		48	
Debtors	62		46	
Cash	8	115	2	96
		275		276

Analysis of accounting statements

	Ordinary share capital	100	100
	Share premium	20	20
	Retained profits	32	40
	10% Debenture stock	60	60
	Trade creditors	50	47
	Accrued expenses	13	9
		275	276

Profit and Loss Account

1983			1984
£000			£000
135		Sales	154
90		Cost of sales	109
45		Gross profit	45
	14	Distribution expenses	17
	8	Administrative expenses	10
22			27
23		Operating profit	18
6		Interest payable	6
17			12
6		Ordinary dividend paid	4
11			8
21		Retained profits b/f	32
32		Retained profits c/f	40

(a) From the information provided calculate the following ratios for 1984:

> Current ratio
> Acid test
> Stock turnover
> Debtors' turnover
> Sales to fixed assets
> Gross profit margin
> Return on total assets
> Return on shareholders' funds

(b) Explain the significance of each of the ratios calculated in part (a).

2. Using the following information together with the information provided in problem 1, prepare a Statement of Sources and Applications of Funds for Norse plc for 1984, in accordance with the requirements of SSAP 10.

   (i) Additional plant and equipment was acquired during the year at a cost £60 000. Old equipment was disposed of at its net book value of £7000.
   (ii) Depreciation charged on plant and equipment in 1984 amounted to £33 000.

3. The summarised Balance Sheet and Profit and Loss Account of Alba plc for 1984 are given below:

Alba plc
Balance Sheet at 30 June 1984

1983 £000				1984 £000
12 000	Ordinary share capital			14 500
700	Share premium			2 300
3 460	Retained profits			4 850
16 160				21 650
4 000	7% Redeemable preference shares			2 500
8 000	10% Debenture stock			6 000
28 160				30 150
6 000	Freehold land and buildings			5 800
9 400	Plant and machinery			7 600
	8 950	Stocks	9 760	
	11 220	Debtors and prepayments	15 470	
	180	Cash	950	
	20 350		26 180	
	7 590	Trade creditors and accruals	9 430	
12 760				16 750
28 160				30 150

Alba plc
Profit and Loss Account for the year ended 30 June 1984

1983 £000			1984 £000
64 800	Sales		72 400
52 450	Cost of sales		59 300
12 350	Gross profit		13 100
(5 650)	Distribution expenses	6 410	
(2 980)	Administrative expenses	3 420	9 830
3 720	Operating profit		3 270
1 000	Interest payable		800
2 720			2 470
	Dividends paid and proposed:		
(600)	Ordinary shares	800	
(350)	Preference shares	280	1 080
1 770			1 390
1 690	Retained profit b/f		3 460
3 460	Retained profit c/f		4 850

Average accounting ratios for 1984, for the industrial category to which Alba plc belongs are as follows:

Analysis of accounting statements

	Industrial average
Total assets turnover	1.5
Long-term debt to total assets	20%
Stock turnover	8 times
Debtors turnover	6 times
Current ratio	2.25
Acid test	1.5
Gross profit margin	20%
Operating profit margin	8%
Return on shareholders' funds	$16\frac{2}{3}$%

Required
- (a) Compute each of the above ratios for Alba plc for 1984 (and 1983 where available).
- (b) Comment on any differences between the ratios for Alba and the industrial averages and identify any areas to which the management of Alba plc should pay specific attention.
- (c) Using a total assets figure of £100, prepare in a summarised form, a Balance Sheet and Profit and Loss Account based on the 1984 industry averages. Assume that the typical company in the industry grouping has no preference capital and pays interest at the rate of 10 per cent on any debenture capital outstanding. Assume further that the industry average ratios have been calculated based on closing Balance Sheet figures.

4. (a) From the information provided in the financial statements for Braemar Ltd for 1983 prepare a report to management covering each of the following:
   - (i) asset utilisation;
   - (ii) liquidity and solvency;
   - (iii) profitability.

Include relevant ratios in your report together with comparative figures for 1982.
- (b) Identify any additional information which you would wish to obtain in order to clarify any issues raised in the report in (a).

Braemar Ltd
Profit and Loss Account for the year ended 31 December 1983

1982 £000		1983 £000
245	Sales	258
150	Cost of sales	170
95	Gross profit	88
32	Distribution expenses	27
24	Administrative expenses	31
39		30
3	Interest payable	4
36	Profit before tax	26
6	Corporation tax on profits	8
30	Profit after tax	18
16	Dividends paid and proposed	8
14	Retained profit for year	10
(8)	Retained profit brought forward	6
6	Retained profit carried forward	16

Braemar Ltd
Balance Sheet at 31 December 1983

	31 Dec 1982 £000	31 Dec 1982 £000	31 Dec 1983 £000	31 Dec 1983 £000
Fixed assets:				
Land and buildings		30		46
Other fixed assets:				
at cost	70		80	
less: accumulated depn	30		40	
		40		40
		70		86
Research and development expenditure:		10		30
Current assets				
Trade debtors	15		20	
Stocks	20		16	
Cash	5		4	
		40		40
		£120		£156
Share capital and reserves:				
Ordinary share capital		50		60
Share premium		5		12
Undistributed profits		6		16
		61		88
10% Debenture stock		30		44
Current liabilities:				
Trade creditors	13		14	
Taxation payable	6		8	
Dividends payable	10		2	
		29		24
		£120		£156

(c) From the information provided in the financial statements for Braemar Ltd, together with the additional information given below, prepare a Statement of Sources and Applications of Funds in accordance with the requirements of SSAP 10.

Additional information:
(i) Depreciation on buildings during the year amounted to £4000.
(ii) Other fixed assets, which had cost £24 000 some years previously were sold in 1983 for £8000. The net book value of these assets at 31 December 1982 was £14 000.
(iii) Amortisation of development expenditure during 1983 amounted to £4000.
(iv) A 'one for five' rights issue was made during 1983 at a price of £1.70 per share.
(v) An issue of £14 000, 10% debenture stock was made during 1983.

15 Accounting for Inflation

15.1 Introduction

As the title suggests, the current chapter considers the issue of accounting for inflation. Although there have been many problems and issues confronting the accounting community in recent years, none has occupied so much time and energy, or produced so much heated debate, as this issue. Although the attention given to this issue is partly due to the importance of the subject itself, other contributing factors include the amount of government involvement[1] in the issue, and also the nature of the proposed solutions.

As will be explained in later sections, proposals have been advanced for two types of accounting adjustment for inflation. The first, using 'stabilised' accounts, involves the replacement of the monetary unit with units of 'general purchasing power', while the second, based on a system of current cost accounting, involves the replacement of the traditional system of historic cost accounting itself.

The term 'inflation' itself has no universally accepted definition, although common usage seems to imply a general increase in the price of goods and services, leading to a consequent fall in the general purchasing power of money. Early attempts to deal with the problem of financial reporting during periods of instability in the unit of currency adopted this definition and tended to concentrate on solutions which produce a stable unit of measurement, based on general purchasing power.

Opponents of this approach have suggested that the concept of general inflation and purchasing power has little validity as the consumption patterns of individuals and of businesses differ so markedly from one another. Counter-proposals which have emerged were based instead on adjustment for changes in the price of the specific goods and services acquired by each business. These proposals have themselves been criticised as measures which are not concerned with accounting for inflation, but with changing the basis of valuation of accounting 'whether there is any general inflation or not'.[2]

15.2 The history of inflation accounting

Interest in the subject of accounting for inflation is not confined either to the United Kingdom or even to this present generation. Rather the issue is one which has occupied the minds of accountants in most developed economies over many years. Indeed, early attempts to come to grips with the issue must be traced to continental Europe in the 1920s and 1930s, and in particular to France and Germany. In both countries rampant inflation in the years following the end of the First World War had made the preparation of accounting reports, based on a highly unstable unit of currency, a meaningless exercise. The solution adopted to deal with the problem was to prepare supplementary reports based on a stable unit of measurement; the gold franc being adopted by France and the gold mark by Germany. As the rates of inflation in each country eventually fell the supplementary reports were abandoned.

During the period between the two World Wars a number of writers in the United States also addressed themselves to the problem of accounting for inflation. The writings of H. W. Sweeney in particular, influenced the views of many of his contemporaries, and also his successors.[3] Sweeney advocated the use of a replacement cost system of accounting, but with additional adjustments to reflect changes in the general level of prices. As has been the case recently, interest in the subject of accounting for inflation waned on both sides of the Atlantic when the rate of inflation itself fell. Only when the rate of inflation began to rise again in the late 1940s and early 1950s did interest in the accounting issue also pick up.

After the end of the Second World War there had been expectations that the level of inflation experienced during the war years would slow down. That this did not take place was due in part to the commitment of the post-war governments to a policy of full employment and the adoption of different monetary policies. As the level of inflation increased, so the interest of the accounting profession increased. The research committees of both the Association of Certified and Corporate Accountants, and the Institute of Cost and Works Accountants produced reports which advocated the adoption of a system of replacement cost accounting.[4] The Institute of Chartered Accountants in England and Wales (ICAEW), however, rejected any move away from the traditional system of historic cost accounting. By the mid-1950s the level of inflation had once again fallen to a sufficiently low level for the interest of the accounting bodies to fall also.

By the late 1960s the rate of inflation was once again rising. The research committee of the ICAEW produced a report in 1968[5] advocating the production of statements prepared on the basis of adjustments for changes in the general purchasing power of money, as supplements to the basic historic cost statements. In January 1973, shortly after the establishment of the Accounting Standards Steering Committee (ASSC) an exposure draft, ED8 'Accounting for Changes in the Purchasing Power of Money' was issued, based largely on the recommendations of the ICAEW research document. Supplementary accounting statements were to be prepared based on a common unit of measurement, i.e., units of 'current purchasing power' at the closing Balance Sheet date. Similar proposals were proposed in an exposure draft issued in 1974 in the United States.[6]

In July 1973, shortly before the discussion period on ED8 was due to expire, the government announced that it was itself setting up a committee of enquiry into the subject. This committee held its first meeting in January

1974. (It was later known as the Sandilands Committee.) Meanwhile the ASSC issued a Provisional Statement of Standard Accounting Practice, PSSAP 7,[7] based on the recommendations of ED8.

The report of the Sandilands Committee, eventually published in 1975, rejected the proposal for a system of stabilised accounting based on historic costs and proposed instead a system of current cost accounting based on a concept of 'value to the business'.

The accounting bodies reacted to the recommendations of the Sandilands Report by forming a sub-committee of the Accounting Standards Committee (formerly the ASSC) under the chairmanship of Douglas Morpeth, with a brief to produce an exposure draft based on a system of current cost accounting. In November 1976, ED 18 'Current Cost Accounting' was available, setting out in detail a comprehensive system of financial reporting based on current cost accounting. By this time, however, opposition to the implementation of a system of current cost accounting was also emerging amongst the 'grass roots' of the accounting profession. This opposition had achieved sufficient support to require an extraordinary general meeting of the ICAEW in July 1977 at which a resolution was passed preventing the adoption of a compulsory system of current cost accounting. As a result of that resolution, ED 18 was withdrawn and the ASC forced to rethink its ideas.

New proposals were presented in November 1977 to the ASC, the so-called Hyde guidelines,[8] recommending a simplified form of current cost accounting, to be used in statements supplementary to the basic historic cost statements. These guidelines were adopted subject to minor modifications in ED 24, published in April 1979, and subsequently in SSAP 16, Current Cost Accounting, published in March 1980.

The system of current cost accounting advocated in SSAP 16 should be seen therefore, as a compromise between a system of stabilised accounting, based on historic costs, and a comprehensive system of current costs. Opponents and proponents of each system continue to argue the merits of their own favoured system and to reject the alternatives. There are those who support a more comprehensive system of current cost accounting and there are those amongst the accounting profession, particularly amongst the small practitioners, who view the system described in SSAP 16 as one imposed on the accounting profession from outside. There is even a group who advocate that inflation has once again fallen to a level where it is no longer necessary to consider the issue of accounting for inflation.

15.3 Inflation and historic cost accounting

Introduction

Earlier chapters have commented upon deficiencies in historic cost accounting, in particular the allocation problem, even during periods in which inflation is low or even non-existent. The additional difficulties presented by rapidly changing prices have led to increased questioning of the wisdom of retaining the historic cost system. Many of the arguments relating to the inadequacy of a system of historic cost accounting during inflationary periods are inextricably linked with the basic deficiencies in the system itself. It is, however, possible to identify three broad areas of criticism of historic cost accounting which relate, in the main, to the effects of inflation. These three areas are:

(i) Non-additivity of financial statement figures;
(ii) Lack of comparability of accounting reports;
(iii) Non-maintenance of capital.

Criticisms of historic cost

(a) *Non-additivity of data*
This criticism rests on the view that to be meaningful, the addition of figures and indeed their subtraction, must be based on the use of the same unit of measurement for all figures. Accounts based on historic costs will include items acquired over a number of years at prices based on different units of measurement, i.e., different levels of purchasing power. The addition of these items, it is argued, is similar to adding items denominated in different foreign currencies and expecting to arrive at a meaningful total.

(b) *Non-comparability of data*
This criticism relates to the fact that it will be difficult, if not impossible, to compare the financial results of business enterprises in a meaningful manner, if similar items were acquired or expended at different points in time. This lack of comparability will relate both to comparisons between different firms in the same period of time and for the same firm across a number of years.

Illustration 1
Assume Business A acquires an asset in Year 1 at a cost of £1000. Business B acquires an identical asset in Year 2 but the price of this asset has since risen to £1500. During Year 2 both assets generate net income to their respective businesses of £150.

The reported rate of historic cost profits earned on the gross asset of each business, ignoring depreciation will be:

Business A	Business B
$\frac{£150}{£1000} \times 100\%$	$\frac{£150}{£1500} \times 100\%$
$= \underline{\underline{15\%}}$	$= \underline{\underline{10\%}}$

It appears, therefore, that Business A is more efficient than Business B when in fact the return generated on the asset owned by each business is equal.[9] In fact if the asset acquired was also a depreciating asset, then it is quite likely that Business A will also show a higher reported profit figure than B because it will almost certainly have a lower depreciation expense in Year 2 (unless the depreciation pattern adopted involves an annual increase in the depreciation expense).

(c) *Non-maintenance of capital*
During periods of rising prices, profits calculated on the basis of historic cost

Accounting for inflation

rules will not be distributable to owners and still ensure the maintenance of the physical amount of capital invested.

Illustration 2

Consider a firm, ABC Products, which sells a single commodity X and which carries out all transactions on a cash basis. Initial investment by the owners is £10 which is sufficient to buy one unit of the commodity. No other assets are held by the firm. During Year 1 the commodity is sold at a price of £20 and the historic cost profit is distributed to the owners. The historic cost profit, and amount available for distribution, is calculated as follows:

	£
Sales	20
Less cost of goods sold	10
Profit available for distribution	£10

Assume that the firm wishes to continue as a going concern, and in the same line of business, but that inflation has increased the cost price of the commodity to £12 at the commencement of Year 2.

The Balance Sheet of the firm, as illustrated in Table 15.1 shows that the funds available will be insufficient to purchase the replacement unit of X. The firm must either borrow additional funds, or else require an additional investment by the owners. Hence it is argued that the historic cost profit calculation understated the amount which should have been set aside to provide for maintenance of business operations.

Obviously the above illustration presents an over-simplified situation and in fact businesses are normally involved in continuous replacement of expired resources. However, the point which may be drawn from the illustration is that the historic cost profit will not be available for distribution, if that is what the owners desire, and still ensure that the business can continue at the same level of operations as previously, without borrowing additional funds or requiring additional investments.

Some commentators have argued that this problem is not one of capital maintenance but one of financing ongoing operations during periods of inflation.[10] Others have accepted that the problem involves capital maintenance, but as we shall see, have disagreed over the appropriate definition of capital to be maintained.

TABLE 15.1

ABC Products
Balance Sheet

Assets	Time 0	End of Year 1
	£	£
Commodity X	10	—
Cash	—	10
	10	10
Owners' interest	10	10

15.4 Current purchasing power accounting

Introduction

Proposed solutions to the problems of financial reporting during periods of inflation range from the use of piecemeal adjustments, such as Lifo stock valuation, to the comprehensive system of current cost accounting proposed by Sandilands. In betwen these extremes, are two other proposals which have at different times been advocated and accepted in the United Kingdom. The first of these involves the adjustment of all items in financial statements for changes in the general level of inflation and is described as general purchasing power, or *stabilised*, accounting. The second proposal adopted involves the adjustment of selected items for specific changes in their cost from their date of acquisition. It has been suggested that these two approaches reflect different perceptions of the nature of business enterprises; the first involving a 'proprietorship viewpoint', identifies each business as an extension of the owners and advocates maintenance of ownership capital; the second involves an 'entity viewpoint' with each business being regarded as separate or distinct from the owners and advocates maintenance of the operating (or earnings) capacity of the business.[11] Both approaches will be considered together with the comprehensive system advocated by the Sandilands Committee.

General purchasing power adjustments

General purchasing power accounting involves restatement of all historic cost account figures into units of what are described as 'general purchasing power'. These units are further identified with a specific point in time. ED 8 and PSSAP 7 adopt the closing Balance Sheet date as the appropriate point in time, and hence describe the units as 'current purchasing power' (CPP) units. The restatement process involves an adjustment for the changes in an index measuring the general level of prices, with the retail price index (RPI) being adopted in the United Kingdom.

Illustration 3

Consider the illustration given earlier for ABC Products and the sale of the single unit of commodity X. Assume that the initial unit of X was acquired when the RPI stood at 100 and that it was sold on the last day of the accounting year, when the RPI stood at 120. Adjustment of the cost of the initial unit of X would be undertaken as follows:

CPP cost: £10 × 120/100 = £12.

As the selling price is already in units of CPP, the revised CPP Income Statement for Year 1 becomes:

	£
Sales revenue	20
Less restated cost of goods sold	12
CPP profit	£ 8

Advocates of this form of adjustment argue that restatement in terms of a common unit of currency overcomes the problem of non-additivity as all items are now stated in the same unit. Critics, however, have argued that the unit chosen is meaningless and that individual investors and business enterprises are not subject to general rates of inflation, but rather to rates which are specific to their own individual consumption and investment patterns.[12]

Restatement in terms of a general index will not remove the lack of comparability of results of different enterprises, unless the costs of their resources also change in line with the general index. However, comparability may be increased within a firm for certain items by the use of CPP adjustments, e.g., to identify the 'real' change in the levels of revenues or expenses. Even in this latter case, however, such adjustments imply that the prices of the items being compared move in line with the general index of price changes.

It may also be argued that adjustments to CPP does not allow for maintenance of the general purchasing power of shareholders' capital or wealth. It has already been pointed out that shareholders will have individual purchasing patterns and will therefore be affected by specific, not general, levels of inflation. In any event, shareholders' wealth (or capital) is not maintained (except in legal terms) by considering the amount recorded in business accounts, whether stated in CPP terms or any other. Rather, shareholders' wealth will only be maintained if the market value of the investment is equal to its original cost, after making suitable adjustments, if so desired, for changes in the individual investor's specific level of inflation.

In summary, CPP adjustments do not appear to remove the specific deficiencies introduced into historic cost accounts by changes in price levels and the approach advocated by PSSAP 7 should therefore be discarded.[13]

One issue raised by advocates of CPP adjustments and included in PSSAP 7 is, however, worthy of further consideration. This involves the distinction between monetary and non-monetary items.

PSSAP 7 defined monetary items as 'assets, liabilities or capital, the amounts of which are fixed by contract or statute in terms of pounds regardless of changes in the purchasing power of the pound'.[14] Non-monetary items are defined as 'all items which are not monetary items, with the exception of the total equity interest'.[15] The latter is regarded as neither a monetary nor a non-monetary item.

The effect of this distinction was to introduce into the statement the notion that shareholders made losses or gains on holding net monetary assets, or net monetary liabilities. As will be seen later, this idea has been carried into SSAP 16, although in a slightly modified form. The identification of gains and losses on monetary items is illustrated in the worked example on CPP adjustments given in the Appendix at the end of this chapter.

15.5 The Sandilands Committee

Introduction

The Sandilands Committee rejected the CPP approach and proposed instead a comprehensive current cost accounting system based on what was described as 'value to the business'.

The main recommendations were:

(i) Assets and liabilities to be included in the Balance Sheet at 'value to the business', while 'operating profit' is calculated after charging the 'value to the business' of assets consumed during the period;
(ii) Holding gains to be excluded from operating profits and shown separately;
(iii) Current cost accounts to become the basic published accounts with historic cost information relegated to a supplementary status;
(iv) No adjustments for CPP to be made or to be provided in supplementary statements.

As the concept of 'value to the business' is considered to be central to the proposals of the Sandilands Committee a brief explanation is given in the next section of the nature of this concept.

Value to the business

Three alternative general bases of asset valuation are suggested by the Sandilands Committee:

(i) Current replacement cost (RC);
(ii) Net realisable value or disposal value (NRV);
(iii) Present value of the expected future earnings, or Economic Value (PV).

There are six ways in which these three bases may be ranked in order of magnitude, namely:

1. NRV > PV > RC
2. NRV > RC > PV
3. PV > RC > NRV
4. PV > NRV > RC
5. RC > PV > NRV
6. RC > NRV > PV

The value of an asset to a business is identified as an *opportunity loss*, or *deprival value*, with the following definition, given originally by Professor J. C. Bonbright, adopted by the Sandilands Committee:

> The value of a property to its owner is identical in amount with the adverse value of the entire loss, direct and indirect, that the owner might expect to suffer if he were to be deprived of the property.[16]

Value to the business in the six combinations of PV, NRV and RC listed above is as follows:

(i) In cases 1 and 2 the firm is better off by disposing of the asset rather than using it as NRV > PV. However, the maximum loss which the firm would suffer if deprived of the asset is RC, since by purchasing another asset of the same type the firm will once again be able to gain the NRV by disposing of it.
(ii) In cases 3 and 4, the firm would be better off by using the asset rather than disposing of it, since PV > NRV. However, the maximum loss that

the firm would suffer if deprived of the asset is RC since this is the amount required to replace the asset.

(iii) Only in cases 5 and 6 will RC not equal the value of the asset to the business. In case 5 the value will be PV, while in case 6 the value will be NRV.

In the view of the Sandilands Committee the low likelihood of occurrence of cases 5 and 6 suggests 'that in the great majority of cases it' (i.e., replacement cost) 'will correctly represent the value of an asset to a business'.[17]

Current cost profit

In an historic cost accounting system the measurement of profit includes not only gains and losses from the operations of the accounting period under examination but also realised *holding gains* and *losses*.

Holding gains (and losses) are 'the difference between the measured value to a company of an asset at any point of time and the original cost incurred by the company in purchasing that asset (less depreciation where appropriate)'.[18] Holding gains may be either realised or unrealised gains. A realised gain will arise from the sale or disposal by a business of any form of goods, services, assets or liabilities. Unrealised holding gains arise when the measured amount of any asset held by a business increases during the year and the asset is still retained at the end of the year.

Illustration 4

XYZ Ltd own a fixed asset which was acquired at Time 0 at a cost of £100. The asset is depreciated on a straight line basis over a two-year useful life, assuming no salvage value at the end of that time. Annual net revenues, before depreciation, of £80 per annum are obtained from use of the asset.

Assume that the 'value to the business' i.e., replacement cost, of a similar asset is £120 at the end of Year 1. Historic cost profit of £30 for each of the two years of useful life of the asset are reported as shown in Table 15.2.

The historic cost profit for Year 1 includes a realised holding gain on the assets of £10, i.e., £$(120-100) \times \frac{1}{2}$. An unrealised holding gain of a further £10 is excluded from Year 1 profits.

Similarly, the historic cost profit of Year 2 includes £10 holding gain realised in Year 2, but arising in Year 1 as shown in Table 15.3.

The Sandilands Committee suggested that only the operating profit should be considered to be the profit of a business, with holding gains excluded and

TABLE 15.2

XYZ Ltd
Historic Cost Income Statement

	Year 1 £	Year 2 £
Net Revenues	80	80
Less depreciation	50	50
Historic cost profit	£30	£30

TABLE 15.3

XYZ Ltd
Operating versus Holding Gains

	Year 1 £	Year 2 £
Net Revenues	80	80
Less		
depreciation based on 'value to the business'	60	60
Operating profit	20	20
Realised holding gain	10	10
Historic cost profit	30	30
Unrealised holding gain	10	—

shown separately. Operating profit would then be calculated by deducting from revenues the value to the business of resources consumed in generating these revenues. By adopting this approach it was argued that the operating capacity of the business would be maintained.

The unit of measurement would continue to be the money unit, without adjustments for changes in the purchasing power of the unit of currency. It may also be argued that both additivity of data and comparability would be restored through the application of the same criteria to the data to be included, i.e., each should represent 'value to the business'.

Operating profit, or current cost profit, was to be calculated, according to the recommendation of the Sandilands Committee, after adjusting depreciation and cost of goods consumed to their value to the business. No further adjustments were considered necessary to the historic cost profits: 'so far as the profit and loss account is concerned, we think that these two adjustments to historic cost accounts, *and these two alone*, constitute a comprehensive system of accounting for inflation'.[19]

The Sandilands Committee considered whether any adjustment to profits should be made for gains and losses on monetary items but concluded that as the accounts were drawn up in terms of the monetary unit no such gains or losses would arise.[20]

15.6 SSAP 16: Current cost accounting

Introduction

As was mentioned earlier, the recommendations of the Sandilands Committee were to a large extent included in the proposals of ED 18. The exposure draft, however, did go one stage further than the Sandilands Committee in recommending not only that current cost accounts should replace historic cost accounts as the main form of published reports, but that the underlying records should also be prepared on a current cost rather than an historic cost basis. After the rejection of ED 18 by the ICAEW membership in July 1977, the ASC introduced a modified form of CCA adjustments in the interim Hyde Guidelines from which ED 24 evolved in April 1979 and SSAP 16 in March 1980.

Current Cost Profit and SSAP 16

SSAP 16 was described in its explanatory foreword as 'based upon a concept of capital which is represented by the net operating assets of a business'.[21] Net operating assets were defined as including fixed assets, stock and monetary working capital, and represented, according to SSAP 16, the operating capability of the business.

Current cost operating profit is identified by making three adjustments to historic cost profit (before interest charges):

(i) depreciation adjustment;
(ii) cost of sales adjustment;
(iii) monetary working capital adjustment.

The first and second of these adjustments are equivalent to adjusting depreciation and cost of goods sold from an historic cost basis to a 'value to the business' basis, as recommended earlier by the Sandilands Committee. The third adjustment, not mentioned in the Sandilands Report, is intended to 'represent the amount of additional (or reduced) finance needed for monetary working capital as a result of changes in the input prices of goods and services used and financed by the business'.[22]

Current cost operating profit is thus described as 'the surplus arising from the ordinary activities of the business in the period, after allowing for the impact of price changes on the funds needed to continue the existing business and maintain its operating capability *but without taking into account the way in which it is financed*'.[23]

A further adjustment is also recommended in SSAP 16 in order to arrive at 'current cost profit attributable to shareholders'. In arriving at this profit, *a gearing adjustment* was proposed to take into account the way in which the business is financed and the gains or losses which may accrue to shareholders as a result of debt financing.

SSAP 16, therefore, not only reintroduced adjustments for gains and losses on monetary items rejected by the Sandilands Committee, but also distinguished between those arising on net monetary working capital, and those arising on long-term borrowings.

The derivation of the two concepts of current cost profit identified in SSAP 16 from historic cost profit is illustrated in Table 15.4 using the figures provided in the Appendix to SSAP 16.

The recommended adjustments are made by reference to specific indices relating to groups of similar assets, where it is not possible to identify actual replacement costs.

Other Features of SSAP 16

(i) SSAP 16 recommended that the accounts prepared on a current cost basis should either be supplementary to the historic cost accounts or else be

TABLE 15.4 *Current cost profit and SSAP 16**

	£000
Historic cost profit before interest and taxation	2900
Less Current cost operating adjustments:	
Depreciation	950
Cost of sales	460
Monetary working capital	100
	1510
Current cost operating profit	1390
Interest payable less receivable	200
	1190
Taxation	730
Current cost profit after interest and taxation	460
Gearing adjustment	166
Current cost profit attributable to shareholders	626

*From the Appendix to SSAP 16.

the main accounts with historic cost information provided as supplementary accounts. A further alternative allowed the provision of sufficient historic cost information to meet the requirements of company law and to allow identification of historic cost profits as supplementary to the main current cost accounts. The freedom to choose whether the main account should be prepared on a current cost or an historic cost basis was later retained in the 1981 Companies Act.

(ii) SSAP 16 only applies to business entities falling within certain categories, excluding unlisted companies below a certain size, wholly owned subsidiaries of UK or Eire registered companies, not-for-profit organisations, and insurance and investment organisations.

(iii) A current cost Balance Sheet must be prepared, with fixed assets and stocks included in accordance with their value to the business, and current assets (other than stocks) and liabilities included on an historic cost basis. A current cost reserve should be shown in the Balance Sheet to include all 'revaluation surpluses or deficits and to allow for the impact of price changes in arriving at current cost profit attributable to shareholders'.[24]

(iv) Additional voluntary disclosures are suggested, including a statement comparing CCA profits and capital employed over a number of years for comparative purposes, e.g., 5 or 10 year statements, but with the figures included in these adjusted *to a common price basis*, i.e., adjusted for changes in general purchasing power.

Current cost operating adjustments

In this section the calculation of the current cost operating adjustments is illustrated using methods described in the appendices to the guidance notes for implementation of SSAP 16.[25]

Accounting for inflation

The historic cost accounts of Anon Ltd on which the adjustments are based are shown in Tables 15.5 and 15.6.

The following additional information is also relevant:

Historic cost expenses:
- Depreciation £10 000
- Cost of goods sold £80 000

All the fixed assets were assumed to have been acquired at the same time,

TABLE 15.5

Anon Ltd
Historic Cost Balance Sheet at 31 December 1983

31.12.82			31.12.83	
£000	£000		£000	£000
100		Fixed assets, at cost		100
20		Less accumulated depreciation		30
80				70
		Current assets		
	20	Stocks	36	
	15	Debtors and prepayments	25	
	5	Cash	14	
	40		75	
		Current liabilities		
	15	Trade creditors and accruals	25	
25		Net current assets		50
105				120
85		Share capital and reserves		100
20		10% Debenture stock		20
105				120

TABLE 15.6

Anon Ltd
Historic Cost Profit and Loss Account
for the year ended 31 December 1983

	£000
Turnover	180
Trading profit	36
Interest payable	2
Profit before taxation	34
Taxation	16
Profit attributable to shareholders	18
Dividend paid and proposed	3
Retained profit for the year	15

when the specific index relating to that category of assets stood at 40. Subsequent changes in the index are as follows:

31 December 1982	60
30 June 1983	68
31 December 1983	72

The three current cost operating adjustments are intended to identify (i) the additional expenses which would have been incurred if stocks and depreciating assets had been acquired at average cost during the year rather than at the price prevailing at their original acquisition date, and (ii) the additional cost of providing 'the specific monetary working capital necessary to maintain the business'.[26]

(a) *Depreciation adjustment*

The current cost depreciation charge for the year is based on average current cost over 1983. For simplicity, all the fixed assets are assumed to be covered by the same index. The charge is calculated as follows:

	£000
Gross current cost 1 January 1983:	
(£100 000 × 60/40)	150
Adjusted to average current cost for the year:	
£150 000 × 68/60	170
The year's current cost depreciation charge is	
£10 000 × 68/40	17
Less historic cost depreciation already charged	10
Depreciation adjustment	7

(b) *Cost of sales adjustment (COSA)*

It is assumed, for the purposes of this illustration, that stock levels rise at an even rate throughout the year and that the historic cost of goods sold has been calculated on a Fifo basis.

The relevant index numbers here relate to the average date of acquisition of the stocks and not to the dates prevailing at the beginning and end of the year, and are as follows:

	Index
Opening stocks	100
Closing stocks	120
Average for the year	105

The average for the year is assumed to be calculated on the basis of a simple monthly average. Where purchases occur unevenly, a weighted average should be calculated.

(i) From the historic cost of the closing stock, is deducted the historic cost of the opening stock to determine the total change in stocks, i.e.,

£36 000 − £20 000 = £16 000

Accounting for inflation

(ii) The effect of the volume (i.e., quantity) change in stock levels is then eliminated by deducting the average current cost of the opening stocks from the average current cost of the closing stocks as follows:

$$(\text{HC closing stock} \times \frac{\text{Average index number}}{\text{Closing index number}})$$
$$-(\text{HC opening stock} \times \frac{\text{Average index number}}{\text{Opening index number}})$$
$$=(£36\,000 \times 105/120) - (£20\,000 \times 105/100)$$
$$=£31\,500 - £21\,000$$
$$=\underline{\underline{£10\,500}}$$

Deducting the volume change from the total change in stocks the price increase may be identified:

$$\text{Cost of sales adjustment} = £16\,000 - £10\,500$$
$$= \underline{\underline{£5\,500}}$$

(c) *Monetary Working Capital Adjustment (MWCA)*

Monetary working capital is assumed, for purposes of this example, to include trade debtors and prepayments plus cash, less trade creditors and accruals. As monetary working capital is used to finance the day-to-day operations of the firm it is normally assumed that the same index may be used as was adopted for the cost of sales adjustment. Indeed, SSAP 16 allows the COSA and MWCA to be combined in the current cost accounts.

Opening and closing MWC and index levels at the average date on which these arose is:

	£000	Index
Opening MWC	5	102
Closing MWC	14	118
The average index is, as before		105

A similar calculation to that used to identify the COSA is used for determination of the MWCA, i.e., first the total change in MWC is identified:

$$£14\,000 - £5000 = £9000$$

Secondly, the volume change is eliminated by deducting the opening MWC from the closing MWC after adjusting both figures to the average 'price' for the period:

$$(\text{HC closing MWC} \times \frac{\text{Average index number}}{\text{Closing index number}})$$
$$-(\text{HC opening MWC} \times \frac{\text{Average index number}}{\text{Opening index number}})$$
$$=(£14\,000 \times 105/118) - (£5000 \times 105/102)$$
$$=£12\,458 - £5147$$
$$=\underline{\underline{£7311}}$$

Deducting the volume change from the total change gives the price change, i.e., the MWCA.

$$\text{MWCA} = £9000 - £7311$$
$$= £1689$$

The gearing adjustment

The gearing adjustment is perhaps the most contentious of all the current cost adjustments proposed in SSAP 16.[27] The Hyde guidelines had introduced a gearing adjustment as an abatement of the depreciation and cost of sales adjustments; reducing these by the proportion financed by borrowings, to reflect a reduction in the burden borne by the ordinary shareholders. The gearing adjustment adopted by SSAP 16 acts in a similar manner to that proposed in the Hyde guidelines, but as an abatement of the three current operating profit adjustments. The adjustment is intended to indicate 'the benefit or cost to shareholders which is realised in the period, measured by the extent to which a proportion of the net operating assets are financed by borrowing'.[28]

The calculation of gearing, advocated in SSAP 16, is based on average net borrowings for the year, excluding those items included in monetary working capital, and also excluding preference share capital. The gearing adjustment for Anon Ltd is calculated as follows:

Opening and closing net borrowings	= £20 000
i.e., average net borrowings	= £20 000

From the current cost Balance Sheet*

Opening net operating assets	= £125 800
Closing net operating assets	= £157 200
Average net operating assets	= £141 500

Gearing percentage $= \dfrac{£20\,000}{£141\,500} \times 100\% = \underline{14.13\%}$

Current cost operating adjustments:

Depreciation	£7 000
COSA	5 500
MWCA	1 689
	14 189 × 14.13% = £2006

The current cost Profit and Loss Account may now be prepared as shown in Table 15.7.

*In order to calculate the amount of current cost net operating assets the current cost Balance Sheet must first be constructed. Not all the figures in the current cost Balance Sheet will be capable of identification in advance of the determination of the gearing adjustment. However, total assets and total liabilities will be capable of determination and it is these which are used to determine net operating assets, i.e.

Net operating assets = Total assets − Total liabilities.

TABLE 15.7

Anon Ltd
Current Cost Profit and Loss Account
for the year ended 31 December 1983

	£	£
Turnover		180 000
Historic cost trading profit		36 000
Less: Current cost operating adjustments:		
Depreciation	7 000	
COSA	5 500	
MWCA	1 689	14 189
Current cost operating profit		21 811
Gearing adjustment	(2 006)	
Interest on borrowing*	2 000	(6)
Current cost profit before taxation		21 817
Taxation		16 000
Current cost profit attributable to shareholders		5 817
Dividends paid and proposed		3 000
Retained current cost profit of the year		2 817

*Alternative presentation to that illustrated in Table 15.4.

For the sake of order an explanation of the preparation of the current cost Balance Sheet is delayed until later.

Current Cost Reserve

(a) *Introduction*

The current cost Balance Sheet will include one additional reserve to those included in an historic cost Balance Sheet. This reserve, known as the current cost reserve, will include unrealised surpluses (or holding gains) on the revaluation of fixed assets, investments and stocks which are held by a company at the end of the financial year. In addition, the reserve will also include any realised surpluses (or holding gains) which have arisen since the date on which current cost accounts were first prepared by the company. Annual additions to realised surpluses will include both the current cost adjustments identified in the previous sections (depreciation, COSA, MWCA, gearing) and also realised revaluation surpluses on assets disposed of during the year. The latter surpluses would include a reclassification of previously unrealised surpluses accruing up to the date of disposal of the assets.

(b) *Opening balance*

The opening balance on the current cost reserve of Anon Ltd includes the unrealised holding gains on fixed assets and stocks from their date of acquisition to 1 January 1983.

(i) Unrealised holding gains on fixed assets are:

	£000
Net historic cost	80
Net current cost: 80 × (60/40)	120
Unrealised holding gain	40

(ii) Unrealised holding gains on stocks may be calculated as follows:
Assume that the specific index relating to stocks stood at 104 on 1 January 1983:

Historic cost:	£20 000
Current cost: £20 000 × (104/100)	20 800
Unrealised holding gain	800

(iii) Current cost reserve 1 January 1983   £40 800

(c) *Gains during 1983*

(i) *Revaluation of fixed assets* The specific index relating to fixed assets has risen from 60 at the commencement of the year to 72 at the end of the year. Gross current cost of fixed assets will therefore have risen from £150 000 to [£150 000 × (72/60)], i.e., £180 000, giving rise to an unrealised holding gain of £30 000.

Accumulated depreciation has also risen by the same ratio, i.e., current cost accumulated depreciation = £30 000 × (72/60) = £36 000. This adjustment to the *opening* balance of accumulated depreciation gives rise to what is known as a 'backlog depreciation charge' which is, however, debited to the current cost reserve rather than to the current cost Profit and Loss Account. The current cost depreciation charge for the year includes a realised holding gain of £7000. This amount will be debited to the current cost reserve.

The current cost depreciation charge which was calculated on the basis of the mid-year index of 68 must also be adjusted to reflect the rise in the specific index to 72 at the end of the financial year.

An additional backlog depreciation charge will arise amounting to:

$$£17\,000 \times (\frac{72-68}{68}) = \underline{\underline{£1000}}$$

This amount will also be debited to the current cost reserve. The net increase to the current cost reserve in respect of fixed assets in 1983 is therefore £16 000, i.e.

£30 000 − £(6000 + 7000 + 1000).

(ii) *Revaluation of stocks* Unrealised revaluation surpluses on stocks may be calculated by deducting the historic cost of stocks from their current cost at opening and closing Balance Sheet dates. The revaluation surplus on opening stocks has already been calculated in (a) as £800. Assuming that the specific index relating to stocks stood at 124 on 31 December 1983, the

Accounting for inflation

unrealised revaluation surplus on closing stocks may be calculated as follows:

Historic cost	£36 000
Current cost: £36 000 × (124/120) =	£37 200
Unrealised revaluation surplus 31 December 1983 = £1200	
Increase in revaluation surplus = £400	

(iii) *Realised holding gains* Realised holding gains occurring during the year and reported in the current cost Profit and Loss Account will also be transferred to the current cost reserve, i.e.,

Depreciation	7 000
COSA	5 500
MWCA	1 689
Gearing	(2 006)
	£12 183

(d) *Closing balance*

The current cost reserve at 31 December 1983 will consist of:

		£
Opening balance		40 800
Gains during 1983:		
Fixed assets (net)	16 000	
Stocks	400	
Realised gains	12 183	28 583
Balance 31 December 1983		£69 383

Current cost Balance Sheet

The current cost Balance Sheet for Anon Ltd may now be prepared on the basis of the calculations described in earlier sections. The Balance Sheet is shown together with the comparative figures for 1982 in Table 15.8.

Unlike the CPP Balance Sheet shown in the appendix to this chapter, the previous year's figures are not updated to the current cost at the closing Balance Sheet date.

A recent report by a working party on SSAP 16 suggested that the current cost Balance Sheet is 'widely regarded as misleading since it may be taken to show the current value of the company's assets, which it does not do'.[29] The working party suggested, in the light of the previous comment, that the requirement for a current cost Balance Sheet should be dropped.

15.7 Summary

One of the major issues with which the accounting profession has had to contend in recent years, is the problem of accounting for the effects of inflation.

TABLE 15.8

Anon Ltd
Summarised Current Cost Balance Sheet at 31 December 1983

1982 £	£		£	1983 £
150 000		Fixed assets		180 000
30 000		less depreciation		54 000
120 000				126 000
		Current assets		
	20 800	Stocks	37 200	
	15 000	Debtors and prepayments	25 000	
	5 000	Cash	14 000	
	40 800		76 200	
		Current liabilities		
	15 000	Trade creditors and accruals	25 000	
25 800		Net current assets		51 200
145 800				177 200
85 000		Share capital and reserves		87 817
40 800		Current cost reserve		69 383
20 000		10% Debenture stock		20 000
145 800				177 200

One suggested solution involves the use of a general index of changes in the price of goods and services to adjust financial accounting information to a common unit of measurement, i.e., general purchasing power units. This approach while having many supporters, particularly among practising accountants, was rejected in the United Kingdom following the publication of the Sandilands Report in 1975.

Alternative suggestions involve the adjustment of selected items for specific changes in prices since their date of acquisition. Such suggestions, including the proposals advocated in SSAP 16, involve restatement of selected assets and expenses in accordance with their 'value to the business'. In practice, the restatement often involves the application of specific indices to reflect the change in prices of these assets and expenses from their date of acquisition.

The use of general purchasing power adjustments is advocated by those who accept a concept of capital maintenance based on the 'real' (i.e., inflation adjusted) amount of shareholders' funds, while the use of specific adjustments is advocated by those who favour a concept of capital maintenance based on 'operating capacity'.

Appendix Preparation of Current Purchasing Power (CPP) Statements

Balance Sheet

The method of preparing CPP Statements described in this section is that

Accounting for inflation

outlined in Appendix 3 to PSSAP 7. Although this method is not the only one available it was probably the most widely used by those companies who produced CPP Statements.

Four stages are involved in the adjustment process as follows:

Stage 1

Translate all items in the historic cost Balance Sheet at the beginning of the period into units of CPP at that date. This involves:

(i) Adjustment of the amounts of all non-monetary items for the change in the RPI between their date of acquisition, or subsequent valuation, and the beginning of the year; and
(ii) including all monetary items in the restated opening Balance Sheet at the amounts shown in the historic cost Balance Sheet.

This first stage will only be necessary during the first year of introduction of the CPP method. In the second, and subsequent years, the closing CPP Balance Sheet of the previous year will be used as the opening Balance Sheet of the year of account.

Illustration 1

The Balance Sheet of Sparta Ltd at 31 December 1983 based on historic cost is as follows:

	£000	£000
Fixed assets, at cost		80
accumulated depreciation		20
		60
Current assets:		
Stocks	48	
Trade debtors	24	
Cash	15	
	87	
Current liabilities:		
Trade creditors	36	
		51
		£111
Owners' interest		81
Long-term loan		30
		£111

All the fixed assets were acquired when the RPI stood at 120. Stocks were, on average, acquired when the RPI stood at 160. At 31 December 1983, the RPI stood at 180.

Updating the non-monetary items:

(a) *Fixed assets*

	£H	Conversion factor	CPP Restatement: £C 1.1.84
Cost	80 000	× 180/120	120 000
Accumulated depreciation	20 000	× 180/120	30 000
Net book value	60 000		90 000

(b) *Stocks*

Cost	48 000	× 180/160	54 000

The updated opening Balance Sheet is shown in Table A15.1 with Owners' Interest representing the balancing item. Historic cost accounts are denoted by the use of '£H' while current purchasing power amounts are denoted by the use of '£C' with the date for which these units apply also appended.

TABLE A15.1

CPP Adjusted Balance Sheet at 1.1.84 (in £C 1.1.84)

		£000
Fixed assets:		120
less depreciation		30
		90
Current assets:		
Stocks	54	
Trade debtors	24	
Cash	15	
	93	
Current liabilities:		
Trade creditors	36	57
		£147
Owners' interest		117
Long-term loan		30
		£147

Stage 2

All items in the converted opening Balance Sheet are updated to CPP units relating to the date of the end-of-year Balance Sheet. Updating takes place using a conversion factor of:

$$\frac{\text{RPI index at end of year}}{\text{RPI index at beginning of year}}$$

The updating process is intended to allow the figures in the opening Balance Sheet to be compared with the closing Balance Sheet figures by stating both in terms of the same unit of measurement, i.e., units of 'closing Balance Sheet date purchasing power'.

Accounting for inflation

Illustration 2
Using the information provided in Illustration 1 the updated opening Balance Sheet for Sparta Ltd is shown in Table A15.2 based on a value of the RPI at 31 December 1984 of 240.

Notice that during the updating process, monetary items are also updated in order to identify their amounts in terms of purchasing power at the year end.

Stage 3
Items in the end-of-year historic cost Balance Sheet are converted into units of current purchasing power at the end of the year by:

(a) adjusting all non-monetary items by the change in the RPI from the date of acquisition or revaluation (including earlier conversion); and
(b) making no adjustment for monetary items since these are already expressed in units of CPP at the year end.

Illustration 3
During 1984 Sparta Ltd acquired additional fixed assets at a cost of £66 000. The RPI stood at 220 at the date of purchase. Depreciation was charged during 1984 as follows:

On existing assets	£10 000
On new assets	£ 6 600

Stocks held at the year end were acquired on average when the RPI stood at 230. At the end of the year the RPI stood at 240. Using the above information together with that provided in Illustrations 1 and 2, the historic cost ending Balance Sheet of Sparta Ltd was converted to £C 31.12.84 as shown in Table A15.3.

TABLE A15.2

CPP Updated Balance Sheet at 1.1.84 (in £C 31.12.84)

		£000 C.1.1.84		Conversion factor		£000 C.31.12.84
Fixed assets:			120	240/180		160
Less depreciation			30			40
			90			120
Current assets:						
Stocks		54			72	
Trade debtors		24			32	
Cash		15			20	
		93			124	
Current liabilities:						
Trade creditors	36				48	
		57				76
			147			196
Owners' interest			117			156
Long-term loan			30			40
			147			196

Table A15.3
Sparta Ltd CPP Balance Sheet at 31.12.84

	£H		£C 31.12.84
Fixed assets		146 000	232 000
less depreciation		36 600	67 200
		109 400	164 800
Current assets			
Stocks	46 000		48 000
Trade debtors	47 000		47 000
Cash	18 000		18 000
	111 000		113 000
Current liabilities			
Trade creditors	69 000		69 000
Net current assets		42 000	44 000
		£151 400	£208 800
Owners' interest		121 400	178 800
Long-term loan		30 000	30 000
		£151 400	£208 800

Stage 4

The final stage in the CPP conversion process involves a comparison of the updated Balance Sheet for 1.1.84 with the CPP Balance Sheet for 31.12.84. This comparison for Sparta Ltd reveals that owners' interest has increased from £156 000 (in £C 31.12.84) at 1.1.84 (from Table A15.2) to £178 800 (in £C 31.12.84) at 31.12.84 (from Table A15.3). CPP profit for the year for Sparta Ltd is therefore £22 800 (in £C 31.12.84), as compared to an historic cost profit of £40 400 (i.e., £121 400 less £81 000).

Profit and Loss Account

Although SSAP 7 did not require the preparation of an updated Profit and Loss Account, the historic cost Profit and Loss Account may also be updated to units of CPP at 31.12.84.

Illustration 4
Assume that the sales, purchases and operating expenses for Sparta Ltd accrue evenly throughout the year and that the historic cost Profit and Loss Account for 1984 was as follows:

	£000	£000
Sales		220.0
Less cost of goods sold		135.0
		85.0
Operating expenses	25.3	
Depreciation	16.6	
Loan interest	2.7	
		44.6
Profit for year		£40.4

Accounting for inflation

The following information relating to the RPI is also relevant:

Weighted average RPI during the year	220
Loan interest paid when index was	240
Debtors arose on average when index was	235
Creditors arose on average when index was	230

The company uses the Fifo basis for stock cost recognition. The CPP Profit and Loss Account for 1984 may be prepared by updating the historic cost amounts as follows:

£C 31.12.84

(a) Sales: £H220 000 × 240/220 = 240 000

(b) *Cost of goods sold*

	£H000	£C.000 (31.12.84)
Stock 1.1.84	48 × 240/160	72
Purchases	133 × 240/220	145
	181	217
Less Stock 31.12.84	46 × 240/230	48
Cost of goods sold	135	169

Cost of goods sold consists of the opening stock of goods bought when the RPI stood at 160 and purchases made during the year when the index on average stood at 220. Purchases are identified by deducting the historic cost value of opening stock from the total of 'cost of goods sold plus closing stock'.

(c) *Operating expenses*

£H25 300 × 240/220 = £C27 600

(d) *Depreciation*

as per Illustration 3   £C27 200

(e) *Loan interest*
£H2700 × 240/240   £C2700

(f) *Debtors*

	£H.000	£C.000
Balance b/f	24 × 240/180	32
Sales	220	240
	244	272
Less cash received*	197	224
Balance c/f	47 × 240/235	48
	Less actual	47
	monetary loss	(1)

*Balancing figure.

(g) *Creditors*

	£H.000	£C.000
Balance b/f 1.1.84	36 × 240/180	48
Purchases	133 × 240/220	145
	169	193
Less cash paid*	100	121
Balance c/f 31.12.84	69 × 240/230	72
	Less: actual	69
	monetary gain	3

*Balancing figure.

(h) *Cash*

	£H.000	£C.000
Balance b/f	15 × 240/180	20.0
Cash received	197	224.0
	212	244.0
Less payments:		
purchase of assets	(66) × 240/220	(72.0)
trade creditors	(100)	(121.0)
operating expenses	(25.3)	(27.6)
loan interest	(2.7)	(2.7)
	(194)	(223.3)
Balance c/f 31.12.83	18	20.7
	Less: actual	18.0
	monetary loss	(2.7)

(i) *Long-term loan*

	£H.000	£C.000
At 1 January 1984	30 × 240/180	40
	Less: actual	30
	monetary gain	10

(j) *Monetary gains and losses*
   Summarising (f) to (i) above:

	£C
Debtors	(1 000)
Cash	(2 700)
Creditors	3 000
Long-term loan	10 000
Net monetary gains	9 300

These net monetary gains represent the reduction over the year, in purchasing power terms, of the cost of repaying the net monetary liabilities.

Using the information obtained in (a) to (j) above, the CPP Profit and Loss Account for Sparta Ltd for 1984 is prepared as shown in Table A15.4.

TABLE A15.4

Sparta Ltd
CPP Profit and Loss Account for the year ended 31 December 1984

		£C 31.12.84
Sales		240 000
Cost of goods sold		169 000
		71 000
Operating expenses	27 600	
Depreciation	27 200	
Loan interest	2 700	57 500
		13 500
Add net monetary gains		9 300
CPP profit for 1984		£22 800

Questions

1. Identify the major strengths and weaknesses of historic cost accounting.
2. Explain what is meant by each of the following:
   (a) general inflation;
   (b) stabilised accounting;
   (c) monetary items;
   (d) non-monetary items;
   (e) purchasing power gains and losses.
3. What is the significance of the 'value' attached to fixed assets under a stabilised accounting system?
4. Identify the major strengths and weaknesses, including the practical limitations, of stabilised accounting.
5. Distinguish between the following possible interpretations of the concept of 'capital maintenance':
   (a) money capital maintenance;
   (b) purchasing power capital maintenance;
   (c) operating capital maintenance.
6. Explain what is meant by the concept 'value to the business'. How does the adoption of the above concept as the valuation base to be adopted in accounting differ, if at all, from the adoption of a system of replacement cost accounting?
7. Identify the major strengths and weaknesses of the adoption of a system of financial reporting based on the concept of:
   (a) 'value to the business';
   (b) replacement cost accounting.
8. 'The use of specific indices to adjust historic cost data to a current cost basis eliminates any benefits obtainable from the adoption of a system of replacement cost accounting.'
   Explain what is meant by the above statement and whether you agree with the sentiments expressed.
9. Explain which accounting base you would expect to find most supported by each of the following groups: (a) investors; (b) creditors; (c) employees; (d) auditors; (e) government.

10. Distinguish between 'current cost operating profit' and 'current cost profit attributable to shareholders' as defined in SSAP 16.
11. Explain the nature and significance of each of the following adjustments required by SSAP 16: (a) depreciation; (b) cost of sales; (c) monetary working capital; (d) gearing.
12. Distinguish between realised and unrealised holding gains and losses. Explain which, if any, should be included in current cost operating profit.

Problems

1. Methuselah Ltd and Peter Pan Ltd are two companies operating in the mineral extraction industry. Methuselah Ltd is a well-established company while Peter Pan Ltd is a relative newcomer to the industry. The mineral extraction industry has experienced a rapid level of development in recent years particularly in relation to the increased sophistication of highly expensive exploration equipment.

   Recently published financial accounts of the two companies suggest that Methuselah Ltd is earning a much higher rate of return on invested capital than Peter Pan Ltd. Summarised accounts of the two companies are given below.

   What possible reasons are there for the difference in performance of the two companies?

   Balance Sheets

	Methuselah Ltd £m	Peter Pan Ltd £m
Land and buildings	25	35
Plant and equipment	45	25
Net current assets	30	15
	100	75
Shareholders' funds	60	55
Debenture capital	40	20
	100	75

   Profit and Loss Accounts

	Methuselah Ltd £m	Peter Pan Ltd £m
Revenues	42	25
Less operating expenses	16	11
Operating profits	26	14
Interest expenses	4	2
Net profit before tax	22	12
Corporation tax payable	6	3
Profit after tax	16	9

2. Revelstone Products has recently commenced business. Stock records for the first year of operations revealed the following movements in the stock of Product Z:

Purchases:	3 January	1000 units at £5
	17 April	2400 units at £5.25
	28 September	2000 units at £5.50
	30 December	1800 units at £5.75
Sales for the year		6000 units.

Accounting for inflation

The company operates a periodic system of stock valuation using the FIFO basis of cost recognition.

(a) Calculate cost of goods sold and closing stock values for Product Z on each of the following bases:
  (i) Fifo, historic cost;
  (ii) Weighted average cost;
  (iii) End-of-year replacement cost.

(b) Assuming the following movements in the retail price index (RPI) for the first year of operations of Revelstone Products, calculate the cost of goods sold and closing stock value for Product Z based on end-of-year current purchasing power values.

	RPI
3 January	100
17 April	108
28 September	115
30 December	120
31 December	120

(c) Explain which of the cost of goods sold figures calculated in (a) above most closely reflects the value to the business of goods sold.

(d) Explain which of the closing stock figures calculated in (a) above most closely reflects the value to the business of closing stock.

3. Ogura Ltd are retailers of oriental tea. Stock records for one of their brands revealed the following information for 1983:

Stock 1.1.83	£52 500
Stock 31.12.83	£79 200
Historic cost of goods sold	£340 000

Sales and purchases of this particular brand of tea are relatively stable throughout the year. The opening stock was acquired when the cost of this brand of tea was £17.50 per 100 kilo. Closing stock was acquired when the cost of tea was £19.80 per 100 kilo. The average cost of 100 kilos of this particular brand of tea, during 1983, was £19.00.

(a) Calculate in accordance with the requirements of SSAP 16:
  (i) the cost of sales adjustment for 1983;
  (ii) the Balance Sheet stock value at 31 December 1983, together with the comparative figure at 31 December 1982.

(b) Explain the significance of the transfer to the current cost reserve of the credit entry relating to the cost of sales adjustment.

4. Acquisitions of plant and equipment by Tanaka Engineering plc together with movements in the specific index relating to the category of capital goods in which their acquisitions fall, are as follows:

Date	Amount (£000)	Specific index
1 April 1978	1800	150
2 January 1980	2400	180
1 July 1982	4200	210

The company depreciates plant and equipment on a straight-line basis over 10 years assuming no salvage values. Depreciation is charged only for the part of the year during which an asset is owned. The company's accounting year end is 31 December.

(a) Calculate:
  (i) the historic cost depreciation expense for each of 1982 and 1983;
  (ii) the amounts to be shown in the historic cost Balance Sheet, relating to plant and equipment, at 31 December 1982 and 31 December 1983, separating gross asset cost from accumulated depreciation.

(b) The specific index relating to the plant and equipment acquired by the company stood at the following levels during the 1982 and 1983 accounting years.

1982	Specific index
1 January	200
30 June	210
31 December	215
1983	
30 June	230
31 December	250

Calculate in accordance with SSAP 16

  (i) the current cost depreciation charges for 1982 and 1983;
  (ii) adjusted current cost Balance Sheet figures at each of 31 December 1982 and 31 December 1983, together with comparative figures for the previous year.

(c) Movements in an index reflecting general purchasing power were as follows:

		Index
1978	1 April	120
1980	2 January	125
1982	1 January	135
	30 June	140
	31 December	148
1983	30 June	152
	31 December	160

Calculate:
  (i) The depreciation expenses, for each of 1982 and 1983, together with comparative figures for the previous year, on the basis of the current purchasing power at the end of each year.
  (ii) The amounts to be shown in the Balance Sheets at 31 December 1982 and 31 December 1983 using the relevant end-of-year current purchasing power in each case and showing separately the comparative figures for the previous year.

5. The directors of Cornton Products Ltd have requested the preparation of financial statements adjusted for the effects of inflation. The historic cost accounts of the company are shown below:

Balance Sheet

	31 Dec. 1982	31 Dec. 1983
	£000	£000
Fixed assets		
Land and buildings	230	225
Plant and equipment	160	185
	390	410

Accounting for inflation

Current assets				
Stock		160		210
Debtors and prepayments		78		106
Cash		40		64
		278		380
Less Current liabilities				
Trade creditors and accrued expenses		90		104
Dividends payable		24		56
Taxation payable		36		80
		150		240
			128	140
			518	550
Shareholders' funds				
Ordinary share capital			286	286
Share premium			54	54
Retained profits			78	110
			418	450
Debenture stock			100	100
			518	550

Profit and Loss Account for the year ended 31 December 1983

	£000
Sales	1680
Less cost of sales	1146
	534
Less operating expenses	346
Operating profit	188
Interest charges	10
Profit before taxation	178
Less corporation tax	90
Profit after tax	88
Less dividends proposed	56
Retained profits for the year	32

Additional information relating to Cornton Products Ltd is as follows:

(i) Freehold land and buildings were acquired in 1965 when the general price index stood at 60. The cost of buildings, amounting to £200 000, is being depreciated on a straight-line basis over 40 years, including the year of acquisition.

(ii) Plant and equipment was purchased during the following years when the general index stood at the amounts shown:

	£000	General index
1980	60	200
1981	80	225
1982	60	240
1983	50	250

Depreciation is charged at 10 per cent per annum on a straight-line basis assuming no resale value of plant and equipment, with a full years' charge being made in the year of acquisition.

(iii) The total depreciation expense, both on buildings and plant and equipment, is allocated to operating expenses.

(iv) Stock at 1 January 1983 was acquired when the general index stood at 250.

(v) Purchases were made evenly through the year and amounted to £1 196 000. All purchases were made on credit terms.

(vi) The closing stock at 31 December 1983 was acquired when the general index stood at 270.

(vii) Dividends are paid on 31 March each year. At 31 March 1983, the general index stood at 260.

(viii) The debenture stock was issued on 1 January 1980. Interest is paid annually on 31 December.

(ix) All cash payments on operating expenses are assumed to accrue evenly throughout the year, as are sales revenues and payments to trade creditors.

(x) 1982 taxation was paid on 30 September 1983 when the general index stood at 270.

(xi) The general index of prices stood at the following levels:

31 December	Index
1979	200
1980	220
1981	230
1982	254
1983	280

You are requested to prepare for the directors of Cornton Products Ltd the following statements on an end-of-year current purchasing power basis:

(a) Profit and Loss Account for the year ended 31 December 1983.
(b) A Balance Sheet at 31 December 1983, including comparative figures for the previous year (restated on an end-of-year current purchasing power basis).

6. The directors of Cornton Products Ltd are dissatisfied with the preparation of accounts based on general purchasing power (Problem 5) and wish instead to receive annual financial statements prepared in accordance with the requirements of SSAP 16. The following information is available relating to the movement in specific indices for the assets of Cornton Products Ltd.

(i)

	Specific index	
	Freehold land	Buildings
Date of acquisition	120	90
1 January 1982	300	150
31 December 1982	320	160
30 June 1983	330	170
31 December 1983	350	180

(ii) *Plant and equipment*

	Specific index
At date of acquisition in 1980	180
1981	200
1982	240
1983	250
1 January 1983	248
30 June 1983	250
31 December 1983	255

(iii) *Stocks*

	Specific index
At date of acquisition of opening stock	160
Index at 1 January 1983	162
Index at 31 December 1983	170
At date of acquisition of closing stock	168
Average index during 1983	166

Using the above information, together with the information provided in Problem 5, prepare the following statements in accordance with the requirements of SSAP 16:

(a) Current Cost Profit and Loss Account for the year ended 31 December 1983;
(b) Current Cost Balance Sheet at 31 December 1983, together with comparative figures for the previous year.

16 Group Accounts

16.1 Introduction

Few UK companies of any great size operate independently of other companies. Rather most of the major companies belong to a 'group' of companies.[1] A group relationship exists when one company has sufficient equity investment in one or more other companies for these to be considered to be subsidiaries of the investing or holding company.

Company law allows the parent company–subsidiary relationship to be defined on the basis of either direct or indirect equity interest. The 1948 Companies Act, Section 154(1), defined one company as the subsidiary of another if, but only if:

(a) that other either
    (i) is a member of and controls the composition of its board of directors; or
    (ii) holds more than half in nominal value of its equity share capital; or
(b) the first company is a subsidiary of any company which is that other's subsidiary.

If a holding company–subsidiary relationship is established then group accounts must be published, subject to certain exceptions explained later. Group accounts published by UK holding companies take the form of consolidated financial statements, in which the assets and liabilities of the subsidiary (or subsidiaries) are combined or consolidated with those of the holding company.

16.2 Historical developments

Company legislation

The idea of investing companies, holding substantial equity stakes in other companies, originated in the United States in the nineteenth century partly as a means of circumventing the Sherman Anti-Trust Law of 1890.[2] Holding companies did not, however, 'play a significant role in business organisations in Britain'[3] prior to 1925.

Accounting for groups of companies first became a major issue in the UK during the 1920s. The Greene Committee, meeting in 1925 to consider possible amendments to the Companies Acts, received evidence on the above issue. A minority of witnesses to the committee suggested that holding companies be required to present to shareholders either consolidated statements or else separate financial statements for each subsidiary. The Greene Committee report[4] tended to side with the majority view which opposed the introduction of consolidated statements and accordingly no such requirement was introduced into the 1929 Companies Act.

By the time the next review of company law was under way the weight of informed opinion had swung in favour of the publication of consolidated financial statements. The Cohen Committee, meeting over the period 1943–5, received evidence from a variety of witnesses advocating the publication of consolidated statements. The subsequent report of the Cohen Committee[5] recognised the need for additional disclosure and made a number of recommendations which were, in the main, incorporated into the 1947 Companies Act (and subsequently into the 1948 Act).

The 1948 Companies Act allowed a number of alternative ways in which the additional information might be presented as follows:

That the holding company may, in addition to its own balance sheet, prepare:

(i) Consolidated statements for the entire group; or
(ii) Sub-sets of consolidated statements, i.e. by dividing the subsidiaries into several groups; or
(iii) Separate statements for each subsidiary; or
(iv) Statements expanding the information about the subsidiaries in the holding company's own accounts; or
(v) Any combination of the above.

As can be seen a considerable amount of discretion was given to directors as to the form in which information concerning subsidiaries should be provided to the shareholders of the investing company. In addition discretion was given to the directors to omit from the consolidated statements the results of a subsidiary on a number of grounds, including impracticality (i.e. impossibility), insignificance, expense (in time or money), potential harm to the business, or if 'the business of the holding company and that of the subsidiary are so different that they cannot reasonably be treated as a single undertaking'.[6]

The reason why any subsidiary has been omitted from full consolidation is required to be provided in a statement annexed to the group accounts.

The Accounting Standards Committee have also addressed the broad disclosure requirements of group accounts in SSAP 14.[7] Among other issues recommendations were made that all members of the group should adopt uniform accounting policies and should have the same accounting year end. Where either of the above conditions are not met then this fact should be disclosed to shareholders together with additional information relating to the effect of the non-compliance.

Factors influencing the development of group accounts

In the previous section a brief description was given of the change of attitude to the preparation of group accounts in the UK. The current section will attempt to explain why the change in attitude came about.

R. G. Walker identified the early UK attitudes to the issue of how to account for investments in other companies as being related to the application of rules which had arisen when distinguishing between 'fixed' and 'floating' assets.[8] 'If holdings of publicly traded securities were regarded as "floating" assets, then they were to be valued at the lower of cost and market price. If investments were deemed to be "fixed" assets, then "cost" was appropriate.'[9]

The adoption of the above so-called conservative attitude to investment valuation continued with little opposition during the early years of the twentieth century. As mentioned a number of witnesses to the Greene Committee had made recommendations to improve the reporting requirements of holding companies but these were mainly ignored. The committee chose rather to follow the prevailing 'wisdom' of (a) not asking the courts to do what shareholders were supposed to be able to do for themselves, and (b) expecting management to provide that financial information which it was in the interests of shareholders to receive.[10]

The attitude to financial disclosure of the details of investments in subsidiaries is one further example of the general inadequacy of financial disclosure rules at the time and the influence which the preparers of financial statements and the directors of reporting companies had over the content of financial statements. During the 1930s, however, three factors helped to change the balance of opinion.

The first factor was the entry into the area of financial reporting regulation by the Stock Exchange. The main impetus for the involvement of the Stock Exchange was the collapse of the stock market in 1929. In order to restore the confidence of investors and help reduce the likelihood of future losses the Stock Exchange began to introduce rules increasing the information disclosure requirements of quoted companies. By 1939 the Stock Exchange had introduced a formal requirement for the publication of consolidated financial statements by companies which applied for listing.

The second factor involved an investigation into the financial affairs of the Royal Mail Steam Packet Company Ltd (RMSPC hereafter) in 1929. The main facts of the case are well documented,[11] particularly in relation to the creation and use of 'secret reserves'. The case was also important in highlighting the inadequacy of the existing rules for the accounting treatment of investments in subsidiary companies.

The established practice when accounting for investments in subsidiary companies was to record these at cost in the Balance Sheet and include as income for the period only dividends received or receivable. Over a number of years prior to 1929 the RMSPC and its subsidiaries had made operating losses. Shareholders had been unaware of these losses partly because the directors had transferred back into the Profit and Loss Account provisions that were no longer required, i.e. secret reserves built up out of over-provisions in previous years. Additionally, the directors had declared dividends for the subsidiary companies, out of accumulated reserves of previous years, and credited these to the Profit and Loss Account of the holding company. If the holding company had been required to prepare annual group accounts, including the holding company's share of the profits or losses of the subsidiary for the year, the latter misrepresentation to shareholders would not have been possible.

The third factor was the influence of *The Accountant*, a journal produced for practising accountants. R. G. Walker suggests that the above journal may have been 'the greatest influence in British reporting practices'[12] during this period. Initially the journal's attitude to the preparation of consolidated accounts had been, on balance, negative. During the decade of the 1930s, however, a constant stream of articles and comments were produced advocating the production of consolidated financial statements.

As a consequence of the above factors, and others, both the accounting profession and the users of published financial reports had become more amenable to the production of consolidated statements by the time the Cohen Committee began to hear evidence on company law reform.

Forms of group accounts

Before describing the form of consolidated financial statements adopted in the United Kingdom it is useful to consider the various alternatives available. R. H. Parker[13] has identified a number of different approaches to the preparation of consolidated financial statements as identified in Table 16.1.

The 'entity' concept of consolidation developed mainly through the writing of M. Moonitz.[14] Moonitz viewed the purpose of consolidated statements, not as that of expanding the disclosure of information relating to the holding company, but of portraying the affairs of 'economic entities'. All the assets and liabilities of subsidiaries are consolidated with those of the holding company under this approach.

TABLE 16.1 *Approaches to consolidation*

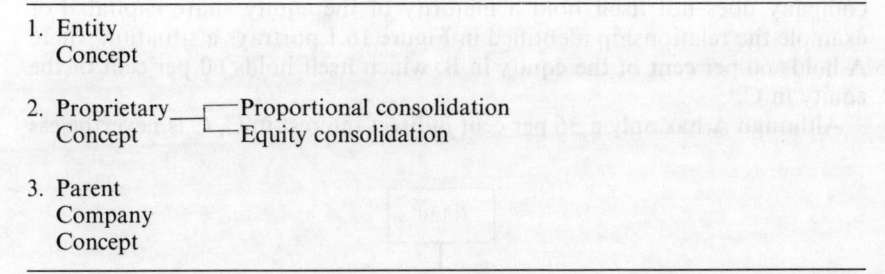

1. Entity Concept

2. Proprietary Concept
   - Proportional consolidation
   - Equity consolidation

3. Parent Company Concept

The 'proprietary' concept of consolidation takes a completely different view of the purpose of consolidated statements to that of the entity theory. The proprietary concept views the preparation of consolidated statements as an extension of the information relating to investments made by the holding company. The means by which this may be achieved is either proportional consolidation of the holding company's 'share' of the assets and liabilities of the subsidiary companies, or else by including only the holding company's share of profits or losses under a heading of investments in subsidiaries (or associates) i.e. 'equity' consolidation.

The third method of consolidation, the 'parent company' concept is broadly that which has been adopted in the United Kingdom. Under this approach the holding, or parent, company is regarded as the dominant shareholder. The main distinction between this approach and the entity approach is that minority shareholders will be credited with a share of any goodwill arising on consolidation[15] (see later) in the entity approach, but not in the parent company approach.

The distinction between the entity and the parent company concepts of consolidation have at times become blurred both in the law relating to group accounts and in the practical aspects of consolidation.

For example, the use of the criterion of control to determine subsidiary relationships has been identified as an extension of the entity concept, whereas an extension of the parent company concept might have been more concerned with the element of materiality of the investment.[16]

Also the preparation of consolidated statements involves the elimination of profits on intra-group transactions as explained later. Appeals to the parent company concept should involve the elimination of the parent company share of profits, while appeals to the entity concept would involve the elimination of all such profits. Actual practice favoured by UK companies appears to be the total elimination of profits on intra-group transactions, possibly on grounds of simplicity rather than appeals to underlying concepts. Investments in associated companies are recorded in group accounts in the United Kingdom under the equity method, with the holding companies share of the profits or losses of the associated company included in the consolidated statements (if prepared).

Subsidiary relationships

The 1948 Companies Act definition of a subsidiary, given earlier, allows one company to be classed as the subsidiary of another even though the parent company does not itself hold a majority of the equity share capital. For example the relationship identified in Figure 16.1 portrays a situation where A holds 60 per cent of the equity in B, which itself holds 60 per cent of the equity in C.

Although A has only a 36 per cent indirect interest in C, C is nevertheless

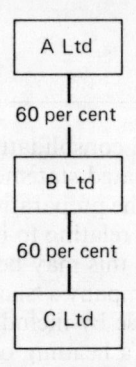

```
        A Ltd
          |
      60 per cent
          |
        B Ltd
          |
      60 per cent
          |
        C Ltd
```

FIGURE 16.1 *Illustration of sub-subsidiary relationship*

considered to be a subsidiary of A because it is the subsidiary of a company, B, which is itself the subsidiary of A.

It is also possible for one company to hold an indirect equity investment of more than 50 per cent in another company without the latter company being a subsidiary of the former. For example, the relationship portrayed in Figure 16.2 shows A having a 40 per cent interest in B and a 90 per cent interest in C, while both B and C have 50 per cent interests in D. D is not the subsidiary of either B or C and hence will not be classed as a subsidiary of A (unless B or C have control over the Board of Directors of D), despite the fact that A has an indirect interest in 65 per cent of the equity of D, i.e. $(40\% \times 50\%) + (90\% \times 50\%)$.

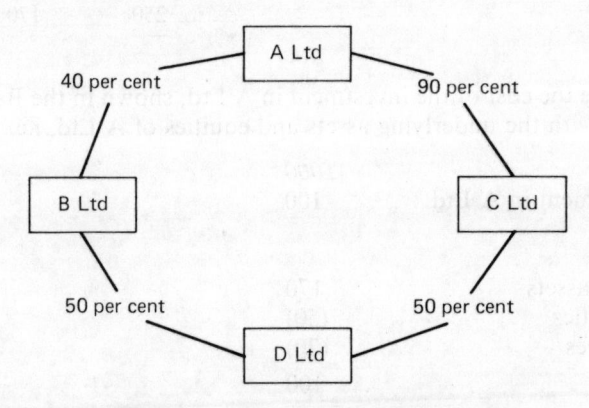

FIGURE 16.2 *Inter-company relationships*

The Jenkins Committee[17] also criticised the definition of subsidiary included in the 1948 Act as allowing one company to be classed as the subsidiary of another without actually controlling it, i.e. if the equity capital did not contain voting rights. The 1948 Act's definition has, however, remained unchanged by subsequent legislation although it is possible that eventual incorporation into company law of the requirements of the EEC Seventh Directive may produce a new definition.[18]

16.3 Balance Sheet consolidation

Introduction

Assume that H Ltd owns all the issued share capital of A Ltd and that the Balance Sheets of the two companies at 31 December 1984 are as shown in Table 16.2.

For the purposes of this initial illustration it is assumed that H Ltd acquired the shares in A Ltd at their nominal value before A Ltd commenced trading.

The principle involved in the preparation of a Consolidated Balance Sheet

TABLE 16.2

H Ltd and A Ltd
Balance Sheets at 31 December 1984

	H Ltd £000	A Ltd £000
Investment in A Ltd at cost	100	—
Other assets	150	170
	250	170
Share capital	120	100
Reserves	50	20
Liabilities	80	50
	250	170

is to replace the cost of the investment in A Ltd, shown in the Balance Sheet of H Ltd, with the underlying assets and equities of A Ltd, i.e. to replace:

	£000
Investment in A Ltd	100

with:

Other assets	170
Liabilities	(50)
Reserves	(20)
	100

The Consolidated Balance Sheet of H Ltd and its subsidiary, A Ltd, at 31 December 1984 is shown in Table 16.3.

Notice that the share capital of the subsidiary, A Ltd is not included in the Consolidated Balance Sheet although the reserves are included (in this illustration).

Minority interests

In the previous section H Ltd was assumed to hold all the share capital of A Ltd. It is possible, however, for one company to be the subsidiary of another without the holding, or parent, company owning 100 per cent of the share capital. The criterion for determining the holding company—subsidiary relationship is clearly established in law as effective control over the affairs of

TABLE 16.3

H Ltd and subsidiary
Consolidated Balance Sheet at 31 December 1984

	£000
Assets	320
Share capital	120
Reserves	70
Liabilities	130
	320

the subsidiary. Suppose H Ltd held only 75 per cent of the share capital of A Ltd. A Ltd is still considered to be the subsidiary company of H Ltd but any consolidation of the Balance Sheets of the two companies should recognise the 25 per cent minority shareholdings.

One possible way to recognise the minority shareholding is to make what is known as 'proportional consolidation', e.g. by consolidating only 75 per cent of the assets and equities of A Ltd.

Proportional consolidation has not, however, gained much support in the UK, possibly because 'most of the early holding companies were the owners of 100 per cent (or near to 100 per cent)'[19] of the issued share capital of the subsidiary companies. Also the 'economic entity' principle has become intertwined with the parent company principle of consolidation with the consequence that the resources at the command of the combined unit are emphasised more than the division of ownership.

Accepted practice for the treatment of minority interests has been to consolidate all the assets and liabilities of the subsidiary and then to identify separately that proportion of the share capital and reserves of the subsidiary belonging to the minority shareholders.

Illustration 1

The Balance Sheets of H Ltd and A Ltd are shown in Table 16.4. H Ltd owns 75 per cent of the ordinary share capital of A Ltd but none of the preference share capital. As H controls more than 50 per cent of the voting shares in A Ltd, despite not owning 50 per cent of the total (of ordinary and preference) share capital, then A is considered to be the subsidiary of H.

Minority shareholders interest in A Ltd may be calculated as follows:

	£000
Ordinary share capital	100
Reserves	20
	120
Minority share 25 per cent thereof:	30
Add minority preference shareholdings	60
Combined minority interest	90

TABLE 16.4

H Ltd and A Ltd
Balance Sheets at 31 December 1984

	H Ltd £000	A Ltd £000
Investment in A Ltd at cost	75	—
Other assets	175	210
	250	210
Ordinary share capital	120	100
Preference share capital		60
Reserves	50	20
Liabilities	80	30
	250	210

The Consolidated Balance Sheet of H Ltd and its subsidiary A Ltd, including minority interests, is shown in Table 16.5.

It is again assumed that H Ltd acquired the ordinary shares in A Ltd at their nominal value before A had commenced trading.

The investment A Ltd shown in the Balance Sheet of H Ltd has been replaced on consolidation with the following assets and equities of A Ltd.

	£000
Total assets	210
Liabilities	(30)
Minority interest	(90)
Reserves	(15)
	75

Note that as the minority shareholders are entitled to 25 per cent of the reserves of A Ltd, the group share is restricted to 75 per cent, i.e. £15 000.

TABLE 16.5

H Ltd and subsidiary
Consolidated Balance Sheet at 31 December 1984

	£000
Total assets	385
Ordinary share capital	120
Reserves	65
Minority interest	90
Liabilities	110
	385

Goodwill and Capital Reserve

In the earlier illustrations, the investment in the subsidiary company was assumed to be acquired at the book value of the net assets involved. This assumption is unlikely to be borne out in practice and it is more likely that the investment will be acquired at a premium or a discount on the book value.

The generally accepted method of accounting for the purchase of subsidiaries is known as the 'acquisition' method. An alternative method, the 'merger' or 'pooling of interests' method will be considered in a later section.

If the cost of an investment in a subsidiary is greater than the holding company's share of the net assets acquired then the difference will normally be described in the Consolidated Balance Sheet as goodwill arising on consolidation. The goodwill so arising should either be written off immediately against group reserves or else amortised in the Consolidated Profit and Loss Account over its estimated useful life, as described in Chapter 8.

If, as occasionally happens, the net book value of the assets acquired is greater than the cost of the investment, then the difference between the two will normally be treated as a Capital Reserve on Consolidation which will not be available for payment of dividends to shareholders of the holding company.

Illustration 2

(i) Assume that X Ltd acquired 75 per cent of the ordinary shares in Y Ltd for £90 000 on 31 December 1984 when the Balance Sheets of both companies were as described in Table 16.6.

From an examination of the Balance Sheet of Y Ltd it can be seen that book value of the net assets acquired by X Ltd amounted to £75 000, i.e.

	£000
Total assets	150
Less liabilities	50
	100
75 per cent thereof	75
Minority interests	25

The excess of the cost of the investment, £90 000, over the book value of the net assets acquired, £75 000, is deemed to be goodwill arising on consolidation, i.e. £15 000. Table 16.7(a) shows the Consolidated Balance Sheet.

(ii) If, in the above illustration, the cost of the investment in Y Ltd had amounted to £65 000 (and the other assets of X Ltd £235 000), then the excess of net asset value over the cost of the investment would amount to £10 000. This amount would be described as Capital Reserve on Consolidation as shown in Table 16.7(b).

Pre-acquisition profits

One further complication arising on preparation of consolidated financial statements is the treatment of profits which have arisen before the date of acquisition of the controlling interest in the subsidiary.

There are at least three possible treatments of these pre-acquisition profits as follows:

(i) to combine the pre-acquisition profits of the subsidiary with those of the holding company and make them available for distribution as dividends to shareholders;
(ii) to make no consolidation of the pre-acquisition profits of the subsidiary;

TABLE 16.6

X Ltd and Y Ltd
Balance Sheets at 31 December 1984

	X Ltd £000	Y Ltd £000
Investment in Y Ltd at cost	90	—
Other assets	210	150
	300	150
Ordinary share capital	100	80
Reserves	60	20
Liabilities	140	50
	300	150

TABLE 16.7

X Ltd and subsidiary
Consolidated Balance Sheet at 31 December 1984

	(a) £000	(b) £000
Total assets	360	385
Goodwill on Consolidation	15	—
	375	385
Ordinary share capital	100	100
Capital reserve on consolidation		10
Reserves	60	60
Minority interests	25	25
Liabilities	190	190
	375	385

(iii) to identify the minority shareholders portion of the pre-acquisition profits and include these as part of the minority interests.

Treatment (i) has in the past been frowned upon in the UK as a practice which allows both the purchase of profits, i.e. the profits of the subsidiary for the current year, and the opportunity for distribution of capital. Distribution of capital is possible under this treatment as dividends paid out of the subsidiary's pre-acquisition profits would involve a return of part of the cost of the investment in the subsidiary to the shareholders of the acquiring company. There are, however, special circumstances in which treatment (i) is now allowed and these are considered in Section 16.6 of this chapter.

Treatment (ii) above might be regarded as an imposition on the minority shareholders who appear to be ineligible for their share of profits arising before a transaction in which they took no part, i.e. the acquisition of control over their company. In actual fact the minority shareholders are not in any way disenfranchised from their share of pre-acquisition profits; the financial statements of the subsidiary not the consolidated statements are the relevant statements as far as the minority shareholders are concerned and these former statements make no distinction between pre- and post-acquisition profits.

The case against treatment (ii) rests rather with the fact that it understates to the shareholders of the holding company their obligation to the minority shareholders. Hence treatment (ii) should be rejected in favour of treatment (iii) which is the treatment normally adopted in the UK.

16.4 Profit and Loss Account Consolidation

Introduction

There are two main tasks involved in the preparation of a Consolidated Profit and Loss Account. The first task, already referred to in the previous section, involves the separation of pre-acquisition and post-acquisition

Group accounts

profits and reserves. The second task involves the elimination of amounts arising as a consequence of intra-group trading, i.e. revenues, expenses and profits or losses on such transactions.

Pre- and post-acquisition profits

(a) *Introduction*

Earlier in this chapter it was explained that profits earned by a subsidiary, prior to the acquisition of control by the holding company, were 'frozen', i.e. not considered to be available for distribution to the shareholders of the holding company. Profits earned by the subsidiary subsequent to acquisition are, however, deemed to be available for consolidation with holding company profits and for subsequent distribution, if desired, to the holding company (after apportionment of minority interests).

When a subsidiary company is acquired other than at the commencement of its financial year, it will be necessary to apportion the profit (or loss) of the subsidiary in the year of acquisition between the pre- and post-acquisition profit (or loss). The normal procedure is to make the apportionment on a time basis although there may be instances where a more exact apportionment may be possible, e.g. where interim financial statements have been prepared up to the date of acquisition.

Illustration 3

P Ltd acquired 60 per cent of the ordinary share capital of Q Ltd on 30 September 1984. Both companies prepare accounts to 31 December annually. Profit and Loss Accounts for both companies for the year ended 31 December 1984 are given in Table 16.8.

The after-tax profits of Q Ltd will be apportioned as follows:

	£000
Minority interests, 40 per cent, i.e.	40
Group interest, 60 per cent, i.e.	60
Pre-acquisition element: 9 months	45
Post-acquistion element: 3 months	15

The group Profit and Loss Account will here include a net credit of £15 000 for the group share of post-acquisition profit. This amount may be credited in one of two ways: either

(i) credit the group Profit and Loss Account with the total group share of pre-

TABLE 16.8

P Ltd and Q Ltd
Profit and Loss Accounts for the year ended 31 December 1984

	P Ltd £000	Q Ltd £000
Profit for the year before tax	420	200
Corporation tax	180	100
Profit after tax	240	100

and post-acquisition profit, and subsequently to debit the pre-acquisition element; or
(ii) credit only the group share of post-acquisition profit.

Method (i) has the advantage of easing the task of comparison of results of the group from one year to the next. Method (ii) has the advantage of simplicity of presentation and reduces the likelihood of misleading the readers of the financial statements. Consolidated Profit and Loss Accounts using both methods are illustrated in Table 16.9.

Notice that under method (ii) 25 per cent of the pre-tax profits and of the corporation tax payable by Q Ltd are included in the Consolidated Profit and Loss Account. Minority interest in the group profits is limited to 40 per cent of the after-tax profits of the post-acquisition period, i.e. 40% × £25 000 = £10 000.

TABLE 16.9

P Ltd and subsidiary
Consolidated Profit and Loss Account for the year ended 31 December 1984

	Method (i) £000	Method (ii) £000
Profit for the year before tax	620	470
Corporation tax	280	205
Profits after tax	340	265
Minority interest	(40)	(10)
Pre-acquisition profits	(45)	—
Profits of the group for the year	255	255

(b) *Dividends from subsidiaries*

When subsidiary companies declare dividends on ordinary shares then a portion of the dividend will accrue to the holding company. On consolidation only dividends declared by the holding company will be shown in the Consolidated Profit and Loss Account.

In the case of a wholly owned subsidiary the amount of dividend declared (i.e. debited) by the subsidiary will be offset (i.e. credited) by the amount of dividend received by the holding company.

In the case of a non-wholly owned subsidiary then part of the dividend will accrue to the minority shareholders. When preparing the consolidated financial statements, however, the group share of the consolidated profits will normally be calculated after deducting minority interests in profits before ordinary dividends. No further adjustment will then be necessary for the minority shareholders' interest in the dividend declared by the subsidiary.

Illustration 4

X Ltd has owned 75 per cent of the ordinary share capital of its subsidiary Y Ltd since incorporation. The Profit and Loss Accounts of the two companies given in Table 16.10 shows that Y Ltd has declared an ordinary dividend for 1984 of £40 000. Included in the profit and loss account of X Ltd is the holding company's share of the dividend of Y Ltd, i.e. 75 per cent × £40 000 = £30 000.

Minority shareholders' interest in the profits of Y Ltd amount to 25 per cent of

TABLE 16.10

X Ltd and Y Ltd
Profit and Loss Accounts for the year ended 31 December 1984

	X Ltd £000		Y Ltd £000
Profit for the year before tax		820	470
Dividend from Y Ltd		30	—
		850	470
Corporation tax		400	230
Profits after tax		450	240
Ordinary dividend			
paid	30		15
proposed	60	90	25	40
Retained profits for year		360	200
Retained profits b/f		830	360
Retained profits c/f		1190	560

the profits after tax, i.e. 25 per cent × £240 000 = £60 000. The minority shareholders interest may also have been calculated on their share of the retained profits and the proposed dividend of Y Ltd, i.e.

25 per cent × £200 000 = £50 000
+25 per cent × £40 000 = £10 000
£60 000

The Consolidated Profit and Loss Account of the group for 1984 is shown in Table 16.11

Note that Group retained profits brought forward included 75 per cent of the retained profits of Y Ltd.

One possible complication to the accounting treatment of dividends received from subsidiaries may arise if the dividends have been declared out of pre-

TABLE 16.11

X Ltd and subsidiary
Consolidated Profit and Loss Account for the year ended 31 December 1984

		£000
Profit for the year before tax		1290
Corporation tax		630
Profits after tax		660
Minority interest		60
		600
Ordinary dividends		
paid	30	
proposed	60	90
Retained profits for year		510
Retained profits b/f		1100
Retained profits c/f		1610

acquisition profits. In such cases the dividends will be deemed to be a partial repayment to the holding company of the purchase consideration for the subsidiary. Thus, in the accounting records of the *holding company* the cost of the investment in the subsidiary will be written down by the amount of the dividend received which relates to pre-acquisition profits. The Profit and Loss Account of the holding company will include only that portion of the dividend from the subsidiary which has been paid out of post-acquisition profits. No further adjustment will be necessary in the Consolidated Profit and Loss Account as dividends received from subsidiaries are excluded in total from this statement.

In order to identify whether a dividend has been declared out of pre- or post-acquisition profits it is normally assumed that the dividend has been paid initially out of post-acquisition profits. If post-acquisition profits are insufficient to cover the total dividend then the balance will be assumed to be paid out of pre-acquisition profits and treated accordingly.

Illustration 5
H Ltd acquired 80 per cent of the ordinary share capital of A Ltd for £125 000 on 30 June 1984. Both companies produce accounts to 31 December annually and their respective Profit and Loss Accounts for 1984 are shown in Table 16.12.

The after-tax profits of A Ltd amounted to £16 000 of which 50 per cent only would be considered to be post-acquisition profits (apportioning on a time basis). As H Ltd is only entitled to 80 per cent of the profits of A Ltd then H's share of post-acquisition profits amounts to £6400. The amount of dividend paid out pre-acquisition profits is therefore £1600. The cost of investment in A Ltd will be reduced in the accounting records of H Ltd as follows:

Original cost	£125 000
Less dividend from pre-acquisition profits	1 600
Revised cost of investment	£123 400

(c) *Intra-group trading*
Many groups contain member companies which trade with one another. However, any profit arising on trading between members of a group is

TABLE 16.12

H Ltd and A Ltd
Profit and Loss Accounts for the year ended 31 December 1984

		H Ltd		A Ltd
		£000		£000
Profit for the year before tax		64		29
Dividend from A Ltd		8		—
		72		29
Corporation tax		26		13
Profits after tax		46		16
Ordinary dividends				
paid	6		10	
proposed	14	20	—	10
Retained earnings		26		6

normally only treated as realised when a further sale (or service) is provided to some third party outside of the group. For purposes of consolidation, therefore, no profit (or loss) will arise on transactions undertaken solely between members of a group. In practice the application of the above principle requires any unsold stock acquired by one member of a group from another to be written down by the amount of profit included in the stock valuation. Similarly any charge paid by one member of a group to another, for services rendered, must be eliminated on consolidation, with the charge paid offset against the charge received.

The question arises as to whether the minority share of any unrealised intra-group transactions should also be eliminated. Although a case can be made for the non-elimination of the minority shareholders portion most accountants would eliminate the total of such profits on the grounds of simplicity of treatment.

In order to avoid possible double-counting and to maintain consistency with the above, Consolidated Profit and Loss Accounts should also exclude sales and cost of sales relating to intra-group transactions.

In addition to the elimination of profits on intra-group transactions other account balances may have to be eliminated or adjusted before preparing consolidated financial statements.

For example, included in the debtors' figure for one member of a group may be an account relating to another member of the group. The latter company will have a corresponding amount included in its own creditors' figure. On consolidation the two balances will be 'netted out', i.e., both excluded from the Consolidated Balance Sheet.

Situations also arise when one member of a group borrows from another and pays interest on the amount borrowed. On consolidation the amount of the loan shown as an asset in the lending members Balance Sheet will be offset against the loan shown as a liability in the borrowing members Balance Sheet. Similarly the interest received in the lending member's Profit and Loss Account will be offset against the interest paid by the borrowing member.

Illustration 6

Y Ltd owns 75 per cent of the ordinary share capital of Z Ltd. The Profit and Loss Accounts and Balance Sheets for the two companies for the year ended 31 December 1984 are given in Tables 16.13 and 16.14.

The following additional information is also relevant:

(a) Turnover for Z Ltd includes sales of £150 000 made to Y Ltd on the basis of cost plus 50 per cent mark-up.
(b) Included in Y's closing stock are goods bought from Z Ltd for £30 000.
(c) Included in the list of Z Ltd's debtors is an amount of £112 000 owed by Y Ltd. A similar amount is included in the creditors of Y Ltd.
(d) Z Ltd has borrowed £100 000 from Y Ltd on the basis of a 10 per cent mortgage debenture secured on the fixed assets of Z Ltd.
(e) At the time of acquisition of the investment in Z Ltd Z's reserves stood at £80 000. No further issues of ordinary shares have been made by Z Ltd since the acquisition.
(f) Goodwill arising on acquisition is being amortised in the Consolidated Profit and Loss Account on a straight-line basis over 20 years. The net book value of goodwill as at 1 January 1984 stood at £160 000.

TABLE 16.13

Y Ltd and Z Ltd
Profit and Loss Accounts for the year ended 31 December 1984

		Y Ltd £000		Z Ltd £000
Sales		2180		970
Cost of Sales		1645		620
Operating profit		535		350
Interest paid/received		10		(10)
		545		340
Dividends from Z Ltd		45		—
Profits before taxation		590		340
Corporation tax		255		160
Profit after tax		335		180
Ordinary dividend				
paid	25		20	
proposed	40	65	40	60
Retained profit for year		270		120
Retained profit brought forward		724		276
Retained profits carried forward		994		396

TABLE 16.14

Y Ltd and Z Ltd
Balance Sheets at 31 December 1984

	Y Ltd £000	Z Ltd £000
Investment in Z Ltd	710	—
Loan to Z Ltd	100	—
Other assets	3830	1179
	4640	1179
Ordinary share capital	2000	440
Reserves	994	396
10 per cent mortgage debenture	—	100
Other liabilities	1646	243
	4640	1179

In order to prepare the Consolidated Profit and Loss Account the following adjustments will be necessary:

(i) *Elimination of inter-group trading*

		£000
Turnover Y Ltd		2180
	Z Ltd	970
		3150
Less intra-group sales		150
		3000

Cost of sales Y Ltd	1645	
Z Ltd	620	
	2265	
less intra-group purchase	150	
	2115	

'Unrealised' profit on goods acquired by Y Ltd from Z Ltd but remaining unsold at the end of the year must also be eliminated.

Accountants differ in their views as to whether the total 'unrealised' profit should be eliminated or only that relating to the holding company's share of the equity. The method adopted in this illustration is to eliminate 100 per cent of the profits, the method favoured by the majority of accountants. Hence, both operating profit and closing stocks will be reduced by:

£30 000 × 50/150 = £10 000

If the method adopted has been to eliminate only the majority shareholders' interest then the adjusting entry would have required a reduction in operating profit and closing stock of only £7500. Minority interest would have then been £2500 higher than the figures shown in the consolidated balance sheet and profit and loss account, in Tables 16.15 and 16.16.

(ii) *Calculation of goodwill amortisation*

	£ 000
Cost of investment in Z Ltd	710
Z Ltd Ordinary share capital	440
Reserves	80
	520
75 per cent thereof	390
Goodwill on consolidation: (710–390)	320
Annual amortisation expense: 5 per cent	16

(iii) The Consolidated Profit and Loss Account will exclude the interest paid by Z Ltd to Y Ltd; one amount will offset the other. Minority shareholders interest in the profits of Z Ltd will, however, continue to be calculated on the amount of £180 000, i.e., after deducting debenture interest.

(g) *Retained profits* The group share of retained profits of Z Ltd will exclude the group share of the pre-acquisition retained profits of £80 000, i.e., £60 000. In addition, group retained profits brought forward will be calculated after adjusting for the amortisation of goodwill on consolidation to 1 January 1984 i.e.

	£000	£ 000
Y Ltd		724
Z Ltd	276	
Less Minority interest (25 per cent)	(69)	
Pre-aquisition reserves	(60)	147
		871
Prior year's amortisation of goodwill		160
Group reserves brought forward 1.1.84		711

The consolidated Profit and Loss Account may now be prepared and is illustrated in Table 16.15. The Consolidated Balance Sheet may also be prepared and is shown in Table 16.16.

TABLE 16.15

Y Ltd and subsidiary
Consolidated Profit and Loss Account for the year ended 31 December 1984

		£000
Sales		3000
Cost of sales		2125
Operating profits of group companies, before taxation		875
Amortisation of goodwill on consolidation		16
		859
Corporation tax on profit for the year		415
		444
Minority share of profit		45
Profit after taxation attributable to the shareholders of Y Ltd		399
Ordinary dividends		
paid	25	
proposed	40	65
Retained profit for the year		334
Balance brought forward		711
Balance carried forward		1045

TABLE 16.16

Y Ltd and subsidiary
Consolidated Balance Sheet at 31 December 1984

	£000
Goodwill on consolidated	144
Other assets	4857
	5001
Ordinary share capital	2000
Reserves	1045
Minority interest	219
Other liabilities	1737
	5001

Goodwill on consolidation has been calculated for the Balance Sheet as follows:

Group accounts

	£000	£000
Goodwill on consolidation		320
Less amounts written off:		
to 1.1.84	160	
in 1984	16	176
Balance carried forward		144

Other assets have been calculated as follows:

	£000	£000
Other assets:		
Y Ltd		3830
Z Ltd		1179
		5009
Less		
Unrealised profit	10	
Intra-group debtor	112	
Dividend receivable from Z Ltd	30	152
		4857

'Other liabilities' have similarly been calculated after eliminating the intra-group creditor and the proposed ordinary dividend of Z Ltd:

	£000	£000
Other liabilities		
Y Ltd		1646
Z Ltd		243
		1889
Less		
intra-group creditor	112	
proposed dividend: Z Ltd	40	(152)
		1737

Minority interest has been calculated as follows:

	£000
Z Ltd: Ordinary share capital	440
Reserves	396
	836
25 per cent thereof	209
Add minority interest in proposed dividend	10
Minority interest at 31.12.84	219

16.5 Associated companies

Introduction

Over recent years it has become increasingly common for one company to hold a substantial equity stake in another, but one that is insufficient to categorise the latter as the subsidiary of the former. One reason for this development is the more frequent use of the consortium or joint venture form of business enterprise. In such circumstances it is insufficiently informative to report on the results of the investments held merely on the basis of dividend income. Accordingly in SSAP 1 the Accounting Standards Committee requires the coverage of consolidated financial statements to be extended to include 'the share of earnings or losses of companies which were defined as associated companies'.[20] For the purpose of SSAP 1, an associated company is defined as:

a company not being the subsidiary of the investing group or company in which:
(i) the interest of the investing group or company is effectively that of a partner in a joint venture or consortium and the investing group or company is in a position to exercise a significant influence over the company in which the investment is made; or
(ii) the interest of the investing group or company is for the long term and is substantial and, having regard to the disposition of the other shareholdings, the investing group or company is in a position to exercise a significant influence over the company in which the investment is made.[21]

Significant influence is defined as participation in the operating and financial policy decisions, but not necessarily control over these decisions. In the absence of a joint venture or consortium form of business organisation, an investment of 20 per cent or more of the voting equity rights in a company is prima facie evidence of associated company status.

Recommended accounting treatment

The accounting treatment of the results of an associated company, when group accounts are prepared, is based on what is known as the 'equity method of accounting'. That is, the Consolidated Profit and Loss Account will include the group's share of the profits or losses of the associated company for the year, and the Consolidated Balance Sheet will include the group's share of post-acquisition retained profits or accumulated losses. SSAP 1 recommends, however, that in the holding company's own accounts the investment in the associated company should continue to be included at cost, or lower, with only dividend income received or receivable credited in the Profit and Loss Account. This latter treatment seems to provide yet more evidence of the inability, or unwillingness, of accountancy to break away from the 'cost basis' of asset valuation proposed by Dicksee and others in the last century.

One effect of the recommended treatment for the accounts of holding companies is that if consolidated financial statements are not prepared then the reporting holding company's share of the investment in the associated company is likely to be understated.

16.6 Merger accounting

Introduction

The method described in the earlier sections of this chapter for consolidating

Group accounts

the results of a subsidiary into the group accounts is known as the 'acquisition' or 'purchase' method. Under this method the net book value of assets and liabilities acquired are recorded at a 'fair market value', i.e., the market value of the resources offered in exchange. Under an alternative method, the so-called 'merger' or 'pooling of interests' method the assets and liabilities of the acquired subsidiary are consolidated at their net book values. Under this latter approach no goodwill or capital reserve on consolidation may arise and no distinction will be made between pre- and post-acquisition profits of the subsidiary. The essential feature of merger accounting is that the nominal value of shares issued by the acquiring company is taken as the purchase consideration. The merger accounting method is demonstrated in the following illustration.

Illustration 7

H has acquired the entire share capital of S Ltd by a share exchange. The agreed fair value of the net assets of S Ltd is £1 100 000. The values agreed for the shares of each company are as follows:

H Ltd: £6 per £1 ordinary share
S Ltd: £4 per £1 ordinary share

The terms of the acquisition of S Ltd involves the exchange of two shares in H Ltd for every three held in S Ltd, i.e., 200 000 shares of H Ltd will be issued.

The summarised balance sheets of the two companies before the share exchange are shown in Table 16.17. The Consolidated Balance Sheet of H Ltd and S Ltd under the merger method is prepared as follows:

TABLE 16.17

H Ltd and S Ltd
Summarised Balance Sheets

	H Ltd £000	S Ltd £000
Ordinary share capital	1500	300
Reserves	750	660
	2250	960
Net assets	2250	960

(i) Identify the issued share capital of H Ltd after the share exchange;
(ii) Combine the reserves of both H Ltd and S Ltd with no separation of pre- and post-acquisition reserves;
(iii) Combine the net assets of H Ltd and S Ltd at their existing book values (with no calculation of goodwill or capital reserve on consolidation).

The Consolidated Balance Sheet is shown in Table 16.18(a).

In this illustration the merger method gives rise to a capital reserve of £100 000 on the exchange of shares; excess of the nominal value of the shares acquired over the nominal value of the shares offered in exchange.

Under the acquisition method the net assets of S Ltd would be included in the Consolidated Balance Sheet at their 'fair market value', i.e., £1 100 000 with the excess of the agreed value of the purchase consideration over the

TABLE 16.18

H Ltd and subsidiary
Consolidated Balance Sheet

	(a) Merger method £000	(b) Acquisition method £000
Ordinary share capital	1700	1700
Share premium	—	1000
Capital reserve	100	—
Reserves	1410	750
	3210	3450
Net assets	3210	3350
Goodwill on consolidation	—	100
	3210	3450

'fair value' included as goodwill on consolidation. Any excess of value of purchase consideration over the nominal value of shares given in exchange would be transferred to a Share Premium Account, both in the accounts of H Ltd and in the Consolidated Balance Sheet. The Consolidated Balance Sheet under the acquisition method is shown in Table 16.18(b). As can be seen by comparison of the results of the two methods, the net asset total is less under the merger method but the amount included as Reserves available for dividend distribution is greater.

Recommended practice

Until the early 1960s very few UK firms, if any, adopted the merger method of accounting for acquisition. The 1948 Companies Act, Section 56, required all premiums arising on the issue of shares to be transferred to a share premium account. The aforementioned requirement seemed to imply that 'merger accounting' was illegal because it failed to recognise in full the share premium on acquisitions by share exchange. The law was not sufficiently clear on this matter, however, and no attempt was made in the 1967 Companies Act to clarify the issue despite recommendations of the Jenkins Committee.[22]

The 1960s witnessed a tremendous increase in the use of the merger or acquisition route as a means to corporate growth. Many of the companies most actively involved in the acquisition of others during this period made extensive use of the method of acquisition through share exchanges. These acquirers often obtained relatively high price-earnings ratios based on rapid rates of growth in earnings per share. The earnings growth rates were themselves fuelled partly by consolidation of the results of newly acquired subsidiaries. Hence the strategy of growth through acquisition and the means by which the strategy might be implemented were closely related (i.e., a steady increase in reported earnings, achieved partly through the consolidation of the results of newly acquired subsidiaries, was an essential part of the strategy of these companies.

Group accounts

A number of managers of the more active of the acquiring companies found the traditional method of accounting for mergers unpopular for two main reasons:

(i) Pre-acquisition profits of the acquired company were 'frozen', i.e., not available for distribution as dividends to the shareholders of the acquiring company;
(ii) the value of the net assets acquired were consolidated at the 'fair value' and not their book value.

The freezing of pre-acquisition profits prevented acquiring companies from including these profits in the Consolidated Profit and Loss Account for the year of acquisition. Also the recording of net assets of the subsidiary at a fair value often gave rise to a higher asset book value both for depreciation (or goodwill amortisation) and for use as the denominator in any measure of return on capital employed. Opponents of the acquisition method also gained some support from those who argued that a number of business combinations involved the merging of two previously separate companies in partnership rather than the takeover of one by another. In such circumstances of merging it was argued that the capitalisation of pre-acquisition profits was an unfair penalty on the shareholders of the companies concerned. The merger method of accounting for acquisitions was a readily available alternative for those who expressed the above sentiments, although in fact very few companies adopted this approach perhaps because of the unclear legal position. It was not until 1980 that the results of a tax case, only indirectly concerned with merger accounting, clarified the legal position for merger accounting. The case of *Shearer* v. *Bercain Ltd*[23] involved a claim by the Inland Revenue that a company, which had received a dividend from a subsidiary out of pre-acquisition profits, was subject to tax on the dividend received. The company resisted the claim and won its case on the basis that pre-acquisition profits were not available for dividend distribution.

One of the implications of the above case was that merger accounting appeared to have been illegal since 1948. Subsequently in Section 37(1) of the 1981 Companies Act the Government gave retrospective relief for companies which, since 1948, had adopted the merger basis of accounting, and laid down conditions under which it might continue to be adopted, i.e. that:

(a) the merger must have resulted in one company acquiring at least 90 per cent of the nominal value of each class of the equity share capital of another company; and
(b) the merger involves the allotment of equity shares in the issuing company; and
(c) the consideration for the shares issued is either transfer of equity shares in the acquired company or the cancellation of those equity shares of the acquired company not held by the issuing company prior to the merger.

In November 1982 the Accounting Standards Committee (ASC) issued an Exposure Draft, ED 31, 'Accounting for Mergers and Acquisitions'[24] which recommended the following conditions under which merger accounting might be adopted:

(i) The business combination should result from an offer to the holders of all equity shares and the holders of all voting shares which are not already held by the offeror; the offer should be approved by the holders of the voting shares of the company making the offer; and
(ii) The offer should be accepted by the holders of at least 90 per cent of all equity shares and of the shares carrying at least 90 per cent of all votes of the offeree company; for this purpose, any convertible stock is not to be regarded as equity except to the extent that it is converted into equity as a result of the business combination; and,
(iii) Not less than 90 per cent of the fair value of the consideration given for the equity share capital should be in the form of equity capital; not less than 90 per cent of the fair value of the consideration given for voting non-equity share capital should be in the form of equity and/or voting non-equity share capital.

ED31 introduced a proposal that merger accounting should be adopted if the above criteria were satisfied and that the two methods should not be alternatives for the same business combination.

A number of criticisms of the criteria identified by ED31 led to a relaxation of these when the ASC subsequently issued a Statement of Intent[25] on 25 April 1984 relating to accounting for business combinations.

The most significant changes involved a relaxation of the criteria to allow:

(i) a 20 per cent limit on the amount of purchase consideration which may be satisfied other than by equity capital;
(ii) a requirement that, prior to the offer, the offeror should hold less than 20 per cent of the equity and voting shares of the offeree;
(iii) approval by the holders of the voting shares of the offering company is no longer required.

16.7 Summary

Where a group situation occurs there is a need to provide more information to the readers of financial statements than might be available by describing investments in other companies on a cost basis. Since 1947, it has been necessary to provide consolidated financial statements for groups of companies registered in the UK, unless exemption has been allowed by the Registrar of Companies.

The results of subsidiary companies are consolidated with those of the holding company broadly on the basis of a proprietary concept of consolidation. Group accounts are viewed as extending the information provided by the holding company. Assets and liabilities of the subsidiary are combined with those of the holding company. An adjustment is made on the face of the consolidated statements for the proportion, if any, of the subsidiary company's equity held by minority shareholders.

Investments in associated companies are included in group accounts, if any, on the basis of an 'equity' method of accounting. Under this method the annual consolidated financial statements will show the group share of

Group accounts

accumulated profits or losses in the associated company, and of the profit or loss for the current financial year.

The acquisition of a subsidiary may be accounted for either by using the 'purchase' or 'acquisition' method, or else by using the 'pooling of interest' or 'merger' method. The method which should be adopted is determined by the criteria laid down in ED31 as revised by the Statement of Intent published in April 1984.

Questions

1. (a) Explain what is meant by each of the following: (i) Subsidiary Company, (ii) Associated Company.
2. Distinguish between the following concepts of consolidation: (a) entity concept; (b) parent company concept; (c) proprietary concept.
3. 'It may be argued that the creditors and shareholders of a holding company would be better served by receiving the separate financial statements relating to each of the major subsidiary companies rather than consolidated statements for the group.'
   To what extent do you agree with the above statement?
4. (a) Explain whether you agree that the definition of a holding company–subsidiary relationship is based on effective control.
   (b) To what extent do you believe that 'effective control' should be the major criterion in identifying which investments in other companies should be consolidated? What other criterion might be adopted?

For each of the following **circle** the *letter* of *best choice* among the possible solutions presented.

5. A Ltd owns 40 per cent of the equity interest in both B Ltd and C Ltd, while B Ltd owns 40 per cent of the equity interest in C Ltd.

    (a) Both B Ltd and C Ltd are subsidiaries of A Ltd;
    (b) Neither B Ltd nor C Ltd is a subsidiary of A Ltd;
    (c) C Ltd is a subsidiary of A Ltd;
    (d) C Ltd is a subsidiary of B Ltd.

6. W Ltd has invested in X Ltd and Y Ltd while both X Ltd and Y Ltd have invested in Z Ltd. W Ltd wishes to maximise its equity interest in Z Ltd but without Z Ltd becoming the subsidiary of W. The maximum indirect equity interest that W Ltd can obtain in Z Ltd is:

    (a) 25 per cent;
    (b) 50 per cent;
    (c) 75 per cent;
    (d) 100 per cent.

7. P Ltd acquired 80 per cent of the ordinary share capital of Q Ltd on 1 April 1984. Reported profits of Q Ltd for the accounting year ended 31 December 1984 were £160 000 after tax and ordinary dividend of £40 000. The share of post-acquisition profits of Q Ltd to be consolidated in the group financial statements for the year ended 31 December 1984 is:

    (a) £96 000;
    (b) £120 000;
    (c) £128 000;
    (d) £150 000.

8. Nibor Ltd acquired a controlling interest of 75 per cent of the equity capital in Nohj Ltd on 31 December 1984. Both companies produce accounts to 31 March. Profit and Loss Appropriation Accounts for the two companies to 31 March 1985 are as follows:

	Nibor Ltd		Nohj Ltd	
	£000	£000	£000	£000
Balance at 1 April 1984		246		108
Net profit (loss) for the year after investment income, interest, and taxes		92		(24)
Ordinary dividends:				
paid	16		12	
proposed	8	(24)	—	(12)
Balance at 31 March 1985		314		72

The interim dividend of Nohj Ltd was paid in January 1985.

Group share of the consolidated profit (loss) of Nibor Ltd and its subsidiary Nohj Ltd for 1985 is:

(a) £65 000;
(b) £68 000;
(c) £74 000;
(d) none of the above.

9. Ben Ltd is a wholly owned subsidiary of Bill Ltd. During the year ended 30 June 1985, Bill Ltd sold to Ben Ltd goods, which had originally cost £120 000 at a mark-up of 50 per cent on original cost.

At 30 June 1985 closing stock of Ben Ltd included goods acquired from Bill Ltd at a price of £45 000. Ben Ltd also owed Bill Ltd £60 000 for goods acquired.

In relation to the reported results of the two individual companies, the Consolidated Financial Statements will require the following adjustments in respect of the above items:

(a) Reduce net profits by £45 000 and net assets by £105 000;
(b) Reduce net profits by £45 000 and net assets by £45 000;
(c) Reduce net profits by £15 000 and net assets by £75 000;
(d) Reduce net profits and net assets by £15 000.

10. Dun Ltd acquired a 75 per cent controlling equity interest in Blane Ltd on 31 December 1984 for £122 000. Blane Ltd achieved a reported profit for the accounting year ended 30 June 1985 of £24 000 but this had been achieved as follows:

	£000
Profit, half-year to 31 December 1984	34
Loss, half-year to 30 June 1985	(10)
	24

The group's share of the profit (or loss) of Blane Ltd for the year ended 30 June 1985 is:

(a) £7500;
(b) £(10 000);
(c) £18 000;
(d) £24 000.

11. Blane Ltd in the above Question (10) declared a final ordinary dividend for 1985

Group accounts

of £8000. The following adjustment must be made in respect of the above dividend to the cost of the investment in the accounts of Dun Ltd and to the goodwill arising on consolidation:

(a) Both to be reduced by £6000;
(b) Both to be reduced by £8000;
(c) Cost of investment to be reduced by £8000, goodwill to remain unchanged;
(d) Cost of investment to be reduced by £6000, goodwill to remain unchanged.

Problems

1. The following is a summary of the Balance Sheets of Blue Ltd and Bird Ltd at 31 March 1985:

	Blue Ltd £000	Bird Ltd £000
£1 Ordinary shares	300	100
7% Preference shares	—	80
Reserves	162	75
12% Debenture	—	50
Current liabilities	94	62
	556	367
Fixed assets (net)	211	179
Investment in Bird Ltd at cost	225	—
Current assets	120	188
	556	367

The following additional information is also relevant:

(i) Blue Ltd acquired the shares in Bird Ltd on 30 June 1984
(ii) The investment in Bird Ltd consists of the following:

  75 000 £1 Ordinary shares, at cost of £165 000
  60 000 7% Preference shares, at cost of £60 000

(iii) The balance of the Reserves of Bird Ltd is made up as follows:

		£
Profit for the year ended 31 March 1985		37 600
Less proposed dividends:		
Pref. dividend	5600	
Ord. dividend	8000	13 600
		24 000
Balance brought forward 1 April 1984		51 000
Balance carried forward 31 March 1984		75 000

(iv) Proposed dividends payable by Bird Ltd are included in the current liabilities of Bird Ltd. Dividends receivable by Blue Ltd are included in the current assets of that company.

You are required to prepare a Consolidated Balance Sheet for Blue Ltd and its subsidiary company as at 31 March 1985.

2. The summarised Balance Sheets of Red Ltd and its subsidiary Rum Ltd on 30 June 1985 were as follows:

	Red Ltd £000	Rum Ltd £000
£1 Ordinary shares	200	100
Reserves	148	55
Current liabilities	46	29
	394	184
Fixed assets	250	74
Investment in Rum Ltd, at cost	84	—
Current assets	60	110
	394	184

Red Ltd acquired 60 000 shares in Rum Ltd on 31 August 1984. Profit and Loss Accounts for Red Ltd and Rum Ltd for the year ended 30 June 1985 are as follows:

	Red Ltd £000		Rum Ltd £000	
Net profit after interest and taxes		61		48
Dividends on Ordinary Shares				
paid		—	5	
proposed	22	(22)	10	(15)
Retained profits for year		39		33
Retained profits brought forward		109		22
Retained profits carried forward		148		55

The final dividend for 1984 of 8 pence per share was paid by Rum Ltd on 30 September 1984, while an interim dividend for 1985 was paid in January 1985. Only the dividend declared in respect of the year ended 30 June 1985 had been included in the net profit for Red Ltd in 1985. Any goodwill arising on consolidation is to be written off immediately against group reserves.

Assuming that the profits of Rum Ltd accrue evenly throughout the year you are required to prepare a Consolidated Profit and Loss Account for the year ended 30 June 1985 for Red Ltd and its subsidiary, and a Consolidated Balance Sheet on that date.

3. The following are the trial balances of Hope Ltd and its subsidiary Anchor Ltd at 30 June 1985:

	Hope Ltd £000	Anchor Ltd £000
Fixed assets (net)	134	20
Investment in Anchor Ltd, at cost	30	—
Closing stocks	20	8
Trade debtors	42	7
Cash	3	1
Interim dividend paid	2	—
Expenses	98	25
	329	61
Share capital, £1 Ordinary shares	70	16
Reserves, 1 July 1984	84	8
Trade creditors and accruals	45	5
Sales	130	32
	329	61

Group accounts

The following additional information is relevant:
  (i) Hope Ltd acquired 12 000 shares in Anchor Ltd on 1 July 1984.
  (ii) Sales by Hope Ltd to Anchor Ltd for 1985 amounted to £9000, priced on the basis of cost plus 50 per cent. Included in the closing stock of Anchor Ltd at 30 June 1985 are goods acquired from Hope Ltd during 1985 at a price of £3000.
  (iii) Anchor Ltd owes Hope Ltd £2500 for goods acquired during 1985.
  (iv) Both companies have proposed a final ordinary dividend of 10 pence per share for 1985.
  (v) Estimated Corporation Tax for the year to 30 June 1985 is:

Hope Ltd	£14 200
Anchor Ltd	£ 2 600

  (vi) Any goodwill arising on consolidation is to be amortised over a period of 10 years.

On the basis of the above information you are required to prepare a Consolidated Profit and Loss Account for Hope Ltd and its subsidiary for the year ended 30 June 1985 and a Consolidated Balance Sheet on that date.

4. Using the information provided in Problem 3 above, but assuming that Hope acquired 100 per cent of the ordinary share capital in Anchor Ltd on 1 July 1984, prepare a Consolidated Profit and Loss Account for the year ended 30 June 1985 and a Consolidated Balance Sheet on that date but using the Merger Method of Consolidation. For the purposes of this problem assume that the purchase consideration for Anchor Ltd had been satisfied by the issue of 30 000 £1 Ordinary shares in Hope Ltd at their nominal value.

5. Lyle Ltd acquired 40 per cent of the ordinary share capital of Mark Ltd on 1 January 1984 for £125 000. The Consolidated Profit and Loss Account of Lyle Ltd and its subsidiaries, and that of Mark Ltd for the year ended 30 June 1984 are given below, together with their respective Balance Sheets at that date.

	Lyle Ltd and its subsidiaries		Mark Ltd	
	£000		£000	
Profit for the year before taxes	126		65	
Income from investment in Mark Ltd	4		—	
	130		65	
Corporation tax	48		29	
Profits after tax	82		36	
Ordinary dividends:				
paid	8		—	
proposed	16	24	10	10
Retained profits for the year		58		26
Retained profits brought forward		213		85
Retained profits carried forward		271		111

You are required:
  (a) To prepare the revised Consolidated Profit and Loss Account of Lyle Ltd for the year ended 30 June 1984, incorporating the group's share of the profits of Mark Ltd;
  (b) To show how the investment in Mark Ltd will be presented in the Consolidated Balance Sheet of the group at 30 June 1984.

Notes and References

1 Introduction: the scope and historical background of accountancy

1. One recent example was the government enquiry into inflation accounting, set up under the chairmanship of Sir Francis Sandilands in 1973.
2. Similar disagreements about the nature of other subjects are not uncommon. For example, a series of lectures was given by the distinguished historian, E. H. Carr, in 1961 under the title, 'What is History?' These were later published by Macmillan in 1961 and more recently by Penguin in 1977 as a paperback entitled *What is History?*
3. Other simplistic definitions might also identify an accountant with membership of one of the recognised chartered institutes.
4. J. B. Sykes (ed.) *The Concise Oxford Dictionary*, 6th edition (Oxford: Clarendon Press, 1976) p. 8.
5. E. L. Kohler, *A Dictionary for Accountants*, 4th edition (Englewood Cliffs NJ: Prentice-Hall, 1970) p. 6.
6. Ibid., p. 7.
7. The Companies Act 1967, s.14 (3)a.
8. For a more complete description of the case, see E. Woolf, *Auditing Today*, 2nd edition (London: Prentice-Hall/International, 1979) pp. 380–85.
9. S. Paul Garner, *Evolution of Cost Accounting to 1925* (University of Alabama Press: Alabama, 1976) p. 2.
10. Factory overheads include all costs of manufacturing additional to those labour and material costs which are directly identified with a finished product. Further explanation of factory overheads is provided in Ch. 9.
11. See H. R. Hatfield, 'An Historical Defence of Book-keeping', p. 2. The paper was first presented to the American Association of University Instructors in Accounting on 29 December 1923 and has since been reprinted in a number of compilations including W. T. Baxter and S. Davidson (eds), *Studies in Accounting*, 3rd edition (London: Institute of Chartered Accountants in England and Wales 1977) pp. 1–10.
12. Luca Pacioli, *Summa de Arithmetica, Geometria, Proportioni et Proportionalita* (Venice, 1494).
13. B. S. Yamey, on p. 7 of the introduction to *Studies in the History of Accounting*, B. S. Yamey and A. G. Littleton (eds). (First printed in 1956 by R. D. Irwin, Homewood, Ilinois, reprinted by Arno Press Inc., New York, 1978.)
14. B. S. Yamey, 'The Development of Company Accounting Conventions', in T. A. Lee and R. H. Parker (eds), *The Evolution of Corporate Financial Reporting* (London: Nelson, 1979) p. 234.
15. Ibid., p. 235.

16. 'Total net assets' is defined as total assets less total liabilities. 'Net current assets' on the other hand, is defined as current assets minus current liabilities. These terms are explained more fully in Ch. 4.
17. *Lee* v. *Neuchatel Asphalte Co.* (1889) 41 Ch.D. 1.
18. *Verner* v. *General and Commercial Investment Trust* (1894) 2 Ch.D. 239.
19. In *Re National Bank of Wales Ltd* (1899) 2 Ch.D. 629, and *Ammonia Soda Co.* v. *Chamberlain* (1918) 1 Ch.D. 266.
20. W. H. Beaver, *Financial Reporting: An Accounting Revolution* (Englewood Cliffs, N.J.: Prentice-Hall, 1981) p. 2.
21. Ibid., p. 18.
22. *The Corporate Report* (Accounting Standards Steering Committee, London, 1975) p. 17, para. 1.8.

2 Users and objectives of financial information

1. See, for example, R. W. Campbell, *Accounting in Soviet Planning and management* (Cambridge Mass.: Harvard University Press, 1963).
2. J. Boswell, *The Rise and Decline of Small Firms* (London: Allen and Unwin, 1973) particularly ch. 3.
3. Gospel of Luke, Ch. 19 verses 12–27.
4. R. B. Jack, 'The Legal Aspects', in *Financial Reporting and Accounting Standards: Conference Papers* (Glasgow: University of Glasgow, 1978) p. 65.
5. The Accounting Standards Steering Committee, *The Corporate Report* (London, 1975).
6. Ibid., p. 15 para. 1.5.
7. Ibid., p. 17 para. 1.8.
8. Ibid., p. 9 para. 0.2.
9. W. H. Beaver, 'What should be the FASB's Objectives?', *The Journal of Accountancy*, vol. 36, August 1973, pp. 45–56. Reprinted in R. Bloom and P. T. Elgars (eds), *Accounting Theory and Policy* (New York: Harcourt Brace Jovanovich, 1981) p. 173.
10. *The Times*, 21 October 1982, p. 24.
11. *The Corporate Report*, p. 25 para. 2.36.
12. There is, however, a school of thought which views developments in accounting theory from a scientific viewpoint. For a critical review of the scientific approach refer to K. V. Peasnell, 'Statement of Accounting Theory and Theory Acceptance: A Review Article', *Accounting and Business Research*, vol. 8, no. 31, Summer 1978, pp. 217–28. Reprinted in Bloom and Elgars, *Accounting Theory and Policy*, pp. 62–75.
13. *The Corporate Report*, p. 28 para. 3.2.
14. APB Statement No. 4, *Basic Concepts and Accounting Principles underlying Financial Statements of Business Enterprises* (New York: AICPA, 1970).
15. Ibid., para. 73.
16. *Objectives of Financial Statements*, Report of the Study Group on the objectives of Financial Statements (New York: AICPA, 1973).
17. This objective was also adopted later in *Statement of Financial Accounting Concepts No. 1* (SFAC 1) (FASB, 1978).
18. R. G. May and G. L. Sundem, 'Research for Accounting Policy: An Overview', *The Accounting Review*, vol. 51, no. 4, Oct. 1976, pp. 747–63. Reprinted in Bloom and Elgars, *Accounting Theory and Policy*, pp. 2–19.
19. For a dissenting view, refer to D. Solomons, 'The Politicization of Accounting', *The Journal of Accountancy*, vol. 146, no. 5, Nov. 1978, pp. 65–72. Reprinted in Bloom and Elgars, *Accounting Theory and Policy*, pp. 141–51.

20. An FASB discussion memorandum entitled, *Conceptual Framework for Accounting and Reporting: Consideration of the Report of the Study Group on the Objectives of Financial Statements* (Stamford, Conn: FASB, 1974), was produced as a follow-up to the report of the Trueblood Committee and led eventually to the publication by the FASB of *Objectives of Financial Reporting by Business Enterprises*, Statement of Financial Accounting Concepts, no. 1, in 1978.
21. R. Macve, *A Conceptual Framework for Financial Accounting Reporting: The Possibilities for an Agreed Structure* (London: ICAEW, 1981).
22. Ibid., p. 17.
23. Ibid., p. 14.

3. Accounting principles and practice

1. May and Sundem, 'Research for Accounting Policy', p. 3.
2. Whether these reporting methods are allowed by law is another matter.
3. Committee on Concepts and Standards for External Financial Reports, *Statement of Accounting Theory and Theory Acceptance* (American Accounting Association, 1977) (SOATATA).
4. The methods adopted by deductive and inductive theorists are not confined to the 'classical' approach but are also found in the other two approaches.
5. Y. Ijiri, *Theory of Accounting Measurement*, Studies in Accounting Research, No. 10 (American Accounting Association, 1975) p. 28.
6. Ibid., preface p. ix.
7. SOATATA, p. 10.
8. There are also two other forms of the EMH, the *weak form* in which security prices are said to reflect all past information on security price movements, and the *strong form* in which security prices are said to reflect all information relevant to the security, whether publicly available or not. Further references to the EMH and its relevance to financial reporting may be obtained by consulting S. M. Keane, *Stock Market Efficiency* (Oxford: Philip Allan, 1983).
9. SOATATA, p. 21.
10. For further discussion, see S. Zeff, 'The Rise of "Economic Consequences"', *The Journal of Accountancy*, vol. 146, no. 6, Dec. 1978, pp. 56–63. Reprinted in Bloom and Elgars, *Accounting Theory and Policy*, pp. 152–62.
11. Solomons, 'The Politicization of Accounting', p. 148.
12. Peasnell, 'Statement of Accounting Theory and Theory Acceptance', p. 224.
13. J. R. Hicks, *Value and Capital*, 2nd edn (Oxford: Clarendon Press, 1946) p. 172.
14. For a readily accessible resumé by Fisher, see I. Fisher, 'Income and Capital', in R. H. Parker and G. C. Harcourt (eds), *Readings in the Concept and Measurement of Income* (The University Press, Cambridge, 1969) pp. 33–53.
15. See, for example, E. O. Edwards and P. W. Bell, *The Theory and Measurement of Business Income* (Berkeley: University of California Press, 1961).
16. See L. Revsine, *Replacement Cost Accounting* (Englewood Cliffs, NJ: Prentice-Hall, 1973).
17. See R. J. Chambers, *Accounting, Evaluation and Economic Behavior* (Englewood Cliffs, NJ: Prentice-Hall, 1966).
18. The Companies Act, 1948, s.149, as amended by the Companies Act 1967, s.9.
19. Jack, 'The Legal Aspects', p. 61.
20. The committee was originally formed as the Accounting Standards Steering Committee.
21. Accounting Standards Steering Committee, '*Disclosure of Accounting Policies*', SSAP No. 2 (1971).

22. The Companies Act 1981, Schedule 1, Part II, Section A, paras 10–14.
23. SSAP, No. 2, p. 2.
24. E. S. Hendriksen, *Accounting Theory*, 4th edn (Homewood, Illinois: R. D. Irwin, 1982) p. 64.
25. Ibid., p. 65.
26. Ibid., p. 83.
27. R. R. Sterling, *Theory of the Measurement of Enterprise Income* (Lawrence: University Press of Kansas, 1970) p. 259.
28. SSAP No. 2, part 2, para. 14 (b).
29. AICPA Professional Standards, *Statement of Financial Accounting Concepts No. 3*, para. 1230.028.
30. M. Moonitz, *The Basic Postulates of Accounting*, Accounting Research Study No. 1 (AICPA, 1962).
31. There is, however, a growing body of opinion which believes that accounting for human resources is both desirable and possible.

4 Financial statements and income measurement

1. B. S. Yamey, 'Some reflections on the writing of a general history of accountancy', *Accounting and Business Research*, vol. XI, no. 42, Spring 1981, p. 132.
2. 'Accounting Principles No. 18', *Preparation of Balance Sheet and Profit and Loss Account* (Institute of Chartered Accountants in England and Wales, 1958).
3. There are also a number of sub-categories, including intangible assets and investments, which are considered later, in Ch. 8.
4. In order to distinguish total gains or losses earned on all transactions undertaken during an accounting period from the gain or loss on a single transaction, the term business income is used temporarily to describe the former. In later chapters terminology adopted will revert back to that commonly used in the United Kingdom, i.e., 'net profit' rather than 'business income'.

5 The accounting recording process (I)

1. Not all business accounting systems record expenses in the Purchase Journal. Many adopt an alternative method of recording, involving the posting of actual payments made directly to the relevant expense ledger account with subsequent end-of-year journal entry adjustments for any prepaid or accrued expenses.

6 The accounting recording process (II)

1. A suspense account is the title given to an account in which a transaction is initially entered when there is some doubt as to the nature of the transaction. Once the transaction has been analysed an adjusting entry will be made to transfer the suspense account entry to the appropriate ledger account.

7 Fixed asset measurement (I)

1. Corporate legislation did not, in fact, include any formal requirement for depreciation to be provided on fixed assets until after the passage of the Companies Act 1981.

2. A. L. Thomas, *The Allocation Problem in Financial Accounting Theory: Studies in Accounting Research, 3* (American Accounting Association, 1969) p. 1.
3. M. Chatfield, *A History of Accounting Thought*, revised edition (New York: Robert E. Krieger Publishing Company, 1977) p. 234.
4. Accounting Standards Committee, *Accounting for Depreciation*, SSAP 12 (1977) para. 1.
5. Ibid., para. 1.
6. The Companies Act 1981, Schedule 1, Part II, para. 26.3(b).
7. Thomas, *The Allocation Problem in Financial Accounting Theory*, p. 77.
8. SSAP 12, para. 7.
9. Ibid., para. 8.

Appendix

1. Chambers, *Accounting, Evaluation and Economic Behavior*.
2. W. T. Baxter, *Depreciation* (London: Sweet and Maxwell, 1971) p. 32.
3. Ibid., p. 36.
4. *Inflation Accounting: Report of the Inflation Accounting Committee* (Chairman F. E. P. Sandilands), Cmnd 6225 (London: HMSO, 1975).
5. Accounting Standards Committee, *Current Cost Accounting*, SSAP 16 (1980).

8 Fixed asset measurement (II)

1. SSAP 12, para. 9.
2. Ibid., para. 6.
3. B. S. Yamey, 'The Development of Company Accounting Conventions', in Lee and Parker (1979), *The Evolution of Corporate Financial Reporting*, p. 235.
4. Goodwill may also arise from other causes including the establishment of a skilled workforce or an experienced management team, etc.
5. Accounting Standards Committee, *Accounting for Goodwill*, ED30 (1982) part 3, para. 56.
6. Accounting Standards Committee, *Accounting for Research and Development*, SSAP 13 (1977).
7. *The Accountant*, vol. 164, no. 5017, 11 Feb. 1971, pp. 169–71.
8. SSAP 13, para. 5.
9. Accounting Standards Committee, *Accounting for Investment Properties*, SSAP 19 (1981) para. 2.
10. In the 1984 Budget Statement, made on 13 March 1984, the Chancellor of the Exchequer proposed a staged reduction in the rate of first year allowance as follows:

    To 75 per cent, in respect of expenditure incurred on or after 14 March 1984;
    To 50 per cent, in respect of expenditure incurred on or after 1 April 1985;
    To nil, in respect of expenditure incurred on or after 1 April 1986.
11. The 1984 Budget Statement proposed a staged reduction in the rate of initial allowance as follows:

    To 50 per cent, in respect of expenditure incurred on or after 14 March 1984;
    To 25 per cent, in respect of expenditure incurred on or after 1 April 1985;
    To nil, in respect of expenditure incurred on or after 1 April 1986.
12. Accounting Standards Committee, *The Accounting Treatment of Government Grants*, SSAP 4 (1974) part 1, para. 5.

9 Current assets (I)

1. Accounting Standards Committee, *Stocks and Work-in-Progress*, SSAP 9 (1975) para. 17.
2. Ibid., para. 3.
3. Ibid., para. 2.
4. Ibid., para. 6.

10 Current assets (II)

1. Accounting Standards Committee, *Stocks and Work-in-Progress*, SSAP 9 (1975) Appendix 1, para. 12.
2. Ibid., para. 22.
3. Ibid., para. 27.
4. Ibid., Appendix 1, para. 23.
5. Formerly M. J. H. Nightingale and Co. Ltd.

11 Forms of business organisation (I): sole traders and partnerships

1. Other less common forms include workers co-operatives, syndicates and joint ventures.
2. *Report of the Committee of Inquiry on Small Firms* (Chairman: J. E. Bolton), Cmnd 4811 (London: HMSO, 1971).
3. *Report of the Committee to review the functioning of Financial Institutions* (Chairman: The Rt Hon. Sir Harold Wilson), Cmnd 7937 (London: HMSO, 1980).
4. Notes on the preparation and presentation of accounts from incomplete records (ICAEW, Guidance Notes 57, Dec. 1965) para 1.
5. Ibid., para. 7.
6. *Value Added Tax: Scope and Coverage*, HM Customs and Excise Notice No. 701, revised Nov. 1977.
7. Accounting Standards Committee, *Accounting for Value Added Tax*, SSAP 5 (April 1974) part 1, para. 5.
8. The Partnership Act, 1890, Section 1(1).
9. E. H. Scamell, *Lindley on Partnership*, 13th edn (London: Sweet and Maxwell, 1971) p. 10.
10. An alternative course of action involving limited partnership liability is possible, but only if responsibility for day to day management is given up by the limited (liability) partners.

12 Forms of business organisation (II): incorporated businesses

1. Companies Act, 1948, part 1 section 1, amended by the Companies Act 1981, Schedule 3.
2. The sole director of a private company cannot also be the company secretary.
3. Companies Act, 1948, part 4, section 196(i).
4. *Committee to review the functioning of Financial Institutions*, p. 209, para. 735.
5. Companies Act 1981, part III s.46(i).
6. In the case of companies defined as *close companies*, shareholders may also be liable to income tax on their share of non-trading profits of the company, whether distributed or not.

A close company is any UK resident company which:

(a) is under the control of its directors who are also participators (i.e., have a financial interest in the profits of the company); or
(b) is controlled by five or fewer participators (Section 282, Income and Corporation Taxes Act 1970).

7. Minimum applying for the 1983–4 tax year.
8. *The Stock Exchange Fact Book*, various years.
9. 'The Unlisted Security Market', *Bank of England Quarterly Bulletin*, vol. 23, no. 2, June 1983, p. 228.
10. *The Times*, 15 August 1983, p. 14, Investors' Notebook.
11. *Investors Chronicle*, vol. 65, no. 821, 29 July–4 August 1983, p. 44.
12. *The Times*, 19 May 1978, p. 21; 25 May, p. 24.
13. *Investors Chronicle*, vol. 65, no. 823, 12–18 August 1983, p. 53.
14. *The Times*, 19 August 1983, p. 13.
15. *Investors Chronicle*, vol. 65, no. 817, 1–7 July 1983, p. 43.
16. The Companies Act 1981, Schedule 1, 3(2). Preliminary expenses may alternatively be written off against share premium account, if available.

13 Corporate financial reporting requirements

1. The Companies Act, 1948, Schedule 8, part II section A. Revised by the Companies Act 1981, Section (1).
2. Ibid., Schedule 8, part II, Section A 14.
3. Ibid., Schedule 8, part III, paras 38–51.
4. Accounting Standards Committee, *Accounting for Contingencies*, SSAP 18 (1980).
5. The Companies Act, 1948, Schedule 8, part III, paras 52–57.
6. Accounting Standards Committee, *Extraordinary Items and Prior Year Adjustments*, SSAP 6 (1974).
7. Accounting Standards Committee, *Accounting for post Balance Sheet Events*, SSAP 17 (1980).
8. That is, those recognised as qualified by the Chartered Institutes of England and Wales, Scotland, and Ireland, and the Association of Certified Accountants and persons with overseas qualifications recognised by the Department of Trade.
9. The Companies Act 1967, section 14, (3) (a).
10. The Companies Act 1980, part III, section 39 (2).
11. '*The determination of realised profits and disclosure of distributable profits in the context of the Companies Acts 1948 to 1981*' (TR 481), para. 10, *Accountancy*, vol. 93, no. 1070, October 1982, pp. 122–6. See also the Companies Act 1948, 8 Sch. 90; Sec. 1(2), 1 Sch.
12. Ibid., Appendix para. 3.
13. The Companies Act, 1980, part III, section 40.
14. M. A. Firth, 'An empirical investigation of the impact of the announcement of capitalisation issues on share prices', *Journal of Business Finance and Accounting*, vol. 14, no. 1, Spring 1977, pp. 47–60.
15. Accounting Standards Committee, *The Treatment of Taxation under the Imputation System in the Accounts of Companies*, SSAP 8 (1974), part 1, para. 8.
16. Accounting Standards Committee, *Accounting for Deferred Tax*, SSAP 15 (1978), part II, para. 26.
17. Accounting Standards Committee, *Accounting for Deferred Tax*, ED33 (1983), part 3, para. 20.

14 Analysis of accounting statements

1. Institute of Chartered Accountants in England and Wales, *Statement of Intent on Accounting Standards in the 1970s* (ICAEW, 1969).
2. See Keane, *Stock Market Efficiency*, Ch. 4.
3. Named after the company which is often given credit for the initial formulation of a pyramidal structure of ratios for management control purposes.
4. See, for example, W. H. Beaver, 'Market Prices, Financial Ratios and the Prediction of Failure', *Journal of Accounting Research*, vol. 6, no. 2, Autumn 1968, pp. 179–92.
5. Accounting Standards Committee, *Statements of Sources and Applications of Funds*, SSAP 10 (1978), para. 7.
6. American Institute of Certified Public Accountants, *Reporting Changes in Financial Position,* Accounting Principles Board, Opinion No. 19 (March 1971), para. 2021.05.
7. P. Mason, *Cash Flow Analysis and the Funds Statement, Accounting Research Study*, no. 2 (AICPA, 1961).
8. APB Opinion 19, para. 2021.06.
9. SSAP 10, part II, para. 8.
10. Ibid., Appendix A, Example 1.

15 Accounting for inflation

1. Some observers may have described this rather as 'government interference'.
2. D. R. Myddelton, 'The Neglected Merits of CPP', p. 90, from Leach and Stamp (eds), *British Accounting Standards: The First Ten Years*' (Cambridge: Woodhead-Faulkner, 1981).
3. H. W. Sweeney, *Stabilised Accounting* (New York: Harper, 1936).
4. *The Accountancy of Changing Price Levels* (Institute of Cost and Works Accountants, 1952), and *Accounting for Inflation* (Association of Certified and Corporate Accountants, 1952).
5. Research Foundation of the Institute of Chartered Accountants in England and Wales, *Accounting for Stewardship in a Period of Inflation* (ICAEW, 1968).
6. Financial Accounting Standards Board, *Financial Reporting and Changing Prices*, Statement of Financial Accounting Standards, No. 3 (Sept. 1979).
7. Accounting Standards Steering Committee, *Accounting for Changes in the Purchasing Power of Money*, PSSAP 7 (1974).
8. Accounting Standards Committee, *Inflation Accounting – An Interim Recommendation* (1977).
9. It may be argued that business A has indeed operated in a more efficient manner than business B as the same level of profits has been generated in the former, although on an older asset. In order to avoid controversy caused by such arguments the asset in the illustration may be considered to be one of infinite useful life, e.g., farm grazing land.
10. See, for example, W. Godley and A. Wood, *Stock Appreciation and the Crisis of British Industry* (1974), available from the Department of Applied Economics, Sidgewick Avenue, Cambridge. Also, a series of articles was published by various authors on this point in the *Financial Times*, during November 1974.
11. These different perceptions do not, however, refer to the legal nature of the business enterprise.
12. See, R. S. Gynther, 'Why use General Purchasing Power?', *Accounting and Business Research*, vol. 4, no. 14, Spring 1974, pp. 141–57.

13. This conclusion may also apply to any proposal to include CPP adjustments in addition to specific price change adjustments.
14. PSSAP 7, part III, para. 28.
15. Ibid., part II, para. 29.
16. J. C. Bonbright, *The Valuation of Property* (New York: McGraw-Hill, 1937), p. 71, quoted in Sandilands, para. 208.
17. Sandilands Report, para. 222.
18. Ibid., para. 70.
19. Ibid., para. 535.
20. Ibid., para. 537.
21. Accounting Standards Committee, *Current Cost Accounting*, SSAP 16 (1980), para. 3.
22. Ibid., para. 11.
23. Ibid., para. 6.
24. Ibid., para. 54.
25. Issued by the ASC together with SSAP 16.
26. G. Whittington, 'Inflation Accounting – What Next?', from Leach and Stamp, *British Accounting Standards*, p. 75.
27. According to G. Whittington, ibid., 'the present (SSAP 16) gearing adjustment carries compromise and caution to the extent of satisfying neither the proponents nor the opponents of the gearing method', p. 79.
28. SSAP 16, para. 18.
29. Statement by the Accounting Standards Committee on SSAP 16 'Current Cost Accounting', para. 4.10, published in *Accountancy*, June 1983, pp. 116–18.

16 Group accounts

1. For information on accounting treatment of groups of companies see *Survey of Published Accounts*, London, ICAEW, various years.
2. R. M. Wilkins, *Group Accounts: The fundamental principles, form, and content* (London: ICAEW, 1975) p. 16.
3. Hein, L. W., *The British Companies Acts and the Practice of Accountancy 1844–1962* (New York: Arno Press Inc., 1978) p. 272.
4. 'Report of the Company Law Amendment Committee', House of Commons, *Sessional Papers*, 1926 (Cmnd 2657), IX, 477.
5. 'Report of the Committee on Company Law Amendment', House of Commons, *Sessional Papers*, 1944–45 (Cmnd 6659) IV, 793.
6. The Companies Act, 1948, Section 150 (2) (b).
7. Accounting Standards Committee, *Group Accounts*, Statement of Standard Accounting Practice, 14 (Sept., 1978).
8. The distinction between fixed, or permanent, and floating, or current, assets owes much to the writings of Dicksee in the late nineteenth century. Dicksee distinguished between permanent assets, i.e. 'those *with* which [a firm] carries on business'; and 'floating' assets, i.e. 'those *in* which [a firm] carries on business'. L. R. Dicksee, *Auditing – a Practical Manual for Auditors* (London: Gee & Co., 1892) p. 121.
9. R. G. Walker, *Consolidated Statements: A History and Analysis* (New York: Arno Press, 1978) p. 41.
10. Ibid., p. 74.
11. For further information refer to Sir Patrick Hastings, 'The Case of the Royal Mail', in W. T. Baxter and S. Davidson (eds), *Studies in Accounting Theory* (London: ICAEW, 1977) 3rd edition, pp. 339–46.

12. Walker, *Consolidated Statements*, p. 81.
13. R. H. Parker, 'Concepts of Consolidation in the EEC', Accountancy, vol. 88, no. 1002 (February 1977), pp. 72–5.
14. M. Moonitz, *The Entity Theory of Consolidated Statements* (American Accounting Association, 1944).
15. Parker, 'Concepts of Consolidation in the EEC', p. 72.
16. Walker, *Consolidated Statements*, p. 111.
17. 'Report of the Company Law Committee' [The Jenkins Committee Report] (London: HMSO, 1962 Cmnd 1749).
18. For a comment on the likely implications of the Seventh Directive for UK company legislation see P. Rutteman, 'Scrutinising the Seventh Directive', *Accountancy*, vol. 94, no. 1078, June 1983, pp. 129–30.
19. Walker, *Consolidated Statements*, p. 270.
20. Accounting Standards Committee, *Accounting for Associated Companies*, SSAP 1 (Jan. 1971, revised April 1982), para. 4.
21. Ibid., para. 13.
22. Jenkins Committee Report, para. 187.
23. *Shearer (Inspector of Taxes)* v. *Bercain Ltd, Times Law Report* 7, March 1980, See also *Simons Tax Cases*, 1980, p. 359.
24. Accounting Standards Committee, *Accounting for Acquisitions and Mergers*, ED31 (November, 1982).
25. Statement of Intent, ICAEW April 25, 1984, TR 545.

Glossary of Terms

The following is a glossary of the more important accounting terms used in the early chapters of the book. It is not intended that the glossary should be comprehensive, rather the purpose is to provide a brief introduction to terms which are explained to readers in more detail in later chapters of the text.

Allocation
The process by which costs are charged to cost centres in proportion to some measure of use. The cost centre may be a product, process, department or some other identifiable area of activity.

Asset
An economic resource, owned by an enterprise, giving rise to a claim as to potential future benefits or services. Assets may be categorised as either current or fixed assets.

Balance sheet
A statement of financial position of an organisation, disclosing the assets, liabilities and net worth of that organisation at a particular point in time.

Capital
The amount invested in an enterprise by its owners.

Capital expenditure
Expenditure which is normally expected to benefit future periods, in contrast to revenue expenditure. Capital expenditure involves the acquisition of fixed assets.

Capital Reserve
Reserves of a company which are regarded as not being available for withdrawal by the owners.

Capital structure
The permanent long-term financing of a business.

Contingent liability
An obligation relating to some past event or transaction, which may arise depending on the outcome of some future event.

Current asset
Assets which are reasonably expected to be realised in cash, or sold, or otherwise consumed during the normal operating cycle of the business or within one accounting year, if longer.

Glossary of Terms

Current liability
A short-term debt or obligation which is expected to be satisfied within one accounting year.

Depreciation
The diminution in value of a tangible fixed asset, however arising.

Distributable profits
The proportion of the profits of a business which is available for distribution to members or owners, in accordance with legal requirements or the constitution of the business.

Dividends
The part of the profits of a company which is distributed to the shareholders, normally by means of a cash payment in proportion to the number of shares held.

Double-entry book-keeping
The method of recording the dual aspect of an accounting transaction.

Expense
Cost, or other decrease in an asset, associated with the revenues earned during that accounting period.

Fixed asset
Assets which are held for use rather than realisation and which are intended to provide services or generate revenues over future accounting periods.

Goodwill
An intangible asset representing the value of a business in excess of the combined value of the individual net assets.

Gross profit
The trading profit of a business represented by sales revenue less the cost of the goods sold. Also described as gross margin.

Income statement
A summary statement of the revenues and expenses of a business organisation for a specified period.

Intangible asset
An asset which has no physical existence but which none the less gives rise to future expected benefits.

Liability
Obligations, or debts of a business enterprise. Classified as either current, i.e. maturing within the next accounting year, or long-term.

Limited company
A company, whose members have their liability limited either by the amount of guarantees made or else by the paid-up value of share capital subscribed for.

Net assets
Total assets less total liabilities. Also known as net worth.

Net current assets
Total current assets less total current liabilities. Also described as working capital.

Prime cost
The direct labour and materials component of the cost of manufacturing a product.

Profit
The excess of revenues over expenses for a particular accounting period.

Profit and loss account
The ledger account to which the totals of revenues and expenses are posted (transferred). The term is also used in the UK to refer to the published income statement.

Registered company
A company which has been formed through the process of registration with the Registrar of Companies.

Reserve
The amount of net worth of a company which is in excess of the nominal value of the issued share capital.

Retained profit
That portion of the profits of the current year (or of previous years) which has not been distributed to owners but rather reinvested within the business.

Revenue
Income arising from the sale of goods or the provision of services.

Revenue expenditure
Expenditure which is expected to benefit a current accounting period only.

Revenue Reserve
Reserves which are regarded as available for distribution to owners.

Share capital
The nominal value of shares either authorised by a company or actually issued to the members.

Statement of financial position
Alternative name for a balance sheet.

Index

Absorption costing 171-9
Accountant 1
Accountant, The 371
Accountancy
  defined 1-2
  historical developments 6-11
  sub-classifications 2-6
Accounting
  concepts and conventions 33-7
  historical developments 32-3
  model of the firm 41-55, 62-3
  policy determination 11, 21-2, 29-30
Accounting Standards Committee (ASC),
    formerly Accounting Standards
    Steering Committee (ASSC),
  aims 229-300
  and Corporate Report 17
  formation 33
Accounts payable *see* Trade creditors
Accruals 35-6, 53, 101-5
Accumulated fund 114-15
Acid-test 312
Acquisition method 376-7
Adjusting entries 100-8
Advanced Corporation Tax (ACT) 275
Allocation 33, 123-4
  asset cost 105-8
  depreciation 125-31
  expense 40-1, 52
Allotment, 256-7
Alternative accounting rules 261
American Accounting Assocation
    (AAA) 27
American Institute of Certified Public
    Accountants (AICPA) 21
Amortisation 154
Analysis of financial statements 299-326
APB No. 4 21-2
Application for shares 256-7
Appropriation account 232-3
Articles of Association 242-3
Assets
  classification 43, 122-5
  current 43
  definition 35
  fixed 43
  intangible 154-7
  long-lived 135
  monetary 123
  non-monetary 123-5
  revaluations 9, 142-6, 142-6, 148-50
  valuation 122-3
Asset utilisation ratios 308-10
Associated company 158, 385-6
Association of Certified Accountants 3,
    334
Attributable cost, and non-attributable
    cost 169-70
Attributable profit 197-201
Auditor
  appointment and qualifications 3, 10, 272
  duties 3, 270, 272
  external and internal 3-4
  remuneration 267
  report 272-3
  resignation 272
Authorised share capital 244
Average collection period 309-10
Average cost inventory valuation 195-7

Bad and doubtful debts
  general and specific provisions 96-100
  written-off 96
Balance sheet
  and accounting equation 44
  form and content 277-82
  income measurement 41-9
  origin 7, 32
  structure 42-6
Balancing allowance and balancing
    charge 160-1
Bank balance 203-5
Bank reconciliation 204-5
Bankruptcy prediction 312
Bank statement 204
Baxter, W. T. 145
Bespac plc 250
Bolton Committee 215
Bonbright, J. C. 340
Bonus issue 273-4
Books of prime entry 65-71
Break-even analysis 173-7

British Petroleum plc (BP) 257
Britoil plc 253, 257

Capital
  authorised 244
  fixed and floating 9
  issued 293
  non-distributable 8–9
  partnership 232
  and revenue items 8–9, 43, 73–4, 128
Capital allowances 159–61
Capital expenditure 128
Capital gearing 249, 311
Capital issues 273
Capital maintenance 338–9
Capital reserve 149, 374–5
Cash 201
  control 205–6
  day book (or journal) 66–71, 202–4
  holding motives 206
Cash discounts 93–5, 129
Cash flow
  ratios 312
  statement 323–7
Cash sales 50, 69
Changing prices, accounting for 334–5
Chambers, R. J. 145
Charitable contributions 270
Charities 112
Chartered Accountants see Institutes of, in England and Wales, in Ireland, of Scotland
Classical approach 27–8
Closing entries 111–2
Cohen Committee 367, 369
Companies Acts
  1900 10
  1907 10
  1928 10
  1929 367
  1948: disclosure requirements 260; filing of accounts 10; group accounts 368, 370–1, 388
  1967 10
  1976 272
  1981: basic accounting principles 34, 261; current cost accounting 344; form and content of accounts 10, 262–269, 276–94; group accounts 157–8, 389; preliminary expenses 253; share repurchases 244; stock valuation 177; see also Disclosure requirements
Company
  categories of 241–2
  conversion from partnership 254–5
  formation 253
  memorandum and articles 242–4
  separate legal entity 244–5

Comparability 23
Completeness 23
Computerisation 3, 11, 73
Conceptual framework 22, 27–30
Conservatism principle 33–6, 123
Consistency 23, 36
Consolidated accounts see Group accounts
Consultative Committee of Accountancy Bodies (CCAB) 33–4
Contingent liabilities 266, 267
Contra items 204
Contracts, long-term see work-in-progress
Control
  accounts 91–3
  cash 205–8
  systems 108
Controlling interest 157, 366, 371
Convertible securities 247, 248
Corporate report 17–20
Copyright 156
Corporation tax 5, 274–6
Cost and managerial accounting 4
Cost allocation 169–71
Cost convention see Historic cost
Cost flow 182–4
Cost of goods sold 194–7
Cost of sales adjustment (COSA) 343, 346–7
Credit entry 63
Credit sales 50, 92–4
Creditor(s) 93–4
Cumulative preference shares 247
Current account 232–5
Current assets 167
Current cost accounting 342–51
Current cost balance sheet 351–2
Current cost operating adjustments 344–9
Current cost profit 341, 342, 343
Current cost reserve 349–51
Current liabilities 43
Current purchasing power accounting (CPP) 338–9, 352–9
Current ratio 311–2
Current value accounting 20, 31–2

Day book 65–71
Debenture capital 247–9, 264
Debit entry 63
Debtor 44
Decision usefulness approach 28–9
Deferred expenditure 156
Deferred liabilities 275–6
Deferred revenues 162
Deferred taxation 275–6
De Lorean Motors 19
Departmental accounts 186–9
Depreciation 125–36
  adjustments 147–52
  allocation 127–36
  current cost 343, 346

Index

Deprival value 145, 340
Development expenditure 156
Direct cost 169
Directors
  appointment 243
  removal 243
  remuneration 243, 268–9
  report 269–71
  responsibilities 7, 243–4
Disclosure requirements
  and 1981 Act 261–73
  origins 7–8, 260
Discounted present values 31, 140–4
Distributable profits 273–4
Dividends 267, 270
Division of profits, in partnership accounts 232–3, 234–6
Double-entry book-keeping
  illustrated 76–80
  introduced 62–4
  origins 6–7
Double declining depreciation 133
Doubtful debts 96–100
Drawings 219, 232
Dual aspect of accounting transactions 41, 62–3
Du-pont system 302–3

Earnings per share 264, 291
Economic income
  and accounting income 30–2
  and asset valuation 139–46
Economic value 28, 145
Efficient markets hypothesis (EMH) 29
Employees
  disclosure requirements 268
  information needs 18
Employment report 20
Entity
  consolidation 369–70
  convention 37
Entry value 145–6
Environmental postulates 37
Equity 41
Equity accounting 369, 386
Equity Funding Corporation 3
Equivalent units of production 180–1
Errors
  of practice 72–3
  of principle 73–4
  of transposition 73
European Economic Community (EEC) 10, 274, 371
Eurotherm 252
Exceptional items 269
Exit value 146
Expected benefits, and depreciation 130
Expense
  accrued 53
  definition 36
  matching 51–3
  recognition 34–6
Exposure draft
  ED8, Accounting for changes in the purchasing power of money 338
  ED18, Current cost accounting 335, 342
  ED24, Current cost accounting 335, 343
  ED30, Accounting for goodwill 155
  ED31, Accounting for mergers and acquisitions 389–91
  ED33, Accounting for deferred tax 402
Extraordinary items 268, 269

Factory overhead, 169
FIFO (first-in, first-out) 195–8
Financial Accounting Standards Board (FASB) 22
Financial management 5–6
Financial reports
  desirable characteristics 23
  internal and external users 13–20
  objectives 17–20, 20–3, 26–7
Financing ratios 310–12
Fisher, I. 31
Fixed assets
  acquisition cost 128–30, 151–2
  classification 123–5
  defined 43
  depreciation 125–36, 147–54
  disclosure requirements 264–5, 270
  and floating assets 368
  revaluations 148–51
Flow of cost 182–4
Flow of information 74–5
Fundamental accounting principles 33–8
Funds
  defined 313–4
Funds flow statement 313–23
  form and content 314–5
  objectives and uses 313
  preparation of 315–23

Gearing 249, 311
Gearing adjustment 343, 348
General purchasing power 338–9
Generally accepted accounting principles 33
Going concern 34
Goodwill 154–5, 374–5
Granville & Co. see Over the Counter Market
Green Committee 366–7, 368
Gross profit (or gross margin) 56
  percentage 221–2
Group accounts
  alternative concepts 369–70
  consolidated statements 371–85
  historical development 366–9
Guarantees 266–7

Hicks, J. R. 30–1
Historic cost accounting 32–7
  deficiencies 335–7
  disclosure requirements 261
  income measurement 40
Holding company 366, 367, 380
Holding gains and losses 341–2
Hyde Guidelines 335, 343

Imputation tax 274
Income
  concepts 30–2
  measurement 40–53
Income and expenditure account 113–5
Income statements *see* Profit and loss account
Income tax 5
Incomplete records 216–27
Inflation accounting 11
  history of 333–5
Information economics approach 29–30
Information usefulness 26
Institute of Chartered Accountants
  in England and Wales 3, 216, 334, 335, 342
  in Ireland 3
  of Scotland 3
Institute of Cost and Management Accountants 334
Institute of Taxation 5
Intangible assets 154–7
Internal control 3
Intra-group trading 380–1
Introduction (Stock Exchange) 249–50
Inventories *see* Stocks
Investments
  classification 157–9
  disclosure requirements 265
  listed *v.* unlisted 208–9
Investment grants 161–2
Investors' information requirements 18
Issued share capital 293

Jenkins Committee 371
Joint Stock Companies Acts
  1844 7
  1855 8
  1856 8
Journal entries 6, 64–5

Ledger accounts 71
Lee *v* Neuchatel Asphalte Co. 9
Leverage *see* Gearing
Liabilities
  classification 43
  contingent 266, 267
  current 43
  deferred 276
  defined 35–6
  long-term 43

LIFO (Last-in, first-out) 195–8
Limited liability 8, 33, 242, 245
Lindley, L. J. 9
Liquid assets 208
Liquidity ratios 310–2
Listed securities 208–9
Long-term contracts 197–201

Macve, R. 22
Mainstream corporation tax 275
Management accounting *see* cost and managerial accounting
Manufacturing accounts 184–7
Marginal cost 177
Matching convention 52–3
Materiality 37
  (*see also* Relevance)
Memorandum of Association 242–4
Merger accounting 386–90
Midland Bank plc 251
Minority interests 372–6
Monetary assets 123
Monetary items 339
Monetary working capital adjustment (MWCA) 343, 347–8
Money measurement convention 37
Moonitz, M. 37, 369
Morpeth, D. 335

Net realisable value 32, 145, 178–9, 340–1
Nominal value 244
Non-monetary assets 123–5, 339
Non-trading organisations 112–5

Objectivity (or neutrality) 23, 33, 123
Obsolescence 127
Oceonics plc 252
Offer for sale 252
Operating capacity 343
Operating cycle 43
Operating ratios 307–8
Opportunity cost 129
Ordinary shares 245–6
Overheads 168–71
Over the Counter Market (OTC) 209, 250

Pacioli, Luca 6
Parent company concept 369–70
Parker, R. H. 369
Partly paid shares 257
Partnership 215
  accounts 231
  agreement 230–1
  changes 233–4
  conversion to limited company 236, 254–5
  division of profits 232–6
  nature of 230
Patent rights 156–7
Pay As You Earn (PAYE) 5

Index

Peasnell, K. V.   30
Perfect market conditions   140, 145
Performance measurement   304
Periodic income measurement   40
Periodic inventory systems   196
Perpetual inventory systems   196
Petty cash   207–8
Placements: private and stock exchange   252
Plant register   148
Political contributions   270
Pooling of interests   *see* Merger accounting
Post-balance sheet events   269
Pre-acquisition profits   377–80
Preference shares   246–7
Preliminary expenses   253
Prepayments   52, 101, 104–5
Present value   340–1
Price level accounting   *see* Current purchasing power
Process cost   179–82
Production basis depreciation   135–6
Profit and loss account
  and income measurement   49–57
  form and content   55–7, 283–7
  origin   7, 32
Profitability ratios   303–7
Property investment   158–9
Proportional consolidation   369
Proprietory concept of consolidation   369
Prospectus issue   251–2
Provisions   266
Prudence concept   *see* Conservatism
Public limited company   242
Purchase Journal (or Day Book)   66–8
Purchase method   *see* Acqusition method

Quick ratio   312

Rate of return   *see* Profitability ratios
Ratio analysis   301–2
Realisation account   254–5
Realisable value   32, 145, 340–1
Realised profit   158, 273
Receipts and payments account   113
Redeemable preference shares   247
Reducing balance depreciation   132–4
Registered company   7
Registrar of Companies   7, 10, 242
Relevance   23
Reliability   23, 32–3
Repairs and renewals   153–4
Replacement cost accounting   32, 145, 340–1
Research and development   154–6, 269
Reserves   266, 270
Residual value   131
Retail price index (RPI)   338, 353
Revaluation of assets   148–51
Revenue expenditure   129

Revenue recognition   34–6, 51–3
Rights issue   251
Rolls-Royce Ltd   156
Royal Mail Steam Packet Company   368–9

Sales Journal (or Day Book)   66–7
Sandilands Committee   145, 335, 338, 339–42, 343
Scrip issue   *see* Bonus issue
Secret reserves   368
Securities
  categories of   208–9, 245–9
  methods of issue   249–53
Security issues, accounting for   253–7
Seventh Directive   371
Share capital
  authorised   244
  disclosure of   263–4
  issued   293
  ordinary   245–6
  partly paid   245, 257
  preference   246–7
Share premium   255–6, 388
Shearer *v.* Bercain Ltd   389
Sherman Anti Trust Laws 1890 (US)   366
Short-term assets   *see* Current assets
Short-term liability   *see* Current liabilities
Sole traders   215–6
Source and application of funds statement   *see* Funds flow statement
Sources of finance   251
S.R. Gent plc   253
Stable monetary unit   333, 334
State of affairs, and auditors' report   272
Statement of Accounting Theory and Theory Acceptance (SOATATA)   27–30
Statement of added value   20
Statement of changes in financial position   *see* Funds flow statement
Statement of financial position   *see* Balance sheet
Statement of Intent TR545   390
Statement of Standard Accounting Practice (SSAP)
  SSAP1, Accounting for associated companies   386
  SSAP 2, Disclosure of accounting policies   34–6, 175, 261, 262
  SSAP 4, The accounting treatment of government grants   161
  SSAP 5, Accounting for value added tax   228, 401
  SSAP 6, Extraordinary items and prior year adjustment   268
  SSAP 7, Accounting for changes in the purchasing power of money   335, 338, 339, 353–9
  SSAP, 8, The treatment of taxation under the imputation system in the accounts of companies   402

SSAP 9, Stock and work-in-progress
    168, 175, 177, 195, 197, 199
SSAP 10, Statements of source and
    applications of funds 313–23
SSAP 12, Accounting for
    depreciation 127, 131, 148, 149
SSAP 13, Accounting for research and
    development 156
SSAP 14, Group accounts 367
SSAP 15, Accounting for deferred
    tax 402
SSAP 16, Current cost accounting 145
    335, 342–51
SSAP 17, Accounting for post-balance
    sheet events 269
SSAP, 18, Accounting for
    contingencies 267
Sterling, R. R. 35
Stewardship function 6–7, 17, 26–7, 32–3
Stocks
    categories 167–8
    cost allocation 169–82
    cost recognition 194–8
    lower of cost and net realisable
        value 178–9
    marginal *v.* absorption cost 171–9
    valuation 168–9
Stock Exchange 208, 249, 368
Straight line depreciation 132–3
Striking price in tender issues 253
Subsidiary
    defined 366, 370–1
    non-consolidation 367
    relationships 370–1
Sum-of-years-digits depreciation 134–5
Suspense account 99
Sweeney, H. W. 334

T-account 62–3
Table A 243
Tangible assets 125
Taxation
    company 274–6
    disclosure 267–8
    general 4–5
Technology for Business plc 252
Tender issue 253
Theory construction 27–30
Thomas, A. L. 123, 130

Time value of money *see* Discounted
    present values
Timeliness 23
Trade discounts 95
Trade mark 156–7
Trade union 112
Trading and profit and loss account 56
Transaction analysis 50–71
    comprehensive illustration 76–80
Trial balance 71–4
True and fair view, and
    auditors' responsibility 2
    balance sheet 43
    disclosure 261
Trueblood report 21–2
Turnover disclosure 268
Turnover ratios 306–9

Underwriters 250
Understandability 23
Unit cost 169
Unit of production depreciation *see*
    Production basis
Unlisted securities 209
Unlisted Securities Markets
    (USM) 249–50, 252
Usage basis of depreciation *see* Production
    basis
Unsecured debentures 248
Useful life, and depreciation 130
Users and accounting information
    external 17–20
    internal 14–17

Valuation bases 30–2
Value added tax (VAT) 5, 227–31
Value to the business 340–2, 343
Variable costing 169–70

Walker, R. G. 368, 369
Weighted-average cost 195–8
Wilson Committee 215, 244
Work-in-progress 44
    long-term contracts 197–201
    process costs 179–82
Working capital 314
Work sheet 108–9

Yamey, B.S. 42–3